W9-AWN-157

Software Engineering

The Production of Quality Software

Software Engineering

The Production of Quality Software

Shari Lawrence Pfleeger
SYSTEMS/SOFTWARE, INC.

Macmillan Publishing Company
NEW YORK

Collier Macmillan Publishers
LONDON

Macmillan Publishing Company
866 Third Avenue
New York, NY 10022

Collier Macmillan Canada, Inc.

Library of Congress Cataloging-in-Publication Data

Pfleeger, Shari Lawrence.
    Software engineering.

    Includes index.
    1. Computer software—Development. I. Title.
QA76.76.D47P5 1987   005.1   86–31249
ISBN 0-02-395720-4

Printing: 1 2 3 4 5 6 7 8   Year: 7 8 9 0 1 2 3 4 5 6

ISBN 0-02-395720-4

DEDICATION

To CPP with affection and gratitude

TABLE OF CONTENTS

PREFACE

Software Engineering is a text for an undergraduate software engineering course. If there is no software engineering curriculum, the text is appropriate for an introductory or survey course, to be used for either one or two semesters. Theoretical software engineering research is shown in practical application, presenting a pragmatic approach to the development of quality software. Theory and practice are blended with examples that relate a student's limited experience to what can be expected on a large software development project.

Key Features

This text has several key features that distinguish it from others.

- *Theory and examples:* The primary function of the text is to present a survey of software engineering theory and principles, supplemented with examples of many available tools and techniques. These examples are detailed enough so that students understand how the method works, why it is helpful, and where it is used best. Automated tools, available on microcomputers as well as on large mainframes, are presented. Most important, an explanation of software engineering is woven from two interdependent points of view: practical experience, and research and development.

- *History of software development:* Current techniques are placed in perspective by reviewing past difficulties with software development and illustrating the need for better methods and tools. Different kinds of software are compared, showing why they are needed, and how they are used. The text explains that software projects differ in complexity, precision and scale, and that techniques and tools can help to solve these problems.

- *Current software engineering methods:* New, more flexible software engineering methods are being espoused today; therefore, flexible approaches such as data abstraction and rapid prototyping are included, along with explanations as to why things have changed and where software engineering is headed.

- *Human issues:* Software engineering is concerned with human as well as technical issues. Recognition is given to the different work styles and needs of the personnel involved on a project, and the student is shown how organizations must be designed to accommodate these differences. The relationships among customer, developer and user are addressed throughout the software development process, emphasizing the connection between these relationships and the production of quality software.

- *Relation to classroom experience:* Discussing concepts and issues *with* students, rather than talking *at* them, the text relates student experience in school to what will most likely be encountered on a job. An emphasis is placed on how analysis, design and programming will be different when done for an employer or a customer. Examples are provided at each stage of software development so that the students understand what is involved at each step.
- *Common example throughout text:* A common example is used throughout the text to give the students an idea of what happens in each stage of software development. The relationships among the customer, developer and user are explored, and examples are given of the interaction among all three.

Thus, this text makes software engineering understandable to the student by tying together the student's experience, practical examples of software engineering, and the underpinnings of computer science. By uniting all three, the student sees how software engineering applies computer science to real-life problems. Moreover, the student views software engineering not just as a set of technical tools but also in a human context.

By communicating at the student's level and relating concepts to what the student understands from his or her academic background, the text allows the instructor to bridge the gap from the theoretical aspects of computer science to the practicalities of software engineering. A software system is viewed as dynamic rather than static; this permits the instructor to present software engineering methods as being flexible and adaptable.

Contents and Organization

Chapter 1 begins with an overview of systems. It investigates why our track record as software engineers has been less than satisfactory. Chapter 2 explains the planning process and the need to estimate cost and schedule before a project even begins. The components of cost are discussed, and several models of cost are examined. In particular, the human element of a project is analyzed, and the effects of work style and project organization on the cost and schedule are investigated.

Each of the next eight chapters addresses a step in the software development process. Chapter 3 investigates the analysis of requirements to ensure that project goals are understood by both customer and developer. Chapter 4 explains how these requirements are translated into a system design to express how the developer plans to solve the customer's problem. Next, chapter 5 describes the way in which the system design is transformed into a program design. The implementation of the program design as actual lines of code is the subject of chapter 6, and guidelines for good programming are included here.

Chapter 7 begins a two-part discussion of testing. First, unit testing is explained, and students are shown the need for thorough integration testing. Chapter 8 goes on to explain the steps involved in function, performance, acceptance and installation testing. When the system is considered to be working properly, it must be delivered to the customer with effective training aids and documentation; chapter 9 describes the tools and techniques available for their development.

The final stage is addressed in chapter 10, where students learn how a system continually evolves, requiring enhancement and modification. It is here that configuration management is described as a technique for controlling system change.

Chapter 11 returns to the issue of past performance by software engineers. Methods that work well in a classroom setting must often be adjusted to suit the political and organizational goals of a business or agency. Typical development problems are discussed, as well as suggested methods for avoiding or handling them.

Teaching Aids

An instructor's manual has been developed to accompany this text. Written by Catherine Hilten, a software engineer with many years of experience in software design and development, the manual provides solutions to all exercises in the text.

ACKNOWLEDGMENTS

Many people have worked very hard to make this book a success. Without Maria Colligan Taylor, I might never have put pen to paper; I thank her for her persistence. I appreciate the help and suggestions of Melissa Wilson, Leon Binder, Robert Kroboth and Robert McDaniel. Many thanks to Bruce Morgenegg, Carol Weaver, Debra Pyatt and Ann Wayburn for the care and speed with which they prepared the manuscript, and to Linda Blake for thorough and professional technical editing. Kristan Mertz was of great help in obtaining permission from vendors to use examples of their products. The comments and suggestions of Bill Haynes, Cathy Hilten, Pat Ehlers and Gary Ford have done a great deal to improve the quality of the text. Laura Welch and the enlightened staff of IPS made the production of the book easy and fun, and I thank them for their expertise and professionalism. Systems/Software, Inc. provided release time to prepare the manuscript and programming support that allowed me to concentrate on the message rather than the medium. Finally but most importantly, I am grateful to Charles Pfleeger for his thorough and careful review of the manuscript, for his encouragement and professional expertise, for his patience and understanding, and for his love and friendship.

S.L.P.

CHAPTER 1

WHY SOFTWARE ENGINEERING?

Computer science is an art as well as a science, and it is important for you as a student of computer science to understand why. Computer scientists not only *study computer mechanisms* and theorize about how to make them more productive or efficient; they also *design computer systems* and write programs to perform tasks on those systems. It is in this latter capacity that computer science can be considered an art. There may be many ways to perform a particular task on a particular system, but some are better than others. One way may be more efficient, more precise, easier to modify, easier to use, or easier to understand. Consequently, *Software Engineering* is about designing and developing high quality software.

We begin by looking at how successful we have been as developers of software systems. After examining the way in which we analyze problems and develop solutions, we show the differences between computer science problems and engineering ones. Our ultimate goal is to produce solutions incorporating high quality software, and we list the characteristics that contribute to that quality.

Next, we look at the people involved in software development. After investigating the roles and responsibilities of customers, users and developers, we turn to a study of the system itself. We see that a system can be viewed as a group of objects related to a set of activities and enclosed by a boundary. Alternatively, we look at a system with an engineer's eye; a system can be developed much as a house is built. Having defined the steps in building a system, we discuss the roles of the development team at each step.

Finally, we discuss some of the possible problems that may arise during development. Because the potential for problems is based to some degree on the characteristics of the system, we build a table of system descriptors and describe how each affects the degree of development difficulty.

1.1

HOW SUCCESSFUL HAVE WE BEEN?

Before we examine what is needed to produce quality software systems, let us look back to see how successful we as computer scientists have been. Are users happy with their existing software and systems? Yes and no. Often systems work, but not

1

exactly as expected. We have all heard stories of systems that just barely work. We have all written programs that still have errors in them but are good enough for a passing grade. Clearly, such behavior is not acceptable when developing a system for a customer.

Our Track Record

There is an enormous difference between an error in a class project and one in a large software system. In fact, software errors and the difficulty in producing error-free software have become frequent topics in recent literature. Some errors are merely annoying; others cost a great deal of time and money. Still others are life threatening. Let us look at a few examples to see what is going wrong and why.

In the early 1980s, the Internal Revenue Service (IRS) hired Sperry Corporation to build an automated federal income tax form processing system. According to the *Washington Post*, the "system has proved inadequate to the workload, cost nearly twice what was expected and must be replaced soon" ([SAW85]). In 1985, an extra $90 million was needed to enhance the original $103 million worth of Sperry equipment. In addition, because the problem prevented the IRS from returning refunds to taxpayers by the deadline, the IRS was forced to pay $40.2 million in interest and $22.3 million in overtime wages for its employees who were trying to catch up.

President Reagan's Strategic Defense Initiative (SDI) has also heightened the public's awareness of the difficulty of producing an error-free software system. Newspapers and magazines ([REN85], [JAC85], [KAN85], [PAR85], for example) have published reports of skepticism in the computer science community. Many computer scientists and software engineers believe there is no way to write and test the software to guarantee adequate reliability.

Many software engineers think that a system for the SDI would require at least ten million lines of code, but some estimates range as high as one hundred million. By comparison, the software supporting the space shuttle consists of three million lines of code, including computers on the ground controlling the launch and the flight; there are one hundred thousand lines of code in the shuttle itself ([REN85]). Thus, an SDI software system may be at least an order of magnitude larger than the largest system in existence.

Many people point to the space shuttle project as an example of the success of software engineering, arguing that the same techniques and tools can be used to build other, more complex software systems. However, a close examination of the space shuttle software reveals that, like many other projects, it too is rife with errors. The first scheduled launch of the shuttle *Columbia* was to be on April 10, 1981— three years late and costing millions of dollars more than planned ([JOY85]). The launch was cancelled because of what was later revealed to be a synchronization problem with the shuttle's five on-board computers. The error was traced to a change made two years earlier, when a programmer reset a delay factor from fifty to eighty milliseconds. This change meant that there was one chance in sixty-seven that the launch would fail. The likelihood of an error was small enough so that the error caused no harm during the thousands of hours of software testing, but created a problem at the actual launch.

The synchronization error was not the only one in the shuttle system. After five years and twenty space flights, the astronauts using the *Columbia* were still being supplied with a book, *Program Notes and Waivers*, a list of known software problems. Some problems were minor, such as the interleaving of two messages on the shuttle display screen. However, the use of a common buffer area shared by the keyboard of the on-board terminal and by ground communications created a more severe problem. If a program or data was being uploaded at the same time that an astronaut was typing, the contents of the buffer were jumbled.

The space shuttle system was developed with over $10 billion of research and development, and yet substantial errors still exist. Moreover, there may be other severe errors that have not yet been discovered. Clearly, there is much yet to be learned about how to build an error-free software product.

According to DeMarco ([DEM82]), the average software product on the market in the U. S. is not error-free. Furthermore, the modifications needed to fix the errors we know exist are sometimes so difficult to make that it is easier to *rewrite* a whole system than to change existing code. Boehm notes that the data processing division of an average corporation has been devoting more and more time to maintenance over the past several decades ([BOE81]). In fact, software maintenance now represents over half of a data processing division's efforts.

Moreover, the longer an error goes undetected, the more *expensive* it is to correct. For example, the cost of correcting an error made during the initial analysis of a project is only one-tenth the cost of correcting a similar error after the system has been turned over to the customer. Unfortunately, we do not catch most of the errors early on. Half of the cost of correcting errors found during testing and maintenance comes from not having found errors that occurred earlier in the life of a system.

Such discoveries tell us that there is much room for improvement in the quality of the software we produce. As students, you are accustomed to developing and testing software on your own. Yet, your testing may be less effective than you think. Fagan ([FAG82]) studied the way in which errors have been detected in the past. He discovered that testing a program by running it with test data revealed only about a fifth of the errors located during system development. However, peer review, the process whereby colleagues examine and comment on each other's design and code, uncovered the remaining four out of five errors found. Thus, the quality of your software can be increased dramatically just by having your colleagues review your work.

1.2

WHAT IS SOFTWARE ENGINEERING?

As computer scientists, we use our knowledge of computers and computing to help solve problems. Often the problem with which we are dealing is related to a computer or an existing computer system, but sometimes the difficulties underlying the problem have nothing to do with computers. Therefore, it is essential that we first understand *the nature of the problem*. In particular, we must be very careful not to impose computing machinery on every problem that comes our way. We must solve the problem first. Then, if need be, we can use technology as a tool to implement our solution. For the remainder of this book, we will assume that our analysis has shown that some kind of computer system is necessary or desirable to solve a particular problem at hand.

Solving Problems

We must begin the investigation of any problem by analyzing it, that is, by breaking that problem into pieces that we can understand and try to deal with. Then we construct our solution from components that address the problem's various aspects. As shown in Figure 1.1, **analysis** is the process of breaking a larger structure into pieces. Figure 1.2 illustrates the reverse: **synthesis** is the putting together of a large structure from small building blocks. Thus, any problem-solving technique must have two parts: analyzing the problem to determine its nature, and then synthesizing a solution based on our analysis.

    To help us solve a problem, we employ a variety of tools and techniques. A **tool** is an instrument or automated system for accomplishing something in a better way. This "better way" can mean that the tool makes us more accurate, more efficient, more productive, or that it enhances the quality of the resulting product. For

Figure 1.1   The Process of Analysis

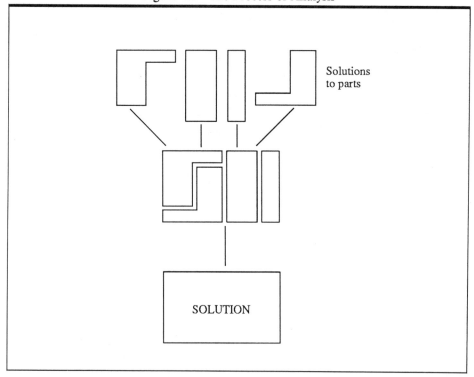

Solutions
to parts

SOLUTION

Figure 1.2   The Process of Synthesis

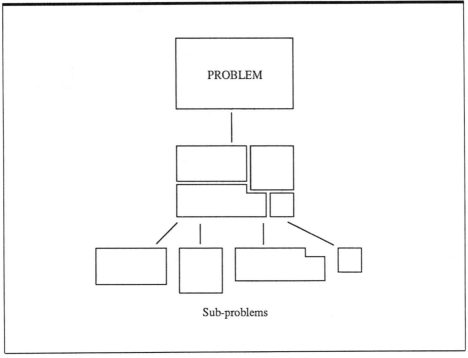

example, we use a typewriter to write letters because the resulting letters are easier to read than our handwriting. Or, we use a pair of scissors as a tool because we can cut faster and straighter than if we were tearing a page.

Sometimes using a procedure or method (but not necessarily a tool) can be similar to using an instrument. We call a **technique** a formal procedure or method for producing some result. For example, a chef may prepare a sauce using a sequence of ingredients combined in a carefully timed and ordered way so that the sauce thickens but does not curdle or separate. The procedure for preparing the sauce involves timing and ingredients but may not depend on the type of cooking equipment used. Here it is the *technique* that makes the sauce better, not the pot or spoon used by the chef.

Computer scientists use tools and techniques to enhance the quality of their software products. Their aim is to use efficient and productive methods to generate effective solutions to problems.

Where Does the Software Engineer Fit In?

To understand how a software engineer fits in the computer science world, let us look to another discipline for an example. Consider the study of chemistry and its use to solve problems. The chemist investigates chemicals: their structure, their interactions, and the theory behind their behavior. Chemical engineers apply the results of the chemists' studies to a variety of problems. Chemistry as viewed by chemists is the object of study. On the other hand, chemistry for a chemical engineer is a tool to be used to address a general problem (which may not even be "chemical" in nature).

We can view computing in a similar light. We can concentrate on the computers and programming languages themselves, or we can view them as *tools* to be used in designing and implementing a solution to a problem. Software engineering takes the latter view, as shown in Figure 1.3. Instead of investigating hardware design or proving theorems about how algorithms work, a software engineer focuses on the computer as a problem-solving tool. We will see later in this chapter that a software engineer works with the functions of a computer as part of a general solution, rather than with the structure or theory of the computer itself.

Quality Software

Just as manufacturers look for ways to assure the quality of the products they produce, so too must computer scientists find methods to assure that their products are of acceptable quality and utility. **Software engineering** is a strategy for producing quality software. Thus, it is important for us to understand what we mean by quality software. What distinguishes "good" software from "bad?"

Characteristics of software quality depend on who is analyzing the software. Users judge software to be of high quality if it does what they want in a way that is easy to learn and easy to use. The software must also be judged by those who are designing and writing the code and by those who must maintain the programs after they are written. Thus, as seen in Figure 1.4, high-quality software has characteristics that address the needs of users, developers, and maintainers.

Figure 1.3   Relationship Between Computer Science and Software Engineering

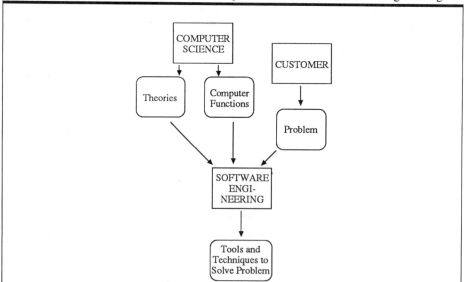

Figure 1.4 Judges of Software Quality

Software Characteristics. Boehm ([BOE78]) views software quality as the incorporation of particular characteristics of software. Figure 1.5 illustrates these characteristics and their interconnection. Note that Boehm's notion of successful software emphasizes not only hardware and software performance but also the needs and expectations of users. Let us examine these characteristics in detail, since insuring their appearance in our software is the focus of the remainder of this book and of software engineering in general.

First, a software system must be *useful*. If it is not, then its development has been a waste of time, money and effort. General utility is a measure of how useful a software system is to those who are supposed to use it. We can consider system utility in three ways, corresponding to the three types of users who remain involved once the system is delivered. The first is the original customer, who is pleased with utility if the system as-is does what the customer wants it to do.

There may be others who want to use the system on another computer at another location. In this case, the system must be **portable**, so that it can be moved from one computer to another and still function properly. The system should also be portable in a slightly different sense. Sometimes an overall configuration remains the same, but the hardware or software is upgraded to a newer model or version. In this case, the system should be able to be moved to the new or different model or version without disturbing the functionality of the system. For example, if one programming language compiler is replaced by another compiler for the same language, the system's functions should not be degraded. Thus, the second type of user of a system is the one involved with this upgraded or changed system.

Finally, the third type of user is the programmer who maintains the system, making any changes that may be needed as customer requirements change or as errors are detected. Programmers must be able to locate the source of an error, find the modules that perform a particular function, understand the code, and modify it.

All three types of users hope that the system is reliable and efficient. By **reliability**, we mean that the system produces the correct result to the correct degree of accuracy. We say in this case that the system has **integrity**. Moreover, if

Figure 1.5   Characteristics of Software

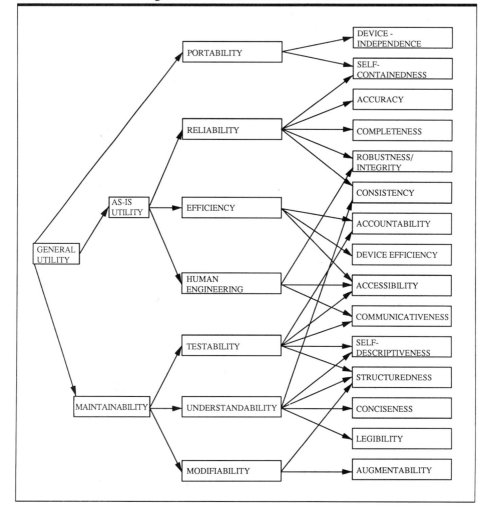

the same set of input data is submitted to the system many times under the same conditions, the results should match. This is called **consistency of function**.

At the same time, the system should produce its results or perform its functions in a timely manner, as determined by the needs of the customer. Thus, data should be *accessible* when needed, and the system should respond to the user in a reasonable amount of time.

Finally, the users and programmers must find the system easy to learn and to use. This *human engineering* aspect can sometimes be the most critical. A system may be very good at performing a function, but if users cannot understand how to use it, the system is a failure.

Thus, **quality software** is software that satisfies the needs of the users and programmers involved with it. We can consider software to be of high quality if:

- It does what the user wants it to do.
- It uses computer resources correctly and efficiently.
- It is easy for the user to learn and use.
- The developers can design, code, test and maintain the system with relative ease.

To produce quality software, it is not enough to know the principles involved in building a computer or developing a computer language. As Figure 1.6 shows us, we must also learn concepts, techiques, and tools to help us design and develop quality programs. Software engineering provides the "tool kit" we need for successful construction of quality software.

Figure 1.6 How to Build Quality Programs

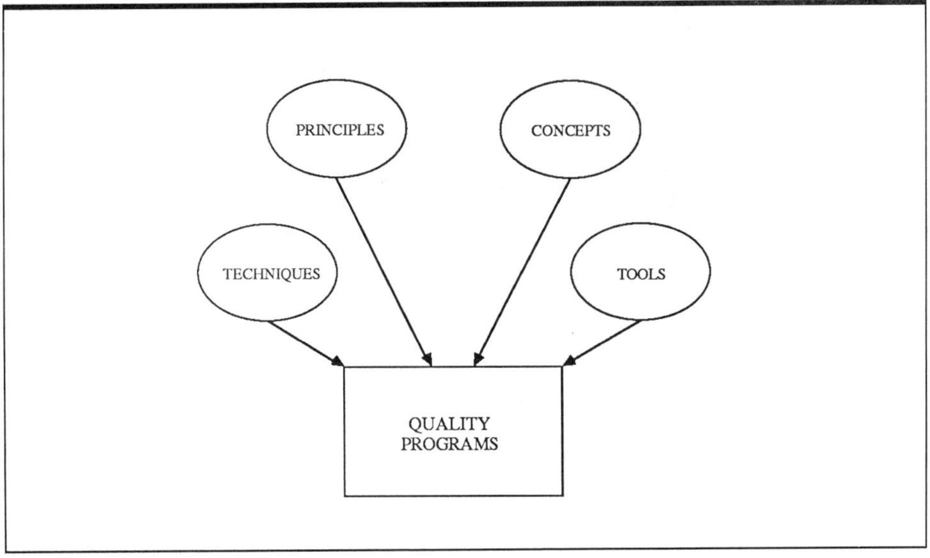

Jobs and Responsibilities

A key component of software development is communication between customer and developer; if that fails, so too will the system. We must understand what the customer wants and needs before we can build a system to help. To do this, let us turn our attention to the people involved in software development.

The number of people working on software development depends on the project's size and degree of difficulty. However, no matter how many people are involved, the *roles* that are played throughout the life of the project can be distinguished. Thus, for a large project, one person or a group may be assigned to each of the roles identified; on a small project, one person or group may take on several roles at once.

Usually, the participants in a project fall into one of three categories: customer, user, or developer. The **customer** is the company, organization, or person who is paying for the software system to be developed. The **developer** is the company, organization, or person who is building the software system for the customer. The **user** is the person or people who will actually use the system: the ones who sit at the terminal or submit the data or read the output. Although for some projects the customer, user, and developer are the same person or group, often these are different sets of people. Figure 1.7 shows the basic relationships among the three types of participants.

The customer, being in control of the funds, usually negotiates the contract and signs the acceptance papers. However, sometimes the customer is not a user. For example, suppose Wittenberg Water Works signs a contract with Gentle Systems, Inc. to build a computerized accounting system for the company. The president of Wittenberg may describe to the representatives of Gentle Systems exactly what is needed, and she will sign the contract. However, the president will not use the accounting system directly; the users will be the bookkeepers and accounting clerks. Thus, it is important that the developers understand exactly what both the customer and users want and need.

On the other hand, suppose Wittenberg Water Works is so large that it has its own computer systems development division. The division may decide that it needs an automated tool to keep track of its own project costs and schedules. By building the tool itself, the division is at the same time user, customer, and developer.

Before we proceed with the investigation of the process of developing a software system, we must know what we mean by the term "system." Such an understanding will help us, as developers, to define what we want to build and determine how the result will fit into the customer's environment.

Figure 1.7 Relationships among Customer, Users, and Developer

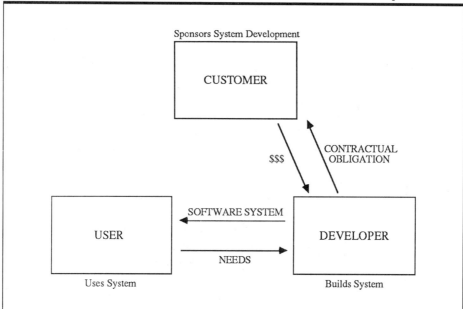

1.3

A SYSTEMS APPROACH

The projects we develop do not exist in a vacuum. Often, the hardware and software we put together must interact with users, with other software tasks, with other pieces of hardware, with existing data bases (that is, with carefully defined sets of data and data relationships), or even with other computer systems. Therefore, it is important to provide a *context* for any project by knowing the boundaries of the project: what is included in the project and what is not. For example, suppose you are asked by your supervisor to write a program to print pay checks for the people in your office. You must know whether your program simply reads hours worked from another system and prints the results or whether you must also calculate the pay information. Similarly, you must know whether the program is to calculate taxes, pensions and benefits or whether a report of these items is to be provided with each paycheck. What you are really asking is, Where does the project begin and end? The same question applies to any system. We must know whether any object or activity is included in the system or not.

The Elements of a System

We can describe a system by identifying how its component parts are related to one another. This is the first step in analyzing the problem presented to us.

Activities and Objects. First, we distinguish between activities and objects. An **activity** is something that happens in the system. The activity transforms one thing to another by changing a characteristic. This can mean that data is moved from one location to another, is transformed from one value to another, or is combined with other data to supply input for yet another activity. For example, an item of data can be moved from one file to another. In this case, the characteristic changed is the location. Or, the value of the data item can be incremented. Finally, the address of the data item can be included in a list of parameters with the addresses of several other data items so that a subprocedure can be called.

The elements involved in the activities are called **objects** or **entities**. Usually, these objects are related to each other in some way. For instance, the objects can be arranged in a table or matrix. Often, objects are grouped as records, where each record is arranged in a prescribed format. An employee history record, for example, may contain objects (called *fields*) for each employee, such as the following:

First name	Zip code
Middle name	Salary per hour
Last name	Benefits per hour
Street address	Vacation hours accrued
City	Sick leave accrued
State	

Not only is each field in the record defined, but the size and relationship of each field to the others is named. Thus, the record description states the data type of each field, the starting location in the record, and the length of the field. In turn, since there is a record for each employee, the records are combined into a file, and file characteristics (such as maximum number of records) may be specified.

Relationships and the System Boundary. Once entities and activities are defined, we match the entities with their activities. The relationships among entities and activities are clearly and carefully defined. An entity definition includes a description of where the entity originates. Some items reside in files that already exist; others are created during some activity. The entity's destination is important, too. Some items are used by only one activity, but others are destined to be input to other systems. That is, some items from one system are used by activities outside the scope of the system being examined. Thus, we can think of the system at which we are looking as having a border or boundary. Some items cross the boundary to enter our system, while others are products of our system and travel out for another system's use.

Using these concepts, we can define a **system** as a collection of things: a set of entities, a set of activities, a description of the relationships among entities and activities, and a definition of the boundary of the system. This definition of a system applies not only to computer systems but to anything in which objects interact in some way with other objects.

Figure 1.8 Respiratory System

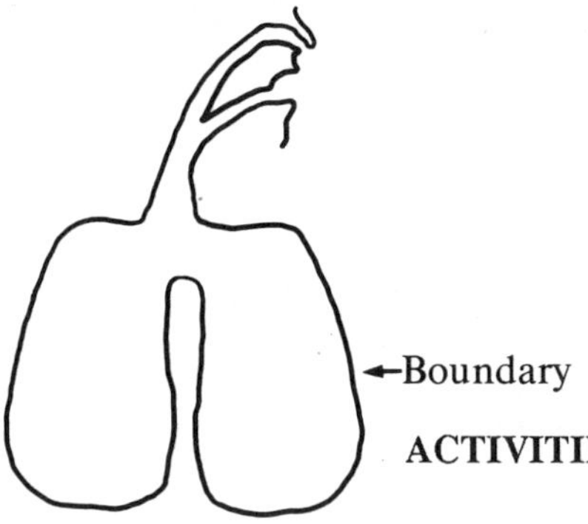

ENTITIES:

Particulate matter
Oxygen
Carbon dioxide
Carbon monoxide
Nitrogen
Nose
Mouth
Trachea
Bronchial tubes
Lungs
Alveoli

Boundary

ACTIVITIES:

Inhale gases
Filtering gases
Transfer molecules to/from blood
Exhale gases

Figure 1.9 Paycheck System

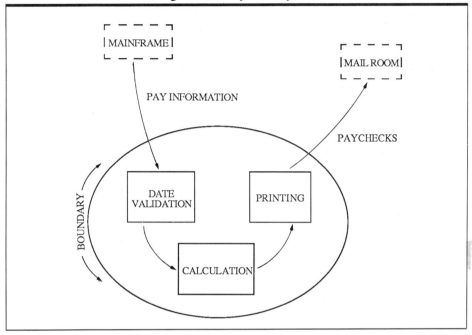

Examples of Systems. For instance, your respiratory system is a bona fide system. You can define its boundary because if you name a particular organ of your body, you know whether or not it is part of your respiratory system. Molecules of oxygen and carbon dioxide are entities or objects moving through the system in ways that are clearly defined. We can also describe the activities in the system in terms of the *interactions* of the entities. If necessary, we can illustrate the system by showing what enters and leaves it; we can also supply tables to describe all entities and the activities in which they are involved. Figure 1.8 illustrates the respiratory system. Note that each activity involves the entities and can be defined by describing which entities act as input, how they are processed, and what is produced (output).

We must also describe our computer systems clearly. We work with prospective users to define the boundary of the system: where does our work start and stop? In addition, we need to know what is on the boundary of the system and thus determine the origins of the input and destinations of the output. In a system that prints paychecks, for example, pay information may come from the company's mainframe computer. The system output may be a set of paychecks sent to the mail room to be delivered to the appropriate recipients. In the system shown in Figure 1.9, we can see the boundary and can understand the entities, the activities, and their relationships.

Interrelated Systems. The concept of boundary is important, because very few systems are independent of other systems. For example, the respiratory system must interact with the digestive system, the circulatory system, the nervous system, and others. The respiratory system could not function without the nervous system; neither could the circulatory system function without the respiratory system. The interdependencies may be complex. (Indeed, many of our environmental problems arise and are intensified because we do not appreciate the complexity of our ecosystem.) However, once the boundary of a system is described, it is easier for us to see what is within and without and what crosses the boundary. In turn, it is possible for one system to exist inside another system.

When we describe a computer system, we often concentrate on a small piece of what is really a much larger system. Such a focus allows us to define and build a much less complex system than the enveloping one. If we are careful in documenting the interactions among and between systems affecting ours, we lose nothing by concentrating on this smaller piece of a larger system.

Let us look at an example of how this can be done. Suppose we are developing a water monitoring system where data is gathered at many points throughout a river valley. At the collection sites, several calculations are done, and the results are communicated to a central location for comprehensive reporting. Such a system may be implemented with a computer at the central site communicating with several dozen smaller computers at the remote locations. Many system activities must be considered, including the way the water data is gathered, the calculations performed at the remote locations, the communication of information to the central site, the storage of the communicated data in a data base, and the creation of reports from the data. We can view this system as a *collection* of systems, each with a special purpose. In particular, we can consider only the communications aspect of the larger system and develop a communications system to transmit data from a set of remote sites to a central one. If we carefully define the boundary between the communications and the larger system, the design and development of the communications system can be done independently of the larger.

The complexity of the entire water monitoring system is much greater than the complexity of the communications system, so our treatment of separate, smaller pieces makes our job much simpler. If the boundary definitions are detailed and correct, building the larger system from the smaller ones is relatively easy. We can describe the building process by considering the larger system in layers, as illustrated in Figure 1.10 for our water monitoring example. A layer is a system by itself, but each layer and those it contains also form a system. The concentric circles of the figure represent the boundaries of the respective systems, and the entire set of concentric circles incorporates the entire water monitoring system.

Recognizing that one system contains another is important, because it reflects the fact that an object or activity in one system is part of every system represented by the outer layers. Since more complexity is introduced with each layer, understanding any one object or activity becomes more difficult with each more-encompassing system. Thus, we maximize simplicity and our consequent understanding of the system by focusing on the smallest system possible at first.

We use this idea when building a system to replace an older version, either manual or automated. We want to understand as much as possible about how both the old and new systems work. Often the greater the difference between the two systems, the more difficult the design and development. This difficulty occurs not only because people tend to resist change, but also because the difference makes

Figure 1.10 Layers of Water Monitoring System

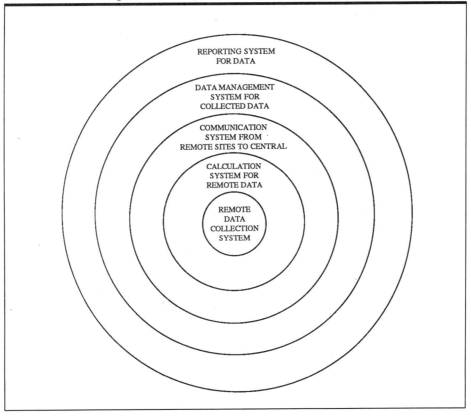

learning difficult. In building or synthesizing our grand system, it helps dramatically to construct a new system as an *incremental series* of intermediate systems, as shown in Figure 1.11. For instance, rather than going from system A to system B, we may be able to go from A to A' to B. By dividing the "distance" from A to B in half, we have a series of small problems that may be easier to handle than the whole.

The target system may be vastly different from the existing one. In particular, it is usually desirable that the target be free of constraints imposed by existing hardware or software. An incremental development approach may incorporate a series of stages, each of which frees the previous system from another such constraint. For example, stage one may add a new piece of hardware, stage two may replace the software performing a particular set of functions, and so on. The system is slowly drawn away from old software and hardware until it is reflects the new system design.

Thus, system development can first incorporate a set of changes to an actual system and then add a series of changes to generate a complete design scheme, rather than trying to jump from present to future in one move. With such an approach, we must view the system in two different ways simultaneously: statically and dynamically. The *static* view tells us how the system is working today, while the

Figure 1.11   Incremental Steps from Old System to New System

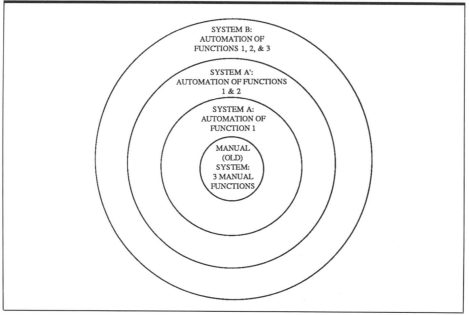

dynamic view shows us how the system is changing into what it will eventually become. One view is not complete without the other.

1.4

AN ENGINEERING APPROACH

Once we understand the system's nature, we are ready to begin its construction. At this point, the "engineering" part of software engineering becomes relevant and complements what we have done so far. Recall that we began this chapter by acknowledging that computer science is an art as well as a science. The art of producing systems involves the craft of software production. As artists, we develop techniques and tools that have proven helpful in producing useful, high-quality products. For instance, we may use an optimizing compiler as a tool to generate programs that run fast on the machines that we are using. Or, we can include special sort or search routines as techniques for saving time or space in our system. These are used just as techniques and tools are used in crafting a fine piece of furniture or in building a house. Indeed, a popular collection of programming tools is called the _Programmer's Workbench_, because programmers rely on them as a carpenter relies on a workbench.

Because building a system is similar to building a house, we can look to house building for other examples of why the "artistic" approach to software development is important.

Building a House

Suppose the Ehlers hire someone to build a new house for them. Because of its size and complexity, a house usually requires more than one person on the construction team. The Ehlers hire McMullen Construction Company. The first event involved in house building is a conference between the Ehlers and McMullen so that the Ehlers can explain what they want. This conference explores not only what the Ehlers want the house to look like but also what features are to be included. Then McMullen draws up floor plans and an architect's rendering of the house. After the Ehlers discuss the details with McMullen, changes are made. Once the Ehlers give their approval to McMullen, construction begins.

During the construction process, the Ehlers are likely to inspect the construction site, thinking of changes that they would like. Several such changes may occur during construction, but eventually the house is completed. During construction and before the Ehlers move in, several components of the house are tested. For example, electricians test the wiring circuits, plumbers make sure that pipes do not leak, and carpenters adjust for variations in wood so that the floors are smooth and level. Finally, the Ehlers move in. If there is something that is not constructed properly, McMullen may be called in to fix it, but eventually the Ehlers become fully responsible for the house.

Let us look more closely at what is involved in this process. Since many people are working on the house at the same time, documentation is essential. Not only are floor plans and the architect's drawings necessary, but details must be written down so that specialists such as plumbers and electricians can fit their products together as the house becomes a whole. Second, it is unreasonable to expect the Ehlers to describe their house at the beginning of the process and walk away until the house is completed. Instead, the Ehlers may modify the house design several times during construction. Furthermore, because of unforeseen complications, McMullen may recommend some changes after construction has begun, and the Ehlers may change their minds about a feature of the house even after that feature is completed. Third, McMullen must provide blueprints, wiring and plumbing diagrams, instructions manuals for the appliances, and any other documentation which would enable the Ehlers to make modifications or repairs after they move in.

We can summarize this construction process in the following way:

- Determining and analyzing the *requirements*.
- Producing and documenting the *overall design* of the house.
- Producing detailed *specifications* of the house.
- Identifying and designing the *components*.
- *Building* each component of the house.
- *Testing* each component of the house.
- *Integrating* the components.
- Making *final modifications* after the residents have moved in.
- Continuing *maintenance* by the residents of the house.

Again, the participants remain flexible and allow changes in the original specifications at various points during construction.

Construction of a house is done in the context of the city or county building codes and regulations. The McMullen employees are licensed by the city or county, and they are expected to perform according to building standards. The construction site is visited by building inspectors who make sure that the standards are being followed. The building inspectors set standards for quality, and the inspections serve as *quality assurance* for the building project.

Building a System

Software projects progress in a way similar to the process of building a house. The Ehlers were the customers and users and McMullen the developer in our example. Had the Ehlers asked McMullen to build the house for Mr. Ehlers' parents to live in, the sets of users, customers, and developer would have been distinct. In the same way, software development involves users, customers, and developers. If we are asked to develop a software system for a customer, the first step is meeting with the customer to determine the *requirements*. These requirements describe the system, as we saw above. Without knowing the boundary, the entities, and the activities, it is impossible to describe the software and how it will interact with its environment.

Once requirements are defined, we create a *system design* to meet the specified requirements. As we will see in chapter 4, the system design shows the customer what the system will look like from the customer's perspective. Thus, just as the Ehlers looked at floor plans and an architect's drawing, we present the customer with pictures of the video display screens that will be used, the reports that will be generated, and any other descriptions that will explain how users will interact with the completed system. If the system has manual backup or override procedures, those are described as well. At first, the Ehlers were interested only in the appearance and functionality of their house; it was not until later that they had to decide on such items as copper or plastic pipes. Likewise, the system design phase of a software project describes only appearance and functionality.

The design is then reviewed by the customer. When approved, the overall system design is used to generate the designs of the individual programs involved. Note that it is not until this step that programs are mentioned. Until functionality and appearance are determined, it makes no sense to consider coding. In our house example, we would now be ready to discuss types of pipe or quality of electrical wiring. We can decide on plastic or copper pipes because now we know where water needs to flow in the structure. Likewise, when the system design is approved by all, we are ready to discuss *programs*. The basis for our discussion is a well-defined description of the software project as a system; the system design includes a complete description of functions and interactions involved.

When the programs have been written, they are tested as individual pieces of code before they can be linked together. This first phase of testing is called *module* or *unit testing*. Once we are convinced that the pieces work as desired, we put them together and make sure that they work properly when joined with others. This second testing phase is often referred to as *integration testing*, as we build our system by adding one piece to the next until the entire system is operational. The final testing phase, called *system testing*, involves a test of the whole system to make sure that the functions and interactions specified initially have been implemented properly. In this phase, the system is compared with the specified requirements; developer, customer, and users check that the system serves its intended purpose.

At last the final product is delivered. As it is used, discrepancies and dislikes are uncovered in the system. If this is a **turnkey system,** the customer assumes responsibility for the system after delivery. Many systems are not turnkey systems, though, and the developer or other organization provides maintenance if anything goes wrong or if needs and requirements change.

The Software Development Life Cycle

Thus, development of software includes the following steps:

1. Requirements analysis and definition
2. System design
3. Program design
4. Writing the programs (program implementation)
5. Unit testing
6. Integration testing
7. System testing
8. System delivery
9. Maintenance

In an ideal situation, the steps are performed one at a time; when you reach the end of the list, you have a completed software project. However, in reality, many of the steps are repeated. For example, in reviewing the system design, you and the customer may discover that some requirements have yet to be documented. You may work with the customer to add requirements and possibly redesign the system. Similarly, when writing and testing code, you may find that a device does not function as described by its documentation. You may have to redesign the code, reconsider the system design, or even return to a discussion with the customer about how to meet the requirements.

As we proceed with our investigation of software engineering, we will examine each development step to see what it involves and to find out what tools and techniques are available to help us. For convenience, we discuss the steps in the order listed above. However, as Figure 1.12 shows, there is always the possibility that we will return to a previous step to revise or redefine something based on new information. Our goal in studying the development steps is to understand the software development process and to combine that knowledge with principles, tools, and methods that will result in quality software systems. Our function is similar to that of the building inspectors: we recommend standards and procedures that build a minimum degree of quality into the final product. A **software quality assurance** or **review process** is performed to make sure that the system is not delivered unless it is of acceptable quality.

Figure 1.12   The Development Cycle

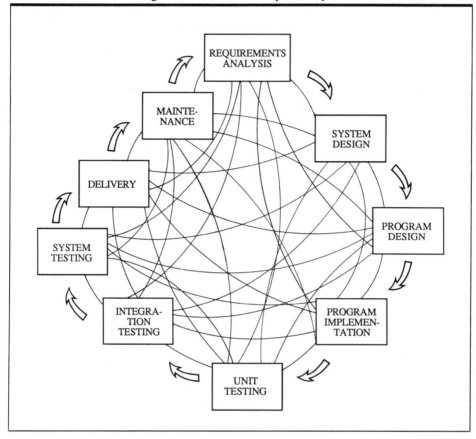

Members of the Development Team

Before we embark on our investigation of software development, we consider who will be involved in the development work. Earlier in this chapter, we saw that customers, users, and developers play major roles in the definition and creation of the new product. The developers are software engineers, but each engineer may specialize in a particular aspect of development. Let us look in more detail at the role of the members of the development team.

The first step in the development process is finding out what the customer wants and documenting the requirements. As we have seen, analysis is the process of breaking things into their component parts so that we can understand them better. Thus, the development team includes one or more *analysts* to work with the customer, breaking what the customer wants into discrete requirements.

Once the requirements are known and documented, analysts work with *designers* to generate a system-level description of what the system is to do. In turn, the designers work with *programmers* to describe the system in such a way that programmers can write lines of code that implement what the requirements specify.

After the code is generated, it must be tested. Often, the first testing is done by the programmers themselves; sometimes, additional *testers* are also used to help catch errors that the programmers overlook. When units of code are integrated into functioning groups, a team of testers works with the implementation to verify that as the system is built up by combining pieces, it works properly and according to specification.

When the development team is comfortable with the functionality and quality of the system, attention turns to the customer. The test team and customer work together to verify that the complete system is what the customer wants; they do this by comparing how the system works with the initial set of requirements. Then, *trainers* show the users how to use the system.

For many software systems, acceptance by the customer does not mean the end of the developer's job. If errors are discovered after the system has been accepted, a *maintenance team* fixes them. In addition, the customer's requirements may change as time passes, and corresponding changes to the system must be made. Thus, maintenance can involve analysts who determine what requirements are added or changed, designers to determine where in the system design the change should be made, programmers to implement the changes, testers to make sure that the changed system still runs properly, and trainers to explain to users how the change affects the use of the system. Figure 1.13 illustrates how the roles of the development team correspond to the steps of the development cycle.

As a student, you often work by yourself or with small groups as a development team for class projects. The documentation requested by your instructor is minimal; you are usually not required to write a user manual or training documents. Moreover, the assignment is relatively stable; the requirements do not change over the life of the project. Finally, your systems are likely to be discarded at the end of the course; their purpose is to demonstrate your ability but not necessarily to solve a problem for a real customer. Thus, program size, system complexity, need for documentation, and need for maintainability are relatively small for class projects.

However, for a real customer the system size and complexity may be large, and the need great for documentation and maintainability. For a project involving many thousands of lines of code and much interaction among the members of the development team, control of the various aspects of the project may be difficult. To support everyone on the development team, several people may become involved with the system at the beginning of development and remain involved throughout. *Librarians* prepare and store documents that are used during the life of the system, including requirements specification, design descriptions, program documentation, training manuals, test schedules, and such. Working with the librarians are the members of a *configuration management* team. Configuration management involves the maintaining of a correspondence among the requirements, the design, the implementation and the tests. This cross-reference tells developers what program to alter if a change in requirements is needed, or what parts of a program will be affected if an alteration of some kind is proposed.

The development roles can be assumed by one person or several. For small projects, two or three people may share all roles. However, for large projects, the development team is often separated into distinct groups based on their function in

Figure 1.13   Roles of the Development Team

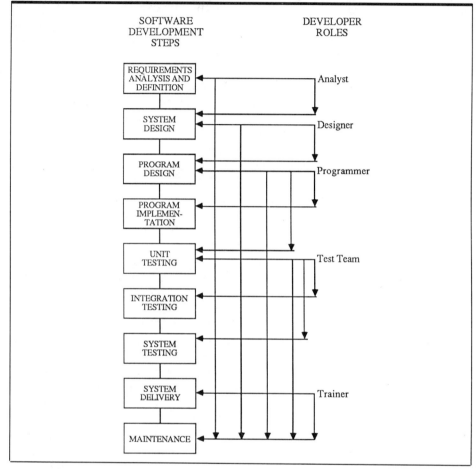

development. Sometimes, those who maintain the system are different from those who design or write the system initially. For a very large project, the customer can even hire one company to do the initial development and another to do the maintenance.

1.5

PROBLEMS WITH SOFTWARE DEVELOPMENT

We have compared the building of software to the building of a house. Each year, hundreds of houses are built across the country, and satisfied customers move in. Each year, hundreds of software products are built by developers, but customers are often very unhappy with the result. Why is there a difference? If it is so easy to enumerate the steps in the development of a system, why are we as software engineers having such a difficult time producing quality software?

Changing Constraints and Requirements

Think back to our house-building example. During the building process, the Ehlers continually reviewed the plans. They also had many opportunities to change their minds about what they wanted. In the same way, software development allows the customer to review the plans at every step and to make changes in the design. After all, if a developer produces a marvelous product that does not meet the customer's needs, the resultant system will have wasted everyone's time and effort.

For this reason, it is essential that our software engineering tools be used with an eye toward flexibility. In the past, we as developers have assumed that our customers know from the start what they want. That is not usually the case. As the various stages of a project unfold, constraints arise that were not anticipated at the beginning. For instance, after having chosen hardware and software to use for a particular project, we may find that a change in the customer requirements makes it difficult to use a particular data base management system to produce menus exactly as promised to the customer. Or, we may find that another system with which ours is to interface has changed its procedure or the format of the expected data. We may even find that hardware or software does not work quite as the vendor's documentation had promised. Thus, we must remember that each project is unique and that tools must be chosen that reflect the constraints placed on the individual project.

Phased Development Systems

Many development projects generate replacements for or additions to existing systems. Consequently, development can be much more complex than the step-by-step approach described above. For such projects, the system *evolves* over a period of time, and development incorporates the building of several systems, each one increasingly more complex than the previous one. In this process, pieces of the new system are built and merged one by one with the existing system; such an approach is called **phased development** and is illustrated in Figure 1.14. We begin with an existing system, and build and install phase one to include several changes from the existing system. Then we build phase two to replace phase one; phase two is closer to the required system because it implements more requirements than phase one. We continue in this way until the final phase is the complete system requested by the customer.

For example, suppose we are building a system to control telephone switching for the state of Pennsylvania. Telephone company customers would not be pleased to have their phones out of service while we install and test our new system. We must work out some sequence of implementation so that our new system replaces the old one gradually, with minimal disruption to the telephone customers. We may define phase one as a system where all telephone exchanges beginning with

Figure 1.14 Phased Development

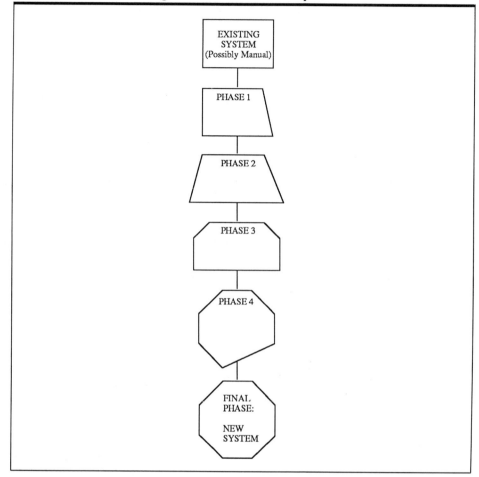

the number 1 use the automated system, while exchanges beginning with 2 through 9 continue to use the old system. Phase two may include exchanges beginning with both 1 and 2, phase three may include exchanges beginning with 1, 2, and 3, and so on, until all exchanges are using the new system.

In cases where we are replacing a manual system with an automated one, we may have the further complication of providing a manual override or auxiliary system so that users have a chance to learn the new system at a comfortable pace. Here, the phases may be defined in terms of how much of the manual system is replaced by the automated one.

When systems are enhancements to or replacements for systems of great sensitivity, or if one phase is to be developed while the previous phase is in use, we often work with two systems concurrently: a **development system** and a **production system**. The development system is used to design, code, and test parts of the new system or next phase in phased development. When we are convinced that the new phase is ready to be merged with or replace the existing system, the new code is combined with the old on the active production system. A successful merger requires planning, design, and coordination. In addition, we usually duplicate many of the development steps; care is taken to document and track changes not only on the production system but also on the development system. Obviously, there is a great deal of room for error; the techniques used previously have not always been able to handle the complexities of phased development.

Interactions with Other Systems

We must also acknowledge that most systems do not stand by themselves. They interface with other systems, either to receive or to provide information. Developing such systems is complex simply because they require a great deal of coordination with the systems with which they communicate. This complexity is especially true of systems that are being developed concurrently. In the past, developers have had difficulty assuring the accuracy and completeness of the documentation of interfaces among systems. In subsequent chapters, we will address the issue of controlling the interface problem.

The Nature of Computer Systems Themselves

So far, we have mentioned problems with software development that involve the imprecision of communication or the difficulty of dealing with change or with phased implementation. We must also address the difficulties inherent in working with computers themselves. In a paper to the professional computing community, Parnas ([PAR85]) discusses why computing is different from other disciplines. He reminds us that it is not always appropriate to compare the kind of work we do with that of other engineers and scientists, since we work with different types of systems and different types of tools.

Discrete and Continuous Systems. The systems we deal with are either discrete, continuous, or a combination of both. **Discrete systems**, sometimes called **digital systems**, can be described with a countable number of stable states. The stability of the states is important, since it assures us that things do not change. On the other hand, **continuous systems**, sometimes called **analog systems**, must be described with an uncountable number of stable states, the behavior of which is described by a continuous function. **Hybrid** systems are mixtures of these two types.

Most engineering disciplines deal with continuous systems and use the mathematics of continuous functions for description and understanding. When we call a function **continuous**, we mean that we can draw a picture of its behavior from beginning to end without lifting our pencil from the paper; there are no gaps. Thus, we know the behavior of the function at any point. In addition, small changes in the input to the function result only in small changes to the output. Therefore, the very nature of these systems allows us to keep components within their operating ranges, guarantees us no surprises, and assures reliability. For example, an engineer can assess the stress on a bridge by knowing about temperature, load, and material strength. None of these will fluctuate wildly or rapidly, so the bridge can be built to withstand an expected level of stress plus a margin for safety.

However, as computer scientists, we deal with discrete systems. In the past, the number of states of our systems was relatively small. We could test our systems thoroughly by examining all possible states or logic paths. This compensated for our lack of the kinds of testing methods available to engineers. When systems are hybrid, we can combine the two approaches, identifying a number of states with discrete behavior and using the mathematics of continuity for analysis.

Today, because we work with discrete systems with an increasingly large number of states, it is not always possible to structure our systems so that they are composed of repetitive pieces of simpler systems. The states are very different from one another, and each state's behavior must be described. Many times, the behavior of a state cannot be described with a continuous function, so engineering methods and tools do not help us to understand the complexities of the system. Hence, it is much more difficult for us to test our systems and to guarantee a high degree of reliability. Figure 1.15 summarizes these differences in method between computer science and engineering.

Figure 1.15　Comparison of Engineering with Computer Science

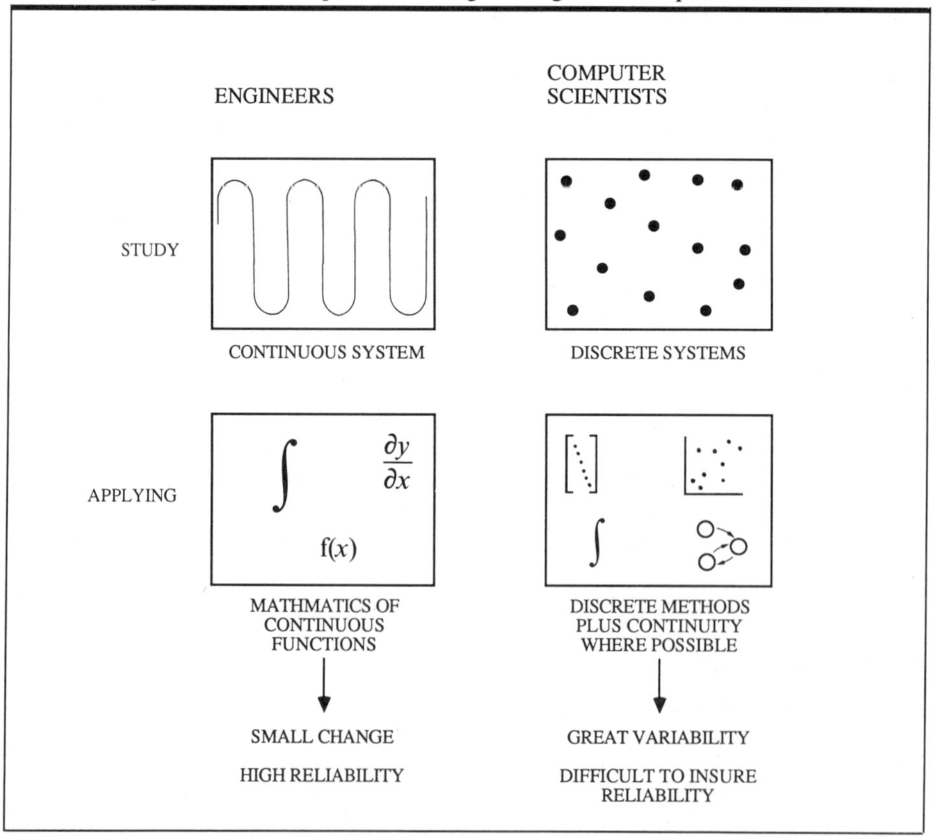

The Logic of Software Development. Since an analysis of our systems is not always possible using continuous functions, we can turn to *mathematical logic* for assistance. However, because the number of states is large and the software is lacking in regularity or repetition, the logical expressions of system behavior tend to be extraordinarily complex and unwieldy. The use of computers to analyze the behavioral expressions is not possible using today's technology.

More important, the logic employed in processing information is different from the logic that we are used to. We tend to work through a problem sequentially, breaking the problem into component parts, and then handling each of the parts one at a time. Today's technology handles several components concurrently, and it is difficult for us as humans to understand the interactions of the components as concurrent processing occurs. This inability to juggle many things in our minds at once, to keep track of many variables and how they change and affect each other, leaves room for much error. Our testing methods are often based on sequential, logical exercise of various parts of a system, but they do not accommodate concurrency at all.

Thus, the sequential processing and testing approaches on which we have relied in the past are inadequate for handling many problems that confront us today. Whenever a solution requires concurrent processing, our testing methods cannot always guarantee the speed, accuracy, or function required. If we can build a system at all to solve such a problem, we cannot assure the system's reliability.

Software engineering addresses these development problems. Other problems arise from personnel matters and from the characteristics of the projects themselves. In chapter 2 we will learn more about the people who work on development projects. First, let us look at other characteristics of a project that affect its complexity and difficulty.

1.6

TYPES OF SOFTWARE PROJECTS

The development process we have described involves a series of steps, from requirements definition to maintenance of the completed system. As we will see, each step incorporates steps of its own to produce a product used in the next step. It is useful to have some notion of the *size* of a project to tell us to what degree we must track development. For example, the amount of documentation and cross-referencing needed to write a fifty-line Pascal program to compute your grade-point average is much smaller than that needed for a year-long project to automate a factory's production line. Knowing the number of lines of code is not enough, since some very complex algorithms can be implemented in just a few lines; the difficulty lies in understanding the problem and developing the algorithm, rather than in actually writing the code. Thus, when we say that we are working on a large project, we often mean that we are working on a *difficult* or *complex* project.

Degree of Difficulty of Development

We can classify a project as being of low, medium or high difficulty, depending on several characteristics. Some of the characteristics involve issues of precision, complexity, and scale when considering the technical problem itself. Others depend on the expertise of the developers and the degree to which the requirements may change during the period of development. The characteristics are summarized in Table 1.1.

To understand these characteristics, suppose we are developers evaluating the difficulty of a proposed project. Our first consideration is the *number of functions* performed by the proposed system. If the new system is to do primarily one thing, such as calculate tax from a table, then its design is simpler than a system that does many jobs, such as one that accesses several tables and optimizes a route to be traveled by a salesperson. Here, as in other rows of Table 1.1, the values indicated in each column are guidelines, not strict delineations of rigid categories. Thus, we can think of the number of functions performed as a continuum, where a small number of functions is easier to implement than a large number.

The *novelty* of the functions is also important. Some systems are developed to do something that has been done before in a way that is standard or straightforward. However, other systems are built to do what has been done before but in a new and different way. The novelty of the method often adds difficulty to the development. Likewise, a system may use a new theory or approach and may do something that has never before been done. Such a system is more difficult still.

We also consider the number of users requiring *multi-user or concurrent access* to the proposed system. If only one person is to use the system at a time, the design is much simpler than if several need access at once. For example, the larger the number of users of the system, the greater the need for tracking the concurrent activities involved. Such a system must include methods for arbitrating among users who are trying to access to the same resource simultaneously. Similarly, implementing a system with no *multi-tasking* is much easier than one requiring that many tasks run at once.

The *type of access* needed by users can also affect the difficulty of development. If batch access is all that is necessary or if only some minimal interaction is required between user and system, then development is much easier than for a highly interactive system where users are frequently responding to queries from the system or providing additional information.

The degree of interaction with users and with other systems can generate requirements for *response time* to be within certain limits. Response time constraints can affect the difficulty of development, especially when real-time (that is, essentially instantaneous) response is needed. A cashier at the check-out counter in a grocery store cannot tolerate a several-second delay between the time an item is entered in the automated register and the time the price is displayed. Special design techniques may be needed to insure required response.

The need for *distributed processing* also affects development difficulty. If no distributed processing is required, the system can be developed on one computer. If two processors are required, then the types of processing are divided between the two, and communication is established to transfer information back and forth. However, if more than two processors are involved, communications are much

Table 1.1 Degrees of Difficulty for Project Development

Characteristic	Low	Moderate	High
Number of functions performed	Small	Medium	Large
Novelty of function	Standard application	Similar to existing systems but with a few new functions	New theory or approach; never been built before
Number of users requiring multi-user or concurrent access	1	Several	Many
Multi-tasking	No	Some	Yes
Interactive vs. batch access	Batch or some minimal interaction	Highly interactive	Highly interactive
Response-time requirements	Off-line; non-critical	Interactive; moderate response time acceptable	Real-time
Need for distributed processing	None	2 computers	3 or more computers
Amount of data stored	Will fit on single disk (storage device)	Requires 2 or more disks	Requires system to manage disk access
Structure of data	Simple data relationships	Moderately complex relationships	Highly complex relationships
Accuracy of data	Low degree	Moderate degree	High degree
Transaction size	Small	Medium	Large
Remote vs. local	Local only	Remote	Remote access
Criticality; tolerance for downtime	Can tolerate several hours of downtime	Can tolerate short periods of downtime	Can tolerate no downtime
Security needs	None	Moderate	High
Interaction with other systems	None	Some but well-defined	Much; possible parallel development
Number of phases of development	None	Few	Many
Need for manual override	No	No	Yes
Dependence on hardware	Independent of hardware	Some	Tied to specific hardware constraints
Stability of specification	Fixed customer requirements	Some changes may occur	Frequent changes in specification
User sophistication	Familiarity with automated systems	Some familiarity with automated systems	Naive
Developer sophistication	Has developed similar systems with similar tools	Experience with tools, not with application	No experience

more complex. In this case, care is taken to design a system that can handle simultaneous requests for transmission to a single processor, to try again when a processor is busy, and to control the information traffic flowing among the processors.

The *amount of data* stored by the system is a key factor. If all data can fit on a single disk or storage device, then the system needs to address only one device. However, if two or more devices are involved, the design must designate the type of data belonging on each device. If a file is so big that it overflows one device, pointers must be defined to link the one part of the file with the other. If the amount of data is so large that the system includes a subsystem to manage device access, then the degree of difficulty of the overall system is increased further.

The *structure of data* can affect development difficulty, too. Simple relationships among data are relatively easy to implement, compared with data that are intricately related. For example, if data can be pictured as a table from which rows and columns are selected for reporting purposes, implementation will be easier than if the data for a report resides in multiple tables with complex connections among them. In this case, a data base management system may be required to track data element relationships.

Accuracy requirements also affect system complexity. The more accurate the results must be, the more difficult it may be to design a system. Accuracy may also affect the choice of computer, because a large word size may be preferable. For scientific calculations requiring more precision, special routines may be needed that yield an accuracy greater than that normally provided by the word size on a particular processor. Program designers and programmers must be very careful to choose instructions that preserve the precision needed by the system.

The *size of transactions* can affect the difficulty of development. Small transactions are easier to handle than large ones, especially when communication is involved. If an error occurs during a large transaction, the recovery process takes more time and may be more complex than for a small transaction.

Some systems are used only by the those whose offices are located in the same building as the main processor. This makes communication with the processor fairly easy, since the user can be connected directly to the computer. However, if users are at *remote locations*, a communications subsystem must be included in the overall system to allow remote users to do their work using telephone or satellite connections. Thus, communications increases the difficulty of design and development.

Many systems involve data or functions that are not critical. The system can be "down" (that is, nonfunctional) for a period of time without adversely affecting the performance of a user's or customer's job. However, other systems have *critical applications* that cannot be interrupted for any reason. For example, a hospital's automated life support system cannot tolerate any interruption at all. System criticality and accompanying low tolerance for downtime are difficult to design.

Critical systems often require a great deal of redundancy. Two systems are **redundant** if one system does exactly what the other does and takes over if the first fails for any reason. The space shuttle on-board computer system is composed of a main computer and several redundant others, since absolutely no down time can be tolerated.

Security concerns many systems. If access must be controlled to files, to records in files, or even to fields in records, the system design becomes complex. Sometimes some users are allowed to exercise a particular program or function while others are not. This too is a security consideration. If the system communicates information that must be encoded or encrypted, the system complexity increases.

Self-contained systems are much easier to develop than those that must *interact with other systems*. Problems are introduced whenever interaction is defined. For each external system to communicate with the development system, an interface must be documented, explaining the method of communication and the structure and content of the data to be transferred. If the interface is clearly and explicitly defined, the development of the new system is not necessarily hampered by the existence of the other system. However, sometimes several systems are developed in parallel, and the interface has never before been documented or tested. Here development can be very difficult, because changes to one system may affect all other systems interfacing with it.

A similar consideration must be made for systems using *phased development*. The more phases involved, the more coordination, documentation, and testing are needed, so the more difficult the development. If the phases incorporate a requirement for a manual override of automated processes, the development is more difficult still.

The *hardware requirements* may affect the system, too. If the system is independent of any hardware constraints, designers have a freer reign over the way in which the system is implemented. However, if the customer includes specific hardware constraints, then development may be more complicated. For instance, if the customer requires that a particular multiplexer be used in communications, the designers are not free to choose a multiplexer with whose interface they are already familiar. Moreover, if the customer is building the multiplexer, we must include extra testing procedures to be sure that the multiplexer developed acts the way the customer intended in the initial documentation.

In general, the more *stable the specifications* of the customer, the easier the development. If the customer's requirements can change as development progresses, then difficulty increases in proportion to the amount by which the specifications change. Sometimes, changes in specification are unavoidable, especially when development occurs over a period of years; then, the technology may change, or products may be superseded by upgraded versions that work in slightly different ways.

Finally, we consider the *experience and sophistication* of those involved in development. If the customer or users have never been involved in producing a software system, communication with us as developers may be very difficult. We may speak a different language, so it will be hard for us to draw out what the customer wants in terms that we and the members of our team can understand. Often a knowledge of the customer's business is helpful in understanding why the system is wanted and how it will aid the customer. Such knowledge also enables us to suggest requirements that the customer may have overlooked. When all requirements are documented, we must be able to translate the customer requirements into specifications that designers and programmers can understand.

At the same time, our experience with the tools and techniques to be used in this particular development project affect the difficulty of development. A system involving a data base management system, an automated design tool, and a communications system will be much harder for someone who has never used such things than for one who has.

Keep in mind that no system falls neatly into one column of Table 1.1. Every system has some aspects that are easy and others that are difficult. To determine overall difficulty, we must examine all of the system's characteristics in the areas denoted by the rows of the table. If our evaluation shows that a system falls mostly in one column or another, we can loosely describe the difficulty of the system by that column. For example, if we find that a system has four or five items that are of a low degree of difficulty, three or four that may be high, but all others that fall in the middle of our chart, we can say that the system is moderately difficult to implement. As we will see in the next chapter, understanding these characteristics and the level of difficulty will help us estimate how long it will take to build the system.

1.7

EXAMPLE: A RESOURCE TRACKING AND SIMULATION SYSTEM

In the chapters that follow, we will examine in more detail the various stages of software development. For each stage, we will investigate tools and techniques that can improve the quality of the resulting product. To help us understand of how the tools and techniques work, we will use a common example throughout the text: a resource tracking and simulation system. Following is a brief description of the project; when we learn about requirement specification in chapter 3, we will see more details of the system's components.

In our example, the Weaver Farm National Recreation Area is a new tract of several thousand acres in the National Park Service system. There is a large lake at Weaver Farm, plus meadowland, heavily forested areas, and a winding river that empties into the lake. Many of the forested areas are traversed by old logging trails that are maintained now for hiking and bicycling. The administrators of Weaver Farm want to develop a computer-based system to help them in several ways.

1. The system will store descriptions of various natural parts of the recreation area. A map of the area will be divided into 100-square-foot cells, and ecological characteristics will be associated with each cell. These characteristics include measures of soil quality, soil type, plant and tree cover, water table height and water quality in the lake and streams.

2. The system will also store descriptions of any constructed facilities in the area, including barns, lodges, restrooms, log bridges, lake docks, picnic tables, shelters, tennis courts, and others.

3. The system will generate a maintenance schedule for Weaver Farm, including natural areas and constructed facilities.

4. In addition, the system will simulate the effects on the environment of a variety of uses of different natural areas of the Farm. This will enable the administrators to decide how best to use the various areas, providing recreation but preserving the environment.

Let us compare what we know about the Weaver Farm project with the categories in Table 1.1 to determine if the project is of low, moderate, or high difficulty. As you can see from the description above, many functions are involved. The data requirements force our system to perform all functions of a data base management system, and the simulation requirements tell us that a great deal of computation will be necessary. The functions are likely to be variations on things that have been done in the past. However, at this point we do not know if the administrators have a new or different way of evaluating environmental impact for their simulation, so there may be some novelty involved.

Two or more users may require access at once; one user may generate a maintenance schedule while another is simulating resource allocation. The reporting may be done with a minimum of user interaction, but the simulation requires a great deal of interactive activity. The response time for all functions must be sufficient to support interactive work, but the system can tolerate minor delays. Moreover, nothing in the system is critical, so a few hours of downtime can be tolerated.

The data requirements add much complexity to the system. To store the large amounts of resource data and to simulate effects of usage, the system will require several storage devices and a subsystem to manage the data. The relationships among the data are likely to be complex, since interactions among data elements will be needed to track the effects of resource use or change. Because the simulation will require more processing time, it may be useful to devote one processor to the management of data and another to the simulation of activity or usage.

Development may be easier if phased, so that the data management functions are provided to the administrators first and the simulation functions added later on. This will also allow the users to become accustomed to the system, and any changes they want to make can be incorporated before the simulation functions are installed.

We summarize our discussion of the Weaver Farm project in Table 1.2. Each complexity value is noted as being of low (L), medium (M) or high (H) difficulty, corresponding to Table 1.1. The characteristics are of low difficulty in five places, moderate difficulty in eleven places, and high difficulty in five places. Thus it is likely that the Weaver Farm project will be of moderate difficulty to develop.

1.8

CHAPTER SUMMARY

This chapter has introduced the idea of software engineering as the application of computer science techniques and tools to a variety of problems. As software engineers, we are problem-solvers rather than theoreticians. Our goal is the production of quality software, but we have not always been successful at building computer-based systems that meet our customers' needs.

Table 1.2   Difficulty of Weaver Farm Project Development

Characteristic	Probable Value For Farm	Difficulty
Number of functions performed	Large	H
Novelty of function	Similar to existing systems but with a few new functions	M
Number of users requiring multi-user or concurrent access	Several	M
Multi-tasking	Some	M
Interactive vs. batch access	Highly interactive	H
Response-time	Interactive; moderate response time acceptable	M
Need for distributed processing	2 computers	M
Amount of data stored	Requires system to manage disk access	H
Structure of data	Highly complex relationships	H
Accuracy of data	Moderate degree	M
Transaction size	Large	H
Remote vs. local	Local only	L
Criticality; tolerance of downtime	Can tolerate several hours of downtime	L
Security needs	Moderate	M
Interaction with other systems	None	L
Number of phases of development	Few	M
Need for manual override	No	L
Dependence on hardware	Independent of hardware	L
Stability of specification	Some changes may occur	M
User sophistication	Some familiarity with automated systems	M
Developer sophistication	Experience with tools, not with application	M

Thus the purpose of this text is to examine software development to see how we can improve our track record. As a first step, we have seen that a problem must be viewed as a set of component parts. Then, as a solution we try to design a system that will help our customers and users to do their jobs better. The system is considered as a set of interrelated smaller subsystems that are easier to understand than the whole. At the same time, we must also view the system in a larger context, so that we know the boundary of our target system.

Complementing our system view is an engineering one, allowing us to construct a software-based system much as we construct a house. The software development cycle presents the construction of our system as a sequence of steps, each of which addresses a particular part of the overall problem. From the requirements analysis and definition stage that finds out exactly what the problem is, to the testing stages that insure that we have built what the customer wants, to the maintenance stage that allows the system to grow and change, we have seen that there are different roles to be played by software engineering specialists.

At the same time, we have looked at those aspects of development that can present problems: changing requirements, phased development, and interaction with other systems. In later chapters, we will study software engineering techniques to help us to avoid such problems. However, some problems are intractable. Parnas has reminded us that the nature of the systems with which we deal includes aspects that are beyond our comprehension right now. Software engineering today holds no solution to the problem of how our sequential minds can understand concurrent processes.

To help us estimate the difficulty of a project before we embark on it, we have investigated those project characteristics that can add to the degree of difficulty involved. Finally, we introduced an example of a system to be developed; this example will be used throughout the book to illustrate the concepts and techniques we present.

Before we examine in detail the stages of development and the methods and tools available for use in each step, we look more closely at the *project* considerations involved in development. In the next chapter, we investigate what is involved in defining, planning and managing a project.

1.9

EXERCISES

1. Consider the automobile engine as a system. Describe the boundary, and list the entities and activities involved.

2. In building the Ehlers house, what documents should be generated? When during the development cycle are they reviewed and updated?

3. Your development group is asked to build a system for your company's office of legal counsel. The counsel receives questions and comments from the chief executive officer and must prepare responses. To respond, the

office of the counsel must itself request information from other offices of the
company, evaluate the information, prepare its response, and communicate
the response to the chief executive officer's office. Diagram the system
involved. Be sure to include the system boundary, the interfaces, the entities,
and the activities. If the chief executive officer returns the response for
additional comment or elaboration, how does such a request appear in your
system diagram?

4. Is every system developed on a personal computer always of low difficulty to
   develop? If yes, explain why. If no, give examples of systems developed on
   personal computers that are of moderate and high difficulty, and explain
   why they are considered as such.

C H A P T E R 2

PROJECT PLANNING

As we saw in the previous chapter, the development cycle includes many steps, some of which are repeated until the construction of the computer system is complete and customer and users are satisfied. However, before committing funds for a software development project, a customer usually wants an estimate of how much the project will cost and how long development will take. This chapter examines the planning of a project and the concepts of cost and schedule estimation.

In the past, estimates of a project's schedule and cost have been far from accurate. To give you an idea of how far from the estimates are the *actual* schedule and cost, consider these "Laws of Project Management" distributed by International Systems, Inc. (King of Prussia, Pennsylvania) with their project management software.

Laws of Project Management

- No major project is ever installed on time, within budgets, with the same staff that started it. Yours will not be the first.

- Projects progress quickly until they become 90 percent complete; then they remain at 90 percent complete forever.

- One advantage of fuzzy project objectives is that they let you avoid the embarrassment of estimating the corresponding costs.

- When things are going well, something will go wrong. When things just can't get worse, they will. When things appear to be going better, you have overlooked something.

- If project content is allowed to change freely, the rate of change will exceed the rate of progress.

- No system is ever completely debugged. Attempts to debug a system inevitably introduce new bugs that are even harder to find.

- A carelessly planned project will take three times longer to complete than expected; a carefully planned project will take only twice as long.

- Project teams detest progress reporting because it vividly manifests their lack of progress.

Software engineers are keenly aware of our inability to estimate accurately. A major goal of software engineering is to include in development the measures needed to have more control over a project's progress. These measures help us generate our initial estimates, guide development as it proceeds, and revise our estimates along the way. This chapter examines the planning process. In later chapters, we will return to some of the problems mentioned here and explain how they affect the various steps of development.

We begin our discussion by looking at the project schedule and the personnel needed for development. Teams or committees can contribute to the project's success, and we examine several popular organizational structures. The roles of the personnel are investigated, and we see how work styles may affect the project's development. Then, we turn to the costs involved in building a system, looking at ways to estimate cost before the system has been designed.

Every customer expects the developer to outline the schedule and estimated cost of a project in a project plan. We list the components of a project plan and describe what the customer expects to see at the beginning of the project, during system development, and when the project is complete.

Finally, we look at an example to see how project planning might be used in our resource tracking and simulation system.

2.1

THE PROJECT SCHEDULE

Software is useful only if it performs a desired function or provides a needed service. Thus, a typical project begins when a customer approaches you to discuss a perceived need. For example, an accountant who keeps records in ledger books may ask for help because she or he would like to store the records on some magnetic medium; this method of storage would allow the accountant to sort or search through information more rapidly. Or, you may be contacted by marine biologists who would like a system to connect with their water monitoring equipment and perform statistical analyses of the data gathered. Usually, customers have several questions to be answered:

1. Do you understand my problem and my needs?
2. Can you design a system that will solve my problem or satisfy my needs?
3. How long will it take you to develop such a system?
4. How much will it cost to have you develop such a system?

Answering the last two questions requires a well thought-out project schedule. A **project schedule** describes the *software development cycle* for a particular project. It enumerates the *phases or stages* of the project, breaks each into discrete *tasks* or *activities* to be done, portrays the *interactions* among these pieces of work, and estimates the *time* that each task or activity will take.

As we saw in the last chapter, a customer will probably work with our development team to decide exactly how the system will function. Moreover, the system is defined globally at first, with the specific program parts being defined fairly late in development. Then how is it possible for us to write down a schedule of exactly what is to be done and how much it will cost?

Deliverables

We begin by working to understand what the customer and users want; we make sure that they are comfortable with our knowledge of their needs.

First, we list all items that the customer expects to see during the development of the project. These items are called **deliverables** and can include anything the customer wants demonstrated or delivered as part of the contract:

- Documents
- Demonstrations of function
- Demonstrations of accuracy
- Demonstrations of reliability and subsystems

Activities and Milestones

Second, we analyze the development and designate certain clearly defined events as **milestones**. These indicate that a measurable level of progress has been made. Often, a milestone is the completion of a deliverable, which is a measurable level of progress, since the milestone is complete when we can turn over or demonstrate the deliverable to the customer. For instance, a milestone can be the completion of a user's manual, the performance of a certain specified sequence of calculations, or a demonstration of the system's ability to communicate to another computer system.

In our analysis of the project, we distinguish between milestones and activities. An **activity** is a part of the project that takes place over a period of time, and a milestone is the completion of an activity.

Thus, a milestone is a particular point in time, while an activity has a beginning and an end. For example, the customer may want the system to be accompanied by an online operator tutorial. The development of the tutorial and its associated programs is an activity; it culminates in the demonstration of those functions to the customer: the milestone.

Phases of the Schedule

By examining the project in this light, we separate development into a succession of *phases*. Each phase is composed of *steps*, and each step can be subdivided further if necessary. Figure 2.1 illustrates how this is done. Let us look at an example as outlined in Table 2.1. If we are building a house, we can break the project into two phases: landscaping the lot and building the house. Then each phase is further

Figure 2.1   Separating Project into Activities

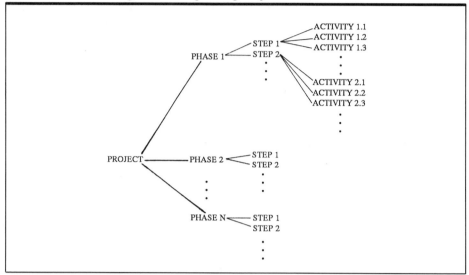

divided into steps: preparing the site, finishing the exterior, and building the interior. Finally, we view each step as a series of activities to be accomplished. For simplicity in this example, we focus on the second of the two phases.

Each of the activities indicated in Table 2.1 is a measurable event; that is, we can tell when the activity is completed. Thus, the endpoint of each of the activities can be a milestone in the construction. Table 2.2 shows these milestones.

This analytical breakdown gives us and our customer an idea of what is involved in the house construction. Likewise, the analysis of a development project gives us and our customers a better grasp of what is involved in the building of a system.

Work Breakdown Structure and Activity Graphs

Analysis of this kind is sometimes referred to as generating a **work breakdown structure** for a given project, because it exhibits the project as a set of discrete pieces of work. Notice that the activities and milestones are items that both customer and developer can understand and use to track development. At any point the customer may want to follow our progress. We as the developer can point to activities, indicating what work is in progress, and to milestones, indicating what work has been completed. However, the work breakdown structure of a project gives no indication of the interdependence of the work units; neither does it show which parts of the project can be developed concurrently. Consequently, a graph is used to depict the dependencies, as shown in Figure 2.2. The nodes of the graphs are the milestones of the projects, and the lines linking the nodes represent the activities involved. We call this type of graph an **activity graph**.

Table 2.1   Phases, Steps and Activities of Building a House

Phase 1: Landscaping the lot

   Step 1: Clearing and grubbing
   Step 2: Seeding the turf
   Step 3: Planting shrubs and trees

Phase 2: Building the house

   Step 1: Site preparation
      Activity 1.1: Surveying
      Activity 1.2: Obtaining permits
      Activity 1.3: Excavating
      Activity 1.4: Obtaining materials

   Step 2: Building exterior
      Activity 2.1: Foundation
      Activity 2.2: Outside walls
      Activity 2.3: Exterior plumbing
      Activity 2.4: Exterior electrical
      Activity 2.5: Exterior siding
      Activity 2.6: Exterior painting
      Activity 2.7: Doors and fixtures
      Activity 2.8: Roof

   Step 3: Finishing interior
      Activity 3.1: Interior plumbing
      Activity 3.2: Interior electrical
      Activity 3.3: Wallboard
      Activity 3.4: Interior painting
      Activity 3.5: Floor covering
      Activity 3.6: Doors and fixtures

Table 2.2   Milestones in Building a House

1.1 Survey complete
1.2 Permits issued
1.3 Excavation complete
1.4 Materials on hand

2.1 Foundation laid
2.2 Outside walls complete
2.3 Exterior plumbing complete
2.4 Exterior electrical work complete
2.5 Exterior siding complete
2.6 Exterior painting complete
2.7 Doors and fixtures mounted
2.8 Roof complete

3.1 Interior plumbing complete
3.2 Interior electrical complete
3.3 Wallboard in place
3.4 Interior painting complete
3.5 Floor covering laid
3.6 Doors and fixtures mounted

An activity can be described with a set of parameters: the precursor, duration, due date, and endpoint. A **precursor** is an event or set of events that must occur before the activity can begin; it is that which allows the activity to begin. The **duration** is the length of time it will take to complete the activity. The **due date** is the date when the activity must be completed, frequently because of a contractual deadline. Signifying that the activity has ended, the **endpoint** is usually a milestone or deliverable.

Figure 2.2 is an activity graph for phase two of our housing example. There are many important characteristics of the project's development that become apparent when the project is viewed in this form. For example, it is clear that neither of the two plumbing activities can be started before milestone 2.2 is reached. Thus, 2.2 is a precursor to both the interior and exterior plumbing activities. Furthermore,

Figure 2.2 Activity Graph for Building a House

Figure 2.3 Activity Graph with Duration of Activity

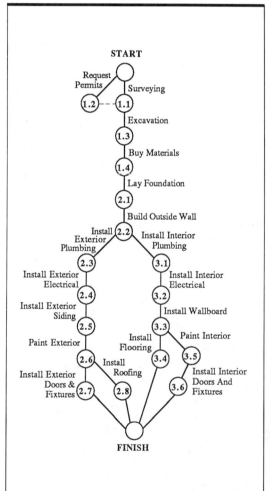

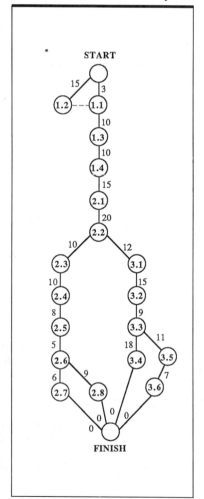

several things can be done simultaneously. For instance, some of the interior and exterior activities are independent (such as installing wallboard, connecting exterior electrical plumbing, and others leading to milestones 2.4 and 3.3). The activities on the left-hand path do not depend on those on the right for their initiation, so they can be worked on concurrently. Note that there is a dashed line from requesting permits (node 1.2) to surveying (node 1.1). This line indicates that these activities must be completed before excavation (the activity leading to milestone 1.3) can begin. However, since there is no real activity that occurs after reaching milestone 1.2 in order to get to milestone 1.1, the dashed line indicates a relationship without an accompanying activity.

Estimating Completion

Such a graph is more useful when time estimates are added to the links between nodes. We can estimate the duration of each activity. Then we label each link of the graph with this estimate, and the result shows us additional information about the project. For example, to each activity of Table 2.1 we append an estimate of the number of days required for its completion. The result is shown in Table 2.3.

Figure 2.3 shows the graph of this project with the durations added. Note that milestones 2.7, 2.8, 3.4, and 3.6 are precursors to the finish; that is, they must all be reached in order for the project to be complete. The zeros on the links from those nodes to the finish show that no additional time is added. There is also a zero on the link from node 1.2 to 1.1, since no additional time is accrued on the dashed link.

Table 2.3   Activities and Time Estimates

Activity	Time Estimate
Step 1: Site preparation	
Activity 1.1: Surveying	3 days
Activity 1.2: Obtaining permits	15 days
Activity 1.3: Excavation	10 days
Activity 1.4: Obtaining material	10 days
Step 2: Building Exterior	
Activity 2.1: Foundation	15 days
Activity 2.2: Outside walls	20 days
Activity 2.3: Exterior plumbing	10 days
Activity 2.4: Exterior electrical	10 days
Activity 2.5: Exterior siding	8 days
Activity 2.6: Exterior painting	5 days
Activity 2.7: Doors and fixtures	6 days
Activity 2.8: Roof	9 days
Step 3: Finishing interior	
Activity 3.1: Interior plumbing	12 days
Activity 3.2: Interior electrical	15 days
Activity 3.3: Wallboard	9 days
Activity 3.4: Interior painting	18 days
Activity 3.5: Floor covering	11 days
Activity 3.6: Doors and fixtures	7 days

This graphical depiction of the project tells us a lot about the project's schedule. For example, since we estimated that the first activity would take three days to complete, we cannot hope to reach milestone 1.1 before the end of day 3. Similarly, we cannot reach milestone 1.2 before the end of day 15. Because the beginning of excavation (activity 1.3) cannot begin until both milestones 1.1 and 1.2 are reached, excavation cannot begin until the beginning of day 16.

Critical Path Method. Such an analysis of the paths among the milestones of a project is known as the **critical path method** or **CPM**. We can use the paths to show the minimum amount of time it will take to complete the project, given our estimates of the duration of each activity. Moreover, the critical path method reveals those activities that are most critical to completing the project on time.

To see how the critical path method works, we return to our house-building example. First, we note that the activities leading to milestones 1.1 (surveying) and 1.2 (requesting permits) can occur concurrently. Since excavation (the activity culminating in milestone 1.3) cannot begin until day 16, surveying has fifteen days in which to be completed, even though it is only three days in duration. Thus, surveying has fifteen days of available time but takes only three days of real time. In the same way, for each activity in our graph, we can compute a pair of times: real time and available time. The **real time** or **actual time** for an activity is the estimated amount of time required for the activity to be completed, while the **available time** is the amount of time available in the schedule for the activity's completion. **Slack time** for an activity is the difference between the available time and the real time for that activity:

$$\text{slack time} = \text{available time} - \text{real time}$$

Another way of looking at slack time is to compare the *earliest* time an activity may begin with the *latest* time the activity may begin without delaying the project. For example, surveying may begin on day 1, so its earliest start time is day 1. However, because it will take fifteen days to request and receive permits, surveying can begin as late as day 13 and still not hold up the project schedule. Therefore,

$$\text{slack time} = \text{latest start time} - \text{earliest start time}$$

Let us compute the slack for our example's activities to see what it tells us about the project schedule. We compute slack by examining all paths from the start to the finish. As we saw, it must take fifteen days to complete milestones 1.1 and 1.2. An additional 55 days are used in completing milestones 1.3, 1.4, 2.1, and 2.2. At this point, there are four possible paths to be taken:

1. Following milestones 2.3 through 2.7 on the graph requires 39 days.

2. Following milestones 2.3 through 2.8 on the graph requires 42 days.

3. Following milestones 3.1 through 3.4 on the graph requires 54 days.

4. Following milestones 3.1 through 3.6 on the graph requires 54 days.

Because milestones 2.7, 2.8, 3.4, and 3.6 must be met before the project is finished, our schedule is constrained by the longest path. As you can see from Figure 2.3 and our calculations above, the two paths on the right require 124 days to complete, while the two paths on the left require fewer days. To calculate the slack, we can work backwards along the path to see how much slack time there is for each activity leading to a node. First, we note that there is zero slack on the longest path. Then, we examine each of the remaining nodes to calculate the slack for the activities leading to them. For example, 54 days are available to complete the activities leading to milestones 2.3, 2.4, 2.5, 2.6, and 2.8, but only 42 days are needed to complete these. Thus, this portion of the graph has 12 days of slack. Similarly, the portion of the graph for activities 2.3 through 2.7 requires only 39 days, so we have 15 days of slack along this route. By working forward through the graph in this way, we can compute the earliest start time and slack for each of the activities. Then, we compute the latest start time for each activity by moving from the finish back through each node to the start. Table 2.4, shows the results, the slack time for each of the activities in Figure 2.3. At milestone 2.6, the path can branch to 2.7 or 2.8. (The latest start times in Table 2.4 are calculated by using the route from 2.6 to 2.8, rather than from 2.6 to 2.7.)

Table 2.4   Slack Time for Project Activities

Activity	Earliest Start Time	Latest Start Time	Slack
1.1	1	13	12
1.2	1	1	0
1.3	16	16	0
1.4	26	26	0
2.1	36	36	0
2.2	51	51	0
2.3	71	83	12
2.4	81	93	12
2.5	91	103	12
2.6	99	111	12
2.7	104	119	15
2.8	104	116	12
3.1	71	71	0
3.2	83	83	0
3.3	98	98	0
3.4	107	107	0
3.5	107	107	0
3.6	118	118	0
Finish	124	124	0

The longest path has a slack of zero for each of its nodes because it is the path that determines whether or not the project is on schedule. For this reason, it is called the **critical path**, the one for which the slack at every node is zero. As you can see from our example, there may be more than one critical path. Since the critical path has no slack, there is no margin for error when performing the activities along its route.

PERT and Other Methods.   Critical path analysis of a project schedule tells us who must wait for what as the project is being developed and which activities must be completed on schedule to avoid delay. This kind of analysis can be enhanced in many ways. For example, our example supposes that we know exactly how long each activity will take. Often, this is not the case. Instead, we have only an estimated duration for an activity, based on our knowledge of similar projects and events. Thus, to each activity we can assign a probable duration according to some probability distribution, so that each activity has associated with it an *expected value* and a *variance*. In other words, instead of knowing an exact duration, we estimate a window or interval in which the actual time is likely to fall. The expected value is a point within the interval, and the variance describes the width of the interval. You may be familiar with a standard probability distribution called a *normal distribution* whose graph is shaped like a bell. The Program Evaluation and Review Technique (PERT) is a popular critical path analysis technique that assumes a normal distribution. (See [HIL67] for more information about PERT.) PERT determines the probability that the earliest start time for an activity is close to the scheduled time for that activity. Using information such as probability distribution, latest and earliest start times, and the activity graph, computer programs can calculate the critical path and identify those activities most likely to be bottlenecks in the schedule.

For example, Figure 2.4 is a portion of a bar chart typical of those produced by an automated project management package. It lists the activities of a development project, including information about the early and late start dates. The horizontal bars represent the duration of each activity; those bars comprised of asterisks indicate the critical path. Activities depicted by dashes and Fs are not on the critical path, and an F represents *float* or slack time.

Later in this chapter, we will look at another example of an automated project management tool. Many use the CPM and PERT methods. However, these methods are of great value only to projects in which several activities are taking place concurrently. If the project's activities are mostly sequential, then almost all activities are on the critical path and are candidates for bottlenecks.

Figure 2.4   CPM Bar Chart

CPM BARCHART

Description	: Early Date	: Late Date	: JAN 1	JAN 8	JAN 15	JAN 22	JAN 29	FEB 5	FEB 12	FEB 17	FEB 24
Test of phase 1	1/1/87	2/5/87	**********************								
Define test cases	1/1/87	1/8/87	*****								
Write test plan	1/9/87	1/22/87		*********							
Write test plan	1/9/87	1/22/87		*********							
Init testing	1/23/87	2/1/87				*******					
Init testing	1/23/87	2/1/87				---FFFF					
Init testing	1/23/87	2/1/87				-----FF					
System testing	2/2/87	2/17/87						**********			
System testing	2/2/87	2/17/87						-----FFFFF			
System testing	2/2/87	2/17/87						----FFFFFF			
Document results	2/17/87	2/24/87									****

2.2

PROJECT PERSONNEL

To determine the project schedule and estimate the associated costs, we need some idea of the number of people who will be working on the project, what tasks they will perform, and what abilities and experience they must have in order to perform their jobs effectively. How do we decide who does what and how many people we need?

Project Roles

The development schedule, sometimes called the *system development life cycle*, is a broad outline for what is to be done. We can examine the work breakdown structure or list of necessary tasks and from it derive the kinds of jobs involved in development. For example, in any project, someone works with customers and users to determine requirements. Others may design the system, and still others may code the programs. In other words, the development team must do the following.

1. Requirements analysis
2. System design
3. Program design
4. Program implementation
5. Testing
6. Training
7. Maintenance
8. Quality assurance

As we saw in chapter 1, not every task is performed by a different person or group; who does how much of what depends to a large extent on the size of the project. However, there is a great advantage in assigning different responsibilities to different sets of people; that way, we have a "checks and balances" approach to project development.

Suppose the test team is separate from those who design the system and the programs. The testing stage of development includes an *acceptance test* to demonstrate to the customer the capabilities of the completed system. The test team must define and document the way in which this test will be conducted and the criteria for the customer's acceptance of the system. The test team can generate its acceptance test plan from the requirements specified by the customer without knowing how the internal pieces of the system are put together. The test team has no preconceptions about how the software and hardware work, and it can concentrate on the functionality of the system as described by the customer. Thus, it is easier for the test plan to catch errors and omissions that the designers may have made.

Likewise, it is useful for the program designers and system designers to be different groups of people. Program designers become deeply involved with the details of the code, and they sometimes neglect the larger picture of how the system should work. We can use techniques such as walkthroughs and reviews (investigated in chapters 4 and 5) to bring the two sets of designers together and provide continuity in the development process. In this way, separating system designers from program designers makes errors less likely to continue through to the testing stage.

We saw in chapter 1 that other development jobs are not evident from the life cycle. For instance, the configuration manager tracks changes to the requirements and to the system. If the customer decides to add to or change the functionality of the system, a member of the project team must update the documentation of the requirements and make sure that changes are made to the system design, program design, program code, test plans, and training information.

Personnel Characteristics

Once we know the roles of project team members, we then decide how many of which kinds of people to assign to those roles. Project personnel may differ in many ways. It is not enough to say that a project needs an analyst, two designers, and five programmers, for example. Two people with the same job title may differ in at least one of the following ways:

- Ability to perform the work
- Interest in the work
- Experience with similar applications, tools or techniques
- Training
- Ability to communicate with others
- Ability to share responsibility with others
- Management skills

Each of these characteristics can affect an individual's ability to perform productively. These variations help to explain why one programmer can write a particular routine in a day, while another requires a week. The differences can be critical not only to the estimation of the schedule and the cost, but also to the success of the project.

Differences in Background. To understand each worker's performance, we must know his or her *ability* to perform the work at hand. Some are good at viewing "the big picture" but may get mired in detail if asked to work on a small part of a large project. Such people may be better suited to system design or testing than to program design or coding. Sometimes ability is related to *comfort*. In your classes, you may have worked with people who are more comfortable programming in one language than another. On class projects, some students feel more confident about their design abilities than their coding prowess. This feeling of comfort is important; people are usually more productive when they have confidence in their ability to perform.

Interest in the work can also determine someone's success on a project. Although very good at doing a particular job, an employee may be more interested in trying something new than in repeating something done many times before. Thus, the novelty of work is sometimes a factor in generating interest in it. On the other hand, there are always people who prefer doing what they know and do best rather than venturing into new territory. It is important that whoever is chosen for a task be excited about performing it, no matter what the reason.

Given equal ability and interest, two people may still differ in the amount of *experience* or *training* they have had with similar applications, tools, or techniques. The person who has already been successful at using Ada to write a communications controller is more likely to write another communications controller in Ada faster (but not necessarily more clearly or efficiently) than someone who has neither experience with Ada nor knowledge of what a communications controller does. Thus, the selection of people to work on a project involves not only individual ability and skill but also experience and training.

On every software development project, members of the development team *communicate* with one another, with users, and with the customer. The progress of the project is affected not only by the degree of communication but also by the ability of individuals to communicate their ideas. Errors in software can result from a breakdown in communication and understanding, so the number of people needing to communicate with one another can affect the quality of the resulting product. If there are n workers on a project, there are $n(n-1)/2$ pairs of people who must communicate, and there are $2^n - 1$ possible teams that can be created to work on smaller pieces of the project. Figure 2.5 shows us how quickly the lines of communication can grow. Increasing a work team from two to three people *triples* the number of lines of communication. A project involving only ten people requires that 45 different lines of communication be established. If this project requires a great deal of interaction or coordination, maintaining 45 open channels can be difficult. Moreover, there are 1,023 possible committees or teams that can be formed to handle subsystem development of various kinds!

In addition, projects involving several people must involve some *shared responsibility*. Those who are working on one aspect of project development must trust other team members to do their parts. In your classes, you are usually in total control of the projects you do. You begin with the requirements (usually prescribed by your instructor), design a solution to the problem, outline the code, write the actual lines of code, and test the resulting programs. However, when working in a team, either in school or for an employer or customer, you must be able to share the workload. Not only does this require verbal communication of ideas and results, but it also requires written documentation of what you plan to do and what you have done. You must accept the results of others without redoing their work. Many people have difficulty giving up control in this way.

Control is an issue in *management* of the project, too. Some people are good at directing the work of others. This aspect of personnel interaction is also related to the comfort people feel with the jobs they have. Those who feel uncomfortable with the idea of pushing their colleagues to stay on schedule, to document their code, or

Figure 2.5 Increase in Lines of Communication

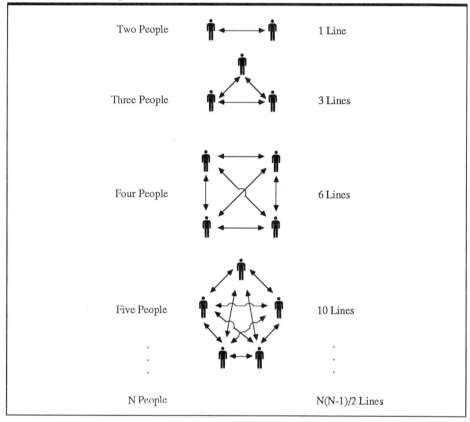

to meet with the customer are not good candidates for development jobs involving management of other workers.

Thus, several aspects of a worker's background can affect the quality of the project team, and they are summarized in Figure 2.6. A knowledge of each person's interest and ability is necessary when choosing people to work together on a project. As we will see later in this chapter, employee background and communication among workers can have a great effect on the project's cost and schedule.

Differences in Work Styles. People approach their work—both the problems and the people with whom they work—in different ways. We can think of your approach to work as having two components: the way in which your thoughts are communicated and ideas gathered, and the degree to which your emotions affect decision making. When communicating ideas, some people *tell* others what their thoughts are. Jung ([JUN59]) calls these people **extroverts.** However, if you prefer to *ask* for suggestions before expressing your own opinion, you are an **introvert.** As an introvert, you probably gather as much information as you can before making a decision. Clearly, a preference for asking or telling can affect the way you interact with others on your project.

Figure 2.6 Characteristics that Affect Quality of Work

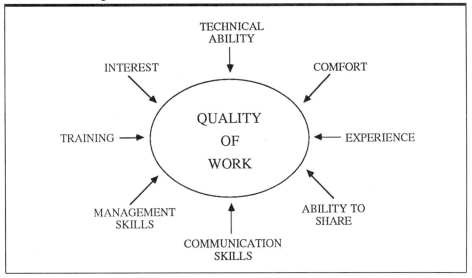

Similarly, **intuitive** people base their decisions on their feelings about and emotional reactions to a problem. Others are **rational** and decide primarily by examining what they regard as facts. If you are rational, you choose a course of action only after careful, reasoned consideration of all options.

We can express these components graphically by placing communication style along the horizontal axis and decision style on the vertical, as illustrated in Figure 2.7. The more assertive you are, the farther to the right the your work style falls on the graph. Similarly, the more emotions play a part in your decisions, the higher up the vertical axis is your work style.

Thus, we can think of people as approaching their work in four basic ways, corresponding to the four quadrants of Figure 2.7. The **rational extroverts** tend to assert their ideas and not let emotions affect decision-making. They tell their colleagues what they want them to know, but they rarely ask for more information before doing so. When reasoning, they rely on logic; "gut feeling" plays no part in what they decide. While the **rational introverts** also avoid emotional decisions, they are always willing to take time to consider all possible options before making a decision. Rational introverts are the information gatherers; they do not feel comfortable making a decision unless they are convinced that they have all facts at hand.

In contrast, **intuitive extroverts** base many decisions on emotional reaction and tend to want to tell others about them, rather than ask for input. They use their intuition to be creative, and they often suggest unusual approaches to problems.

The **intuitive introvert** is creative, too, but only applies creativity after having gathered information. Winston Churchill was an intuitive introvert ([MAN83]); when he wanted to learn about an issue, he read every bit of material available that addressed it. He often made his decisions based on how he felt about what he learned.

Figure 2.7   Work Styles

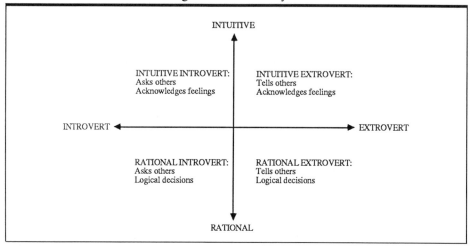

What are other characteristics of these types? We can look at some typical personalities for examples. Pablo, a rational extrovert, judges his colleagues by the results they produce. When making a decision, his top priority is efficiency. Thus, he wants to know only the bottom line. He examines his options and their probable effects, but he does not need to see documents or hear explanations supporting each option. If his time is wasted or his efficiency is in some other way hampered, he asserts his authority to regain control of the situation. Thus, Pablo is good at making sound decisions quickly.

Pablo is very different from his rational introvert colleague, Nancy. She judges her peers by how busy they are, and she has little tolerance for those who appear not to be working hard all the time. She is a good worker and is admired for the energy she devotes to her work. Her reputation as a good worker is very important to her, and she prides herself on being accurate and thorough. She does not like to make decisions without having complete information. When asked to make a presentation or write a report, Nancy does so only after putting all relevant information at her disposal.

Nancy shares an office with Emma, an intuitive extrovert. Whereas Nancy will not make a decision until she has complete knowledge of the situation, Emma prefers to follow her feelings. Often, she will trust her intuition about a problem, basing her decision on professional judgment rather than a slow, careful analysis of the information at hand. Furthermore, since she is assertive, Emma tends to tell the others on her project about her new ideas. She is creative, and she enjoys the recognition of her ideas by others. Thus, Emma enjoys working in an environment where there is a great deal of interaction among the employees.

Fritz, an intuitive introvert, also thrives on the attention he gets from his colleagues. He is sensitive and aware of his emotional reactions to people and problems; it is very important that he be liked by his peers. Because Fritz is a good listener, he is the one to whom others turn to express their feelings. Fritz takes lots of time to make a decision, in part because of his need for complete information and in part because he wants to make the "right" decision. He is sensitive about what others think of his ability and policies. Fritz analyzes situations much as Nancy does, but with a different twist; whereas Nancy looks at all the facts and figures, Fritz examines relational dependencies and emotional involvements as well.

Clearly, not everyone on a project fits neatly into one of the four categories. However, different people have different tendencies. Communication is critical to project success, and work style determines communication style. For example, if you are a project member responsible for a part of the project that is late, Pablo and Emma are likely to *tell* you when your work must be ready. Emma may offer several ideas to get the work back on track, while Pablo will give you a new schedule to follow. However, Nancy and Fritz will probably *ask* when the results will be ready. Nancy, in analyzing her options, will want to know why it is not ready; Fritz will ask if there is anything he can do to help.

Understanding work styles can help you to be *flexible* in your approach to other project team members and to customers and users with whom you may work. Work style gives you information about the priorities of others. If Paul's priorities are different from yours, you can present information to him in terms of things that are important to him. For instance, suppose Paul is your customer. You are asked to make a presentation to him. If Paul is an introvert, you know that he prefers gathering information to giving it. Thus, you may structure your presentation so that it *tells* him a great deal of information about the project. However, if Paul is highly assertive, you can include questions to allow him to *tell you* what is wanted or needed. Similarly, if Paul is intuitive, you can take advantage of his creativity by soliciting new ideas from him. However, if he is rational, your presentation can include facts and figures without reference to professional judgment or feeling.

Thus, work styles affect interaction among customers, users, and developers. The styles can also affect the *choice of worker* for a given task. For example, intuitive employees may prefer design and development (requiring new ideas) to maintenance programming and design (requiring attention to detail and analysis of complex results). In the same way, work styles can also affect the way in which the project is organized.

Project Team Organization

The project's organization can enhance quality, allowing development to progress unencumbered by bureaucracy, and permitting you and your customer to track the actual cost and schedule. There are several ways to organize a project to meet these goals. The choice of organizational structure depends on several things:

- The backgrounds and work styles of the people working on the project
- The number of people working on the project
- The management styles of the customer and the developer

A good project director is aware of different work styles and makes sure that team members are flexible enough to adapt to all four types. The director also knows that some project organization structures are more appropriate for certain work styles than for others.

One popular organizational structure is the **chief programmer team**, first used at IBM ([BAK72]). On a chief programmer team, one person is totally responsible for the project's design and development. All other team members report to this *chief programmer* who has final say on everything. The chief programmer not only supervises all others, but also designs the programs and allocates portions of code to be written by other team members. Assisting the chief is a programmer designated as an *understudy* whose principal job is to substitute for the chief programmer whenever necessary.

A *librarian* assists the team and is responsible for maintaining all documentation related to the project. The librarian also enters, compiles, links, and does preliminary testing of the code written by the other programmers. This allows the other programmers to concentrate entirely on what they do best: programming.

Being entirely responsible for the outcome of the project, the chief programmer makes all decisions about problems arising during development. This reduces the amount of communication and coordination needed among team members; rather than working out a problem themselves, they simply approach the chief programmer for an answer. Similarly, rather than having peer reviews of design and code, the chief programmer alone does a final review.

A chief programmer team has a hierarchical structure, as depicted in Figure 2.8. Although everyone ultimately reports to the chief programmer, groups of workers may be formed to accomplish specialized tasks. For example, one or more people may form an administrative group to report on the status of the project's cost and schedule.

Clearly, the chief programmer must be good at making decisions quickly. Consequently, you may choose someone with an extrovert work style for that position. However, if most team members are introverts, the chief programmer team may not be the best structure for the project.

Figure 2.8   Structure of Chief Programmer Team

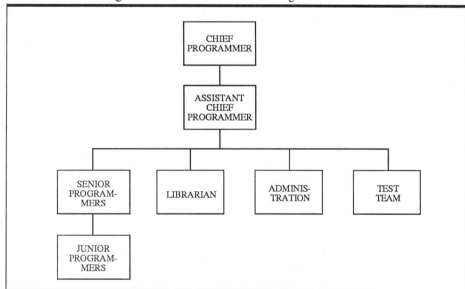

Figure 2.9 Egoless Programming Structure

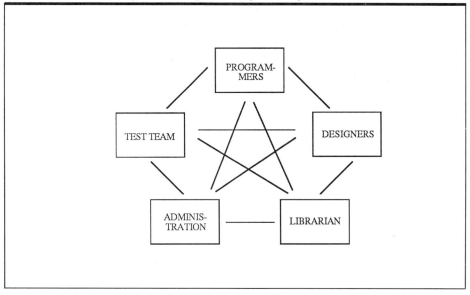

An alternative structure is based on the idea of "egoless" programming, as described by Weinberg ([WEI71]). Whereas the chief programmer is responsible for a project, an egoless approach holds everyone equally responsible. In an egoless structure, the project is separated from the individuals; criticism is directed to the result, not to individuals. This structure, shown in Figure 2.9, is more democratic; all team members vote on decisions, whether they concern design considerations or testing techniques.

Which structure is preferable? The more people there are on the project, the more need there is for a formal structure. Certainly, a development team with only three or four members does not always need an elaborate structure. However, a team of several dozen workers must have a well-defined organization. The managers in a participating company or agency may also impose a structure on the development team. For instance, your customer may insist that the test team be totally independent from program design and development. Or, your supervisor may designate someone as chief programmer or may insist that a previously successful structure be used again.

Studies have been made to determine which organizational structure is best suited for which kinds of projects. A National Science Foundation ([NAT83]) investigation found that projects with a high degree of certainty, stability, uniformity, and repetition can be accomplished more effectively by a hierarchical organizational structure such as the chief programmer team. These projects require little communication among project members, so they are well suited to an organization that stresses rules, specialization, formality, and a clear definition of organizational hierarchy.

On the other hand, when there is much uncertainty involved in a project, a more democratic approach may be better. For example, if the requirements may change as development proceeds, the project has a degree of uncertainty. Likewise, suppose your customer is building a new piece of hardware to interface with a system; if the exact specifications of the hardware are not yet known, then the level of uncertainty is high. Here, participation in decision making, a more loosely defined hierarchy, and the encouragement of open communication among project members can be effective.

We can summarize the characteristics of the two types of organizational structure in Table 2.5.

Table 2.5   Comparison of Organizational Structures

Highly Structured	Loosely Structured
High certainty	Uncertainty
Repetition	New techniques or technology
Large projects	Small projects

The two types of structures may be combined. For example, programmers may be asked to develop a subsystem on their own using an egoless approach within a hierarchical structure. Similarly, the test team of a loosely structured project may impose a hierarchical structure on itself and designate one person to be responsible for all major testing decisions.

2.3
COST OF BUILDING A SYSTEM

Once we have established a schedule for our project and know who will be doing the work, the next step is to determine how much the project will cost.

Types of Costs

To estimate cost, we enumerate the items that will generate costs. We include not only technical considerations but also human ones, placing the costs in five categories:

1. Computer-related

2. Facilities

3. People

4. Project complexity

5. Project methods and tools

In the sections that follow, we investigate each category.

Computer-related Cost. First, there are hardware and software costs for items purchased for development. This category includes computer *hardware*, such as the main processing computers, front-end processors (computers whose special purpose is to process the incoming data before the main processor handles the data), array processors (computers that process all elements of an array at once rather than single pieces of data), data base machines (computers whose main function is to store and retrieve data from a large data base), and so on. In addition, terminals, printers, disk drives, tape drives, plotters, and other *peripheral devices* are necessary. Often, other hardware is needed. Communications requires modems, phone lines, multiplexers, concentrators or controllers, for example. *Cables* connect the devices, and racks and other *furniture* hold the equipment. Finally, we need storage media and supplies: disks, tapes, print wheels, paper, and so on.

Accompanying the computer is *software* of various kinds. An operating system, compilers, interpreters, and assemblers are supplemented by software tools to help in tracking requirements, designing the system, testing it, and documenting. A data base management package, graphics program, communications procedure, simulation tool, or other specialized software may be purchased, too.

The resources available can generate indirect costs by enhancing or hindering the productivity of the project team. For example, suppose your project has an inadequate number of video display terminals or inadequate computer time on the development system. You may waste time waiting for resources to become available. Deadlines are sometimes missed because the computer has insufficient disk space or memory for the large amount of compile time or disk searches needed.

Sometimes the *technology* itself can help or hinder the project. For instance, suppose development for your project is done on a new, state-of-the-art computer. The computer was chosen because it uses a powerful nonprocedural language. Although the nonprocedural language may speed program development, no one on the team is familiar with the new computer and how it works. Because the project has a tight deadline, the computer was delivered before the vendor completed testing. Your unfamiliarity coupled with the continual appearance of computer system errors can hold you back and actually slow development.

Cost of Facilities. Additional costs relate to the renting or building of *space* to house you and your development team. The team may have to acquire space, build a raised floor, install special security aids (such as controlled access to the computer room), regulate the temperature or humidity, and buy office furniture and supplies for the workers. Lights, heat, telephones, photocopiers, and access to other facilities add to the total costs.

Inadequate space may cause hidden costs. Studies by DeMarco and Lister ([DEM85]) and McCue ([MCC78]) indicate that a programmer needs a minimum amount of space and quiet to be able to work effectively. McCue reported to colleagues at IBM that the minimum standard for programmer workspace should be 100 square feet of dedicated floor space with 30 square feet of horizontal work surface. The space needs a floor-to-ceiling enclosure for noise protection. In addition, DeMarco and Lister's work suggests that programmers free from telephone calls and uninvited visitors are more efficient and produce a better product.

People Costs. Salary is a major cost of development. A common way to determine this cost is to estimate the effort required for each task in the work breakdown structure. After deciding who is best suited to perform each task, you multiply the hourly estimate by the labor rate (salary plus benefits) for the person assigned to the task and thus have an estimate of personnel cost for the entire project. However, as we have seen, work style, project organization, ability, interest, experience, training, and other worker characteristics affect the estimates. Moreover, when communication occurs among several employees, the cost of an activity is increased by the time needed for meetings, documentation, training, and so on. Thus, whereas the computer-related and space-related costs of a project are relatively easy to estimate, the costs generated by people, their work habits, and their interactions are much more difficult to predict with any degree of certainty.

Cost of Project Complexity. The complexity of a project influences the cost by affecting the speed with which the project is completed. The more complex a project, the longer it will take; the longer it takes, the more it will cost. As we will see in more detail in chapters 4 and 5, the complexity of a system can be evaluated in two ways: by noting the amount of *coordination* required among the scheduled activities, and by looking at the amount of *documentation* required to describe the behavior of some system components with others. For example, if your project is divided into several subsystems, each with a single input and output, your development team needs little time to coordinate the passing of parameters among the subsystems. Indeed, in this sense, the project complexity is equivalent to the complexity of the activity graph of the project schedule.

Subsystem complexity influences cost as each subsystem is designed, tested, and documented. The more complex a subsystem, the more time is required to design efficient processing techniques, to test their effectiveness, and to document the code and design well enough so that the code can be easily tested and maintained.

Understanding the underlying problem affects cost, too. The more complete your understanding of what the customer wants, the more easily and quickly you can attack the problem. Similarly, the stability of the requirements is important. If the requirements evolve as the system does, your project team must continually revise the design and code, much of which may already have been written and tested. These repeated changes to the requirements can increase the cost substantially. Boehm ([BOE78]) has determined that the cost to make a change increases exponentially the farther into the software development life cycle the change is made. The later in development a change is made, the more work must be redone. Thus, a major goal of software engineering is to be as precise and complete as possible to eliminate misunderstandings that can result in changed requirements. A second goal is to build systems *flexibly* so that the impact of change is minimized.

Sometimes the problem to be solved is not extraordinarily difficult by itself, but it is made to seem so by complicated notation or an unsystematic approach to its description or solution. This complication can be eased by expressing ideas and concepts in their most elementary forms from the very beginning of the project. Along with a systematic description of the problem and its solution must be a systematic way to control the changes in the system's design, code, and documentation. Your project can be adversely affected if you change existing code or an existing design without notifying the other members of your team or without determining the impact of the change on the remainder of the system.

The project specifications usually include some kind of reliability constraint or response requirements. After a certain point, the more reliable a system is to be, the more complex the design and the slower the development. Likewise, if the system is to respond in a very short period of time, the design is likely to be more complex. In both cases, the testing phase is lengthened so that as many responses and contingencies as possible can be tested.

Cost of Project Methods and Tools. Project management can also affect productivity. Managing includes setting project standards or procedures for activities such as documenting requirements, keeping track of changes, developing and administering tests, or even holding project staff meetings. The long-term goal of such standards and procedures is to enhance the quality of the final product. An additional goal is to keep costs down by minimizing the time it takes to correct an error or make a change in the system.

Management includes methods for training team members and for tracking the status of their work. Costs may be incurred for training courses or for periodic status meetings. For example, suppose that your project leader wants the team to use structured programming techniques (described in chapter 6) for the project. The programmers attend a three-day training class on structured programming and how to use it with an automated programming tool on the development computer. Some customers permit the cost of the instructor plus the cost of three days' salary for each programmer to be included in the cost of the product. The project leader hopes that these costs will be outweighed by the benefits of structured, more easily maintainable code.

Project methods can have hidden costs, too. The management skills of the project directors and their superiors can aid or hinder communication and understanding both among the team members and with the customer. Lack of communication can result in confusion and error, adding significantly to a project's cost. Management must also set goals that are consistent with the project members' abilities and job categories. Otherwise, project members may fall behind schedule, holding up others on the project and creating costly delays. Finally, effective management techniques can prevent the customer and the developers from straying outside the scope of the project. Sometimes, as a project is being developed, the customer or the developers request enhancements to the original system description. These enhancements may be attractive, but the continual addition of enhancements may alter the intended purpose of the system and unnecessarily hold up the schedule.

Cost Estimation

Many factors affect the cost of a project. Some are difficult to understand or anticipate, and this uncertainty makes accurate prediction of costs very difficult. Still, we must give our customer an idea of what the cost will be. There are several ways to consider cost factors and approach cost estimation. We describe each briefly and then analyze the strengths and weaknesses of each.

1. One approach estimates cost by using *analogies*. If we have already built a system that is very much like the one proposed, we can use the similarity as the basis of our cost estimates. In other words, if system A is very much like system B, then the cost to produce system A should be very much like the cost to produce system B. This same approach can be extended to say that if system A is about half the size (or complexity) of system B, system A should cost about half as much as system B.

2. A second approach to cost estimation examines the individual components of the *work breakdown structure* of a project. An estimate is made of the cost of completing each activity within the project. The cost of the entire system is then the sum of the costs of the individual work units.

3. A third approach estimates the *cost per unit of measurement*; this measurement unit is often a line of code in a program. Then, each activity or module is estimated in terms of lines of code, and the total price for a project can be computed by multiplying the estimated number of lines of code by a previously determined cost per line.

4. The fourth approach to cost estimation describes the project in terms of its components, and then uses an *equation* to relate the cost of the components to the overall project cost. For example, if the system is to use X sets of user menus, Y user functions, and Z tables in its data base, we may be able to estimate the cost of the project as

$$\text{Cost} = a\text{X} + b\text{Y} + c\text{Z}$$

where a, b and c are constants that relate the parameters to the cost of developing these features.

An examination of each approach will reveal those with the most promise.

Estimating Cost Using Analogies. Very often, we base our cost projections on our experience with other projects. This seems to be a reasonable and attractive way of generating an estimate. However, projects that appear to be very similar can in fact be quite different. For example, fast runners today can run a mile in four minutes. A marathon race requires a runner to run 26 miles and 365 yards. If we extrapolate the four minute time, we might assume that a four minute-mile runner should be able to run a marathon in 1 hour and 45 minutes. Yet a marathon has never been run in under two hours. Consequently, there must be characteristics of running a marathon that are very different from running a mile. Likewise, there are often characteristics of one project that make it very different from another project; however, these characteristics are not always apparent.

Even when we know how one project differs from another, we do not always know how the differences affect the cost. The proportional cost strategy is unreliable because project costs are not necessarily linear: two people cannot produce code twice as fast as one. Extra time may be needed for coordination and communication or to accommodate for differences in interest, ability, and experience. For instance, suppose project A and project B are identical in all characteristics except that the ten people developing project A are a different group from the ten people developing project B. Assume, too, that the experience and educational backgrounds of the people on A's team are the same as those of B's. A study ([SAC68]) has shown that there is no easily definable relationship between the experience of programmers and their performance.

When researchers calculated ratios between the best and worst performance, they found that the ratio averaged ten to one on productivity measurements and five to one on program speed and space measurements. Thus, even though the projects appear to have the same characteristics, estimating costs using only the apparent similarities may be misleading.

Estimating Cost Using Work Breakdown Structure. In the title essay of *The Mythical Man-Month* ([BRO75]), Brooks makes a convincing argument that increasing the effort put forth on a project does not guarantee that progress will be made. The more people we place on a project and the longer they work, the higher are the costs. The work breakdown structure is a tool to help measure a project's progress, not the effort expended by those who are doing the work. Thus, using the work breakdown structure to estimate personnel costs can be misleading. The work breakdown structure divides a project into tasks or work units. We can estimate the cost of each work unit by comparing it with the cost of a similar, completed piece of work, or with any other method that seems appropriate. It is tempting to sum the unit costs to estimate the total project cost. However, this method works only when no communication is needed among those working on different tasks. Otherwise, additional costs are generated for communication and training, understanding the underlying design and customer needs, and other project tasks that are not reflected directly in the work breakdown structure.

Further research has confirmed that there seems to be an optimal development time for a given project. Adding extra members to the development team cannot speed development and force the project to be completed before this optimal time. We cannot always estimate this optimum exactly, but Boehm's work ([BOE81]) indicates that development time cannot be compressed below 75% of the optimum, no matter how many people or what kinds of resources are used. Brooks points out that adding people to a late project can only increase the time and cost of the project, since the newcomers must first learn about the project, its progress, and its other resources before being able to contribute anything to the development.

Estimating Cost Using Lines of Code. For many years, the number of lines of source code has been used as an estimate of project size and as a basis for estimating project cost. All of these estimating techniques rely on the quality of the estimator's judgment. For example, you may be asked to estimate the size of a project by supplying an optimistic estimate of lines of code *(a)*, a pessimistic one *(b)*, and an estimate of the most likely number of lines of code *(m)*. Then, a lines-of-code estimate is calculated by using the formula

$$\frac{a + 4m + b}{6}$$

We can extend this idea by looking at completed projects to infer a relationship between lines of code and total cost. Several researchers have examined project histories, including project size and cost. They have generated equations to act as models for new projects. For example, Walston and Felix ([WAL77]) estimate the relationship between effort in person-months (E) and thousands of lines of code (L) to be

$$E = 5.2 \ L^{.91}$$

This kind of model, known as a **resource model**, predicts the effort involved in or the duration of a project. Similar models can be found elsewhere. For instance, Nanus and Farr ([NAN64]) examined a different set of historical data to reach the conclusion that

$$E = k \ L^{1.5}$$

where k is a constant. As you can see, the two equations are quite different. Part of the difference can be attributed to the fact that they are based on two completely different sets of historical data. However, there may be some underlying rule that can be applied to estimate costs; we just have to discover what that rule is.

The drawback to this technique is that it is one-dimensional. It assumes that system cost is related only to one particular system characteristic, namely the number of lines of source code. This approach is unrealistic for several reasons. One is the difficulty in distinguishing two projects that are identical except for the programming language used for implementation. Two programs can be of equal difficulty and development time, but one can have 200 assembler statements while the other has 20 Pascal lines of code. A value for the constant k may be determined that can account for the difference. However, the use of subroutines, functions, macros, and other time- and space-savers complicates matters, too. With the increased use of program generators that supply a great deal of code automatically, it is difficult to tell how much work is required by the development team for each line of code in the result.

Estimating Cost Using Parametric Equations.   The investigation of the relationship between lines of code and cost is not useless. There may be some consistency of cost factors among different projects. Earlier in this chapter, we examined some of the many factors that contribute to the difficulty or complexity of a project and that can affect the cost. Researchers have tried to isolate these factors and generate a set of equations that describes the relationship between factors and cost. Many of these equational models define the project as a function of time; thus, they are called **dynamic models** because the estimates of cost change as the time period changes. A typical dynamic model uses several variables and demonstrates how time affects effort and other project factors. Let us look at some examples of dynamic models to see how they work.

Effort and Work Environment Models.   Putnam ([PUT78]) has generated a model that relates the number of *lines of code* to the *development effort* and the *time* it takes to complete the project. If we represent number of thousands of lines of code by L, the project development time (in years) by T, and the development effort by K, then the relationship demonstrated by Putnam is

$$L = c \, K^{1/3} \, T^{4/3}$$

In this equation, the constant c is a number representing the state of technology; as technology advances, c should increase to show that more lines of code can be generated for the same amount of effort and time.

When you are asked to estimate the time it will take to complete a task, you usually assume that you will work uninterrupted. However, part of your day is devoted to unproductive time, some of it caused by interruptions in your office. Some researchers have incorporated in their models the effects of the *work environment* on individual productivity. These models try to be more realistic by recognizing the nonproductive time in any office. For example, Esterling ([EST80]) has generated equations incorporating the following variables:

a = the fraction of the day spent on administration and work not directly related to the project.

t = the number of minutes in the average work interruption.

r = the number of minutes it takes to recover after an interruption.

k = the number of interruptions per day by people working on the project.

p = the number of interruptions per day by non-project causes.

i = the overhead cost per person as a fraction of base pay.

d = the differential for overtime pay as a fraction of base pay.

g = the number of overtime hours per day.

The resulting model calculates the *useful* working time per person in a standard eight-hour day as

$$w = (1/8)(8 - 8a + g - \frac{4r}{60} - \frac{p(t+r)}{60} + \frac{k(n-1)(t+r)}{60})$$

We can multiply this value by the number of people on the project to find the useful working time of all project members per day. Then multiplying the result by five tells us how much useful work is accomplished during a regular five-day work week:

$$5nw = \text{useful hours of work per week}$$

where n is the number of people working on the project.

If you estimate that a system will take 400 hours to build, you really mean that you need 400 hours of useful time, in Esterling's terminology. You can use

Esterling's model to give you a better idea of how many days to place on the project schedule, accounting for distractions.

The model can also be used to calculate costs. For example, the labor cost per workday for an average employee salary S is computed as

$$c = nS(gd + 8(i + 1))$$

and the project cost per person-day of work is

$$\frac{c}{nw}$$

Types of Work Involved. The most recent research tries to distinguish among *types of projects* to see how each type is related to the work involved in project development. Years ago, it was thought that development effort was the same no matter what kind of project was being developed. For example, Brooks ([BRO75]) estimated that one-third of project development time is spent on planning, one-sixth on coding, one-quarter on unit and integration testing, and one-quarter on system testing. However, other studies present varying distributions. For example, Yourdon ([YOU82]) suggests that time is used in the following way:

Survey	5%
Analysis	35%
Design	20%
Implementation	15%
Remaining activities	25%

The differences in these distributions, depicted in Figure 2.10, may be attributable to project complexity or difficulty.

Boehm ([BOE81]) investigated the variation in effort for different types of projects. By comparing characteristics of a large number of completed projects, he derived three modes of program development. A program's mode depends on its independence from other programs and procedures. An **organic** program is one

Figure 2.10 Comparison of Development Effort

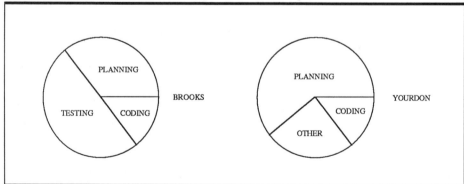

that can be run by itself, possibly incorporating (calling) other programs. Most application programs (that is, programs that perform a function for a user, rather than for the system or the computer) are organic. A **semi-detached** program is used by other programs to perform certain tasks; this type of program usually does not stand by itself. Utility programs (that is, programs that support general system functions rather than particular user functions) are examples of semi-detached programs. An **embedded** program is one that has a great deal of interaction with other programs and passes control back and forth. Many systems programs (that is, programs dealing directly with computer control) are embedded programs.

By examining dozens of projects, Boehm found the relationship between total number of programmer-months of effort (M) and number of thousands of delivered source instructions (I) to be

$$M = 2.4 \ I^{1.05}$$

for organic programs,

$$M = 3.0 \ I^{1.12}$$

for semi-detached programs, and

$$M = 3.6 \ I^{1.20}$$

for embedded programs. Thus, a 60,000-line utility program takes about twice as long to develop as an application program, and a system program takes about three times as long to develop.

Other researchers have generated similar estimates, but the exponents have varied widely. For example, the exponent in the equation for M above has been found to be as low as .91 and as high as 1.83. This range of variation means that our estimate can easily be wrong by a large amount or that we have not based our estimate on the right set of independent variables.

Combining Variables. How can we make our estimates more accurate? One way is to take into account more factors that affect the project. The project characteristics discussed in chapter 1 are good candidates for estimating factors. For example, how reliable must code be? We can determine reliability by considering several requirements:

1. Accuracy of calculation

2. Robustness and consistency of results

3. Completeness (the ability of the system to handle all situations)

Since different systems can tolerate differing degrees of reliability, Boehm proposes five categories of reliability, each representing a tolerance for a given system. For each tolerance, he has used information about completed projects to define a multiplier; the multiplier is used in calculating the amount of development effort required for that kind of system. The more reliable a system must be, the higher the multiplier; this represents the fact that higher reliability requires more effort for building and testing the system. Table 2.6 lists the tolerances, effects, and multipliers for Boehm's reliability categories.

Table 2.6   Reliability Categories and Multipliers

Tolerance	Effect	Multiplier
Very low	Slight inconvenience	.75
Low	Losses easily recovered	.88
Nominal	Loss recoverable with moderate difficulty	1.00
High	High financial loss	1.15
Very high	Risk to human life	1.40

Boehm has considered the use of technology in the same way. The more a project takes advantage of available technology, the faster the project will be completed. For example, a project may use modern design techniques (investigated in chapters 4 and 5) or automated development tools. Boehm suggests that if a project uses no modern practices, its effort is multiplied by 1.24; if it uses all modern practices, its multiplier becomes .82. Similarly, if the project uses only very basic development tools, its multiplier is 1.24; if advanced development tools are available, the multiplier is only .83.

The COCOMO Model. Many other factors have been investigated and quantified in this way. Boehm has incorporated these parameters in a **Constructive Cost Model (COCOMO)**. The model makes initial estimates by looking at the cost of modules and subsystems in terms of lines of source code instructions. Then, just as we have seen for reliability and technology, the model adjusts the estimates with multipliers to account for other aspects of the project that have an effect on the effort expended to develop the system. Table 2.7 lists some of the parameters included in the COCOMO model.

By including a variety of parameters in the cost estimate, the COCOMO model allows us to get some idea of what a project will cost. In addition, the model allows us to work with a customer to determine whether some requirements might be changed to lower the cost or change the focus of the system. The various cost factors, as represented by the parameters of the model, can be played against one another to determine tradeoffs the customer is willing to make. At the end of this chapter, we will see how the COCOMO model can be used to estimate the cost of developing the resource tracking and simulation system for Weaver Farm.

Effort Over Time. The techniques discussed so far are useful for initial estimates of the effort required to build a system. However, the models give project planners no idea of the percentage of effort required for a particular development activity. When building a software project, not everyone on the project team is

Table 2.7   Parameters for which there are Multipliers

System Parameters:
    Required reliability
    Size of the data base(s)
    Complexity of the system

Hardware Parameters:
    Constraints on execution time
    Constraints on storage
    Volatility of the virtual machine
    Response time

Personnel Parameters:
    Ability of the analysts
    Ability of the programmers
    Experience with the application
    Experience with the hardware
    Experience with the programming languages, development tools

Project Parameters:
    Use of modern programming practices
    Use of development tools
    Existence of required development schedule

involved completely from beginning to end. For example, programmers may not begin their work until the program design is complete. Thus, it is helpful to develop estimating techniques that forecast *when* effort will be required as well as how much is needed. These dynamic models allow us to ask questions that cannot be answered by static models. For example, dynamic models allow us to vary the effort involved in each stage of development and see the effect on the project completion date.

Several cost models incorporate development time as a parameter. Norden ([NOR63]) found that the development effort of projects at IBM followed a distribution similar to the Rayleigh curve, shown in Figure 2.11. Others, notably Putnam ([PUT78]) and Parr ([PAR80]), have incorporated several project characteristics in their equations and have generated similar curves. We can use these curves to deter-

Figure 2.11   Rayleigh Distribution of Project Effort

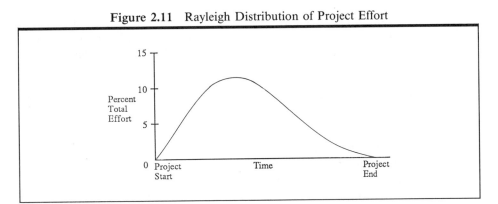

mine the trade-offs between number of people on a project and the expected completion time. For instance, the three curves of Figure 2.12 illustrate three possible
distributions of effort for a given project. The total amount of effort, represented by
the area under each curve, is the same. However, each distribution results in a
different completion date. A complete discussion of the time-sensitive models can
be found in Putnam's tutorial ([PUT80]).

Figure 2.12   Alternatives for Project Effort

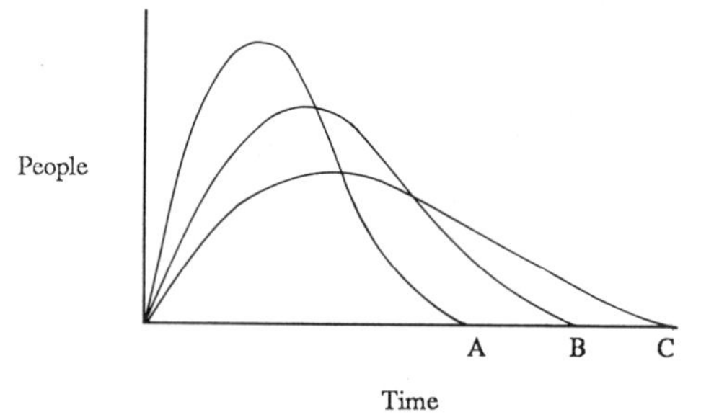

SOURCE: Planning Control International. Used by permission.

2.4

TOOLS AND TECHNIQUES
FOR TRACKING COST AND SCHEDULE

Many tools and techniques are available for keeping track of the project cost and
schedule. All are known as **project management aids**. Some are manual and
others automated, but all help developers in planning, budgeting, and reporting
progress to the customer.

A typical project management aid begins by asking you as the developer to
divide a project into a series of phases, steps, and activities to form a work breakdown structure. Then you enter data about the various resources available (people
and hardware) and their costs, and the package generates estimates of cost and
schedule. Status reports can be printed out during the project's development.

The management aids are available for a variety of types of computers, from
microcomputers to large mainframes. To understand their capabilities, consider
the Easytrak system from Planning Control International (Newport Beach,
California). Figure 2.13 illustrates a work breakdown structure drawn by Easytrak.
The project schedule is depicted as Figure 2.14. This bar chart is known as a **Gantt
chart**, and it shows the project activities in parallel. Such a chart enables the
project director to understand what tasks can be performed concurrently. A similar
chart, shown as Figure 2.15, illustrates all milestones for the project.

Easytrak allows you to graph the resources assigned to project activities to
determine the best assignment. For example, Figure 2.16 is a graph of the relation-

Figure 2.13 Work Breakdown Structure

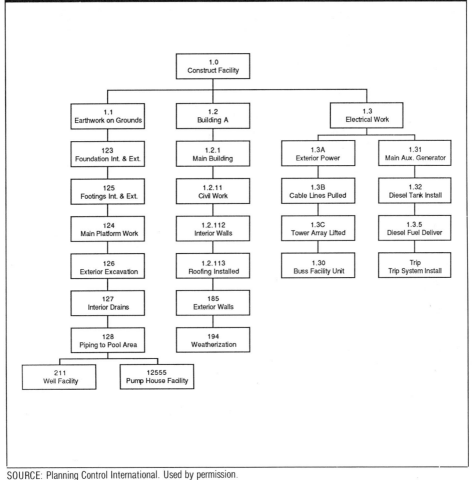

ship between the people assigned to the project and those needed at each stage. The months during which there are too many team members is clearly shown: June 27 to July 25. You can change the resource allocation and see how the project will be affected. Using this capability, you determine "what-if" something changes. By varying resource availability and cost, you watch the schedule change. In this way, you can weigh and compare the effects of various combinations of people, time, and resources.

The Easytrak charts help you decide on the overall project schedule. However, they can also be generated for small time intervals to help with detailed planning. Figures 2.17 and 2.18 are examples of charts comparing predicted cost and progress with the actual results at some point during development. You can use this information to decide if your project is on schedule and within budget. PERT charts, calendars, graphs of estimated versus actual progress, and a host of other visual aids are used not only to view current project status but also to revise estimates and plan for the future.

Figure 2.14   Gantt Chart

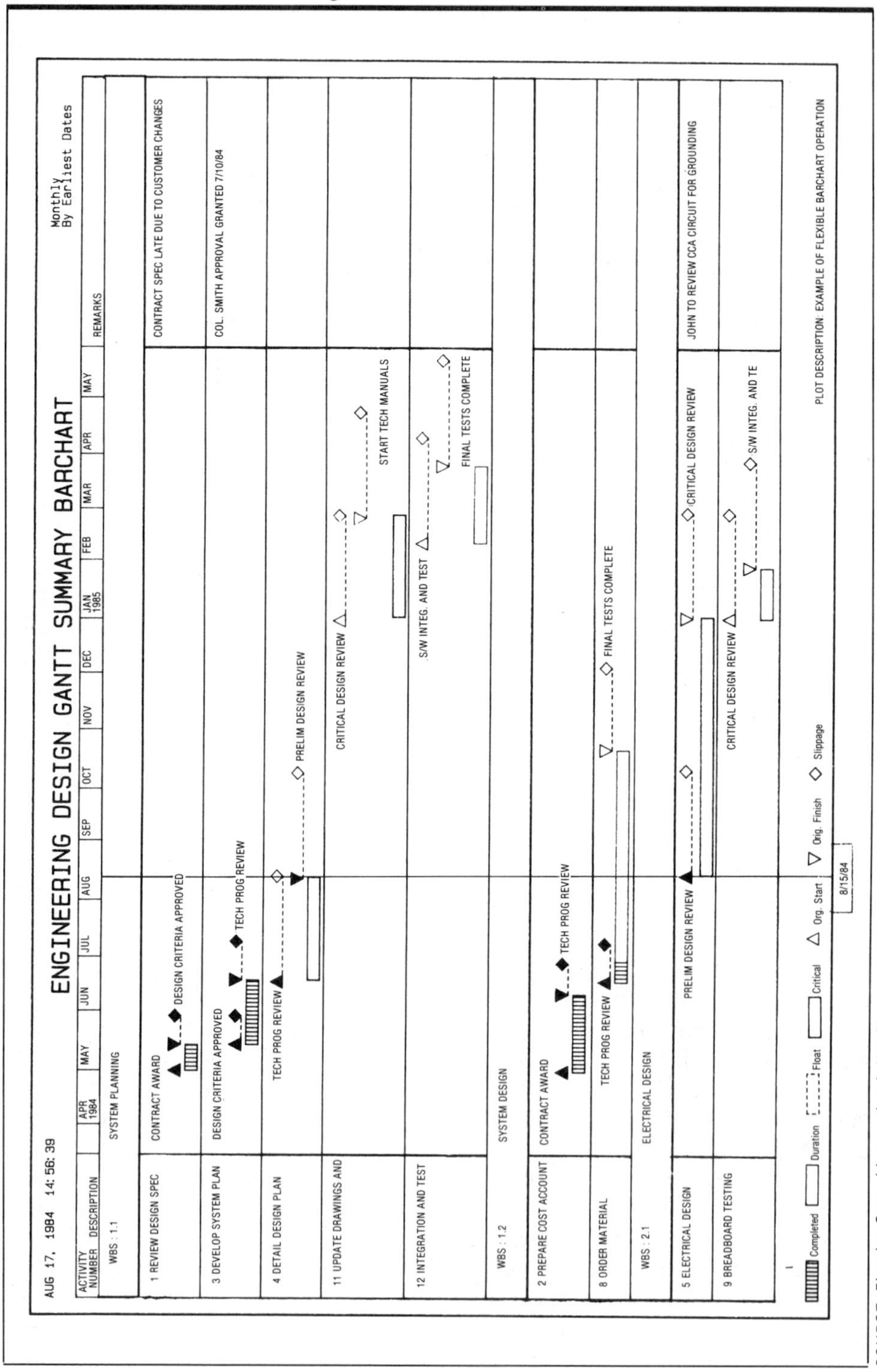

SOURCE: Planning Control International. Used by permission.

Figure 2.15 Milestone Bar Chart

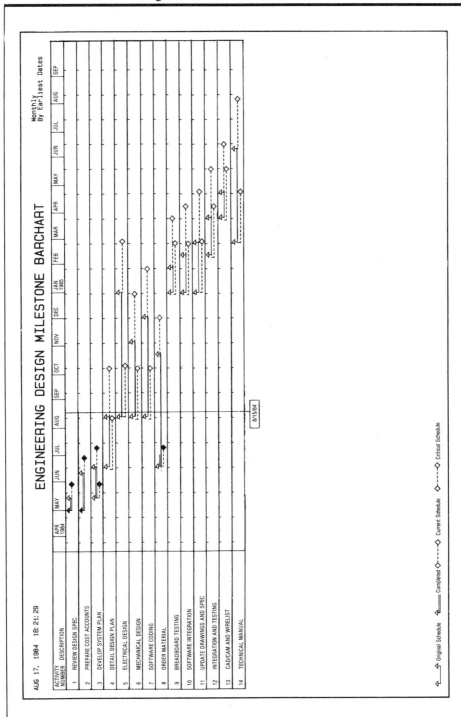

Figure 2.16   Resource Load

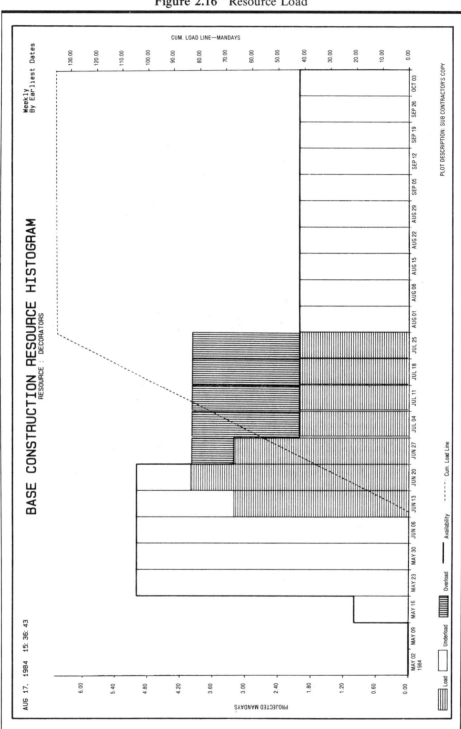

SOURCE: Planning Control International. Used by permission.

Figure 2.17 Comparison of Actual and Planned Costs

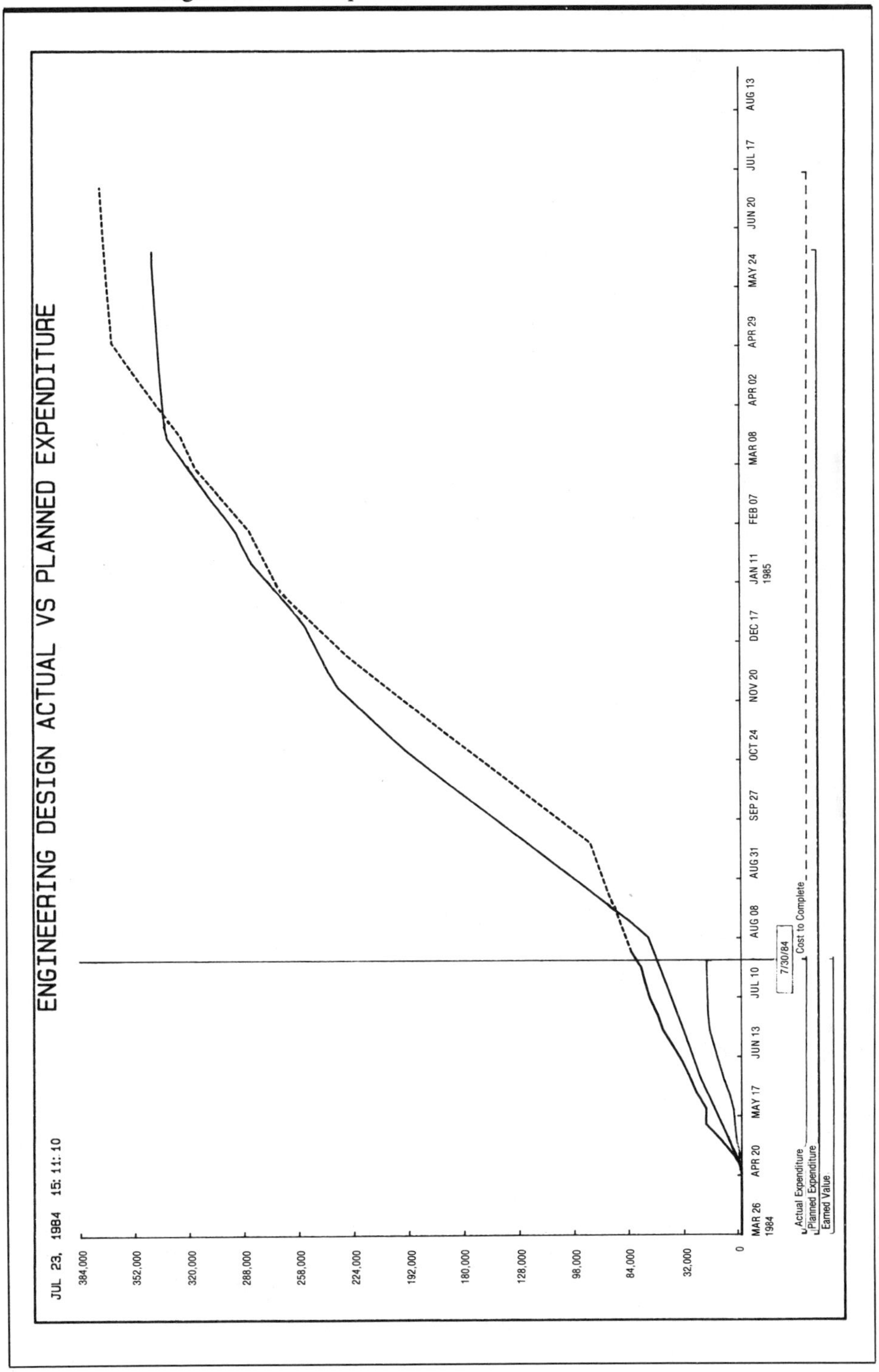

SOURCE: Planning Control International. Used by permission.

Figure 2.18   Activity Completion Report

ENGINEERING REVIEW ACTIVITY COMPLETION REPORT

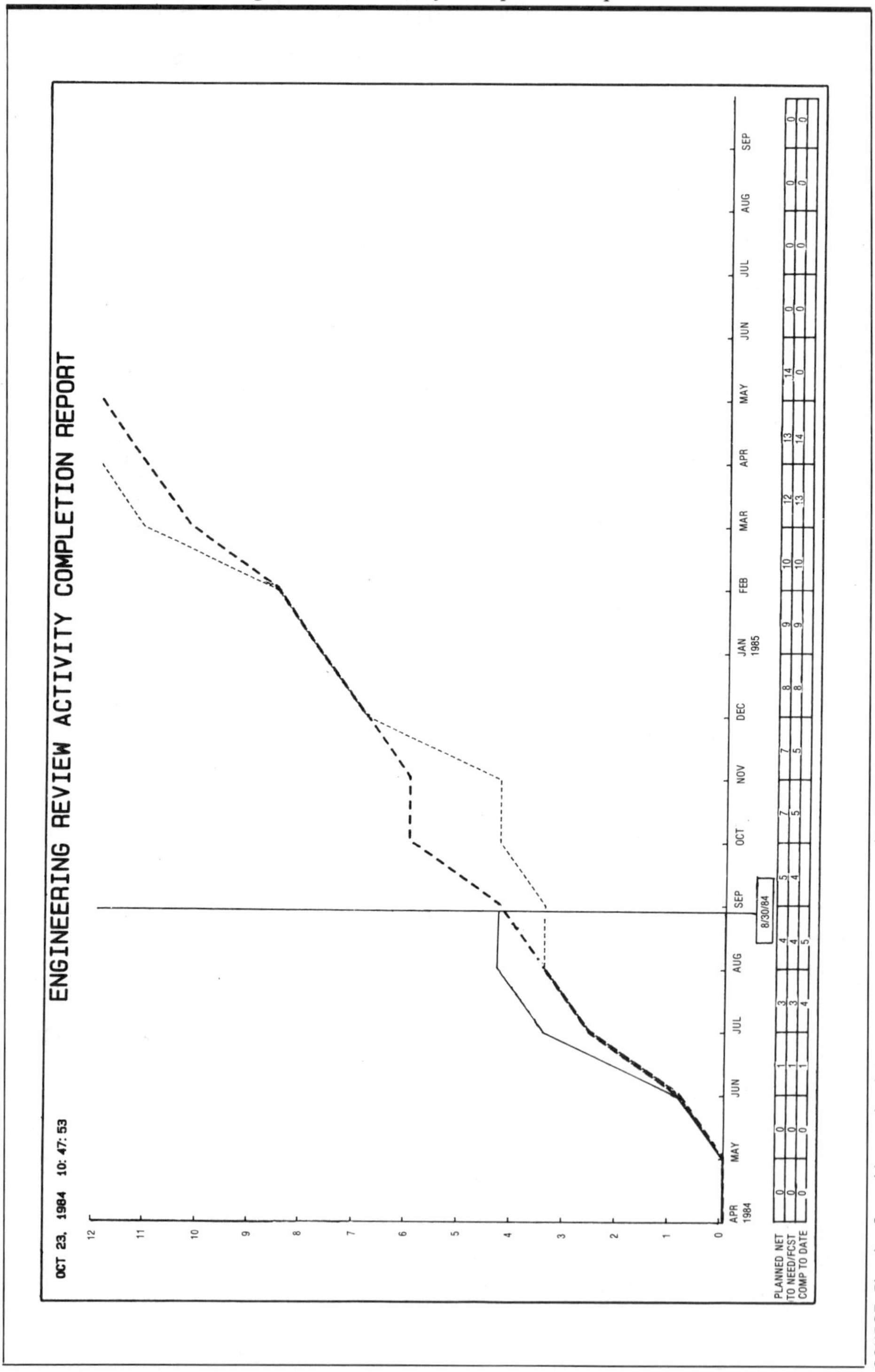

SOURCE: Planning Control International. Used by permission.

2.5

THE PROJECT PLAN

To communicate the project cost estimates, schedule, and organization to a customer, we present a document called a **project plan**. The plan's purpose is to put in writing the customer's needs and what we plan to do to meet those needs. The customer refers to the project plan for an explanation of the activities in the development process. The plan enables the customer to follow the project's progress through development. We can also use the project plan as a tool for confirming with the customer the overall purpose of the system. Finally, the plan acts as the starting point for comparing the project's progress with the proposed schedule and cost.

The components of the plan can be summarized by these items:

1. Project scope
2. Project schedule
3. Project team organization
4. Technical description of the proposed system
5. Project standards, procedures and proposed methodologies
6. Quality assurance plan
7. Special development tools and techniques
8. Configuration management plan
9. Documentation plan
10. Data management plan
11. Resource management plan
12. Test plan
13. Training plan
14. Security plan
15. Maintenance plan

We begin the plan with a description of the project's *scope*. This description assures the customer that we understand what is wanted. The scope is really a definition of the system boundary, as described in chapter 1. It discusses not only what the project includes but also what it does not include.

The project plan also contains the project *schedule*, including the work break down structure, the deliverables, and a timeline to show what will be happening when during the life of the project. A Gantt chart is sometimes provided to give the customer an idea of the parallel nature of the development tasks. Accompanying the tasks is a list of the *people* on the project team, how they are organized, who they are, and what they will be doing.

The project plan contains the *technical description* of the system. Again, we affirm that we will build a system that satisfies the customer's needs. By working together to generate a technical description, we are forced to answer questions that arise and to address all aspects of the problem to be solved. The technical description lists the system hardware and software. For example, if the proposed system is to use a particular brand or type of computer, compiler, or special-purpose piece of equipment, we include their specifications. In addition, interfaces with other computer systems are described. Circuit diagrams and functional descriptions for special-purpose hardware are included in the plan. Also, any special requirements or restrictions for cabling, terminal capabilities, execution time, response time, and so on are listed.

If particular *methods* are to be used or strategies followed, the plan contains an explanation of them. This explanation includes the following:

1. The methods used in system design including any algorithms or techniques to be used, and the use of desing reviews

2. The methods used in program design, including program design languages

3. The methods used in program coding, including programming languages

4. The methods used in testing

We discuss in the plan the accuracy required by the system and how it will be guaranteed, and the ways in which the quality of the software and hardware will be assured. For large projects, it may be more appropriate for us to write a separate *quality assurance* plan.

Sometimes, special *tools* are developed for the designers, programmers, trainers, or testers. The project plan describes the need for these tools, the techniques used to build them, and the ways in which they will help development.

A *configuration management description* outlines the way in which we will keep track of modifications made to the system or its requirements after the initial requirements are defined. Thus, the plan tells the customer how the documentation, code, and design will be changed and how those changes will be communicated to the team.

We also list all *documents* to be produced during development. Accompanying the list is an explanation of how the documents will be generated, who will write them, and when they will be available. In particular, a documentation plan explains how the documents will be changed when the other components of the project change.

Every project involves the input of data, its processing, and the production of output. The project plan includes a *data management* plan to explain to the customer how data will be gathered, how it will be stored and manipulated, and how it will be archived. Similarly, a *resource management plan* describes how physical resources will be used. For example, if removable disk drives are configured with the hardware and the system is to generate large amounts of data, the resource management plan explains how many disk packs will be used and how they may be rotated for backups. Correspondingly, the data management plan explains what data are on each pack.

Each project plan describes to the customer how we will perform testing. The *test description* includes several key items:

1. How test data will be generated

2. How each program module will be tested

3. How program modules will be integrated with each other and tested

4. How the entire system will be tested

5. How directions for the administration of each test will be generated

If the proposed system is to be installed in stages, the test plan addresses the testing of each stage; it explains how the addition of the next stage does not corrupt the functionality of the previous ones.

Users must be trained to employ the resulting system, and we explain how and when *training* will occur. If a series of classes is necessary, the training plan describes each class, what is to be taught, and for whom the class is most appropriate.

For systems requiring some degree of *security*, the project plan addresses the way the system assures the security of data, users, and hardware. The security section explains how passwords will be issued to users, files and documents, how backups will be handled, how access to certain data will be limited, and how the physical security of the system will be guaranteed.

Finally, if we are to maintain the system after it is complete, the project plan explains how maintenance will be performed. The plan lists our responsibilities in changing the code, repairing the hardware, and supporting documentation and training.

Thus, the project plan presents a comprehensive picture of the proposed system to the customer. It helps to clarify exactly what can be expected once development begins.

2.6

RESOURCE TRACKING AND SIMULATION EXAMPLE

Let us return to the Weaver Farm project to see how the project planning concepts discussed in this chapter are applicable. Suppose we are creating a project schedule and estimated cost for the Weaver Farm project. At this point, we have only an overview of the project from discussions with the customer, the administrators of Weaver Farm. We can create a work breakdown structure by dividing the project into phases according to the parts of the system described to us. For example, we must build a data base to contain the desired descriptions of the various aspects of the recreation area. The data base must include two types of data: natural characteristics and constructed facilities. The natural descriptors may include soil, water, air, and vegetation characteristics, while a structure can be described by the type of structure, the materials of which it is composed, the need for maintenance, and so on.

Another part of the project involves a system to generate the maintenance schedule for Weaver Farm. This phase of the system depends on the data base components, and a great deal of documentation and coordination is involved. The last part of the project is the creation of the simulation subsystem. It too relies on the data base for its basic information. Thus, we can describe our work breakdown structure in three phases:

Phase 1: Create data base

Phase 2: Develop maintenance schedule subsystem

Phase 3: Develop simulation subsystem

Next, we further divide the phases into steps. For example, the data base development must begin with the creation of a data dictionary. This involves the definition and description of each data element that will be stored in the data base. Then, we identify the relationships among the data elements. For instance, if the value of an element is generated by computation involving the value of several other elements, the relationships among these elements must be recorded for future use. In this manner, we can describe phase 1 as a sequence of steps:

Step 1.1: Compile data dictionary

Step 1.2: Identify relationships among data elements

Step 1.3: Define data base tables

Step 1.4: Generate required data entry screens

Step 1.5: Develop query capability

Step 1.6: Develop desired report capability

We continue by dividing each step into activities. For example, the activities for step 1.1 may be viewed as:

Activity 1.1.1: List all data elements

Activity 1.1.2: For each data element, define name, type, length, validation requirements, alternate names, source

Activity 1.1.3: Eliminate duplication from data elements

Activity 1.1.4: Form data dictionary from resulting elements

Assume that we have defined a work breakdown structure for the entire project. We can draw an activity graph to illustrate the flow from one activity to another. To do so, we investigate the dependencies of activities on one another. For example, we cannot determine the relationships among data elements until they are defined and placed in the data dictionary. Thus, activity 1.1.4 must be complete before activity 1.2.1 can begin. However, the query and report capabilities can be developed concurrently. Thus, the activity graph can show activities 1.5.1 and 1.6.1 being performed at the same time. The resulting activity graph for phase 1 may look something like Figure 2.19.

Figure 2.19 Activity Graph for Weaver Farm—Phase 1

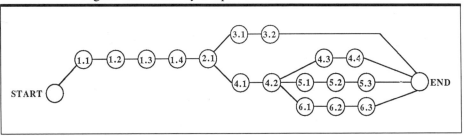

Next, we estimate durations for each activity, and we label the edges of the activity graph with the corresponding time to complete that activity. Using the critical path method discussed earlier in the chapter, we can calculate a completion time for each phase or for the entire project. For example, suppose the durations for phase 1 of the Weaver Farm project are as shown in Figure 2.20. We see that it will take 50 days from the start of activity 1.1.1 to the completion of activity 1.2.1. Then, the path through activity 1.3.1 to the end uses 26 days; from the beginning of activity 1.4.1 through 1.4.4 to the end uses 17 days; from the beginning of 1.4.1 through 1.5.3 takes 23 days; and from the beginning of 1.4.1 through 1.6.3 takes 19 days. Thus, the longest path through this phase is the one beginning at the start and traveling through activities 1.3.1 and 1.3.2. This is the critical path. The total amount of time for the completion of phase 1 must be at least the number of days on the critical path. Thus, phase 1 will take at least 76 days to complete. Activities for steps 1.4, 1.5, and 1.6 have some slack available, because they are not on the critical path.

We can do the same kind of analysis for the entire project activity graph. The exercises at the end of this chapter will give you more experience in determining the critical path and calculating slack.

To estimate the cost of the project, we can choose from among several cost models to help us. Since we investigated the difficulty of the Weaver Farm project in chapter 1, we have some idea of the characteristics of the project. We can use these characteristics to select multipliers for the COCOMO model, and then use the model to generate a cost estimate.

To help us in determining cost with COCOMO, we use an automated tool called Before You Leap (BYL), available from the Gordon Group (San Jose, California). Recall that COCOMO asks us to consider four categories of factors that may affect

Figure 2.20 Activity Graph with Durations—Phase 1

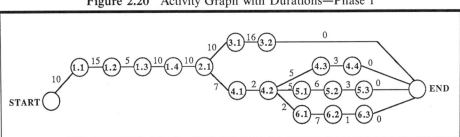

development: system, hardware, personnel, and project. Within each category are several attributes for which Boehm has developed multipliers. BYL presents us with a cost driver screen (Figure 2.21) containing an entry for each attribute. By rating each attribute of the Weaver Farm project, we are automatically selecting the COCOMO multipliers. For example, Figure 2.21 shows that we have rated the project "nominally reliable." As we have seen, this means that a system failure would cause moderate but recoverable losses. Similarly, we have indicated a very large data base size and high project complexity. The BYL documentation contains an appendix that explains the meaning of each attribute and each possible rating.

Notice that our example assumes that the analysts and programmers on our development team are very highly capable and are rated "VERY HIGH." In addi tion, they have a great deal of programming experience; they are rated "HIGH." In the product attributes section, we are assuming a high use of modern programming practices and of software tools. Thus our development team is highly skilled and sophisticated software engineering tools and methods.

After completing the cost driver screen, BYL shows us a project sizing screen (Figure 2.22). To determine project sizing, we must rate the system as organic, semi-detached, or embedded. We have chosen "semi-detached" and have estimated that the project will require ten thousand lines of new source code instructions. Some projects use code that has been adapted from another development project with similar hardware or a similar operating system. If such code is adapted to the current project, the number of lines can be estimated for BYL. Similarly, if code from a system with dissimilar hardware or a dissimilar operating system is modi-

Figure 2.21   Work Styles

```
Before You Leap          COST DRIVER SCREEN
         COST DRIVERS                          RATINGS
PRODUCT ATTRIBUTES
RELY  Required software reliability   VLOW  LOW  NOMINAL  HIGH  VHIGH
DATA  Database size                         LOW  NOMINAL  HIGH  VHIGH
CPLX  Product complexity             VLOW  LOW  NOMINAL  HIGH  VHIGH  XHIGH
COMPUTER ATTRIBUTES
TIME  Execution time constraints                 NOMINAL  HIGH  VHIGH  XHIGH
STOR  Main storage constraints                   NOMINAL  HIGH  VHIGH  XHIGH
VIRT  Virtual machine volatility           LOW  NOMINAL  HIGH  VHIGH
TURN  Computer turnaround time             LOW  NOMINAL  HIGH  VHIGH
PERSONNEL ATTRIBUTES
ACAP  Analyst capabiilty             VLOW  LOW  NOMINAL  HIGH  VHIGH
AEXP  Applications experience        VLOW  LOW  NOMINAL  HIGH  VHIGH
PCAP  Programmer capability          VLOW  LOW  NOMINAL  HIGH  VHIGH
VEXP  Virtual machine experience     VLOW  LOW  NOMINAL  HIGH
LEXP  Programming lang. experience   VLOW  LOW  NOMINAL  HIGH
PROJECT ATTRIBUTES
MODP  Use of modern prog. practices  VLOW  LOW  NOMINAL  HIGH  VHIGH
TOOL  Use of software tools          VLOW  LOW  NOMINAL  HIGH  VHIGH
SCED  Required development schedule  VLOW  LOW  NOMINAL  HIGH  VHIGH
                         F1 = HELP
```

Figure 2.22   Before You Leap Project Sizing Screen

```
┌──────────────────────────────────────────────────────────────────────────┐
│ Before You Leap              PROJECT SIZING SCREEN                          │
│                                                                            │
│   INPUTS                                                                   │
│                                                                            │
│   DEVELOPMENT MODE     ORGANIC │SEMIDETACHED│ EMBEDDED                      │
│   DELIVERED SOURCE NEW INSTRUCTIONS (THOUSANDS) ==      10.00               │
│   DELIVERED SOURCE ADAPTED INSTRUCTIONS (THOUSANDS) ==      0.00            │
│         ADAPTED DESIGN REQUIRING MODIFICATION ==    0.00%                   │
│           ADAPTED CODE REQUIRING MODIFICATION ==    0.00%                   │
│    ADAPTED INTEGRATION REQUIRING MODIFICATION ==    0.00%                   │
│   DELIVERED SOURCE CONVERTED INSTRUCTIONS (THOUSANDS) ==      0.00          │
│      CONVERTED DESIGN REQUIRING MODIFICATION ==    0.00%                    │
│        CONVERTED CODE REQUIRING MODIFICATION ==    0.00%                    │
│ CONVERTED INTEGRATION REQUIRING MODIFICATION ==    0.00%                    │
│        LEVEL OF CONVERSION ANALYSIS AND PLANNING == 0  (0-LOW ... 5-HIGH)   │
│   OUTPUTS                                                                   │
│                                                                            │
│   EFFORT :        22.71 man-months                                         │
│   PRODUCTIVITY :   440.28 new-equiv. delivered source instructions / man-month │
│   SCHEDULE :    7.46 months                                                │
│   AVERAGE STAFFING :     2.05 full-time equivalent software personnel       │
│                             F1 = HELP                                       │
└──────────────────────────────────────────────────────────────────────────┘
```

fied to work on the new project, an estimate of modified lines of code is supplied to BYL. Since Weaver Farm is to be a completely new system, we have indicated zero lines of adapted or modified code.

BYL applies the COCOMO model to the data we supply and produces an estimate of project effort at the bottom of the project sizing screen. Figure 2.22 shows that, given the project attributes and size we specified, the Weaver Farm project will need 22.71 person-months of effort. This means that over a period of 7.46 months, just over three full-time people will be needed for project development.

Figure 2.23 is a BYL cost driver report, summarizing the data we supplied and the staffing results produced. However, we can get more detailed information by asking for a phase distribution report (Figure 2.24). This report shows us the distribution of staff effort during each step of the development cycle. It also tells us how many months should be anticipated for design, programming, and testing. Finally, the aggregate activity report (Figure 2.25) summarize the phase distribution report and estimates the effort needed to plan the project before development actually begins.

In addition to projecting the staff and schedule for the Weaver Farm project, we can use Before You Leap to give us an idea of how staff assignments affect development time. For example, the cost driver screen of Figure 2.26 includes many of the same ratings of attributes that we used before. The differences lie in the ratings for personnel attributes. Here, instead of using staff that are highly capable and familiar with the type of system being built, we substitute staff of average ability

Figure 2.23   Cost Driver Report

```
                                      Cost Driver Report
      *********        SOFTWARE COST MODEL        *********
                     copyright 1985, Gordon Group

Description:

Development Mode: SEMIDETACHED
Thousands of New Source Instructions (KDSI):      10.00

Thousands of Adapted Source Instructions (KDSI):        0.00
    Percentage Requiring Design Modification:        0%
    Percentage Requiring Code Modification:          0%
    Percentage Requiring Integration Modification:   0%

Thousands of Converted Source Instructions (KDSI):       0.00
    Percentage Requiring Design Modification:        0%
    Percentage Requiring Code Modification:          0%
    Percentage Requiring Integration Modification:   0%
    Conversion Analysis and Planning (0-LOW ... 5-HIGH): 0

PRODUCT ATTRIBUTES
RELY  Required Software Reliability:  NOMINAL
DATA  Database Size:                  VHIGH
CPLX  Product Complexity:             HIGH

COMPUTER ATTRIBUTES
TIME  Execution Time Constraint:   NOMINAL
STOR  Main Storage Constraint:     VHIGH
VIRT  Virtual Machine Volatility:  NOMINAL
TURN  Computer Turnaround Time:    NOMINAL

PERSONNEL ATTRIBUTES
ACAP  Analyst Capability:            VHIGH
AEXP  Applications Experience:       HIGH
PCAP  Programmer Capability:         VHIGH
VEXP  Virtual Machine Experience:    NOMINAL
LEXP  Programming Language Experience:  HIGH

PROJECT ATTRIBUTES
MODP  Use of Modern Programming Practices:  HIGH
TOOL  Use of Software Tools:                HIGH
SCED  Required Development Schedule:        NOMINAL


OUTPUTS
 EFFORT:
     22.71 man-months

 PRODUCTIVITY:
     440.28 new-equivalent delivered source instructions/man-month

 SCHEDULE:
     7.46 months

 AVERAGE STAFFING
     3.05 full-time equivalent software personnel, FSP
```

Figure 2.24 Phase Distribution Report

```
                                        Phase Distribution Report
          **********        SOFTWARE COST MODEL        *********
                         copyright 1985, Gordon Group

Description:

PRODUCT SIZE:
       10.00 thousand new-equivalent delivered source instructions
PROJECT SCHEDULE:
       7.46 months
ESTIMATED EFFORT:
       22.71 man-months
```

Phase	Product Design	Programming	Integration and Test
DISTRIBUTION	17.00%	60.75%	22.25%
Activity percentage			
Requirements analysis	12.50	4.00	2.50
Product design	41.00	8.00	5.00
Programming	12.54	56.50	35.17
Test planning	4.54	4.54	2.54
Verification & validation	6.54	7.54	30.88
Project office	11.92	6.96	7.96
Configuration mgmt/QA	2.50	6.46	8.00
Manuals	7.96	5.96	7.96
EFFORT	3.86 MM	13.80 MM	5.05 MM
Activity man-months			
Requirements analysis	0.48	0.55	0.13
Product design	1.58	1.10	0.25
Programming	0.48	7.80	1.78
Test planning	0.18	0.63	0.13
Verification & validation	0.25	1.04	1.56
Project office	0.46	0.96	0.40
Configuration mgmt/QA	0.10	0.89	0.40
Manuals	0.31	0.82	0.40
SCHEDULE	25.08%	51.67%	23.25%
Duration schedule months	1.87	3.85	1.73
AVERAGE STAFFING	2.06	3.58	2.91
Full-time software personnel			
Requirements analysis	0.26	0.14	0.07
Product design	0.29	0.15	0.15
Programming	0.26	2.02	1.02
Test planning	0.09	0.26	0.07
Verification & validation	0.14	0.27	0.90
Project office	0.25	0.25	0.23
Configuration mgmt/QA	0.05	0.23	0.23
Manuals	0.16	0.21	0.23

Figure 2.25   Aggregate Activity Report

```
                                      Aggregate Activity Report
             **********           SOFTWARE COST MODEL          *********
                             copyright 1985, Gordon Group

Description:

PRODUCT SIZE:
        10.00 thousand new-equivalent delivered source instructions
PROJECT SCHEDULE:
        7.46 months
ESTIMATED EFFORT:
        22.71 man-months

                                          Supplemental Plans
            Aggregate                      and Requirements
            Development                (not included in Aggregate)
----------------------------------------------------------------------
    100.00%              DISTRIBUTION              7.00%
                           Activity percentage
        5.11             Requirements analysis     46.92
       12.94             Product design            16.54
       44.29             Programming                4.08
        4.18             Test planning              3.04
       12.56             Verification & validation  4.46
        8.03             Project office            14.42
        6.15             Configuration mgmt/QA      3.00
        6.74             Manuals                    5.96
----------------------------------------------------------------------
    22.71 MM             EFFORT                     1.59 MM
                           Activity man-months
        1.16             Requirements analysis      0.75
        2.94             Product design             0.26
       10.06             Programming                0.06
        0.95             Test planning              0.05
        2.85             Verification & validation  0.07
        1.82             Project office             0.23
        1.40             Configuration mgmt/QA      0.05
        1.53             Manuals                    0.09
----------------------------------------------------------------------
    100.00%              SCHEDULE                  18.17%
        7.46               Duration schedule months   1.35
----------------------------------------------------------------------
        3.05             AVERAGE STAFFING           1.17
                           Full-time software personnel
        0.16             Requirements analysis      0.55
        0.39             Product design             0.19
        1.35             Programming                0.05
        0.13             Test planning              0.04
        0.38             Verification & validation  0.05
        0.24             Project office             0.17
        0.19             Configuration mgmt/QA      0.04
        0.21             Manuals                    0.07
----------------------------------------------------------------------
```

Figure 2.26   Assigning Staff Unfamiliar with Language and Applications

```
Before You Leap          COST DRIVER SCREEN
          COST DRIVERS                        RATINGS
PRODUCT ATTRIBUTES
RELY  Required software reliability   VLOW  LOW [NOMINAL] HIGH  VHIGH
DATA  Database size                         LOW  NOMINAL  HIGH  [VHIGH]
CPLX  Product complexity             VLOW  LOW  NOMINAL [HIGH] VHIGH  XHIGH
COMPUTER ATTRIBUTES
TIME  Execution time constraints           [NOMINAL] HIGH  VHIGH  XHIGH
STOR  Main storage constraints             NOMINAL  HIGH  [VHIGH] XHIGH
VIRT  Virtual machine volatility      LOW  [NOMINAL] HIGH  VHIGH
TURN  Computer turnaround time        LOW  [NOMINAL] HIGH  VHIGH
PERSONNEL ATTRIBUTES
ACAP  Analyst capabiilty        VLOW  LOW [NOMINAL] HIGH  VHIGH
AEXP  Applications experience   VLOW [LOW] NOMINAL  HIGH  VHIGH
PCAP  Programmer capability     VLOW  LOW [NOMINAL] HIGH  VHIGH
VEXP  Virtual machine experience  VLOW  LOW [NOMINAL] HIGH
LEXP  Programming lang. experience [VLOW] LOW  NOMINAL  HIGH
PROJECT ATTRIBUTES
MODP  Use of modern prog. practices  VLOW  LOW  NOMINAL [HIGH] VHIGH
TOOL  Use of software tools          VLOW  LOW  NOMINAL [HIGH] VHIGH
SCED  Required development schedule   VLOW  LOW [NOMINAL] HIGH  VHIGH
                    F1 = HELP
```

```
Before You Leap            PROJECT SIZING SCREEN


  INPUTS


  DEVELOPMENT MODE    ORGANIC  SEMIDETACHED  EMBEDDED
  DELIVERED SOURCE NEW INSTRUCTIONS (THOUSANDS) ==    10.00
  DELIVERED SOURCE ADAPTED INSTRUCTIONS (THOUSANDS) ==    0.00
       ADAPTED DESIGN REQUIRING MODIFICATION ==    0.00%
         ADAPTED CODE REQUIRING MODIFICATION ==    0.00%
   ADAPTED INTEGRATION REQUIRING MODIFICATION ==    0.00%
  DELIVERED SOURCE CONVERTED INSTRUCTIONS (THOUSANDS) ==    0.00
     CONVERTED DESIGN REQUIRING MODIFICATION ==    0.00%
       CONVERTED CODE REQUIRING MODIFICATION ==    0.00%
 CONVERTED INTEGRATION REQUIRING MODIFICATION ==    0.00%
       LEVEL OF CONVERSION ANALYSIS AND PLANNING == 0  (0-LOW ... 5-HIGH)
OUTPUTS


EFFORT :       68.10 man-months
PRODUCTIVITY :  146.85 new-equiv. delivered source instructions / man-month
SCHEDULE :   10.95 months
AVERAGE STAFFING :      6.22 full-time equivalent software personnel
                    F1 = HELP
```

who are unfamiliar with the application and the programming language. The result is that the project requires three times as many person-months for development. More than twice as many full-time people are needed on the project team, and the schedule must be over three months longer.

Next, we make one more change to the cost driver screen. We leave all attributes as they were in Figure 2.26 but change the use of modern programming practices and software tools from high to low. The resulting estimates (shown in Figure 2.27) tell us that the project will take longer still. Now, almost eight people will work for over a year to build the Weaver Farm system. In terms of cost, this estimate tells us that by not using good software engineering tools and techniques, the project will cost us thirty months of extra salary alone!

Tools, such as Before You Leap, can be used effectively in weighing considerations of cost and schedule. If the system must be finished quickly, BYL shows us that we must use experienced people employing modern tools and techniques. If schedule is secondary, we may want to assign less experienced, lower salaried people to work for a longer period of time.

2.7

CHAPTER SUMMARY

In this chapter, we have investigated several aspects of project planning. Before we can begin to develop a software project, we must have some idea of the activities involved, who will do them, how long it will take, and how much it will cost. The project schedule breaks development into a series of tasks known collectively as a work breakdown structure. Within this structure is a series of milestones, representing the completion of a major activity or the delivery of an important item to the customer. We have seen how activity graphs can be used to depict the work breakdown structure and help us determine the critical path through the network of activities. PERT and CPM techniques aid the process, showing us how much slack we have.

Once we understand what to do, we decide who will do the development. We choose personnel for the project based not only on expertise and experience but also on work styles, communications skills, and a host of other factors. It is also important to organize the personnel so that the project development is enhanced, not held back by bureaucracy and structure.

Knowing the salaries of the project personnel is not enough. We must estimate the amount of effort to be expended by each type of employee on the project. These estimates can be based on previous experience, on work breakdown structure, on similar projects, or on a set of project characteristics associated by a variety of mathematical relationships. Estimates can also be used to evaluate trade-offs between personnel assignments and possible completion date.

Project planners present the customer with information in addition to estimated schedule and cost. The project plan is a document that summarizes the problem to be solved by the proposed system, outlines any constraints placed on the solution,

Figure 2.27 Assigning Average Staff with No Software Engineering Methods

```
Before You Leap          COST DRIVER SCREEN
         COST DRIVERS                          RATINGS
PRODUCT ATTRIBUTES
RELY  Required software reliability   VLOW  LOW [NOMINAL] HIGH  VHIGH
DATA  Database size                         LOW  NOMINAL  HIGH [VHIGH]
CPLX  Product complexity            VLOW  LOW  NOMINAL [HIGH] VHIGH  XHIGH
COMPUTER ATTRIBUTES
TIME  Execution time constraints           [NOMINAL] HIGH  VHIGH  XHIGH
STOR  Main storage constraints             NOMINAL  HIGH [VHIGH] XHIGH
VIRT  Virtual machine volatility      LOW [NOMINAL] HIGH  VHIGH
TURN  Computer turnaround time        LOW [NOMINAL] HIGH  VHIGH
PERSONNEL ATTRIBUTES
ACAP  Analyst capability          VLOW  LOW [NOMINAL] HIGH  VHIGH
AEXP  Applications experience     VLOW [LOW] NOMINAL  HIGH  VHIGH
PCAP  Programmer capability       VLOW  LOW [NOMINAL] HIGH  VHIGH
VEXP  Virtual machine experience  VLOW  LOW [NOMINAL] HIGH
LEXP  Programming lang. experience [VLOW] LOW  NOMINAL  HIGH
PROJECT ATTRIBUTES
MODP  Use of modern prog. practices VLOW [LOW] NOMINAL  HIGH  VHIGH
TOOL  Use of software tools         VLOW [LOW] NOMINAL  HIGH  VHIGH
SCED  Required development schedule  VLOW  LOW [NOMINAL] HIGH  VHIGH
                         F1 = HELP




Before You Leap            PROJECT SIZING SCREEN

  INPUTS

  DEVELOPMENT MODE    ORGANIC  SEMIDETACHED  EMBEDDED
  DELIVERED SOURCE NEW INSTRUCTIONS (THOUSANDS) ==    10.00
  DELIVERED SOURCE ADAPTED INSTRUCTIONS (THOUSANDS) ==     0.00
        ADAPTED DESIGN REQUIRING MODIFICATION ==    0.00%
          ADAPTED CODE REQUIRING MODIFICATION ==    0.00%
    ADAPTED INTEGRATION REQUIRING MODIFICATION ==    0.00%
  DELIVERED SOURCE CONVERTED INSTRUCTIONS (THOUSANDS) ==     0.00
      CONVERTED DESIGN REQUIRING MODIFICATION ==    0.00%
        CONVERTED CODE REQUIRING MODIFICATION ==    0.00%
  CONVERTED INTEGRATION REQUIRING MODIFICATION ==    0.00%
        LEVEL OF CONVERSION ANALYSIS AND PLANNING == 0  (0-LOW ... 5-HIGH)
  OUTPUTS


  EFFORT :        99.50 man-months
  PRODUCTIVITY :   100.50 new-equiv. delivered source instructions / man-month
  SCHEDULE :   12.51 months
  AVERAGE STAFFING :     7.96 full-time equivalent software personnel
                         F1 = HELP
```

depicts the project's organization and proposed methods, and in general outlines
what the customer can expect to happen during the life of the project.

Once the customer and developer agree on the nature of the problem and the
need for a solution, it is time for a detailed description of the problem's characteristics. In chapter 3, we will investigate the determination of the customer's requirements.

2.8

EXERCISES

1. You are about to bake a two-layer birthday cake with icing. Describe the
   cake-baking project as a work breakdown structure. Generate an activity
   graph from that structure. What is the critical path?

2. Figure 2.28 is an activity graph for a software development project. The
   number corresponding to each edge of the graph indicates the number of
   days required to complete the activity represented by that branch. For
   example, it will take four days to complete the activity that ends in milestone E. For each activity, list its precursors. For each milestone, compute
   the earliest start time, the latest start time, and the slack. Then, identify the
   critical path.

3. Figure 2.29 is an activity graph. Find the critical path.

4. On a software development project, what kinds of activities can be performed in parallel? Explain why the activity graph sometimes hides the
   interdependencies of these activities.

5. Explain why adding personnel to a project that is behind schedule can
   make the project completion date even later.

Figure 2.28 Activity Graph for Exercise 2.2

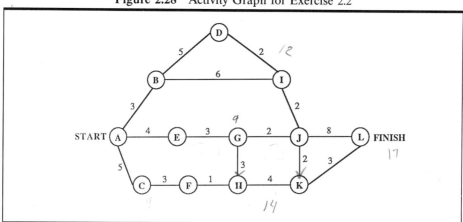

Figure 2.29   Activity Graph for Exercise 2.3

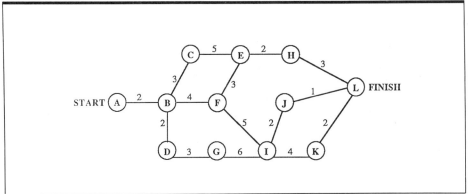

6. A large government agency wants to contract with a software development firm for a project involving 20,000 lines of code. The Hardand Software Company uses Walston and Felix's estimating technique for determining the number of people required for the time needed to write that much code. How many person-months does Hardand estimate will be needed? If the government's estimate is 10% too low, how many additional person-months wil be needed? In general, if the government's estimate is off by k%, by how much must the person-month estimate change?

7. Programmable Problem: Write a program that accepts as input the variables of Esterling's model. The program is to compute the useful working time per day per person (w), the ratio of calendar time to person-days, the labor cost per workday (B), and the project cost per person-day of work (P). Then, the program is to print out a set of tables to show how small changes in the input variables affect w, B and P. For example, show what happens to w, B and P when the number of interruptions per day by non-project causes is decreased by 5%, 10%, and 25%.

8. Explain why it takes longer to develop a utility program than an applications program and longer still to develop a system program.

9. Manny's Manufacturing must decide whether to build or buy a software package to keep track of its inventory. Manny's computer experts estimate that it will cost $325,000 to buy the necessary programs. To build the programs in-house, programmers will cost $5,000 each per month. What factors should Manny consider in making his decision? When is it better to build? to buy?

10. For each of the parameters listed in Table 2.6, explain how the parameter affects the amount of development effort required for a project.

11. Brooks says that adding people to a late project makes it even later. The Putnam curve seems to indicate that adding people to a project can shorten development time. Is this a contradiction? Explain why or why not.

C H A P T E R   3

REQUIREMENTS ANALYSIS

In chapter 1, we discussed the stages of system development. We noted that each step is necessary for successful software development, but some are repeated as development progresses. Figure 3.1 illustrates the major stages of a project; with this chapter, we begin our investigation of what is involved in each stage.

Before we can design a system, we must know what the customer wants the system to do. Thus, our understanding of system intent and function starts with an examination of requirements. We note that requirements are of two types, functional and non-functional, and explore the characteristics of each. Then we discuss the properties of a *set* of requirements, such as completeness and consistency. We look at ways of defining requirements and investigate the difference between static descriptions and dynamic ones. A variety of requirements specification methods are detailed, and examples of both automated and manual methods are presented. When the requirements are defined, we learn how to document them and then review them for correctness and completeness in a *design review*.

Projects vary in their size and scope. At the end of this chapter, we learn how to choose a requirements specification method appropriate to the project at hand. Analyzing requirements involves much more than merely writing down what the customer wants. As we shall see, we must find requirements on which both we and the customer can agree, and with which we can build our test procedures. First, let us examine exactly what a requirement is.

3.1

WHAT IS A REQUIREMENT?

When a customer requests that we build a system, the customer has some notion of what the system will do. Often, the new system replaces an existing system or way of doing things. Thus, the system has a purpose. A **requirement** is a feature of the system or a description of something the system is capable of doing in order to fulfill the system's purpose. For example, suppose we are building a system to generate paychecks for our customer's company. One requirement may be that the checks be issued every two weeks. Another may be that direct deposit of an employee's

Figure 3.1   The System Development Process

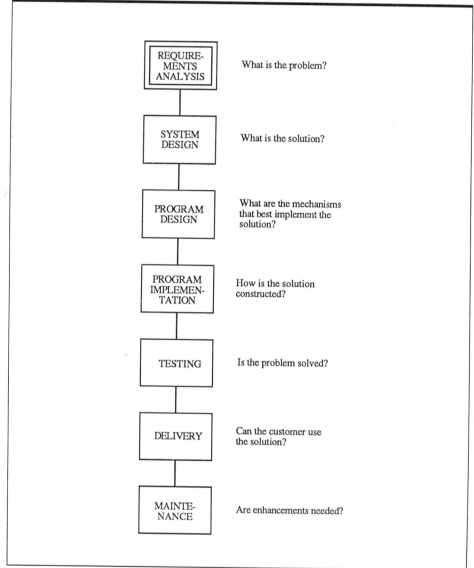

check be allowed for all employees of a certain salary level or higher. The customer may request access to the paycheck system from several different company locations. All of these requirements are specific descriptions of functions or characteristics that address the more general purpose of the system.

Note that none of the above requirements specifies how the system is to be implemented. In other words, there is no mention of what data base management system to use, how much memory the computer is to have, or what programming language must be used to develop the system. These implementation-specific descriptions are not considered to be requirements unless mandated by the customer. In other words, a requirement addresses the *purpose* of the system without regard for how the system is *implemented*. When requirements are viewed in this light, it is easy to see that some system characteristics can be irrelevant. In particular, those that have nothing to do with the purpose of the system should be deleted from any requirements specification.

This distinction becomes clearer if we keep in mind the purpose of requirements analysis. We are at the beginning of development, and our goal is to *determine the nature of the customer's problem*. A discussion of any solution is premature until the problem is clearly defined. Moreover, the problem is most easily stated in terms of the customer's business. Thus, requirements should be *focused on the customer and the problem*, not on the solution or implementation.

Two Sets of Requirements

Because the focus is on the customer's problem, requirements analysis serves two separate but related purposes. On one hand, the requirements analysis yields a **requirements definition document**. Written in terms that the customer can understand, the requirements definition is a complete listing of everything the customer expects the proposed system to do. It represents an understanding between customer and developer of what the customer needs or wants.

Although the requirements definition tells the customer what to expect, the document is not in technical terms that can be used easily by system designers. For example, the requirements definition may state that

> Water quality information must be accessible immediately.

However, a system designer needs more technical information. This requirement may be transformed to say

> Water quality records must be retrieved within five seconds of request.

The *technical* counterpart to the requirements definition document is the **requirements specification document**. The specification document restates the requirements definition in technical terms appropriate for the development of a system design.

There must be a *direct correspondence* between each requirement of the definition document and those of the specification document. It is here that the configuration management methods used throughout the life cycle begin. **Configuration management** is a set of procedures that track

- the requirements that define a system
- the design modules that are generated from the requirements
- the program code that implements the design
- the tests that verify the functionality of the system
- the documents that describe the system

In a sense, configuration management provides the threads that tie the system parts together. Configuration management *unifies* the system components that have been developed separately. During requirements analysis, configuration management documents the correspondence between elements of the requirements definition and those of the requirements specification. (See Figure 3.2.) We will examine these methods in detail in chapter 10. For now, it is important to remember that the customer's view is tied to your developer's view in an organized, traceable way.

Functional and Nonfunctional

Requirements describe a system's *behavior*. We can think of a system as satisfying a *set of conditions* or being in a *state*. The activities of the system, such as a reaction to input, can cause the system to change states. The requirements definitions express the system states and the transitions from one state to another.

To help us describe requirements in this way, Yeh ([YEH82]) and others divide requirements into two categories: *functional* and *nonfunctional*.

Functional Requirements. A **functional requirement** describes an interaction between the system and its environment. For example, to determine functional requirements, we decide what states are acceptable ones for the system to be in. Further, functional requirements describe how the system should behave given certain stimuli. For instance, suppose we are defining the requirements of a system to print weekly paychecks. The functional requirements must answer questions about when paychecks are issued. What input is necessary for a paycheck to be printed? If that input is provided, should a paycheck always be printed? Under what conditions can the amount of pay be changed? What causes the removal of an employee from the payroll list?

Nonfunctional Requirements. The questions we have raised are independent of an implementation of a solution to the customer's problem. We describe what the system will do without discussing the particular computer we might use, the programming language employed, the internal data structures involved, or the kind of paper on which the checks will be printed. A **nonfunctional requirement** or **constraint** describes a restriction on the system that limits our choices for constructing a solution to the problem. For instance, we may be told that the system must be developed on an Aardvark computer or that the paychecks must be distributed to the employees no more than four hours after the initial data is read.

We need a formal requirements analysis because customers are not always good at describing exactly what they want or need. They know their business, but they cannot always describe their business problems to outsiders. Further, if not carefully organized and encouraged, the communication between us and our customers can lead to misunderstanding or incomplete specification. Discrepancies between what the customer wants and what we as developers provide may cost as much as 100 times more than if errors or omissions had not been made in defining requirements ([BOE81]).

Figure 3.2   Two Sets of Requirements

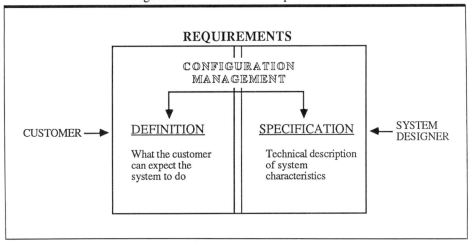

3.2

TYPES OF REQUIREMENTS

The requirements definition describes everything about how the system is to interact with its environment. Included are the following kinds of items.

Physical Environment:
- Where is the equipment to function?
- Is there one location or several?
- Are there any environmental restrictions such as temperature, humidity, magnetic interference?

Interfaces:
- Is the input coming from one or more other systems?
- Is the output going to one or more other systems?
- Is there a prescribed way in which the data must be formatted?
- Is there a prescribed medium that the data must use?

Users and Human Factors:
- Who will use the system?
- Will there be several types of users?
- What is the skill level of each type of user?
- What kind of training will be required for each type of user?
- How easy will it be for a user to understand and use the system?
- How difficult will it be for a user to misuse the system?

Functionality:
- What will the system do?
- When will the system do it?
- How and when can the system be changed or enhanced?
- Are there constraints on execution speed, response time, or throughput?

Documentation:
- How much documentation is required?
- To what audience is the documentation addressed?

Data:
- For both input and output, what should the format of the data be?
- How often will it be received or sent?
- How accurate must it be?
- To what degree of precision must the calculations be made?
- How much data flows through the system?
- Must any data be retained for any period of time?

Resources:
- What materials, personnel, or other resources are required to build, use, and maintain the system?
- What skills must the developers have?
- How much physical space will be taken up by the system?
- What are the requirements for power, heating, or air conditioning?
- Is there a prescribed timetable for development?
- Is there a limit on the amount of money to be spent on development or on hardware and software?

Security:
- Must access to the system or to information be controlled?
- How will one user's data be isolated from others'?
- How will user programs be isolated from other programs and from the operating system?
- How often will the system be backed up?
- Must the backup copies be stored at a different location?
- Should precautions be taked against fire or theft?

Quality Assurance:
- What are the requirements for reliability?
- How must the characteristics of the system be demonstrated to others?
- Must the system detect and isolate faults?
- What is the prescribed mean time between failures?

- Is there a maximum time allowed for restarting the system after a failure?
- How can the system incorporate changes to the design?
- Will maintainance merely correct errors, or will it also include improving the system?
- What efficiency measures will apply to resource usage and response time?
- How easy should it be to move the system from one location to another or from one type of computer to another?

Figure 3.3 summarizes the aspects of a system to be considered as possible requirements. The list of quality software characteristics enumerated in chapter 1 also contains possible system descriptors to be used as a basis for generating software requirements.

Figure 3.3 Types of Requirements

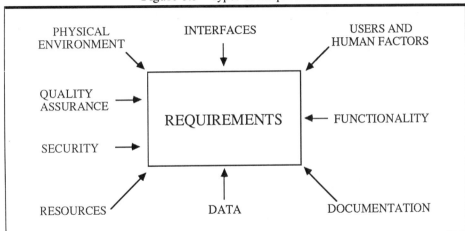

3.3

CHARACTERISTICS OF REQUIREMENTS

As you can see, requirements describe not only the *flow of information* to and from a system and the *transformation of data* by the system, but also the *constraints* on the system's performance. Thus the requirements can serve three purposes. First, they allow us as the developer to explain our understanding of how the customer wants the system to work. At the same time, they tell our designers what functionality and characteristics the resultant system is to have. Third, the requirements tell the test team what to demonstrate to convince the customer that the system being delivered is indeed what was ordered. In particular, the performance characteristics described in the requirements must be *quantifiable* measures, thereby providing a goal for each test.

Because both we and our customers use the requirements, it is important that the requirements be **validated**. The validation process checks for seven criteria:

1. Are the requirements **correct**? Both we and the customer review them to assure that they are stated without error.

2. Are the requirements **consistent**? That is, are there no conflicting or ambiguous requirements? For example, if one requirement states that a maximum of ten users can be using the system at one time, and another requirement says that in a certain situation there may be twenty simultaneous users, those requirements are said to be inconsistent.

3. Are the requirements **complete**? They are complete if all possible situations are described by some requirement. Thus, a payroll system should describe what happens when an employee takes a leave without pay, when someone gets a raise, or when someone needs an advance. We say that a system description is **externally complete** if the description contains all the properties desired by the customer. A description is **internally complete** if there are no undefined references among the requirements.

4. Are the requirements **realistic**? Can what the customer is asking the system to do really be done? Sometimes, when development time is long, the customer can anticipate technological improvements, requesting state-of-the-art requirements. All requirements should be reviewed to insure that they are possible.

5. Does each requirement describe something that is **needed** by the customer? Sometimes a requirement restricts us unnecessarily. For example, the customer may demand that we use an XYZ microcomputer because it has a good reputation. However, XYZ may not be the best processor to use for implementing the desired system. Such requirements do not directly address the goals of the system. We should review the requirements to retain only those that work directly to solve the customer's problem.

6. Are the requirements **verifiable**? Can tests be written so that we can demonstrate that the requirement has been met? This is a common place for difficulties to arise. The customer may demand quick response time without defining an actual speed and the circumstances under which the response is being measured. For example, "quick response time" may be restated in a more verifiable form as "with the maximum number of users on the system (32) using the word processing function, the system can rewrite a user's screen with the next page of a document in under five seconds."

7. Are the requirements **traceable**? Can each system function be traced to a set of requirements that mandates it? Is it easy to find the set of requirements that deals with a specific aspect of the system? For example, to review all communications requirements, would all requirements need to be read?

Examples of requirements can show us how to discern these characteristics. Suppose a requirement for the space shuttle system is proposed as follows:

> Accuracy shall be sufficient to support mission planning.

How can we test the system to see if it satisfies this requirement? The requirement does not tell us what mission planning requires for support. We discuss the meaning of mission planning and reword the requirement:

> Position error shall be less than 50 feet along orbit, less than 30 feet off orbit.

In this case, we can test for position error and know exactly whether or not we have met the requirement.

Similarly, we cannot test this requirement:

> System shall provide real-time response to queries.

We do not know what "real-time response" is. However, if the requirement were to say:

> System shall respond to queries in not more than two seconds.

then we know exactly how to test the system's reaction to response.

Suppose a system requires user access to a main computer located several thousand miles away. The response time for remote users is to be the same as for local users (those whose terminals are connected directly to the main computer). This requirement is unrealistic, since extra time is required for transmission over communication lines.

3.4

HOW TO DEFINE REQUIREMENTS

As with many activities in computer science, requirements definition is often performed best by working down from the top. In other words, we begin by expressing the general attributes of the system at the very highest level; then at subsequent levels the attributes are made more specific. For instance, if a high-level requirement demands reliability, lower levels of definition may restate the requirement in specific terms of robustness, accuracy, completeness and consistency.

For many years, requirements were specified in English (or the customer's natural language). However, it has become clear that there are several problems with using natural language. First, if the requirements are to be useful, all parties using them must interpret their meaning in the same way. If the customer thinks of "accuracy" in one way and we in another, the requirements can lead to confusion. It is unlikely that we and our customers have the same understanding of all words we use. For instance, to a customer, "availability" may mean that anyone can use the system at any time; to us, "availability" may have a much more technical meaning.

When users are unable to use a terminal because system backup is in progress, the customer may consider the system "unavailable" to the user. However, we may say that the system is still *functional* and therefore "available." Thus, natural language may not be the precise and unambiguous medium needed for expressing the system's functionality and the relationship of its relevant parts.

Secondly, requirements are not always easily separated according to the system elements with which they deal. It is sometimes difficult (if not impossible) to trace back from a system characteristic to the requirements that define or affect it. The use of natural language can add an element of confusion here, too.

Therefore, software engineers have investigated many ways to specify requirements in a more rigorous and controlled fashion. Their approaches often use formal notation to describe the system to be built. An advantage to this approach is that accompanying tools can be developed to check the specification for completeness and consistency and to make it easier to trace.

The project being defined is a *system*, in the sense introduced in chapter 1. Thus, any set of requirements must form a complete system definition. The requirements should describe all parts of a system, including the boundary. We need to know what objects or entities are included, what they look like (by defining their attributes), how they relate to one another, and what happens to them as they enter, pass through, or leave the system. All requirements describe the system in terms of these elements, insuring that the description distinguishes the system from its environment. Once the system elements are defined, more detailed representational techniques can be used to generate the specific requirements of the system. Let us investigate some of these techniques.

Static Descriptions of Requirements

A system description lists the system entities, attributes, and their relationships with each other. Thus, we consider a requirements specification to be *relational*, that is, the requirements define the relationships of entities to each other. This view is static because it does not describe how relationships change with time. When time is not a major factor in the system's operation, such a description is useful and adequate. There are several ways to describe a system statically.

Indirect Reference. A system can be described with *indirect reference* to the problem and its solution. For example, suppose the problem is to develop a computational system that solves a series of k equations in n variables. The actual algorithm for the solution is implied but not stated directly. With this kind of definition, the *properties* of the solution are given without stating the solution *method*. Thus, there is no guarantee that a solution even exists.

Recurrence Relations. A similar system description uses a *recurrence relation*. In this kind of description, an initial condition is defined, and the transformation from one condition to the next is described in terms of the previously defined conditions. For example, you may be familiar with Fibonacci numbers that define, among other things, the way a seashell curves and the way rabbits proliferate. The Fibonacci numbers can be generated as

$$F(0) = 1$$
$$F(1) = 1$$
$$F(n+1) = F(n) + F(n-1)$$

In a similar fashion, suppose we are asked to build a system to track a disease's spread throughout a population. The initial outbreak is described, as well as the way in which the disease travels from one group to another. The proposed automated system is to generate a description of the incidence of the disease at any point in time. It may be easy to specify this system with a *recursive function or program*.

Axiomatic Definition. An alternate way of viewing a system is in terms of *axioms*. This approach specifies basic system properties, and the behavior of the system generates new properties from them. The new properties are called *theorems*. The axiomatic method demands a set of axioms that is both complete and consistent; otherwise, the resulting theorems will not express truths about the system. This type of requirements definition is well suited to the development of an *expert system*, since the behavior of such a system involves generating new information from statements of basic knowledge about a particular subject.

Axiomatic definition is often used in specifying abstract data types. The system is described as a set of objects and permissible operations on those objects, and axioms specify the relationships among the objects and the operations. Later in this chapter, we investigate *data abstraction* methods for specifying requirements.

Expression as a Language. When a system processes a set of *strings of data*, we sometimes describe the acceptable strings as expressions that comprise an acceptable language. For example, a compiler for a programming language reads strings of characters and decides which are valid strings in the language and which are not. In another system, strings of information generated by a data capturing device are processed. The system may check the validity of each string before passing it on for further processing.

In these cases, the requirements become a specification of the syntax of the strings. A special category of language called a *regular language* can be recognized by a finite state machine. (For an explanation of how and why, see Pfleeger and Straight ([PFL85]).) By describing requirements as strings of a regular language and viewing the valid strings as valid regular expressions, we can automate the checking of requirements for completeness and consistency.

The Sprinter-2 text processing system from Scenic Computer Systems, Inc. (Redmond, Washington) was developed from requirements expressed as a regular language. The text processor reads strings of characters, interprets them, and formats the result. The Sprinter-2 syntax conditions are written in *Backus-Naur form* as a set of characters and collections of characters as shown on the next page. (See Sammet ([SAM69]) for more information about Backus-Naur form.)

- ASCII characters
- expressions (<expr>)
- terms
- factors
- scale factors (<scale>)
- functions (<func>)
- digits
- letters
- addition operators (<addop>)
- multiplication operators (<mpyop>)

Then, the relationships among the characters are expressed as the following strings:

```
<condition>    ::= <bool-term> | <bool-term> or <condition>
<bool-term>    ::= <bool-factor> | <bool-factor> and <bool-term>
<bool-factor>  ::= <expr> <relop> <expr> | (<condition>)
<relop>        ::= < | ≤ | = | ≥ | > | <>
<expr>         ::= <term> | <expr> <addop> <term> | <addop> <expr>
<term>         ::= <factor> | <term> <mpyop> <factor>
<factor>       ::= <scaled-expr> | <primary>
<scaled-expr>  ::= (<expr>) <scale> | <number> <scale>
<primary>      ::= (<expr>) | <regname> | <number> | <func> (<expr>)
<number>       ::= <integer> | <integer>. | .<integer> | <integer>.<integer>
<regname>      ::= $ <regchar> | <regname> <regchar>
<integer>      ::= <digit> | <digit> <integer>
<regchar>      ::= <digit> | <letter> | <underscore>
<addop>        ::= + | −
<digit>        ::= 0 | 1 | 2 | 3 | 4 | 5 | 6 | 7 | 8 | 9
<func>         ::= abs | trunc
<letter>       ::= A | a | B | b | . . . | Z | z
<mpyop>        ::= * | / | mod
<scale>        ::= c | d | h | i | l | P | p | q | t | v
<underscore>   ::= _ (ASCII character #95)
```

Expressing the conditions for text processing in this way, we can compare each definition with the others (using an automated process, if available) to guarantee that the terms of each definition are themselves defined elsewhere.

Data Abstraction. In many cases, the data manipulated by a system determine the kinds of actions taken. It can be useful to define requirements by focusing on the *data* rather than on the functions themselves. **Data abstraction** is a technique for describing what data is *for*, rather than how it looks or what it is called.

We describe data by forming a *data-type dictionary*. The central idea is to categorize data and group like elements together. Each kind of data is given a name, and the dictionary contains the names in alphabetical order. Data elements are associated by type; two data elements are of the same **data type** if they have the same general form and content.

To see how data types are defined, consider your student record. The university records office keeps track of the number of credits each student takes each semester. Your file contains information about you (your student record), including your name and student number, information about where you live (your address record), the number of semesters you have been enrolled, and information about each of those semesters. Notice that by knowing these four categories of data, you have a grasp of what is in the record, even though we have not listed every data *element* for you.

Knowing the types of data we have in the record, we can define the student record in the following way:

Semester Record
    Semester Type
    Semester date
    Grade point average
    Completed hours

Semester Type
    (Fall, Spring, Summer)

Address Information
    Telephone number
    Street address
    City
    State
    Zip code

Student Record
    Name
    Student number
    Address Information
    Number of semesters
    {Semester record}

All data types are indicated by italics. Thus, the actual definition of the student record type is the last six lines of the listing. Your student record contains your name and student number followed by information about your address. The address information is itself a type and is defined by the five elements containing your address and phone number. After the number of semesters, your record contains a semester record for each semester you attended the university. The braces ({ }) indicate that the semester record type may be repeated.

Notice that the semester data type is defined by listing the three possible entries that may be used. When a data type can be completely defined by listing all choices in this way, we use parentheses and describe each choice. Thus, a semester data type can be only one of Fall, Spring, or Summer for each semester described.

In using data abstraction to specify requirements, we must also explain actions permissible with the data and data types. Data can be acted upon only in four ways: it can be *created, queried, modified,* or *deleted.* Rather than manipulate data directly, we describe **objects** to manipulate the data for us. Thus, object modules are defined that tell us the ways in which we can use the data. Each object module contains three types of information: *states* in which the data can be, *operations* to establish new states, and *probes* to report information about a state. We will see in chapter 4 that data abstraction allows us to extract the substance of a problem and deal with it, without becoming mired in the details of data representation and manipulation.

Dynamic Descriptions of Requirements

When describing a system in terms of the relationships among its entities, there is often no easy way to explain how the system reacts over a period of time to the things that change system behavior. Thus, software engineers have developed techniques for viewing a system in terms of *changes* that occur *over time*. The system is considered to be in a particular state until some stimulus causes it to change its state. Specifying a system in this way makes it easier for us and our customer to describe all possible states and stimuli; the resulting requirements specification is more likely to be complete. In this section, we examine techniques that describe a system in terms of states and stimuli.

Decision Tables. Sometimes, it is convenient to describe a system as a set of possible conditions satisfied by the system at a given time, rules for reacting to stimuli when certain sets of those conditions are met, and actions to be taken as a result. For example, suppose the admissions office at your university is developing a system to determine whom to accept as freshmen. Table 3.1 shows how the decision is made.

Table 3.1   Decision Table

	Rules				
	1	2	3	4	5
High SAT scores	T	F	F	F	F
High grades	–	T	F	F	F
Outside activites	–	–	T	F	F
Good recommendations	–	–	–	T	F
Send rejection letter			X	X	X
Send admission forms	X	X			

The conditions are listed along the left side of the table. Each column represents a set of conditions and is thus a *state* of the system. The action beneath each column illustrates the *rule* to be followed when the system is in the state represented by the column. An entry of 'T' means that the condition denoted by the row is true; 'F' means that the condition is false, an '–' indicates that the truth of the condition does not matter. The possible actions to be taken are shown at the bottom of the table, and an 'X' at the bottom of a column designates the action to take for the set of conditions represented. Thus, if a student has high SAT scores, the admissions forms will be sent, regardless of grades, outside activities, and recommendations. Similarly, if a student has high grades, the admissions forms will be sent. In all other cases, a rejection letter will be mailed.

Thus, the decision table represents actions to be taken when the system is in one of the states illustrated. This kind of representation can generate very large tables, since the number of states is equal to the number of combinations of conditions. If there are n conditions, there are 2^n possible combinations of conditions.

What can we tell about the requirements specification from the table? Certainly, we can see that if every possible set of conditions results in an action, then the specification is complete. Exercise 3 gives you a chance to interpret some of the other aspects of a specification in terms of the format of the table.

Functional Descriptions and Transition Diagrams. We can view a system in a similar manner as a set of states where the system *reacts* to certain possible events. For example, suppose the system is in state A and event X occurs. Event X may cause the system to act in some way: to change to another state, to remain in state A but output a character, and so on. The system's behavior is interpreted as a series of functions, the input to which is a set of conditions and an event and the output from which is a system action:

$$f(\text{state } A, \text{ event } X) = \text{Action } Q$$

We can depict this transition by drawing a diagram of the movement of the system from one state to another. First, we draw a circle for each state in the system. Then, for each state and possible input, we draw a directed arrow to indicate the transition from one state to another. For example, if the system is in state A and an input of X causes the system to go to state Q, we draw an arrow from the initial state to the resulting state (that is, from i to j) and label it with the input X (as shown in Figure 3.4).

Figure 3.4   Transition from State A to Q on Input X

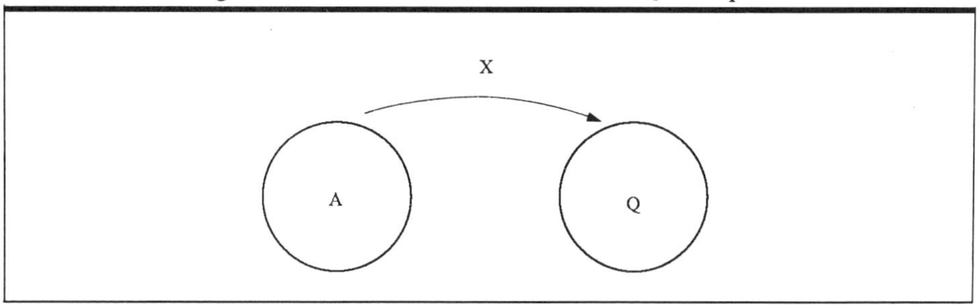

In general, we can express each system transition as

$$f(S_i, C_j) = S_k$$

indicating that when in state S_i, the occurrence of condition C_j causes the system to change to state S_k. Thus, the state changes for a system can be presented in a tabular way by displaying a list of states and the system reaction to input when in that state. Table 3.2 is formed in this way. According to the table, if the system is in state $S1$ and receives a 1 as input, it remains in state $S1$. However, if the system receives a 0 when in $S1$, the system state changes to $S2$. Similarly, the system in state $S2$ stays in $S2$ with a 0 input but changes to $S1$ if 1 is received.

Table 3.2   Transition Table

Current State	Input	Next State
S1	0	*S2*
S1	1	*S1*
S2	0	*S2*
S2	1	*S1*
S3	0	*S1*
S3	1	*S3*

Figure 3.5 is the state transition diagram for Table 3.2. Such a representation is useful for small systems with several states. For example, Figure 3.6 represents the requirements for a device that routes telephone calls into a voice-and-data network. The device waits for a call, detects the presence of a voice connection or a data connection, and routes the call to a handset or computer, accordingly. When the call is complete, the device disconnects and waits for the next call.

Figure 3.5   State Transition Diagram

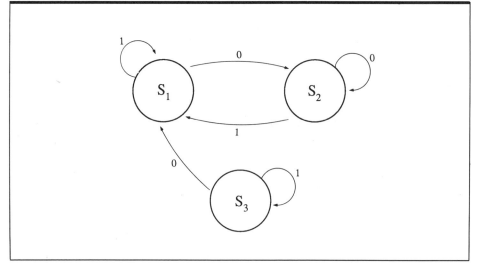

Figure 3.6 Transition Diagram for Automatic Call Router

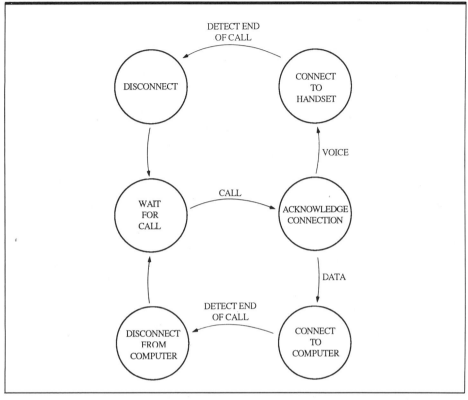

Event Tables. We can represent a system's states and transitions in a different tabular form. We begin, as before, by determining the system's functional decomposition. We then form a table where the vertical axis consists of the *states* or sets of conditions. Along the horizontal axis, we place the *events* that can occur. The cells of the table contain the action or actions that take place when the event at the top of the column occurs while the system is in the state indicated by the row position.

To see how the table is constructed, suppose that Manny's Manufacturing is building an automated system to serve three purposes. In one mode, the computer system acts as a graphics processor that can generate drawings of all sorts. In another mode, the system generates blueprints and architectural drawings for Manny's customers. The third mode is the native computer mode, allowing the programmers to develop applications as needed. We list the three modes of operation along the left side of Table 3.3. Across the top, we place all possible events. Then, in the cells corresponding to each intersection of row and column, we indicate the result of being in the mode for that row and having the event for that column occur.

To see how this table works, suppose Event 2 is the pressing of the "help" key on the terminal. Different actions may occur in different modes. In graphics mode, the pressing of the "help" key moves the user to a screen that displays information about the function being executed (action 8). In architecture mode, the user is shown a screen summarizing the last few functions performed (action 2), followed

Table 3.3   Event Table

Mode	Event 1	Event 2	Event 3	Event 4
Graphics	Action 1	Action 8	0	X
Architecture	X	Action 2 followed by Action 3	Actions 5 and 6 in parallel	0
Native	0	Action 4	Actions 1, 2, 3	Action 7

by a menu asking the user whether to cancel the previous function or continue (action 3). In native computer mode, the user may be shown the prompt for the next desired command (action 4). An 'X' in a cell means that the configuration is not possible; the event represented by the column will never occur in the mode represented by the row. A '0' in a cell indicates that there is no state change and no action. Such conditions may exist if, for instance, the user is in architecture mode and hits a function key that is defined for graphics mode but not for architecture mode.

Petri Nets. There are many other techniques for representing requirements. Choosing the best one depends on the type of system being described, and often the choice is a combination of several techniques. For example, we can describe the data flowing into a system by a set of regular expressions, while the changes of state caused by the data can be represented as a transition table.

The techniques described thus far are most useful for systems whose states and events occur in sequence. When several events occur at once, sometimes a system must perform *parallel processing*, and special computers are used to handle many things concurrently. A major problem in representing concurrent processing is the need to *synchronize* events. Several events may occur in parallel but are performed in an unpredictable order.

To describe synchronization and parallel processing, we can extend the notion of transition that we used above. We begin by representing system behavior as before, viewing a transition as a function. In the simplest case, the system is in state A, an event occurs, and the system moves to state S:

$$f(\text{State } A, \text{ Event}) \rightarrow \text{State } S$$

Alternatively, several events must occur before the system can leave state A and move to state S. For example, a system to print company paychecks must have the proper paper in the printer, enough money in the checking account, and a signal that it is the end of the pay period before the checks can be produced. These three events can occur in any order; the important thing is that all three must occur before the system can move to its check-writing state. In this situation, *several events* trigger the move from one state to the next. We can represent the general case as follows:

$$f(\text{State } A, \text{ Event 1, Event 2}, \dots, \text{ Event } N) \rightarrow \text{State } S$$

In the most general case, we may have several events required to begin the state transition. However, once the transition is initiated, the system moves into *several states* that execute in parallel. We represent the transition as

f(State *A*, Event 1, Event 2, . . . , Event *N*) → State 1, State 2, . . . State *M*

To understand this last case, consider the emergency room in a hospital. Before the patient can be treated, several events must occur. The staff must attempt to find out the name and address of the patient. The blood type of the patient must be determined. Someone must determine if the patient is breathing, and the patient must be examined for bleeding wounds. The events occur in no particular order, but all must occur before a team of doctors begins a more thorough examination. Once the examination can begin (that is, once the transition is made from a preliminary examination to a thorough one), the team of doctors represents a set of new states. The orthopedic doctor checks for broken bones, while the hematologist runs blood tests and the surgeon puts stitches in a bleeding wound. These states are independent of one another, but none can occur until the transition from the preliminary examination takes place.

The complicating factor here is the need for coordination. The activities are occurring in parallel, and we need some way of controlling the use of events or collections of events to change states. None of the techniques mentioned above is appropriate for this synchronization. **Petri net representation** is an alternative that is well-suited for expressing parallel processing requirements. Petri nets represent a system graphically by drawing a node for each *state* and an arrow to mark the *transitions*. Figure 3.7 shows an example of how the three types of transitions discussed above might be displayed. To handle the coordination of events and states,

Figure 3.7   Three Types of Transitions

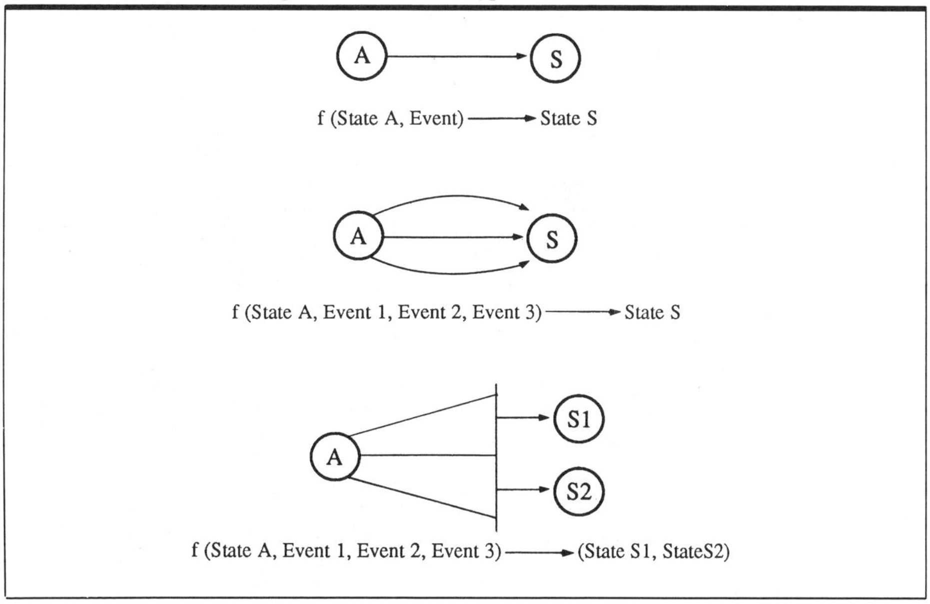

each state of a Petri net is associated with a set of *tokens*. The tokens represent events that occur. Once an event occurs, a token may travel from one state to another. Transitions are described by a set of *firing rules*. Each firing rule explains how tokens are associated with a state; when the correct number and type of tokens are present in one state, tokens are released to travel to another state. Thus, the firing rules correspond to the functions defining the conditions for a transition. The notion of tokens and firing rules allows the Petri net to represent and synchronize activities that may be taking place concurrently.

3.5

EXAMPLES OF REQUIREMENTS SPECIFICATION METHODS

The methods used by software engineers range from manual and semi-formal to formal and highly automated. In this section, we investigate a variety of methods, beginning with a simple but effective manual one, and concluding with several designed to evaluate requirements using a computer.

Manual Methods

Several manual methods can be useful in recording requirements. Especially when the project size is too small to justify the purchase of expensive automated tools, these methods help to *organize* and *standardize* the way in which requirements are specified.

   HIPO Charts. The *Hierarchy and Input-Process-Output (HIPO)* method of specifying requirements has been used by the IBM Corporation for a long time ([IBM74]). HIPO illustrates how system functions relate to one another. To use HIPO, we begin by developing a table of contents to display the hierarchy of functions. This hierarchy is exhibited as a chart in which there is a box for each major function of the system. The boxes are arranged so that one box is connected to another if one is a subfunction of the other. The subfunctional box is lower than its superior. Figure 3.8 is an example of a table of contents for a word processing system. As you can see, the name of the function is indicated in the box, along with a reference number. Note that the boxes represent *functions*, not *design elements*. The purpose of the hierarchy is to show *functional requirements* and their relationships, not the hierarchy of implementation modules.
   Associated with each functional box in the table of contents is a diagram to show what acts as input to the function, what process is involved in the function, and what are the outputs of the function. Thus, the table of contents shows the 'H' (hierarchy), while the corresponding diagrams detail the 'IPO' (input-process-output) of the functions. Figure 3.9 is a diagram for box 1.0.3 of the hierarchy shown in Figure 3.8.

Figure 3.8 Table of Contents for Word Processing System

WORD PROCESSING SYSTEM 1.0
EDIT EXISTING DOCUMENT 1.0.1
CREATE NEW DOCUMENT 1.0.2
PRINT DOCUMENT 1.0.3
DOCUMENT FILING 1.0.4
UTILITIES 1.0.5
EXIT WORD PROCESSING 1.0.6
RENAME DOCUMENT 1.0.4.1
DELETE DOCUMENT 1.0.4.2
COPY DOCUMENT 1.0.4.3
DOCUMENT DIRECTORY 1.0.4.4.
MERGE DOCUMENTS 1.0.4.5

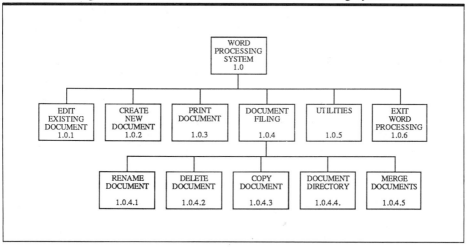

There are several drawbacks to HIPO charts, the major being that they express only functional requirements. Since they have no mechanism for handling non-functional requirements, we need a supplementary method for specifying reliability, performance, and other constraints. There are no checking mechanisms either, so the customer can only verify by careful study that the resulting requirements definition is complete and accurate. At the same time, we must be certain that the system specified is feasible. Both we and our customers are responsible for insuring that each of us understands the meaning of the requirements.

Figure 3.9 Input-Process-Output for Box 1.0.3 of Figure 3.3

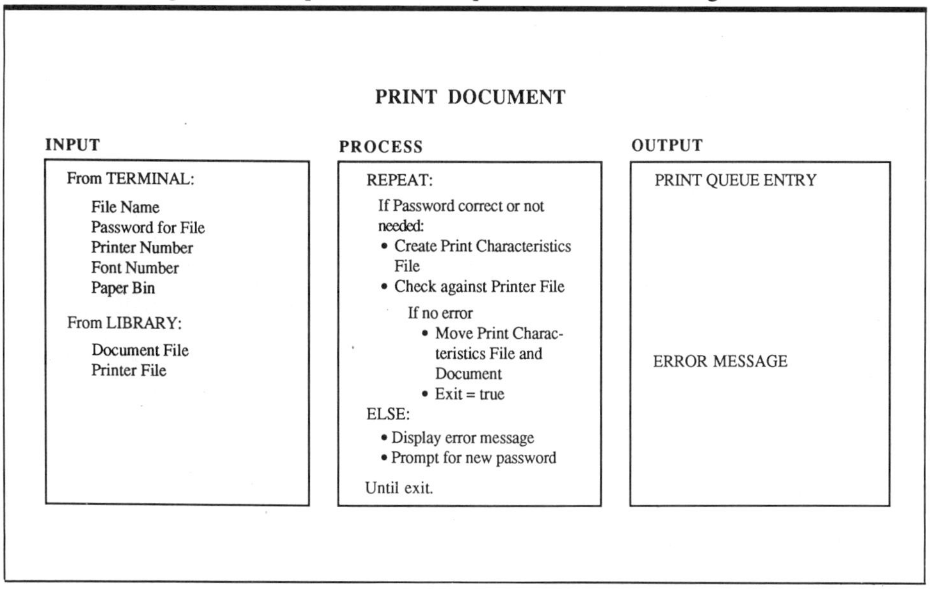

PRINT DOCUMENT
INPUT
From TERMINAL:
File Name
Password for File
Printer Number
Font Number
Paper Bin
From LIBRARY:
Document File
Printer File
PROCESS
REPEAT:
If Password correct or not needed:
• Create Print Characteristics File
• Check against Printer File
If no error
• Move Print Characteristics File and Document
• Exit = true
ELSE:
• Display error message
• Prompt for new password
Until exit.
OUTPUT
PRINT QUEUE ENTRY
ERROR MESSAGE

Hierarchical Data Structure. We can use the concept of a hierarchy in a different way to specify the workings of a system. Instead of focusing on the system functions, we examine how data relationships are defined. There are several popular methods for examining the hierarchical nature of data. As with HIPO, the hierarchical data approach uses many levels of boxes placed in a tree-like fashion to show how data sets are related. If the hierarchy shows box B below and connected to box A, then the data represented by box B is a subset of the data represented by box A.

For example, Figure 3.10 displays a directory of available pharmaceutical products. Since the box labeled "Available Pharmaceuticals" has two boxes directly below it, we know that both "Prescription Products" and "Nonprescription Products" are subsets of the set of pharmaceutical data. Likewise, the figure tells us that prescription products must fall in one of four classes: barbiturates, narcotics, steroids, and other drugs.

Warnier diagrams involve a similar technique, using a tree of items connected with braces ({) and special symbols. The braces differentiate the levels, and the special symbols show conditional relationships among data elements. Whereas the hierarchical data structure diagram shows the hierarchy of data by reading from the top down, a Warnier diagram shows the hierarchy by reading from left to right. In a Warnier diagram, when a name appears to the left of a brace, then the part of the diagram to the right of the brace defines the entire structure of the named data. Operators indicate that data types are either concatenated or are mutually exclusive. For instance, the Warnier diagram in Figure 3.11 displays the same information as the hierarchy of Figure 3.10. The plus enclosed in a circle indicates that the sets of prescription and nonprescription products are mutually exclusive. A solid

Figure 3.10   Hierarchical Data Structure

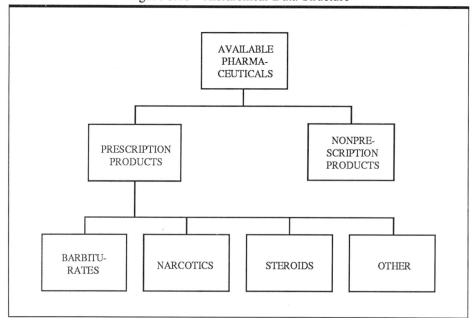

Figure 3.11 Warnier Diagram

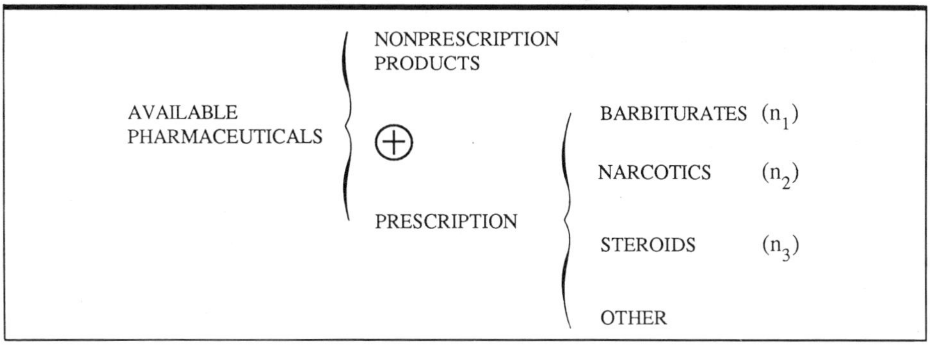

circle is often used as an indicator to show that two types of data are concatenated. When there may be multiple copies of a data type, the number of possible repetitions is usually shown by a number in parentheses after the data name. For example, the numbers in parentheses in Figure 3.11 show the number of times the drug classification is repeated.

As with HIPO charts, the one-dimensional nature of the hierarchical data structure techniques leaves many important requirements to be defined in another way. The techniques are presented here because they are often considered as broad-based design techniques. Requirements specified in this way can be used in the design stage where the basis for design is the organization of the data. We will investigate the idea of *data-structured design* in chapter 4.

Data Flow Diagrams. Methods discussed so far show how the data and processes are organized. However, they do not explain how data flow into, through, and out of a system. To exhibit the requirements for the flow of data, we use **data flow diagrams**. Here again, hierarchy is expressed by layering, so that different levels of detail are shown in different layers. We begin by considering the system as a *transformer* of data. We examine the data that flows into the system, how it is transformed, and how it leaves the system. This is similar to the input-process-output evaluation reflected in HIPO charts. The emphasis is on the flow of the *data*, not on the flow of *control*. As shown in Figure 3.12, the input is an arrow going into a bubble, and the output is an arrow leaving the bubble. Thus, the transformation is represented by the bubble, and the arrows are the data paths.

Figure 3.12 Data Flow Bubble

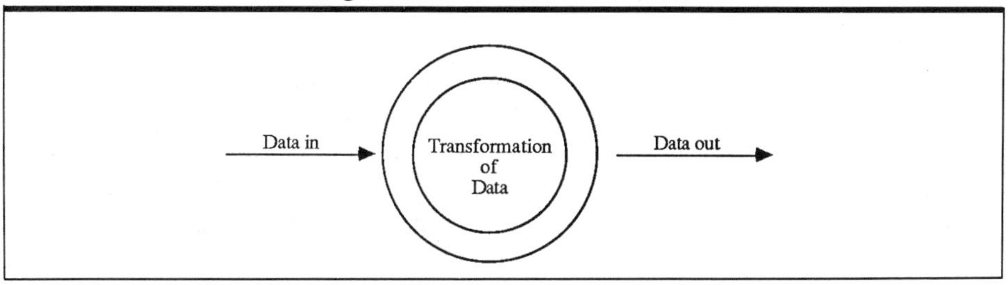

Figure 3.13 is an example of the data flow for a trip to the doctor. As you can see, most of the data paths are both the output from one transformation and the input to another. In three cases, data is required from an external source, rather than as a result of a process. These are represented by two parallel lines. Since the diagram is one of a set of layers, it is easy to see that the "Trip to the Drug Store" is likely to have a diagram of its own to describe how the input is processed to become output.

Figure 3.13   Data Flow Diagram for Physician Visit

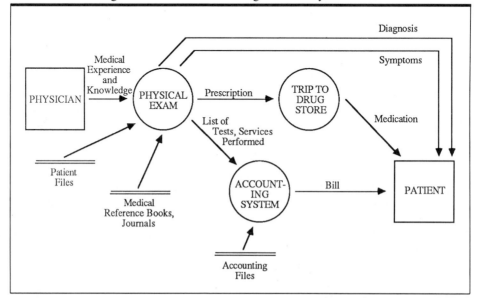

Using this technique, we can represent the data flows for a computer system. For example, Piccolo's restaurant needs an accounting system to report on the various taxes paid each year. Figure 3.14 is a data flow diagram depicting the requirements of the tax subsystem. For each customer who eats at the restaurant, sales tax must be calculated and recorded. Because there are separate tax rates for food and alcoholic beverages, the calculations must be performed separately. Thus, data flow diagrams can be drawn for each subsystem of the accounting system: payroll, inventory, and so on. Additional data flow diagrams can depict how the subsystems work together to form a complete accounting package.

Automated Methods

Some of the methods described above have been supplemented by software tools to aid in their use, but the results must be evaluated manually. For example, there are software packages available on computers ranging from microcomputers to mainframes that can draw activity diagrams and bubble charts. Some of the packages allow the automatic recording of data and process names accompanying the diagrams and build a data dictionary to correspond to the drawings.

Figure 3.14   Data Flow Diagram for Piccolo's Restaurant

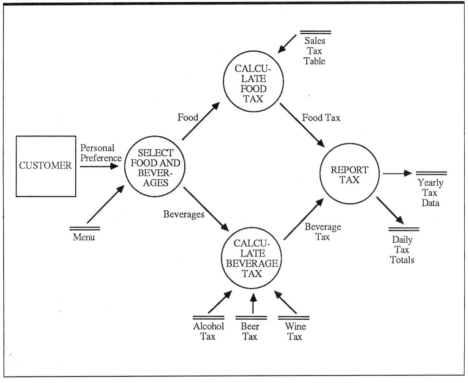

However, several additional methods have been developed especially for use with automated evaluation systems. That is, the requirements are examined by a computer package for characteristics such as consistency, and reports can be produced to show how the requirements are related to one another. Let us examine several of these methods.

PSL/PSA. Several multi-dimensional systems are available for recording requirements. One popular method describes a system as a set of objects with attributes, just as we did in chapter 1. The PSL/PSA method ([TEI77]) uses a *Problem Statement Language (PSL)* to enumerate system requirements. Then, the specification is processed by a *Problem Statement Analyzer* (PSA). The PSA not only produces reports about the requirements but also builds a data base of requirements and system descriptors.

The first step in using this method is to describe the system thoroughly using the PSL language. We begin by describing the *flow of data* between the system and its environment. Thus, the system boundary is defined, and data crossing the boundary are specified. Then the system structure is portrayed as a hierarchy of the objects in the system. Next, the relationships among data elements are described. Because the system acts on these elements in certain ways, the processes or activities of the system are listed. Each data element that is either input to or output from a process is associated with that process.

After listing the processes and related data, we describe in PSL how the data are derived and transformed. The size of the system is included as a requirement, and we estimate the volume of processing needed at various steps. Finally, constraints on the system and its processing are included. Additional information about the management and development of the project can be included with PSL terminology.

A sample description in PSL for the Weaver Farm illustrates the kinds of statements used in the language. Recall that the automated Weaver Farm system must produce a maintenance schedule. In PSL, we can define the process of printing a daily mowing schedule in the following way:

```
PROCESS: daily-mowing-schedule
DESCRIPTION: For week day, schedules areas of farm to be mowed;
GENERATES: mowing-schedule;
RECEIVES: turf-file, history-file, cell-file;
SUBPARTS ARE: check-type, check-frequency, check-history, schedule;
PART OF: daily-maintenance-schedule;
DERIVES: mow-need
USING: turf-file, cell-file;
DERIVES: mow-day
USING: mow-need, history-file;
PROCEDURE:
    1. Check cell file for type of turf.
    2. Check type of turf for frequency of mowing: mow-need.
    3. Determine next mow-day.
    4. If today = mow-day, put on schedule.
HAPPENS: daily
TRIGGERED BY: work-day;
TERMINATION-CAUSES: holiday;
SECURITY IS: none;
```

The PSA analyzer produces reports from the PSL descriptions. These include data dictionaries, object relationship reports, data flows, and other descriptions of data attributes. Reports such as these summarize the information input in PSL and provide valuable tools for reference. Other reports analyze the PSL statements, comparing data descriptions and detecting errors. For example, if there are data items that are described but never used, PSA will point them out. More importantly, if the flow of data is not well-defined (that is, if there is a missing link in the flow of data), then PSA will indicate where the error is. To help keep track of data elements and changes to them, PSA will also generate reports that cross-reference data items and list modifications made to data descriptions.

The PSL/PSA methodology is useful in organizing the requirements specification so that it can be examined for many of the characteristics described early in this chapter. For example, PSA may catch incompleteness and inconsistency among existing requirements. However, we must check some of the desirable characteristics ourselves. For instance, no report produced by PSA can guarantee that all requirements have been generated.

Software Requirements Engineering Methodology. A real-time system is one of the most difficult kinds of systems for which to generate requirements, since there are usually many constraints to be documented and tracked. To address this need, the TRW Corporation has developed a *Software Requirements Engineering Methodology (SREM)* ([ALF77] and [ALF85]). Just as PSL/PSA has two parts, one for specification and one for analysis and reporting, so too does SREM.

To use SREM, we begin by writing the requirements in a *Requirements Statement Language* (RSL). Then, the statements are analyzed by a *Requirements Engineering Validation System (REVS)*. As with PSL/PSA, a system is described in terms of objects and their relationships. However, RSL describes the *flow of processing* in terms of what events initiate which processes. These flows are represented as networks, using both pictures and a written description. Each network, or R-net, specifies how a particular state and single input are transformed into a new state with a set of output messages. By using a network format, SREM allows us to depict what happens when more than one process takes place at the same time within a network; however, only one R-net is active at a given time. Figure 3.15 shows how the network might look for a process involved in an on-line banking system. The circled plus indicates a condition for which the process may branch. In our example, either the right or left path may be taken. The circled ampersand indicates that processes follow that can be performed in parallel or in any order. The triangles indicate points of synchronization, where all parallel processes must be complete before the next process can begin.

Once we draw the network diagrams, we then translate the components of each diagram into their corresponding RSL statements. For example, the R-net depicted in Figure 3.15 is written in the RSL language as follows:

```
R_NET: PROCESS_TRANSACTION
    STRUCTURE:
        INPUT_INTERFACE_ACCOUNT_REQUEST_RECORD
        EXTRACT_DATES
        DO (REQUEST = TRANSACTION)
            RECORD_TRANSACTION
            TERMINATE
        OTHERWISE
            FIND_ACCOUNT-RECORDS
            COMPUTE_SAVINGS_BALANCE
            AND COMPUTE_CHECKING_BALANCE
            AND COMPUTE_MONEY-MARKET_BALANCE
            PRINT_BALANCES
            TERMINATE
        END
    END
```

We can define other elements in addition to the R-net definitions. An ALPHA is a specification for the *functions* in an R-net. For each function, the input to the function, the output, and the description of the transformation are included. Similarly, the *data elements* are described, including the fields of each element, where the element originates, and a general description.

The R-net diagrams exhibit only the functional system requirements. We can think of the *nonfunctional* requirements as descriptions of constraints placed on the flow along various paths. For example, in the network shown in Figure 3.15, the customer may require the account balance to be printed within five seconds after the account record is located. To specify this requirement, we can mark the R-net with validation points. A **validation point** is a place in the diagram used to denote the beginning or end of a measurement. In our example, we mark the "Find Account Records" block as one validation point and the "Print Balances" block as

Figure 3.15   Requirements Network

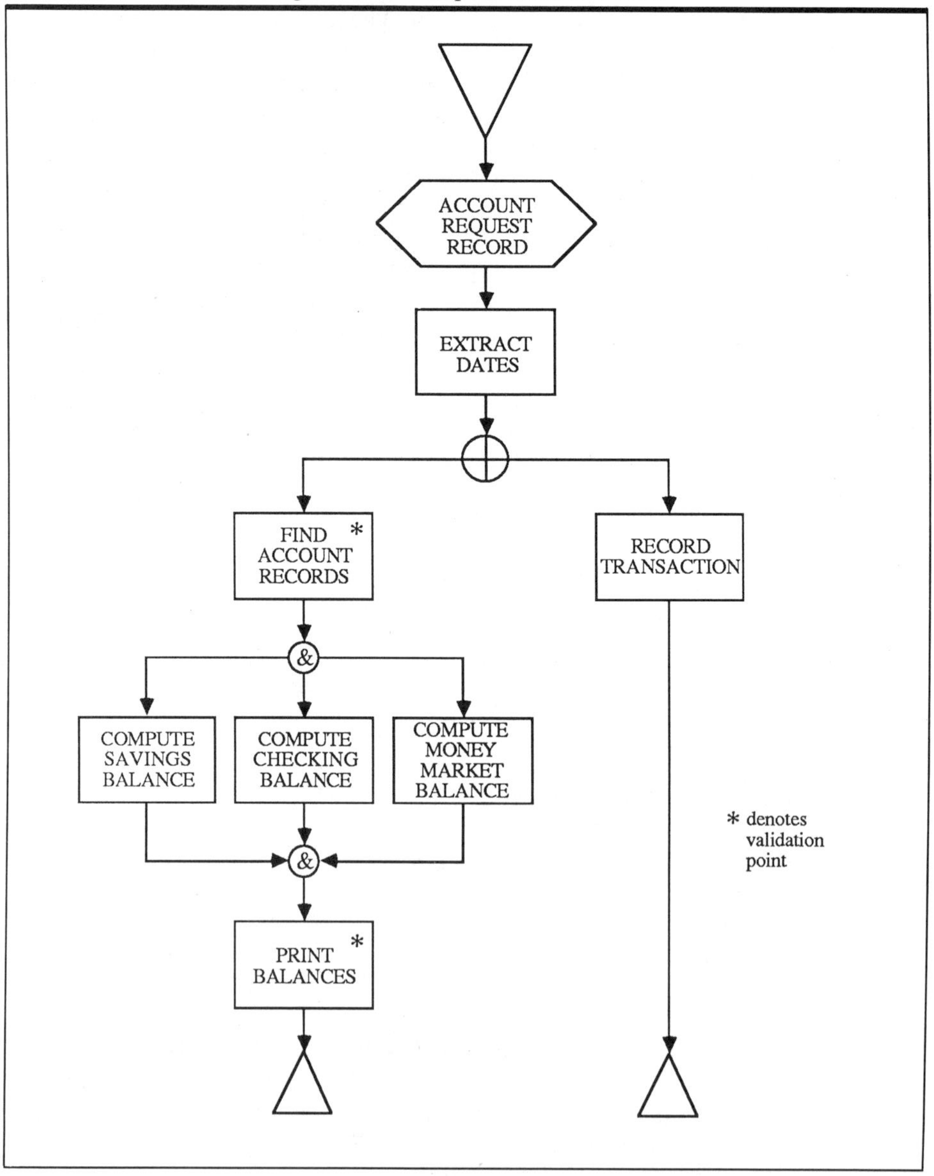

another. Then, our five-second requirement is a descriptor of the path from one validation point to another. We use this general approach in SREM and express nonfunctional requirements as descriptors of the paths through the R-nets.

The RSL elements allow us to tie the requirements to the data elements and to the requirements definition by setting a pointer from the originating requirement to the data and processes generated. This is especially useful for configuration management. When requirements change, it is important to be able to evaluate the impact of the change by looking at the specific system objects that must change accordingly.

After we have used RSL to translate the requirements into a precise description of data elements, processing steps, and their associated functional and non-functional requirements, the REVS system reads the RSL statements as input. REVS translates the RSL statements and forms a data base from them, similar to the way PSA operates on the statements of PSL. This data base, called the *Abstract System Semantic Model (ASSM)*, is accompanied by a set of tools that analyzes its contents and produce a variety of reports. The reports can be of two types. First, REVS produces summary reports that allow us to consider alternative approaches and evaluate the trade-offs among them. Second, REVS simulates the critical processing requirements of the system, allowing us to analyze the overall feasibility of the system under development. The flow of data through the system is depicted with a graphics package, and a simulator builds and runs simulation models of the system. Table 3.4 shows the steps involved in using SREM (adapted from [ALF85]).

Table 3.4   SREM Steps

Phase	Focus	Criteria
Define kernel.	Identify I/O, R-nets, transformations.	All input messages processed. All output messages generated.
Establish baseline.	Clean up data base. Plot R-nets.	All naming consistent.
Define data.	Define input, output for each transformation.	No data used before given a value.
Establish traceability.	Generate consistent traceability requirements.	All top requirements satisfied.
Simulate functionality.	Simulate subsystem functions performed.	Validation that all are processed correctly.
Identify performance requirements.	Define traceable, testable performance subsystem requirements.	Each path constrained by response time and accuracy.
Demonstrate feasibility.	Rapid prototype of all critical algorithms.	Accuracy requirements satisfied by prototype algorithms.

The SREM views the system as a finite state machine. An enhancement to SREM, called *Systems Requirements Engineering Methodology (SYSREM)*, adds a time dimension to this concept. The addition of time allows us to specify a sequence of events or concurrent events. We can also describe performance and function in terms of response to a stimulus. SYSREM expands SREM to a useful design tool, as we shall see in chapter 4.

Both SYSREM and SREM have many advantages. First, it is relatively easy to use RSL to translate requirements into a detailed set of activities and data descriptions. Second, because the system is divided into discrete functional pieces, the interfaces to each piece can be examined for completeness. The REVS processor evaluates alternate approaches and simulates alternative sets of requirements to determine the system's feasibility. This approach is well suited for systems that are to be embedded in other, larger systems.

Structured Analysis and Design Technique

SofTech, Inc. has developed another requirements definition tool that involves graphical representation of a system ([ROS77] and [ROS85]). The *Structured Analysis and Design Technique (SADT)* really consists of two parts: the structured analysis (SA), followed by the design (DT). SA specifies the requirements using two types of diagrams, and then DT explains how to interpret the results.

SA represents a system with an ordered set of *activity and data diagrams*. Each diagram represents a transformation, and at most six diagrams can be used to describe a function. (If more than six diagrams are needed, the function should be redefined as a set of subfunctions.) The diagram includes four factors: an input, a controlling parameter, a human or mechanical mechanism, and an output. Thus, every activity diagram is drawn as a block with three arrows entering and one arrow leaving, as shown in Figure 3.16. Figure 3.17 shows the corresponding diagram for a

Figure 3.16   Structured Analysis Activity Diagram

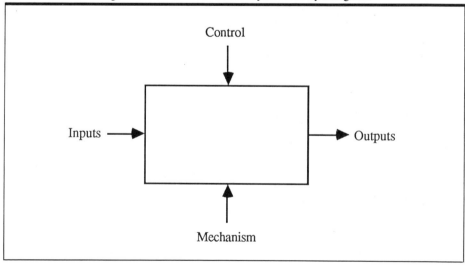

Figure 3.17   Structured Analysis Data Diagram

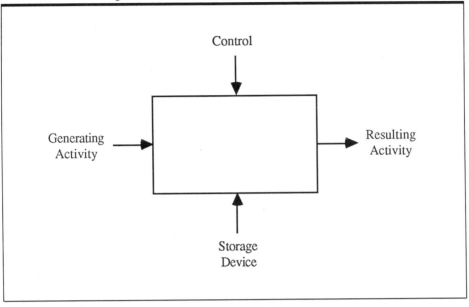

data transformation, where a storage device is a facilitating mechanism, and activities generate the change in the data. In both types of diagrams, the *mechanism* is something external that aids in the process, while the *control* is a piece of data that limits or prescribes the type or degree of transformation. The box in each diagram is called a *node* of the system network, and the arrows are the arcs. As with other methods, the diagrams are arranged in a hierarchy to show more detail at lower levels. Because graphics indicate the system's structure and relationships, we say that SADT generates a "system blueprint."

To see how structured analysis works, we consider the system network shown in Figure 3.18. It illustrates the top-level view of a word processing system. There are four activity diagrams linked together to show that a document can be created, edited, checked for spelling, and printed. The network diagram does not show each activity in complete detail. Figure 3.19 contains examples of the detailed activity and data diagrams needed to accompany the network and complete the picture.

Unlike SREM and PSL/PSA, there is little automated support for the DT phase of requirements analysis, making checks for completeness and consistency difficult. However, SADT is still useful, because, as with other requirement specification techniques, it forces us and our customers to divide a system in a disciplined way into distinct and easily understood pieces.

Structured System Analysis. *Structured System Analysis (SSA)* ([GAN79] and [DEM78]) is part of a more general design technique that also represents the system as a set of diagrams. However, SSA incorporates data base concepts in its system description. The flow of data through the system is shown with data flow

Figure 3.18   Structured Analysis (SA) Network Diagram

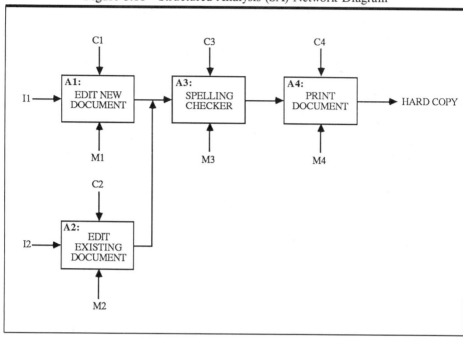

diagrams, and the data are defined in *data dictionaries*. A **data dictionary** is a list of all data elements in a system. It includes a description of the format and content of each data element; it also explains the relationships among data elements. (Since the use of data flow diagrams with data dictionaries is also a design technique, we will look at examples of data dictionaries and data flow diagrams in chapter 4.) Data flow diagrams cannot display sequences of events, so algorithms to be used with the data are described nongraphically, where text describes the processing logic. The relationships among data elements are recorded in relational tables of fields from the data elements.

Because SSA is also a design technique, there is always a possibility that design details will find their way into the requirements specified. In other words, we risk considering implementation options before we understand how the system is to function. Furthermore, there are no automated tools to check for consistency, completeness, and other desirable characteristics that should be verified before the design process begins.

Gist. The Information Sciences Institute has developed a special requirements specification language called *Gist* ([BAL81]). Its clearly defined syntax describes the behavior of a system in terms of a finite state model. Gist forces us to view the system as a set of valid states and actions. The *states* are configurations of the system, while the *actions* cause the system to change from one state to another. We generate a Gist specification by classifying the system's objects into object types. Then we list the ways in which objects can be related to one another. This allows the

Figure 3.19 Structured Analysis (SA) detailed Data and Activity Diagrams

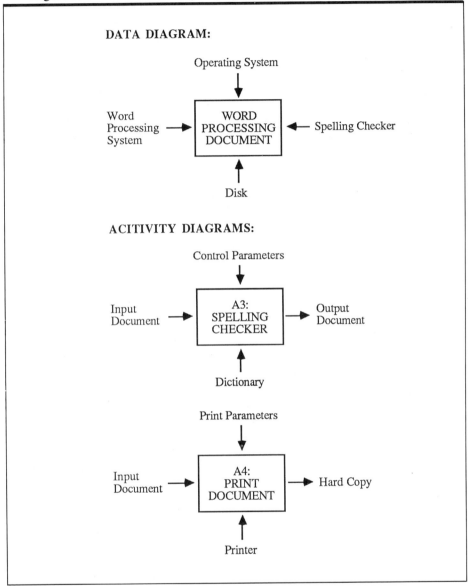

Gist processor to determine all states in which the system might be at a given time. Next, we describe the possible actions that might be taken and the state transitions that will occur with each action. Finally, we record constraints on the states and transitions.

To use Gist, we employ techniques similar to the data abstraction methods discussed earlier in this chapter. First, we classify objects of the system into *object types*. These are abstract data types that describe legal values of objects of a particular type plus legal operations on the objects. For example, on Weaver Farm, the set of trees can be classified as an object type using a Gist statement:

```
type TREE includes (BIRCH, ELM, OAK, PINE, DOGWOOD);
```

For each type, all possible objects of that type are listed. Other descriptors are defined relating to the types, including the grouping of objects or a description of characteristics of the object type. Thus, if TOP is the height of the top of a set of trees and BOTTOM the height of the lowest branches, we can have statements of the form:

```
type CANOPY definition(TOP, BOTTOM);
type HEIGHT definition integer;
```

The relationships among objects are described next. For instance, if one tree is in the shade of a cluster of other trees, we can define this relationship formally. The shade depends on the height of the tree and the height of the canopy. We can express this as

```
relation SHADES(TREE, CANOPY, HEIGHT) where HEIGHT < CANOPY (TOP)
```

We can also define other types derived from the basic ones and relationships among them; this is done by using a set of derivation rules. Static constraints on the types and relationships can be included.

Next, we list the actions that can change the state of the system. These action descriptions include the state of the system before the change, the cause of the change, and the state after the transformation. For example, we may want to cut down a tree that is shaded by a cluster of other trees. An action definition of this logging activity may look like this:

```
action LOGGING(TREE, CANOPY)
    precondition TREE:HEIGHT ≤ CANOPY
    definition if SHADES(TREE, CANOPY, HEIGHT) then HEIGHT = 0
end
```

Not only do we list constraints on the object types and relationships, but we also list constraints on the actions and changes themselves. Finally, we associate classes of common actions into processes.

Once the requirements are completely specified by using the Gist language, an automated testing tool called *Initial Operating Capability (IOC)* can test the resulting requirements. IOC determines whether the requirements are valid by applying them to test data.

3.6

REQUIREMENTS DOCUMENTATION

No matter what method we choose for defining requirements, we must keep a set of documents recording the result. We and our customer will refer to the requirements throughout development and maintenance. Requirements must be written so that they are *meaningful* not only to the customer but also to designers on our development team. Furthermore, the requirements must be *organized* in such a way that they can be *tracked* throughout the system's development. Clear and precise illustrations and diagrams accompanying the documentation should be consistent with the text. Numbering the requirements allows us to *cross-reference* them with the data dictionary and other supporting documents. A *numbering scheme* is also essential to the configuration management team. If any changes are made to the requirements during the remaining phases of development, the changes can be tracked from the requirements document through the design process and all the way to the test procedures. Ideally, then, any feature or function of the system can be traced to its generating requirement and vice versa.

Requirements Definition Document

The system documentation contains a record of the requirements in the customer's terms. This requirements definition document describes *what the customer would like to see.*

1. First, we outline the *general purpose* of the system. References to other related systems are included, and we incorporate any terms and abbreviations that may be useful.

2. Next, we describe the *background and objectives* of system development. For example, if a system is to replace an existing approach, we explain why the existing system is unsatisfactory. Current methods and procedures are outlined in enough detail so that we can isolate those elements with which the customer is happy from those that are disappointing.

3. If the customer has a proposed new approach to solving the problem, we outline a *description of the approach*. Remember though, that the purpose of the requirements documents is to discuss the problem, not the solution; the focus should be how the system is to meet the customer's needs. In particular, if the customer places any constraints on the development or if there are any special assumptions to be made, the definition document should list them.

4. Once we record this overview of the problem, we describe the *detailed characteristics of the proposed system*. We define the system boundary and interfaces across it. The system functions are explained. Also, we include a complete list of data elements and classes and their characteristics. The relationships

among data and functions are detailed, and the input and output to each process or function is described. Specific performance requirements, such as timing, accuracy, and reaction to failure, are also included.

5. Finally, we discuss the *environment* in which the system will operate. We include requirements for support, security and privacy, and any special hardware or software constraints should be addressed.

Requirements Specification Document

The requirements specification document covers exactly the same ground as the requirements definition document. The requirements definition document is written at a level appropriate for the customer and in terms that the customer understands. However, the requirements specification document is written from our own perspective as a developer. For example, the customer may not understand the definition of a requirement in terms of a complex mathematical relation, so the definition document defines the requirement in natural English. The specification document may define the same requirement as a series of equations.

Because there is to be a direct correspondence between the two documents, we establish a numbering scheme or data file for convenient tracking of requirements from one document to another. Often, the configuration management team sets up or extends the numbering system to tie requirements to all other components of the system.

Let us look at an example of how a requirement definition may differ from its specification. A satellite tracking system has in its requirements definition document the following requirement:

4.1.3.1 <u>INITIATE TRACK ON IMAGE</u>. Logical processing shall be done to INITIATE TRACK ON IMAGE. This shall have as input HANDOVER DATA. This shall have as output HOIQ, STATE DATA, and IMAGE ID. This logical processing shall, when appropriate, identify a new instance of IMAGE. This logical processing, when appropriate, shall identify the type of entity instance as being IMAGE ON TRACK. NOTE: A request for pulses is made by entering a formal record into the HOIQ which feeds the pulse-send procedures.

However, in the requirements specification document, the requirement is written in RSL and is tied to the definition document.

```
ALPHA: INITIATE_TRACK_ON_IMAGE.
    INPUTS: HANDOVER_DATA.
    OUTPUTS: HOIQ, STATE_DATA, IMAGE_ID.
    CREATES: IMAGE.
    SETS: IMAGE_ON_TRACK.
    DESCRIPTION: "(4.1.3.1)A REQUEST FOR PULSE IS MADE BY ENTERING A FORMAL
                 RECORD REQUEST INTO THE HOIQ WHICH FEEDS THE PULSE SENDING
                 PROCEDURES"
```

It is clear that the customer can understand the definition document description but may not be capable of understanding the specification of the requirement in RSL.

3.7

REQUIREMENTS REVIEW

Remember that requirements analysis serves two purposes. First, it provides a way for the customer and developer to agree on what the system is to do. Second, the specification provides guidelines for the system designers. Thus, before the requirements can be turned over to the designers, we and our customer must be absolutely sure that each knows the other's intent and meaning. To establish this certainty, we hold a *requirements review*. Representatives from our staff and the customer's examine the list of requirements. These representatives include those who will be operating the system, those who prepare the input, and those who will use the output; managers of these employees may also attend. We provide members present from the design team, the test team, and the configuration management team. What does the requirements review entail?

1. We review the stated *goals and objectives* of the system.

2. We *compare* the requirements with the goals and objectives to verify that all requirements are necessary.

3. We describe the *environment* in which the system is to operate. We examine the interfaces between the system and all other systems, and we verify that they are correct and complete. Then the information flow and structure of the system is reviewed again to insure that the requirements *accurately reflect the meaning and intent* of the customer. The functions of the system should be *consistent* with the scope and intention of the customer. Furthermore, the functions and the constraints should be *realistic* and within our development abilities. All requirements are checked again for omissions, incompleteness, and inconsistency.

4. If any risk is involved in the development or in the actual functioning of the system, it is assessed and documented. We discuss and compare alternatives, and we and our customer agree on the approaches to be used.

5. We talk about testing the system. How will the requirements be verified and validated? How will the test team be sure to check all requirements? Who will provide the test data? If the system is to have a phased implementation, how will the requirements be checked during the intermediate phases?

When the requirements review is complete, we and our customer should feel comfortable about the specification of the requirements. Understanding what the customer wants, we can proceed with the system design. The customer has in hand a document describing exactly what the system will do when it is complete.

3.8

CHOOSING A
REQUIREMENTS SPECIFICATION METHOD

Every project begins with requirements analysis and specification. Project size does not eliminate this step in the development cycle. However, project size can affect the choice of method used to document, evaluate, and track the requirements. For example, suppose we are asked to develop a billing system for a small office of consultants. For this small system, it is unlikely that a set of automated tools such as SREM is necessary to specify the requirements. Since the primary system functions involve data manipulation, we look for a method that captures the data structure and relationships. A manual method based on data structures is a good choice for a system such as this.

On the other hand, suppose we are to build a computerized system to monitor water quality in the lakes and streams of a large watershed. Monitoring equipment is to be placed at the locations to be monitored. Some processing is performed on site, but the data gathered and the results from the on-site processing are to be transmitted to a central site for further analysis. One of the key characteristics of this water monitoring system is that it is an **embedded system**. That is, the data processing part of the system is embedded in a complex of data gathering and analysis equipment. In addition, the system involves a large number of functions whose processing is distributed over several computers. The complexity of this system makes it essential that the requirements be specified exactly and completely. Interfaces must be well-defined, and the requirements should provide enough information so that the test team will know how to verify that the system functions properly. Any confusion at the requirements specification stage will result in a nightmare when testing begins.

Some methods may work better here than others. Automated ones may be preferable to manual methods. Moreover, techniques that allow the system to be checked for consistency and completeness may catch errors in the specification that are not easy to spot otherwise. SREM may be a good specification tool for this system, since it is especially well suited for embedded systems.

If a system has real-time requirements, we must look for techniques that allow us to include the effects of time in our specifications. Moreover, any need for phased development tells us that we will be tracking requirements through several intermediate systems. Not only does that add to the difficulty of tracking requirements, but it also increases the likelihood that the requirements will be modified over the life of the system. As the users work with intermediate versions of the system, they may see new items to add, functions to change, or constraints to incorporate. Thus, we need a sophisticated method that can handle change easily.

To be sure that the requirements have all of the desirable characteristics listed early in the chapter, we look for a method that allows us to revise the requirements, track the changes, cross-reference the data and functional items, and analyze the requirements for as many characteristics as possible. The ability to simulate the system or a subsystem is highly desirable, since development really involves the development of a series of subsystems of progressively increasing functionality.

No one approach is universally applicable to all systems. In fact, in many cases, it may be necessary to combine several approaches to define the requirements completely. Some methods are better at capturing nonfunctional requirements than others, for example, so it may be best to use one approach to record the functional requirements and another to describe the constraints. Likewise, some methods are better at describing data requirements than others, so it may be useful to use one method for data requirements and another to describe processes or time-related activities. Most importantly, we must realize that no requirements specification technique is complete; what may be adequate for designers to deal with may be difficult for the test team to use. Thus, the choice of a specification technique is bound up in the characteristics of the individual project and the preferences of the developers and customer.

3.9
RESOURCE TRACKING AND SIMULATION EXAMPLE

In this chapter, we have seen examples of how requirements can be translated into various requirement specification languages. Our examples assume that we know what those requirements are. In this section, we investigate *how* to work with the customer to determine the requirements.

The director of Weaver Farm is our first point of contact. Either by *questionnaire* or *direct interview*, we begin with questions about *why* the system is being built. We try to determine exactly what problem the director wants to solve. Most of our discussion involves the nature of the business of Weaver Farm, since an understanding of the business is necessary for understanding the problem. Thus, we do the asking and let the customer do the *telling*. Our purpose at this stage of development is to gather information.

Next, we talk with the prospective users of the system. Asking them the same kinds of questions that we asked the director does not always yield the same answers. The users often have a different perspective on the problem that can supply valuable information. For example, the director may describe the need to generate a daily maintenance schedule. However, the users may point out that consideration must be given to the preparation of equipment that will perform the maintenance. Time must be allotted for lubricating and fueling gas-powered mowers and for moving equipment from one part of the recreation area to another.

The question-and-answer process is usually repeated several times. We begin with an overall picture of the situation and systematically refine our understanding of the problem, asking more and more detailed questions. One way to accomplish this is to record our understanding as a set of requirements after each discussion with the customer. Then we review the requirements, looking for those that are not clear, not testable, or in some way not satisfactory. For instance, the director may request real-time response from the simulation functions. We must return and ask exactly what is meant by "real-time response."

The requirements analysis is usually performed by system analysts. Sometimes a program designer or hardware expert is involved if the customer insists on placing hardware constraints on the system. If the director requests the use of a particular data base management system, an expert on that system may be asked to help define requirements. If the customer wants to use a VAX computer, a VAX technical expert may participate in requirements analysis. If the proposed system is to communicate with other existing systems, analysts familiar with those systems should take part in the discussion of requirements.

Thus, we can view the requirements review process as the culmination of the series of question-and-answer sessions. It is the time for final refinement of requirements and for verification that all parties have the same understanding of the problem to be solved.

3.10

CHAPTER SUMMARY

This chapter has examined the first step in the system development process: determining the requirements. In *requirements analysis*, we work with the customer to find out exactly what problem needs a solution. First, we investigated what a requirement is, and we saw that we must attend to functional as well as nonfunctional requirements. In each of these classes, we can target particular characteristics of the desired system and record as a requirement those characteristics that are desirable.

Then we looked at several ways to *define requirements*. Using static techniques such as indirect reference or axiomatic definition, or dynamic techniques such as decision tables or transaction diagrams, we can describe the system in terms of its functions or reactions to stimuli.

To *specify requirements* for use by the developer's designers, we can use manual written or graphic methods such as HIPO or data flow diagrams. Although automated tools help with the generation of these diagrams, there are also other methods designed with automated evaluation in mind. PSL/PSA, SREM, SADT, SSA, and Gist begin with a description of requirements in a formal language or structure so that we can analyze the requirements automatically for characteristics such as consistency and completeness.

The requirements analysis results in two documents: a *requirements definition document* that describes the requirements in the customer's terms, and a *requirements specification document* that reflects those requirements in the developer's more specialized language. No matter how the requirements are enumerated and analyzed, they must be structured so that all system components can be traced back to their roots in the requirements. This traceability is key, not only to testing, so that the tests can determine whether the problem has actually been solved, but also to configuration management, where changes in requirements are followed through the design and into the implementation.

A *requirements review* is a final analysis technique to assure us that we and our customer have a common understanding of the problem and any related issues. Once the review is complete, the we can turn from the problem to its solution. In chapter 4, we look at how to move from considering the requirements to suggesting a solution to the customer's problem.

3.11

EXERCISES

1. Write a decision table that specifies the rules for the game of checkers.

2. If there are two conditions possible for a system, how many combinations of conditions must be represented in a decision table? If there are *n* conditions possible for a system, how many combinations of conditions are there? Write an inductive proof to show that your answer is correct.

3. If a decision table has two identical columns, then the requirements specification is ambiguous. Why is this true? How can we tell if the specification is redundant? Contradictory? What do blank entries in the table indicate about the specification? What would multiple entries mean?

4. Write an event table that describes the output of the algorithm for finding the roots of a quadratic equation using the quadratic formula.

5. Write an event table to specify the process of calculating the determinant of a matrix.

6. Generate a transition table and diagram to illustrate the requirements of an automatic bank teller machine.

7. Generate a transition table and diagram to specify legal moves in the game of Trivial Pursuit.

8. A specification is complete if and only if there is a transition specified for every possible combination of state and input symbol. We can change an incomplete specification to a complete one by adding an extra state, called a *trap* state. Once a transition is made to the trap state, the system remains in the trap state, no matter the input. For example, if 0, 1, and 2 are the only possible inputs, the system depicted by Figure 3.20 can be completed by adding a trap state as shown in Figure 3.21. In the same manner, complete the transition diagrams of Exercises 6 and 7.

Figure 3.20   Diagram for Exercise 3.8

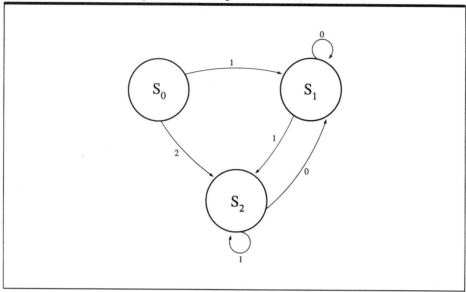

Figure 3.21   Diagram for Exercise 3.8

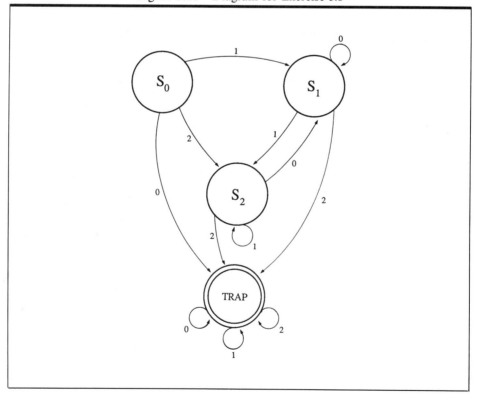

9. Sometimes part of a system may be built quickly to demonstrate feasibility or functionality to a customer. This prototype system is usually incomplete; the real system is constructed after the customer and developer evaluate the prototype. Should the system requirements document be written before or after a prototype is developed? Why?

10. Write a set of HIPO charts to indicate the requirements for an online telephone directory to replace the one that is provided to you by your phone company. The directory should be able to provide phone numbers when presented with a name; it should also list area codes for different parts of the country and generate emergency telephone numbers for your area.

11. Use Structured Analysis (SA) activity and data diagrams to illustrate the functions and data flow for the online telephone directory system specified in the previous problem.

12. What are the benefits of separating functional flow from data flow?

13. What special kinds of problems are presented when specifying the requirements of real-time systems?

CHAPTER 4

SYSTEM DESIGN

In the last chapter, we learned how to work with the customer to determine what the proposed system is to do. As illustrated in Figure 4.1, the next step in development is to translate those desires, as specified in the requirements documents, into a system that will satisfy the customer's needs. In this chapter, we explore what to do and how to do it.

We begin by examining the purpose of a system design and noting that two forms of the design are needed: a *conceptual design* for the customer and a *technical design* for the hardware and software experts. After discussing who designs the system, we look at the characteristics of a good system design. Several design strategies are introduced that help to insure a high-quality design. Then we examine several techniques and tools that can be helpful in specifying a design.

Once specified, a system design is evaluated to be sure that it is a good design that meets all of the customer's requirements. Several methods are suggested for performing this evaluation. Next, we learn why and how to document the design. Finally, we return to our resource tracking and simulation example to see how design concepts and methods can be applied to the Weaver Farm system.

4.1

WHAT *IS* SYSTEM DESIGN?

A customer wants to build a new system either because there is no existing system or there is a major problem with the old system. The customer's need forces us to think of system design in two ways: as a *process* and as a *product*. The creative process of system design is the transformation of the problem into a solution. The resulting product is a description of the solution; this is called the **system design**.

There may be more than one solution to a problem. Returning to our house-building example, it is easy to see that there may be many houses that satisfy the needs of the Ehlers, the family that is to live in the house. Moreover, it is also clear that there may not be a "best" house; several of the houses may be equally satisfactory. Thus, there is a range of houses, all of which will satisfy the Ehlers' requirements. At one end of the spectrum are the solutions with the fewest "extras," and at

Figure 4.1   The System Development Process

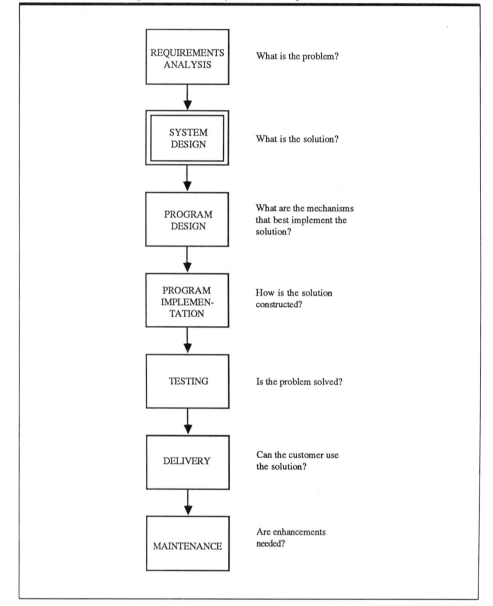

the other end are those that give the Ehlers all that they want plus a lot more that
they haven't even considered.

The same things can be said about system design. We use the requirements
specification to define the problem. Then, we declare something to be a *solution* to
the problem if it satisfies all the requirements in the specification. In many cases,
the number of possible solutions is limitless. Just as the Ehlers can choose the

particular house that they want to build from among their many options, so too can the customer choose the one solution that is to be implemented from several possibilities.

The *nature* of the solution may change as the solution is described or even as it is implemented. For example, when the architect shows a set of plans to the Ehlers, the Ehlers may decide to modify some of the specifications of their house. This decision is neither unusual nor unreasonable. The modifications may not be based on whim but on a change in perception or need. If the Ehlers decide to have a baby, they may need to change the specifications for their house to make room for the child. Or, if the Ehlers realize that they misunderstood something or forgot to mention an important requirement, it makes more sense for them to change the specifications than to learn to live with a house that displeases them or in some way does not suit their needs. In the same way, the description of a system may change during the development cycle. Indeed, often a customer, in concert with the developers, modifies requirements well after the initial requirements analysis is complete.

Thus, to transform requirements into a working system, we as system designers must satisfy both the customer and the system builders on our development team. The customer understands *what* the system is to do. At the same time, the system builders must understand *how* the system is to work. For this reason, system design is really a two-part process. First, we produce a **system specification** that tells the customer exactly what the system will do. This specification is sometimes called a **conceptual system design**. Once the customer approves the conceptual design, we present the system builders with a **technical design** that allows them to build the actual hardware and software. This two-part design mirrors the two parts of requirements description. As illustrated in Figure 4.2, the two design documents describe the same system, but in different ways because of the different uses of the documents. The conceptual design concentrates on the *function* of the system, while the technical design describes the *form* the system will take.

Conceptual Design

The conceptual design tells the customer *what* the system will do. As we saw in chapter 1, the system is described in terms of its boundary, entities, attributes, and

Figure 4.2 Two Parts of System Design

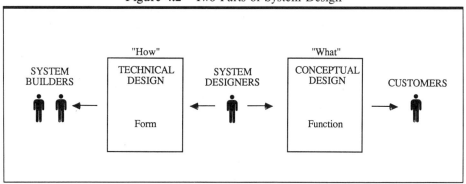

relationships. Where will the data come from? What will happen to it in the system? What will the system look like to users? What choices will users be offered? What will the reports and screens look like? The system specification tells the customer exactly what functionality to expect.

Moreover, the system is described in language that the customer can understand rather than in computer jargon and technical terms. For example, the customer may be told that a menu on a display screen will give users access to the system functions. The system description may even list acceptable user responses and the actions that may result. However, the customer is not told how the data are stored in the system or what kind of data base management system is used for data manipulation. Similarly, the customer may be told in the system specification that messages are routed from one location to another. Yet the networking protocol and topology, which tell *how* the system works rather than *what* the system does, are not specified. The "how" belongs in the technical design. Thus, a good conceptual design should have the following characteristics:

1. Is written in customer's language
2. Contains no technical jargon
3. Describes functions of system
4. Is independent of implementation
5. Derives from requirements document
6. Has cross-reference to requirements
7. Incorporates all requirements in adequate detail

Technical Design

As you can see in Figure 4.3, the technical design explains the system to those hardware and software experts who will implement it. The design describes the

Figure 4.3   Conceptual Design vs. Technical Design

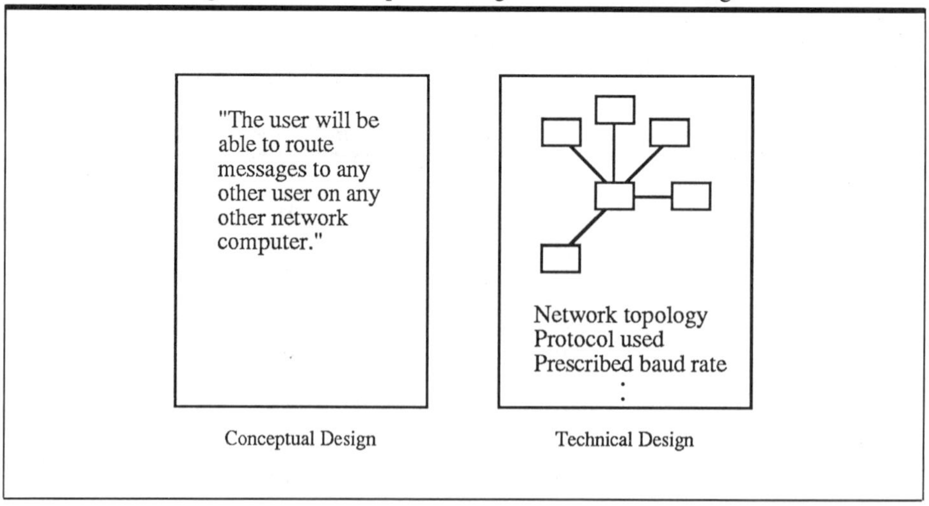

| Conceptual Design | Technical Design |

hardware configuration, the software needs, the communications interfaces, the input and output to the system, the network architecture, and anything else that translates the requirements into a solution to the customer's problem. The design description is a technical picture of the system specification.

The idea of having two different but complementary descriptions of a system is not unusual. In constructing a house, the Ehlers are more likely to be able to visualize what McMullen plans to build if they are presented with an artist's rendering and a floor plan of the design, rather than with construction blueprints. The blueprints and the drawings are two ways of describing the same house, so they complement one another. The Ehlers do not have to become experts in all aspects of building in order to understand exactly what they are getting. Likewise, McMullen does not need to learn all about the Ehlers' private lives to understand what the Ehlers want or need.

In the same way, the conceptual design enables the customer to understand what the system will do by explaining the observable external characteristics of the system. The internal, technical description is left for the technical design. Thus, we include the following items in the technical design:

1. The system architecture: a description of the major hardware components and their functions

2. The system software structure: the hierarchy and function of the software components

3. The data: the data structures and the data flow

4.2
WHO PRODUCES THE SYSTEM DESIGN?

As we noted in previous chapters, systems analysts work with customers to understand their needs and to develop the requirements specification. Next, several members of our development team will be involved in creating the system design and supporting documents.

One or more systems analysts produce the system specification. They are familiar with the customer's needs, and they are good at expressing technical concepts and functions in terms that the customer can understand. The systems analysts know what the technology can do, but they do not have to know exactly how the system will be implemented in hardware and software. The implementation is handled by design specialists who have a deep understanding of the capabilities and functions of a wide variety of hardware and software options; they may know little of the context in which the application is to run. As the designers put together a proposed package of hardware and software components, the systems analysts translate that package into the customer's vocabulary for use by those who develop test procedures, training aids, and documentation.

4.3

APPROACHES TO SYSTEM DESIGN

A system design includes both conceptual and technical designs. To understand design, we begin by examining the way in which we interpret system requirements. First, we view the system in the abstract before we consider its implementation. Phrased simply, we must find a logical solution to the customer's problem before we can describe how that solution will be implemented. This abstract, high-level design allows us to determine whether the solution is complete and consistent before we proceed to lower levels. Again, this procedure parallels that of building a house, in which floor plans are drawn and examined carefully before more detailed blueprints for each aspect of the house are generated.

Thus, in its early stages, a design may not be precise or even practical. However, during these early stages we can insure that all needs of the customer are met and that the pieces of the design fit together properly. In the conceptual design, we verify the following:

1. All information entering the system is completely defined.

2. All required functions are specified.

3. All data produced by the system are in the format expected by the users or other systems with which this one communicates.

It is useful to separate the design into its composite parts. A **design module** is a functional entity with a well-defined set of inputs and outputs. Therefore, each module can be viewed as a component of the whole system, just as each room is a component of a house. A module is **well-defined** if all inputs to the module are essential to the function of the module and all outputs are produced by some action of the module. Thus, if one input were left out, the module could not perform its full function. In addition, well-defined means that there are no unnecessary inputs; every input is used in generating the output. Finally, the module is well-defined only when each output is a result of the functioning of the module, and when no input becomes an output without having been transformed in some way by the module.

A **design** is then a determination of the modules and intermodular interfaces that satisfy a specified set of requirements ([DEM82]). We can develop these modules in two ways: by beginning with a high-level view and dividing the system into modules, or by beginning with data and objects and building modules from them. The first approach is known as **decomposition**, while the second is the **composition** approach to design.

Decomposition

To decompose a design into modules, we begin by writing a high-level description of what goes into the system, how these data are transformed by the system, and

Figure 4.4   Decomposition of System into Levels

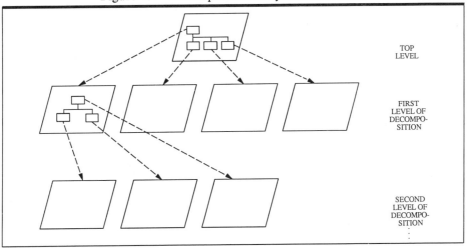

what results are produced by the system. Then we refine and redefine the top level as a more detailed set of modules: the first level of decomposition. In turn, we decompose each set of modules in the first level into a second, even more detailed set of modules. The process, illustrated in Figure 4.4, continues until a set of primitive modules is defined, where each module performs a transformation on exactly one major data structure. We say that a system is **modular** when each activity of the system is performed by exactly one module and when the input and output of each module are well-defined.

Composition

A design can be derived by working from system data descriptions instead of high-level functional descriptions. We begin with data and data type definitions abstracted as described in chapter 3. There we saw how to define data by looking at what they are used for in the system. This functional description included an investigation of the *actions* performed on each data type: creation, query, modification, and deletion. We can build a system from the data types by constructing a set of tools to manipulate them. Thus, we *compose* modules to handle the data types, rather than handling the data directly.

For example, we define an **object module** as a set of actions that apply to a data object. You can think of the object module as a box containing the data: you cannot use the object directly; you must instead use the actions in the object module. Then, we define an **object-type module** as a module to describe a *type* of data. Later in this chapter, we look at an example of an object module and an object-type module when we investigate data abstraction as a design principle.

The result of building up from data and data types is also a set of modules. Figure 4.5 shows how we still have a hierarchy of modules, and for each level, the next lower level contains more detail about the data.

Figure 4.5   Composition of a System from Data

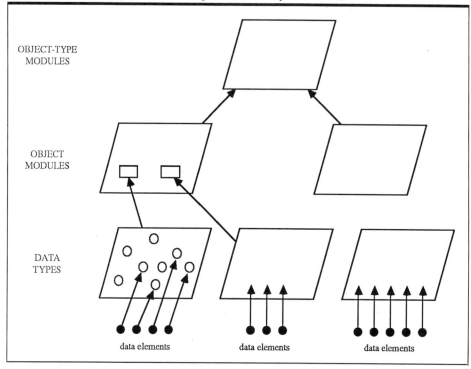

4.4

CHARACTERISTICS OF GOOD DESIGN

No matter whether the design is generated through decomposition or composition, the resulting modules must be easy to understand and modify. *Modifiability* is especially important, since changes to requirements or changes needed for error correction sometimes result in a design change. Thus, let us investigate the characteristics of a good system design.

Modularity

Modularity is a characteristic of good system design. High-level modules give us the opportunity to view the problem as a whole and hide details that may distract us. By being able to reach down to a lower level for more detail when we want to, modularity provides the flexibility we need to understand what the system is to do, trace the flow of data through the system, and target the pockets of complexity. Contrary to popular thinking, breaking a problem into pieces does not magically turn a complex problem into a set of simple ones. However, modularity allows us to isolate those parts of the problem that are the most difficult to handle. In turn, such isolation prevents us from being confused or led astray by unrelated functions and data.

Levels of Abstraction

Because the modules at one level refine those in the level above, we consider the top level to be the most abstract. As we move to lower levels, we find more detail about each module. Thus, modules are said to be arranged in *levels of abstraction*. The levels of abstraction help us to understand the problem addressed by the system. By examining the levels from the top and working down, the more abstract problems can be handled first and their solutions carried through as the detailed description is generated. In a sense, the more abstract top levels hide the detail of the functional components from us. In a similar way, Parnas ([PAR71]) suggests that modules hide the internal details and processing from one another. An advantage to this **information hiding** is that each module hides a design decision from the others. Thus, if design decisions are difficult or are likely to change, the system design as a whole can remain intact while only the module design changes.

Abstraction and information hiding allow us to examine the ways in which modules are related to one another in the overall design. The degree to which the modules are *independent* of one another is a measure of how good the system design is ([PAR72], [WIR71], [STE74]). Independence is desirable for two reasons. First, it is easier to understand how a module works if its function is not intricately tied to others. Second, it is much easier to modify a module if it is independent from others. Often a change in requirements or in a design decision means that certain modules must be modified. Each change affects data or function or both. If the modules depend heavily on each other, a change to one module may mean changes to many others. The more independent the modules, the easier it is to isolate the modules that are affected by the change.

Two criteria help us to evaluate the degree of module independence and, correspondingly, the quality of the design: *coupling* and *cohesion*.

Coupling

Coupling is a measure of how much modules depend on each other. We say that two modules are **highly coupled** if there is a great deal of dependence between them. **Loosely coupled** modules have some dependence, but the interconnections among modules are weak. **Uncoupled** modules have no interconnections at all. (See Figure 4.6.) Coupling depends on several things:

1. The *references* made from one module to another. For example, module A may invoke module B, so the function of module A depends on that of module B.

2. The *amount of data* passed from one module to another. For example, module A may pass the contents of an array to module B, so that module B depends on A.

Figure 4.6   Independent vs. Dependent Modules

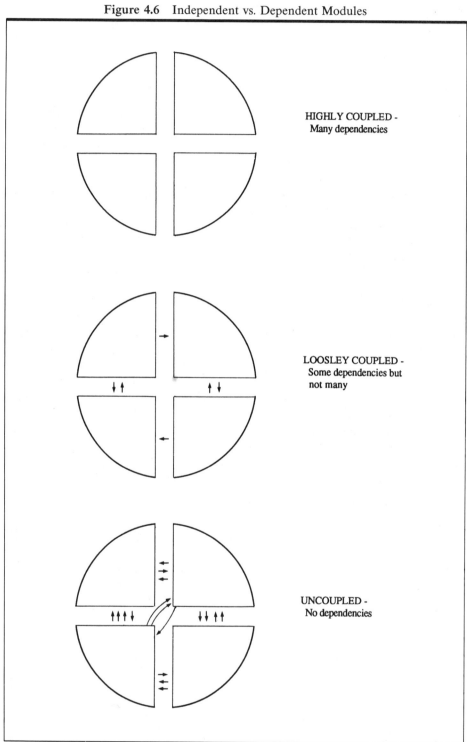

3. The *amount of control* one module has over the other. For example, module A may pass to module B a control flag. The function performed by B depends on the value of the flag.

4. The *degree of complexity* in the interface between one module and another. For example, if module A passes one flag to module B, but modules C and D exchange values before D can complete its function, then the interface between A and B is less complex than that of C and D.

Thus, coupling really represents a range of dependence, from complete dependence to complete independence, as shown in Figure 4.7.

We want to minimize the dependence among modules for several reasons. First, if an element is affected by a system action, we always want to know which module causes the effect at a given time. This knowledge allows us to change a portion of the system design without disrupting a large part of the system. For example, if the customer's requirements change and one function is replaced by another, a modular design with low coupling among modules allows us to replace one module directly with another. Only a few other modules will be affected by the change and might be candidates for modification. Thus, low coupling minimizes the number of modules needing revision.

Second, modularity helps in tracking the cause of system errors. If an error occurs during the performance of a particular function, independence of modules allows us to isolate the defective module more easily.

Some types of coupling are less desirable than others. The least desirable occurs when one module actually modifies another. Then the modified module is completely dependent on the modifying one. We call this **content coupling**. Content coupling might occur when one module modifies an internal data item in another module, or when one module branches into the middle of another module. In Figure 4.8, module B branches into D, even though D is supposed to be under the control of C. A similar instance of content coupling is represented by Figure 4.9. Here, one module branches to the middle of another where the branch point is also in the flow of control. These situations are undesirable because at some points of

Figure 4.7   Types of Coupling

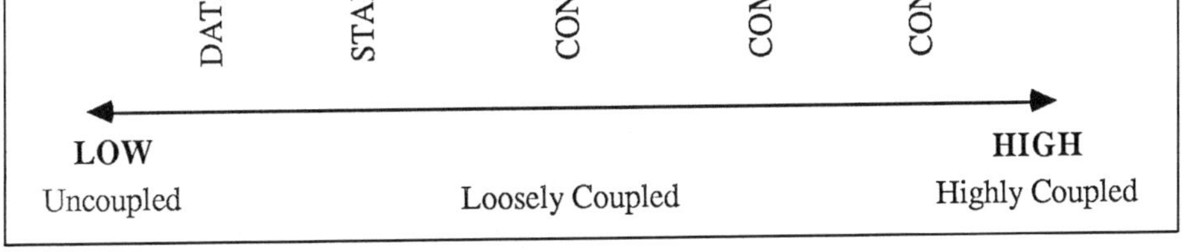

Figure 4.8   Content Coupling

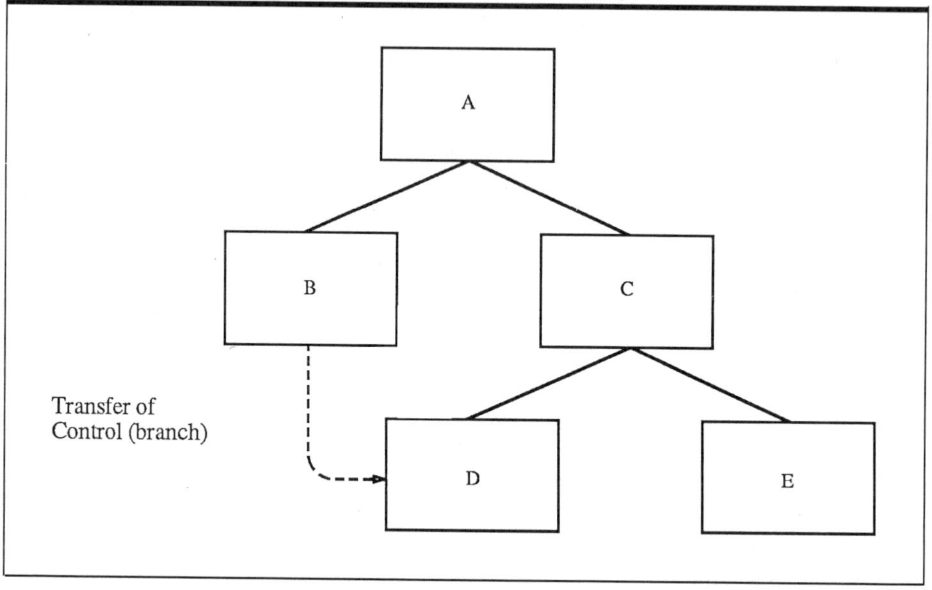

modules D (in Figure 4.8) and G (in Figure 4.9), it is not easy to determine which module (B or C, G or H) led to the point of execution in D or G, respectively.

We can reduce the amount of coupling somewhat by putting data items in a global or common data area (such as in a FORTRAN COMMON block or variables declared in an outermost Pascal or PL/I block). Dependence still exists, since a change in the common data area has effects that must be traced to all modules that access that data. This kind of dependence is called **common coupling**. With common coupling, it can be difficult to determine which module is responsible for having set a variable to a particular value. Figure 4.10 shows how common coupling works.

When one module passes flags to control the activity of another module, we say that there is **control coupling** between the two. It is still impossible for the controlled module to function without direction from the controlling one. An advan-

Figure 4.9   Content Coupling Involving Flow of Control

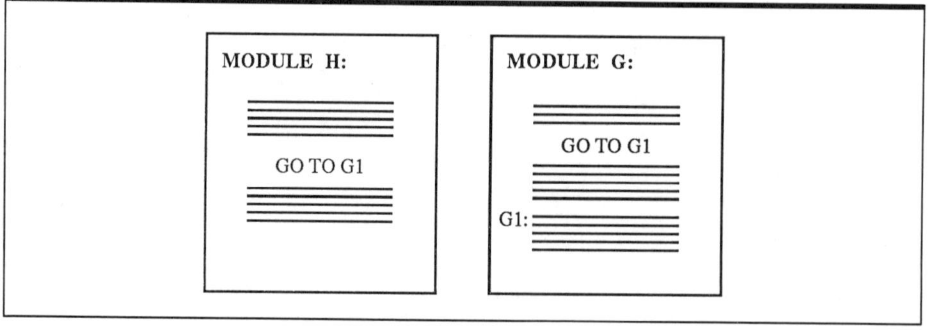

Figure 4.10 Common Coupling

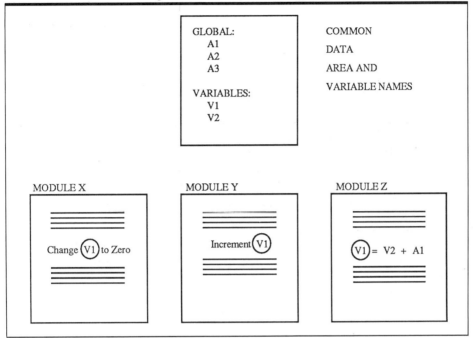

tage to having each module perform only one function is that the amount of controlling information that must be passed from one module to another is minimized. In addition, control is localized to a fixed and recognizable set of control flags forming a well-defined interface.

Suppose that instead of flags, a data structure is used to pass information from one module to another. This data structure allows an argument list to be used, rather than a set of control flags and data items. If the data structure itself is passed, there is **stamp coupling** between the modules; if only data are passed, the modules are connected by **data coupling**. With stamp coupling, the data values, format, and organization must be matched between interacting modules. Thus, data coupling is simpler and leaves less room for error. If coupling must exist between modules, data coupling is the most desirable; it is the easiest through which to trace data and to make changes.

Cohesion

In contrast to measuring the interdependence of modules, cohesion refers to the internal "glue" with which a module is constructed. The more cohesive a module, the more related are the internal parts of the module to each other and to the functionality of the module. In other words, a module is **cohesive** if all elements of the module are directed toward and essential for performing the same function. Just as there are levels of coupling, there are also levels of cohesion. Our goal is to

Figure 4.11   Examples of Cohesion

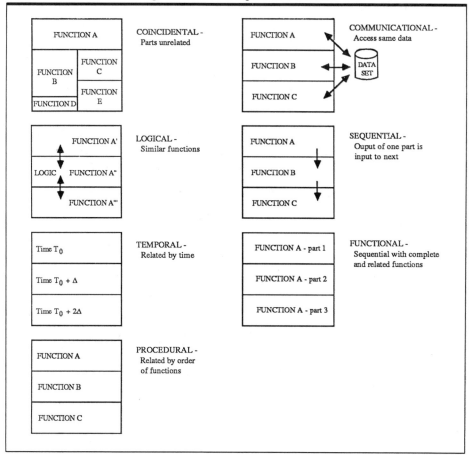

make each module as cohesive as possible, so that every part of a module's processing is related to the module's singular function. Thus, the worst degree of cohesion is found in a module whose parts are unrelated to one another. **Coincidental cohesion** occurs when the parts of a module are completely unrelated. For example, a module that checks a user's security classification and also prints this week's payroll is coincidentally cohesive.

A higher level of cohesion (though still not desirable) is **logical cohesion**, where several logically related functions are placed in the same module. For example, one module may read all kinds of input (from cards, tape, disk, telecommunications port), regardless of where the input is coming from or how it will be used. Because all parts of this module perform input, the module is logically cohesive. Although more reasonable than coincidental cohesion, the elements of a logically cohesive module are not related functionally. In our example, since the input can have different purposes for different modules, we are really performing many unrelated functions in one place.

Sometimes a module is used to initialize a system or a set of variables. Such a module performs several functions in sequence, but the functions are related only because of the timing involved. This kind of module exhibits **temporal cohesion**, since *time* is what the various parts of the module have in common. Both temporally and logically cohesive modules are difficult to change. Suppose a system function X must be changed, so a design modification is necessary. Because logically or temporally cohesive modules perform several different functions, to change the affected function X, you must search through all modules for the parts related to X. If the modules were more cohesive, finding all modules related to a particular function would be much simpler.

Often, functions must be performed in a certain order. When these functions are grouped together in a module just to insure this order, the module is **procedurally cohesive**. Alternatively, we can associate certain functions because they operate on or produce the same data set. Sometimes this construction seems to be convenient because everything can be performed with only one disk or tape access, for instance. Modules constructed in this way are **communicationally cohesive**. However, communicational cohesion often destroys the modularity and functional independence of the design.

If the output from one part of a module is input to the next part, the module has **sequential cohesion**. Because the module still is not constructed based on functional relationships, it is possible that the module will not contain all of the processing related to a function. Our ideal is **functional cohesion**, where every processing element is essential to the performance of a single function. A functionally cohesive module not only performs the function for which it designed, but it performs only that function and nothing else. Figure 4.11 illustrates examples of cohesion, and Figure 4.12 shows the progression from the least desirable to the most desirable types of cohesion.

Control Issues

Suppose our design is composed of modules that are functionally cohesive (to guarantee internal functional consistency), and we connect the modules in such a

Figure 4.12 Types of Cohesion

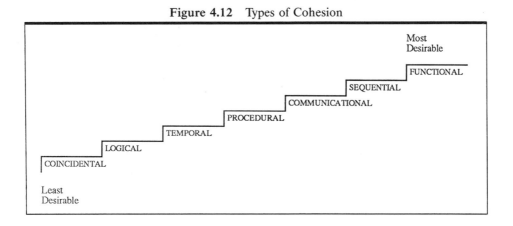

way that we have a low degree of coupling (so that the modules are independent of one another). What else can we examine to tell us about the quality of the design?

One aspect of our design involves the control of several modules by a single module. For example, the modules depicted in Figure 4.13 are two possible designs for the same system. (An arrow from one module to the other means that one module controls the other.) **Fan-in** is the number of modules controlling a particular module, and **fan-out** is the number of modules controlled by a module. Thus, module A has a fan-out of 3 in system 1 but a fan-out of 5 in system 2. Similarly, the fan-in for module C in either system is 1.

Figure 4.13   Example of Fan-In and Fan-Out

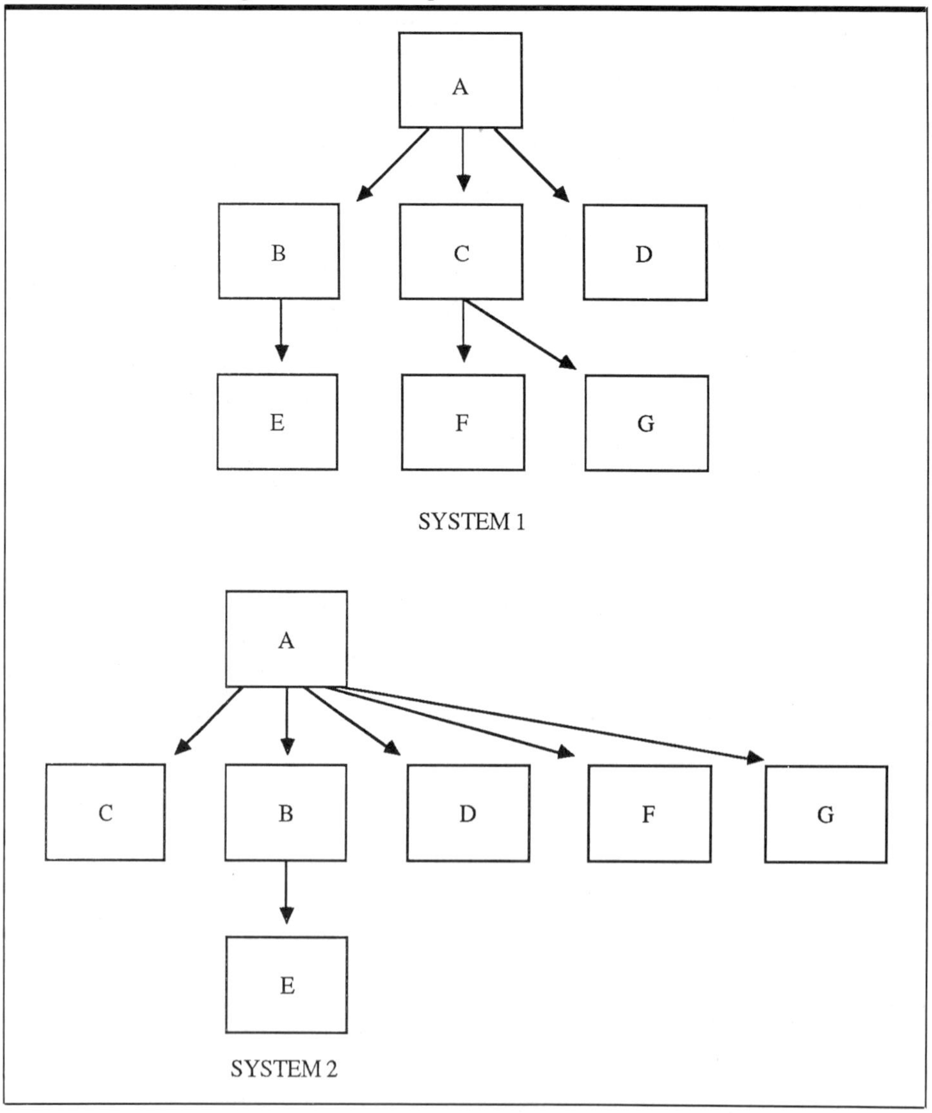

SYSTEM 1

SYSTEM 2

Which is the better design? In general, we want to minimize the number of modules with a high fan-out. A module controlling many other modules usually indicates that the controlling module is doing too much; the controlling module is probably performing more than one function. Thus, system 1 may be a better design than system 2 since its modules have low fan-out. On the other hand, as we increase the number of levels in the design, sometimes we want to use a particular module more than once. For instance, we may need in many cases to search a string for a particular character. If we design one general-purpose module to do that task, and then invoke that module from many others, the resulting design is more efficient and easier to test and modify than one in which there is a proliferation of similar string-searching functions. Thus, for a design with a large number of levels, we create a set of **utility modules**: tools or building block that is used by other modules to perform often-needed tasks. A typical utility module has a high fan-in because it is invoked by many other modules. One of our goals in designing systems is creating modules with high fan-in and low fan-out.

Scope of Control and Effect. Finally, we want to be sure that the modules in our design do not affect other modules over which they have no control. An example will show us why this consideration is important. Look again at system 1 in Figure 4.13. The structure chart leads you to believe that what happens in C affects only F and G. Thus, a change to the design of C should only affect F and G. Suppose, however, that module C resets a pointer in A that then affects the processing in module E. In the structure chart, an arrow connects one module to another only if the first module can invoke the other. For a given module, the set of modules to which arrows are drawn from it is called the **scope of control** of the module. The modules controlled by the given module are collectively referred to as the **scope of effect**. No module should be in the scope of effect if it is not in the scope of control. If the scope of the effect of a module is wider than the scope of its control, it is almost impossible to guarantee that a change to the module will not destroy the entire design.

4.5

INITIAL DESIGN STRATEGIES

In the previous sections, we discussed characteristics of good system designs:

1. Low coupling of modules
2. Highly cohesive modules
3. Minimal number of modules with high fan-out
4. Scope of effect of a module limited to its scope of control

These characteristics are goals for us as system designers because they make the system easier to construct, test, correct, and maintain. It is useful to know these characteristics before we begin to design so that we can build them into our system.

We turn now to the actual design process. We begin by transforming the requirements into conceptual and technical designs.

Reducing Structural Complexity

Before generating a conceptual design, we try to simplify the requirements specification as much as possible without changing the nature of the problem. This simplification allows us to understand the problem more easily and usually leads to a simpler, more easily understood system design. These characteristics percolate through the rest of development, making the software and hardware easier to design, construct, and maintain.

For example, diagrams of system interactions can be reduced in complexity so that they are easier to understand. Figure 4.14a shows a structure diagram that has many arrows crossing over one another. These crossovers make the diagram confusing and difficult to read. It can be redrawn as Figure 4.14b so that there are no crossovers; this depiction of the structure is simpler and more easily understood. In general, graphs and diagrams such as these should be redrawn to reduce the number of crossovers. Redrawing to preserve its relationships but minimize crossovers demonstrates the **planarity** of the graph, the minimum number of crossovers that must be used when drawing the graph on a piece of paper.

Simplifying Decision Tables

Sometimes decision tables that describe system actions can be reduced in complexity. In chapter 3, we examined a decision table for a university admissions office. Let us look at that kind of table in more detail. Admission to the university is based on four factors: high grades, high SAT scores, outstanding recommendations, and extracurricular activities. For each applicant, we can represent the presence of each

Figure 4.14a   Diagram before Simplification

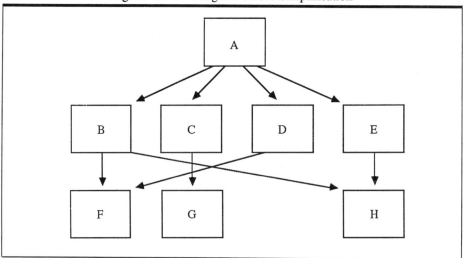

Figure 4.14b   Diagram after Simplification

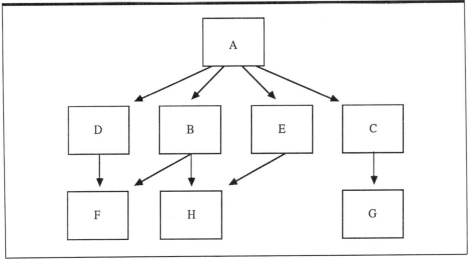

variable by using a "1" and the absence of the variable by a "0." Let the variable assignments be represented as

w = student has a GPA of A or B

x = student has combined SAT scores of 1200 or more

y = student has outstanding recommendations

z = student has extra-curricular activities

The university can take a series of actions based on the particular combination of variables for each student:

A1: invite for early admission

A2: admit for regular semester

A3: invite for honors program

A4: invite for regular program

A5: conditional admission

A6: reject

Table 4.1 shows all possible variable combinations and their consequent actions. For instance, if $w = 1$ and $z = 1$ but x and y are both 0, then actions A2 and A4 are taken: the student is given regular admission into the regular program.

Boolean algebra can be used to describe the relationship among the actions and the variables. (For a more complete discussion of Boolean algebra and how it can be applied to decision tables, see [PFL85].) For each action represented by a column, we write the action as the sum of products, with one term for each row in which there appears an X. For example, in the column labeled for action A1, there

Table 4.1   Decision Table For University Admission

| Variables | | | | Actions | | | | | |
w	x	y	z	A1	A2	A3	A4	A5	A6
0	0	0	0						X
0	0	0	1						X
0	0	1	0				X	X	
0	0	1	1				X	X	
0	1	0	0		X		X		
0	1	0	1		X		X		
0	1	1	0		X		X		
0	1	1	1			X	X		
1	0	0	0		X		X		
1	0	0	1		X		X		
1	0	1	0		X		X		
1	0	1	1		X		X		
1	1	0	0		X	X			
1	1	0	1		X	X			
1	1	1	0	X	X				
1	1	1	1	X	X				

are Xs in the last two rows: where w, x, and y are 1 and z is 0, and where all variables are set to 1. From each such row, we form a product in the following way: whenever the variable is set to 1, use the variable in the product; whenever the variable is set to 0, use the variable's complement in the product. Let us represent the complement of a variable by the variable with a bar over it, writing the complement of x as $\bar{x}$. Thus, we can describe the action A1 by writing the two conditions that result in A1 as the sum of the products $w\,x\,y\,\bar{z}$ and $w\,x\,y\,z$:

$$w\,x\,y\,\bar{z} + w\,x\,y\,z = A1$$

In a similar fashion, we generate all six equations that describe the relationship between the input variables and the resultant actions, as shown in Table 4.2:

Table 4.2   Algebraic Description of Decision Table

$$A1 = w\,x\,y\,\bar{z} + w\,x\,y\,z$$
$$A2 = \bar{w}\,x\,\bar{y}\,\bar{z} + \bar{w}\,x\,\bar{y}\,z + \bar{w}\,x\,y\,\bar{z} + \bar{w}\,x\,y\,z$$
$$\qquad + w\,\bar{x}\,\bar{y}\,\bar{z} + w\,\bar{x}\,\bar{y}\,z + w\,\bar{x}\,y\,\bar{z} + w\,\bar{x}\,y\,z$$
$$\qquad + w\,x\,\bar{y}\,\bar{z} + w\,x\,\bar{y}\,z$$
$$A3 = w\,x\,\bar{y}\,\bar{z} + w\,x\,\bar{y}\,z + w\,x\,y\,\bar{z} + w\,x\,y\,z$$
$$A4 = \bar{w}\,\bar{x}\,y\,\bar{z} + \bar{w}\,\bar{x}\,y\,z + \bar{w}\,x\,\bar{y}\,\bar{z}$$
$$\qquad + \bar{w}\,x\,\bar{y}\,z + \bar{w}\,x\,y\,\bar{z} + \bar{w}\,x\,y\,z + w\,\bar{x}\,\bar{y}\,\bar{z}$$
$$\qquad + w\,\bar{x}\,\bar{y}\,z + w\,\bar{x}\,y\,\bar{z} + w\,\bar{x}\,y\,z$$
$$A5 = \bar{w}\,\bar{x}\,y\,\bar{z} + \bar{w}\,\bar{x}\,y\,z$$
$$A6 = \bar{w}\,\bar{x}\,\bar{y}\,\bar{z} + \bar{w}\,\bar{x}\,\bar{y}\,z$$

As you can see, some of these expressions are quite intricate. However, we can use the property that $x + \bar{x} = 1$ to simplify these formulae. For example, we can reduce A1 in the following way:

$$A1 = w\,x\,y\,\bar{z} + w\,x\,y\,z$$
$$= w\,x\,y\,(\bar{z} + z)$$
$$= w\,x\,y(1)$$
$$= w\,x\,y$$

Exercise 6 (page 183) gives you the opportunity to verify that the expressions in Table 4.2 can be reduced to their equivalents in Table 4.3.

Table 4.3   Simplified Formulae for the Decision Table

$$A1 = w\,x\,y$$
$$A2 = x\bar{y} + \bar{w}\,x\,y + w\,\bar{x}$$
$$A3 = w\,x$$
$$A4 = \bar{x}\,y + \bar{w}\,x + w\,\bar{x}\,\bar{y}$$
$$A5 = \bar{w}\,\bar{x}\,y$$
$$A6 = \bar{w}\,\bar{x}\,\bar{y}$$

Similar methods can be applied to hardware logic design requirements. The results are designs with fewer gates, or wiring diagrams with fewer crossovers. In these cases, simplicity not only enhances understanding, but it also reduces hardware costs and makes testing faster and cheaper.

4.6

SYSTEM DESIGN TECHNIQUES AND TOOLS

There are many techniques and tools available for use in designing a system. The choice of technique or tool depends in part on the characteristics of the system. Following the terminology of DeMarco ([DEM82]), we say that a system is **function-strong** if it can be specified and implemented almost entirely in terms of the operations it performs on data. On the other hand, a system is **data-strong** if it can be described in terms of the data upon which it acts and the relationships among the data, rather than the operations. For example, a system that controls the automation of an assembly line is likely to be function-strong, while a payroll reporting system is more likely to be data-strong. Of course, many systems fall in between; we call these **hybrid systems**.

The techniques and tools presented in this section are a few of many available for designing a system. For the particular projects that you will work on, you may use one of these, a combination of several, another that your company uses, or one that you develop yourself. As long as the result is a high-quality design (that is, it is characterized by modularity, high cohesion, levels of abstraction, and so on), it does not matter which design technique is used.

Data Flow Diagrams

Any system design begins with the requirements specification. Somehow, these requirements must be translated into a design. The requirements specification tells you what the entities of the system are and how they are related to one another. In particular, the data elements are listed. Often, a *data dictionary* is used to reference these data elements. The data items are listed and cross-referenced with the transformations that affect them. In addition, the rules for accepting new data elements are shown, including a set of rules for combining data elements to form new data elements.

We saw in chapter 3 that some requirements specification techniques (such as Structured System Analysis) combine a data dictionary with data flow diagrams. For data-strong systems, the data descriptions in the requirements specification can form a basis for the system design. The functions of a data-strong system are derived from the data *transformations* described in the data flow diagrams.

We can see how the design is generated from the requirements by examining an example. We begin by using operators and equivalence to form new elements. Suppose A, T, X and F are acceptable data elements as defined in the dictionary. The equals sign shows us when two elements are equivalent:

$$C = A$$

Similarly, an asterisk acts as an "and" operator, so that a new element can be formed by combining two existing elements:

$$C = A*T$$

A vertical bar represents an "or" operator, and all possible choices are enclosed in brackets:

$$B = [A | T | F]$$

Here, B is equal to A or T or F. Braces indicate iterations of an element. In this example, A consists of between zero and sixteen copies of X:

$$A = 0\{X\}16$$

Finally, parentheses show that something is optional:

$$C = A(X)$$

The data dictionary lists the basic elements and simple ways of forming new ones. However, it does not always show completely the way the data are related. Bachman originated the idea of displaying the relationships among data elements with diagrams ([BAC69]). Using his technique, we can represent data items by boxes, as shown in Figure 4.15. The arrows connecting the boxes show how the

Figure 4.15 Data Structure Diagram

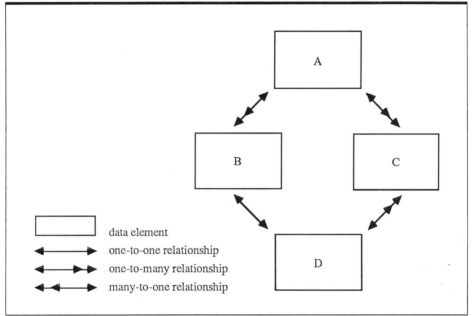

data element

one-to-one relationship

one-to-many relationship

many-to-one relationship

elements relate. For example, there is an arrow from A to C with a single head at A and a double head at C. This arrow indicates that there is a one-to-many relationship between A and C: one copy of A is related to many copies of C. For example, if A is the name of an employee and C is the schedule of hours worked in a week, there may be one A record corresponding to 52 C records. Similarly, the arrows of that diagram show that there is a many-to-one relationship between C and D, but only a one-to-one relationship between B and D.

There are many variations on the original idea of a data flow diagram. For example, DeMarco ([DEM78]) combined the notion of a pictorial representation of the data with its corresponding reference to the data dictionary. Most schemes using data flow diagrams display the system data flow by using a combination of arrows, bubbles, and operators. The bubbles represent centers where transformations of data occur. The name of a bubble is always an action. Arrows go into and out of bubbles, showing the direction and routes on which the data flow. Operators give us additional information about the relationships among arrows.

Figure 4.16 is an example of a data flow diagram for querying a data file. A label on each arrow names the data associated with the arrow. Arrows leading into bubbles depict input data, while arrows leading out of bubbles show output data. Each bubble is a distinct transformation, and the output is different from the input. The asterisk placed near the "Extract Records" bubble, between the search criteria and the data file name, is an operator that indicates an "and" condition between the two input arrows. The transformation requires as input both the search criteria *and* the data file name. Similarly, the "Sort Records" tranformation requires both the records *and* the sort criteria in order to function. A circled plus sign represents the

Figure 4.16 Data Flow Diagram

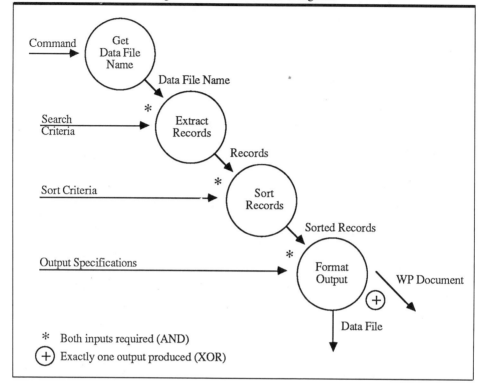

"exclusive or" operator: exactly one of the designated outputs is produced by the transformation. In our example, after the output is formatted, either a word processing document is produced or a data file is formed, but not both. Thus, a circled plus is placed between the arrows corresponding to those outputs from the "Format Output" transformation bubble.

No control or sequence information is represented on a data flow diagram. If two pieces of data are flowing through the system, we cannot tell if they are acted upon in parallel or one before the other. We can tell only what happens to the data, not when or where.

The flow of data through a data-strong system can sometimes determine the system's structure. Jackson ([JAC83]) has created a system design technique based on this notion. He believes that the structure of a problem is reflected in the structure of its data, which in turn determines the structure of a solution to the problem. Thus, he begins the design process by specifying the initial data and how it is transformed. To do this, he uses tree diagrams of the data plus a regular grammar that describes how the elements are built from one another. Figure 4.17 shows an example of how data might be depicted using Jackson's techniques. From these diagrams, a model of the system is built by identifying points of correspondence between the nodes in the trees. This model is then expanded to define the operations needed to solve the problem.

Figure 4.17   Examples of Jackson Data Structure Diagrams

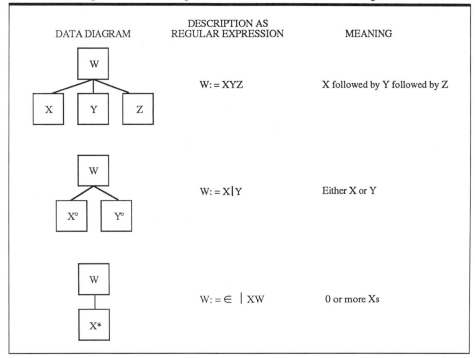

DATA DIAGRAM	DESCRIPTION AS REGULAR EXPRESSION	MEANING
	W: = XYZ	X followed by Y followed by Z
	W: = X|Y	Either X or Y
	W: = ∈ | XW	0 or more Xs

Data Abstraction

There are other ways of using data to help design a modular system. If we have used data abstraction to specify requirements, we can use the composition approach to design and build system modules from data specifications. To understand the technique, we begin by exploring the concept of *abstraction*. Suppose we are designing a system one of whose functions is to rearrange the elements of a list L. We can specify the rearrangement in the following way:

```
Rearrange L in nondecreasing order.
```

This perfectly good description of the "rearrangement" operation on L can be given more detail:

```
DO WHILE I is between 1 and (length of L)-1:
    Set LOW to index of smallest value in L(I), . . ., L(length of L)
    Interchange L(I) and L(LOW)
ENDDO
```

The algorithm provides a great deal of additional information. It tells us the procedure that will be used to perform the rearrangement operation on L.

However, it can be made even more detailed. This final algorithm tells us exactly
how the rearrangement operation will work.

```
DO WHILE I is between 1 and (length of L)-1:
    Set LOW to current value of I
    DO WHILE J is between I+1 and (length of L)-1:
            IF L(LOW) is greater than L(J) THEN set LOW to current value of J
            ENDIF
    ENDDO
    Set TEMP to L(LOW)
    Set L(LOW) to L(I)
    Set L(I) to TEMP
ENDDO
```

Each description of the rearrangement operation serves a purpose. The first is
the most abstract. If we care only what L looks like before and after rearrangement,
the first abstraction is all we need to know. The second algorithm is a lower level of
abstraction than the first. By giving us more detail, it gives us an overview of the
procedure used to perform the rearrangement. If we are concerned only about the
speed of the algorithm, the second level of abstraction is sufficient. However, if we
are writing code for the rearrangement operation, the third level of abstraction tells
us exactly what is to happen. There is little additional information needed.

The purpose of data abstraction is to describe what data is for, regardless of how
it is labeled or structured. Thus, we want to keep the level of abstraction high so as
not to be distracted by extraneous information. Look at the three preceding
rearrangements. If you were presented only with the third level, you might not
discern immediately that the procedure describes a rearrangement. With the first
level, the nature of the procedure is obvious. The third level distracts you from the
real nature of the procedure.

Thus, data abstraction when used for design aims to eliminate extraneous information. To do this, data elements and types are defined as described in chapter 3.
Then, sets of related functions on those elements are grouped together. Finally, an
object module is defined that acts on the data elements to perform the functions.

Consider a system as being in one of many states at a given time. An **object
module** or **state space** describes a behavior of the system. Each object module is
composed of three items: **states** described by global data descriptors, **operations**
that describe how to transform the current state to a new state, and **probes** that yield
information about a state but do not change the current state. All object modules
have at least one operation; an *initialize operation* places the object module in its
initial state.

Object modules are defined to promote **data encapsulation**: the only access to
a data object is through a well-defined data manipulation tool. For example, a *stack*
is a commonly used data structure. Rather than performing stack operations
directly, we apply data abstraction techniques and define an object module to
perform the stack operations for us. The object module *contains* the stack, and we
must use the module, not the stack itself, to manipulate the elements of the stack.

This concept can be understood more easily if we examine an example. The
description that follows defines an object module for a stack (adapted from [ZIM85]).

Discussion: Contains a last-in, first-out data structure.

State Space: A state is a two-way condition, full/not_full, and a sequence i_1, $i_2, \ldots, i_k$ of *items*, where k is a nonnegative integer.

Probes:

top
>   preconditions: k not equal to 0
>   export: *item*
>   description: export i_k

full
>   export: *Boolean*
>   description: export true if and only if full is set

empty
>   export: *Boolean*
>   description: export k = 0

Operations:

initialize
>   description: create an empty sequence; set not_full

push
>   preconditions: not_full is set
>   imports: *item*, i
>   description: $k \leftarrow k+1$
> $i_k \leftarrow i$
>   EITHER
>   set full
>   OR
>   set not_full
>   END

pop
>   preconditions: not *empty*
>   description: $k \leftarrow k-1$; set not_full

The module performs the two possible stack operations, popping and pushing. The probes give us information about the stack—whether it is full or empty and what is on top—without changing the stack's state. Thus, we can use the module instead of manipulating the stack itself.

This general technique is used to build up a system of modules from the initial data requirements. Object modules manipulate data elements, and *object-type modules* manipulate data types. The abstraction of the essential characteristics of types allows us to hide the details of data that are unimportant to us for the manipulations we need to do. A more detailed analysis can be found in Zimmer ([ZIM85]).

Structure Charts

When systems are not very data-strong, additional information must be added to the design of the data to explain control and timing decisions. Thus, to complement data flow diagrams, many design techniques use structure charts. A structure chart displays the hierarchy of the system modules. In a typical structure chart, a module is drawn as a box. When one box is placed above another and connected to it with an arrow, the first box is controlling the second.

Figure 4.18 is a structure chart that corresponds to the data flow diagram of Figure 4.16. The figure contains small arrows next to the lines of control. An arrow with an open circle at the end indicates data passed from one module to another. Thus, the "File Query" module has control over four other modules. The data flowing between "File Query" and the four subordinate modules is described by the data arrows, and the direction of the arrows shows which are input to or output from "File Query."

Denoting Control. When one structure chart module appears above another and they are connected by an arrow, we assume that the one on top controls the one below. When there is no connecting arrow, we presume there is no relationship of control. However, the ordering of modules from left to right has no meaning in structure charts. Thus, if some functions are to be performed in a particular sequence, we must find a way to include this information on the structure chart. We do this by adding control information to the structure chart. For example, Figure 4.19 is a structure chart for part of a system that prints reports. The system produces monthly reports; however, once every three months, it also produces a quarterly report. We use an arrow with a filled circle to denote control information (such as a flag). This notation enables us to show how the function of one module can be controlled by another module. In our example, the value of a flag controls when the quarterly report is generated.

Stepwise Refinement. Levels of abstraction are important in a good design. How can we use structure charts to help us break the design into levels? If we are using a decomposition approach to design, we begin with the top level and work

Figure 4.18   Structure Chart for File Query

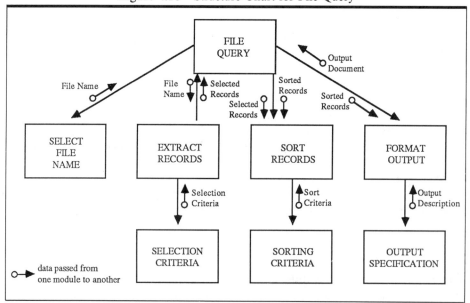

Figure 4.19   Use of Control Flag

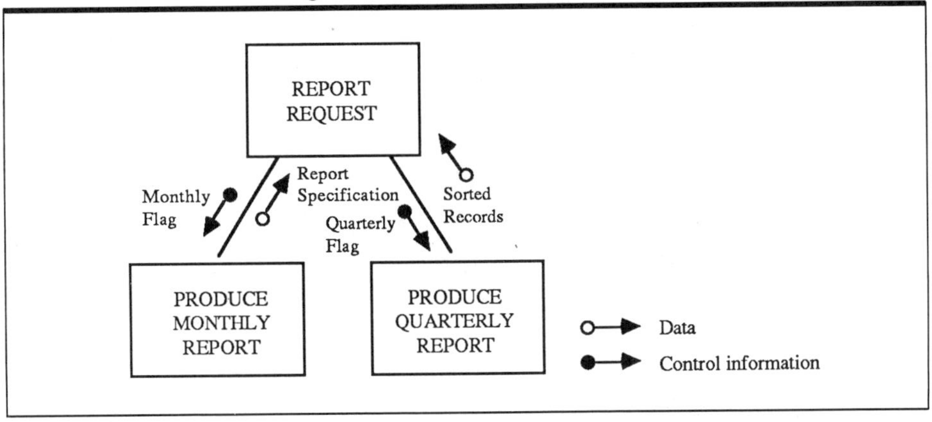

REPORT
REQUEST

Monthly
Flag

Report
Specification

Quarterly
Flag

Sorted
Records

PRODUCE
MONTHLY
REPORT

PRODUCE
QUARTERLY
REPORT

Data

Control information

our way down. Figure 4.20 shows the initial step in designing a file query system. At first, the details of the four subordinate modules do not concern us. We concentrate on what is involved in querying a file and identify the separate functions below. Once we are satisfied with the decomposition of the file query problem into smaller problems, we attack each of the four resultant problems. Figure 4.21 illustrates how we represent some of the smaller modules. We continue this process until we are satisfied that each module in our structure chart performs exactly one transformation on a data structure. This method of generating the design is known as **stepwise refinement**, and it helps assure modularity and levels of abstraction in a system design.

Types of Data Flow. Structure charts provide a great deal of information about system data flow. The relationship of circled arrows to their corresponding module boxes indicates what kind of data flow to which parts of the system. In general, we characterize the flow of data through a module as one of four types: *input, output, transformation,* and *coordination.* Figure 4.22 shows how these data

Figure 4.20   Levels of Structure Charts

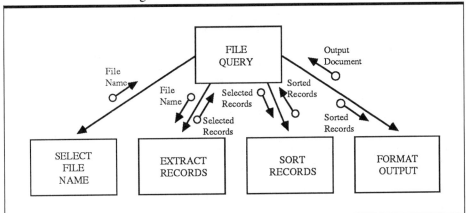

FILE
QUERY

File
Name

File
Name

Selected
Records

Sorted
Records

Output
Document

Selected
Records

Sorted
Records

SELECT
FILE
NAME

EXTRACT
RECORDS

SORT
RECORDS

FORMAT
OUTPUT

Figure 4.21   Second Level of Structure Charts

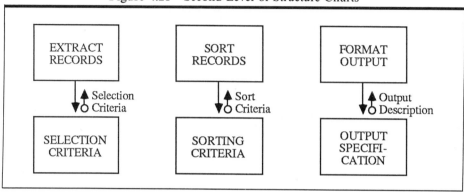

flows look in a structure chart. Module A represents an input flow, where data come from a subordinate module (shown below module A in the structure chart) and pass through A to a superior module (shown above module A in the chart). The data may be used to perform some function within A, but A passes it along untouched. The output flow, shown as module B, is similar, except that the data come from a higher module and flow to a lower one. Module C is very different from A and B because something happens to the data during the functioning of C: transformation to another value. Finally, module D uses the data coming from a module below it to make some control decision about or provide input to another module below it.

The degree to which a system's data controls the choice of system function can also be seen as the *fan-out* of modules. In Figure 4.23, the system consists of modules with low fan-out because the input data is processed in a straightforward manner; little preliminary decision making is necessary. When much of a system's input data is transformed in a straightforward way to output data, we say that the system is **transform-centered**. However, when the input data must pass through some kind of control mechanism to determine the kind of processing needed, the system is known as **transaction-centered**.

Figure 4.22   Four Types of Data Flow

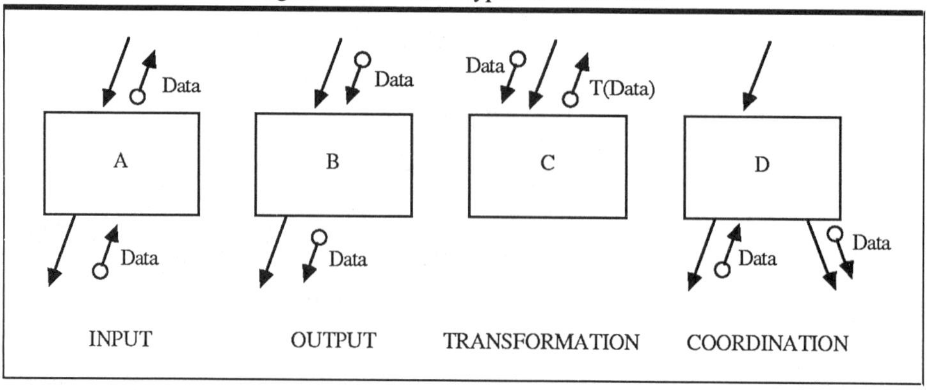

A	B	C	D
Data	Data	Data T(Data)	Data Data
Data	Data		Data
INPUT	OUTPUT	TRANSFORMATION	COORDINATION

Figure 4.23 Transform-Centered System

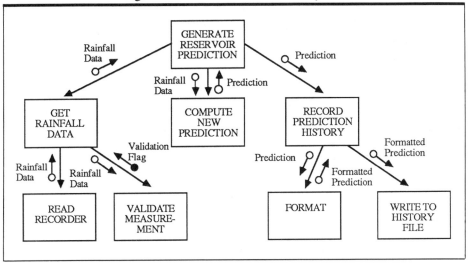

Figure 4.24 illustrates a transaction-centered system: the input data tell the system what type of operation is required. Note that the fan-out for the module determining the type of operation is very high, especially compared to the fan-out values of modules in Figure 4.23.

Structured Design Methodologies. The structure charts presented here are similar to the ones generated by the Structured Systems Analysis (SSA) techniques discussed in the previous chapter. There, we introduced a variety of methods for denoting a system's requirements, some of which are part of an overall scheme for generating a system design. For example, the Structured Analysis and Design Technique (SADT) represents a system as a set of activity and data diagrams; the diagrams are used not only to depict the system but also to generate a system

Figure 4.24 Transaction-Centered System

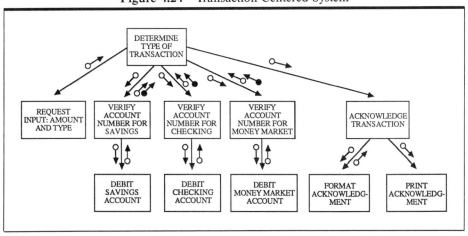

design. Although the particular design techniques differ in their rules of representation, they all produce a set of structure charts and/or data flow diagrams. Moreover, no matter how the design is represented, it must still be evaluated in terms of modularity, cohesion, coupling, and other design characteristics.

Rapid Prototyping

When a customer works with us to determine requirements, sometimes the customer is uncertain of exactly what is required or needed. The requirements analysis may yield a "wish list" of what the customer would like to see, but it is not clear whether the list is complete. In some situations, customers or users are involved in the analysis and design processes so that requirements can be modified as we examine available options. In other cases, the customer knows what is needed or wanted, but we are not certain whether the requirements are realistic. Here, we may investigate options to determine whether the customer's problem has a feasible solution. A technique known as **rapid prototyping** builds sections of the proposed system to determine the necessity, desirability, or feasibility of requirements. The term "rapid" distinguishes the prototype from that used in engineering, where a small system or subsystem is built after design is complete. In rapid prototyping, choices are evaluated before a design is created; the purpose of the rapid prototype is to help us decide on a final design.

Determining Customer Needs. Although a customer's needs are stated in the requirements definition, the customer is sometimes uncertain of details or options desired. By involving customers in design, various requirements or situations are demonstrated and customers can choose among them. For this reason, rapid prototyping is sometimes thought of as a requirements specification tool, rather than as a design technique. In either case, rapid prototyping helps us work with customers to determine what is really wanted or needed.

Let us look at an example to see what customer involvement means. Suppose Milly's Garage contracts with your company to develop a system that will track Milly's customers and their needs. The system is to automate what Milly now does manually:

1. Maintain information about the billing status of each of Milly's customers.

2. Maintain information about the maintenance status of each of Milly's customer's vehicles: when repairs were last done, when routine maintenance was last done, when different kinds of routine maintenance will be needed again.

3. Generate bills for each customer as necessary.

4. Generate reminders to customers when their routine maintenance is needed.

Since Milly does not have much experience with computers, she is not sure exactly what her new computer system can do. To help her, your company works with her in front of a display screen to generate a sample system or subsystem called a prototype. A **prototype** is all or part of a system that looks like the system under consideration but does not have the complete functionality of the real system. Thus, a prototype may have the screens, reports, and menus of the real system; but it does not really perform all the functions of the system. For example, Milly may look at a main system menu that allows her to choose either the billing subsystem or the maintenance subsystem. If she chooses the billing subsystem, she is presented with a menu that, among other things, allows her to "Print This Month's Bills." The actual billing information is not stored in the accompanying data base, so Milly cannot really print out her bills. However, Milly can examine what a bill would look like, how resulting reports would be formatted, and in what order the functions would be performed. This prototype gives her the opportunity to change her mind, try several options, and determine her preferences.

Alternatively, developing a prototype may help to validate the requirements specifications. By forcing us to put together the main components of the system quickly, we find out where our requirements are inconsistent or incomplete.

Prototyping involves both analysts and designers. Analysts explain Milly's options to her. The designers define the system modules, describe the data base and data structures needed, and generate algorithms for performing system functions. Questions of speed and efficiency must still be addressed. However, a prototype gives us the opportunity to "fine-tune" what our customers want or what we think will work best in a design. Thus, the prototype paints a preliminary picture of how some or all of the resulting system might appear.

Determining Feasibility. There are times when a customer requests a system or feature that we are not certain we can build. For example, a customer may ask for a data base management system on a particular microcomputer; we may not be sure that the microcomputer can handle the concurrent access and field-locking characteristics required. We can develop a prototype of the data base management system, implementing only those functions necessary to answer our questions.

Similarly, a feasibility prototype allows us to find out in the design stage whether the system will solve the problem at hand. Thus, a prototype encourages us to communicate with each other and our customers to explore areas that are not well-defined. Such exploration resolves many problems early in development and avoids the creation of many more during testing.

Prototyping Considerations. Prototyping does not replace design. Nowhere in the prototyping process is there a place to address the pockets of complexity that are identified when modularizing a design; although prototyping may be a useful addition to the design phase of a project, it can never replace real design. All but the most trivial problems require the system analyst's creativity and insight, that cannot be mechanized by an automated design tool.

In addition, prototyping is not as useful in function-strong systems as in data-strong ones. Since a prototype omits the details of functionality from the initial system, a prototype of a function-strong system is full of "holes" that must be filled in by the designer. Consequently, it is difficult for the customer to envision how the system will eventually work. Thus, the best candidates for prototyping are data-strong systems or subsystems that are simple and self-contained.

It is also possible to use different prototypes to investigate different aspects of the same system. For example, a small team may be used to generate a prototype for each of several aspects of a problem: one for the interface with the user, one for performance, one for the security, and so on. The final system is then a synthesis of the results generated by the individual prototypes.

When efficiency or real-time response is a key requirement of the system being built, the prototype may not satisfy the customer's needs. As long as the customer realizes that the prototype is a model, not a refined product, prototyping can be useful in helping both us and the customer understand what the system is to do. Because it encourages cooperation and communication, the generation of a prototype also enhances the relationship between customer and developer.

If a prototype is intended to demonstrate *feasibility* or *desirability*, we may not give the same careful attention to the design of the prototype that we would give to a real system. Rather than trying to fill the "holes" left in the prototype or salvage code for some of the prototype's models, we sometimes discard the prototype and build the actual system from scratch. Often a prototype is meant to be discarded; its development is helpful in identifying the unanticipated flaws in a large design. Brooks ([BRO78]) recommends building a system, throwing it away, and building it again. The second system will profit from the mistakes discovered in the process of building the first.

However, recent software engineering research has encouraged the use of rapid prototyping to build and save parts of the prototype for use in the actual system. By using care in defining and developing the tools that higher level modules use, a rapid prototype can answer questions about requirements and design at the same time that it provides building blocks for the final system. In this light, rapid prototyping incorporates specification, design, implementation, and testing in one step. The drawback is that this process must be rapid to be of any value. If the prototype cannot be built more quickly than the actual system, then it has not met its objective.

Thus, there are several trade-offs to be considered when deciding whether a prototype is appropriate for your project. Boehm, Gray, and Seewaldt ([BOE84]) have studied projects well suited to the use of prototypes. They found that products developed using prototypes performed about as well as those developed using traditional design techniques. In addition, 45% less effort was expended and 40% fewer lines of code were generated by the developers who used prototypes. The speed and efficiency of the systems developed with prototypes were almost the same as that of the traditionally developed systems.

Application Generators

In an ideal situation, once system requirements are specified, a designer can sit down at a computer terminal and "write" a system by describing the requirements to the computer. The computer, in turn, generates the system from the requirements. For some applications, such a computer or computer program is available. An **application generator** translates system requirements into the system itself to perform the application specified.

An example of an application generator will show you how the code is produced. The software on a Wang VS computer includes a program called List Management.

By answering questions and filling in forms on the screen, you can generate a complete system that allows you to create data files, add or delete records, modify records, and print out a variety of reports. You provide information to describe the characteristics of the fields of the data file. A data entry screen is generated automatically, and you can alter the order in which the data are entered, the spacing on the screen, and the error checking that is done. Then, you define procedures for querying the data file and printing reports. You design the application, but you neither design the system nor write code; all code is generated by the List Management program itself.

Similarly, the TableTalk package for the FOCUS data base management system presents a user with a menu of questions about data elements, formats, and reports. The user is guided from one set of questions to the next, and when the questions have been answered, TableTalk generates a complete set of FOCUS data bases and reports. The user need know nothing about FOCUS commands or formats; Table-Talk allows the user to move from requirements directly to working system.

Clearly, application generators can be of great benefit in developing a system. Because there is no code written, the program design, implementation, and testing steps in development disappear. The system testing phase is minimized, so the total development time for the system is very short. Users going from requirements to actual system very quickly can even consider the resulting system to be a prototype; after using the system for a while, users can revise their requirements and generate a second, more pleasing system. Figure 4.25 shows how an application generator can be employed in iterative development. The dashed line indicates that intermediate systems may be generated until both the customer and developer are satisfied.

Unfortunately, few systems can be generated with applications generators. The complexity of most systems exceeds the capabilities of applications generators currently available. In these cases, it may be useful to generate some subsystems with applications generators and then incorporate the subsystems in an overall design.

High-Level Languages and Design Tools. It is sometimes advantageous to use an automated design tool, especially when designing a large system. Automation makes the tracking of the parts of a system easier by capturing in a data base the following elements:

- The flow of information
- The functions to be performed by the system
- The data to be processed or produced by the system

By comparing system elements, the tool helps us make sure that nothing has been left out of the system design. Thus, the design data are evaluated to see whether the data, the interfaces, and parameters of all functions are completely defined.

In other words, the design tool takes over the tedious job of making sure that all pieces of the design are defined and fit consistently with other pieces of the design.

Figure 4.25   Application Generator in Herative Development

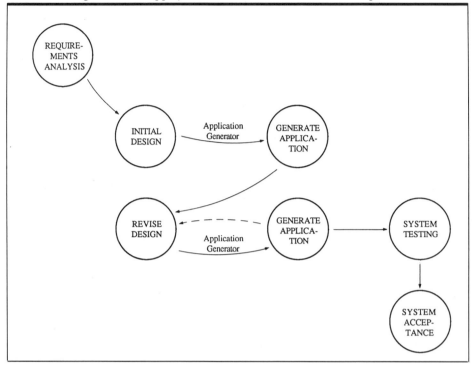

For example, if a function requires parameters PARM1, PARM2, and PARM3 in the data base, an automated tool can insure the following:

1. The function, PARM1, PARM2, and PARM3 are defined in the data dictionary.

2. Every time the function is invoked, the parameters PARM1, PARM2, and PARM3 have acceptable values in them.

3. Whenever the function is invoked, the function calls for all three parameters.

This type of analysis is similar to the checking done by a compiler. In fact, many of these tools are outgrowths of compilers or are high-level compilers themselves.

A worthwhile design tool makes the design clear and understandable to those who use it. Thus, appropriate design tools also depict the design in some consistent way. For example, there are automated tools available that draw structured design bubble charts on a computer display screen. You can manipulate the bubbles and arrows on the screen, and the tool automatically records the changes and adjusts supporting data structures accordingly. Figure 4.26 is an example of a data flow diagram produced by the Visible Systems Corporation (Concord, Massachusetts) Visible Analyst design package.

Figure 4.26 Example of Automated Design Tool

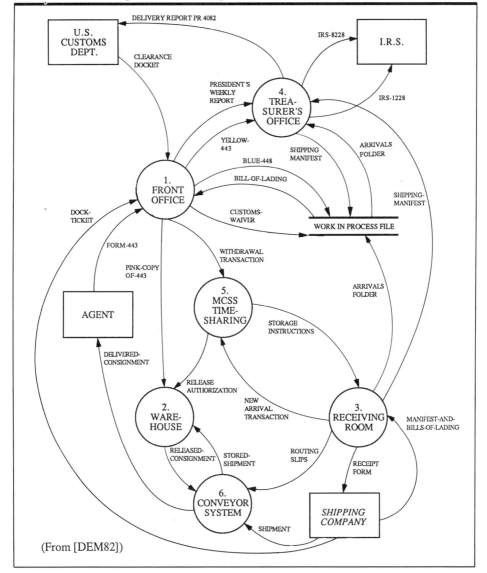

(From [DEM82])

Design languages and tools are also of great value in generating documentation of the design and in building a cross-reference between the design constructs and the system requirements. These capabilities allow the customer to trace the requirements and be assured that the system that is to be built will do everything that he or she wants it to do.

Design tools and languages do not *do* the design; they merely perform some of the repetitive or tedious tasks for us. As with prototyping, the complexities of the design can only be untangled by us, not by the supporting tools.

4.7

DESIGN EVALUATION AND VALIDATION

Once we have designed a system, we check it in two different ways. First, we make sure that the design satisfies all requirements specified by the customer. This procedure is known as **validation of the design**. Then we address the quality of the design: **verification of the design** involves insuring that the characteristics of a good design are incorporated, as we described earlier. Automated tools can help us with both verification and validation. However, these tools cannot perform the whole job. Moreover, we may have several designs or design decisions from which to choose, and we must decide which ones are most desirable. In the following section, we will investigate several ways of validating and verifying a design.

Mathematical Validation

Ideally, we would like to show formally that the system design is correct, in the sense that each system process correctly transforms the input of the process to its expected output. Some researchers have imposed a degree of mathematical rigor on validation by breaking the system into a set of processes. Associated with each process is a set of inputs, a set of expected outputs, and a set of assertions about the process. Then, for each such process, we demonstrate that

1. If the set of inputs is formulated correctly, it is transformed properly into the set of expected outputs.
2. The process terminates without error.

This procedure "proves" that the design is correct. However, to use it formally and to prove each small transformation mathematically correct can be time consuming and expensive. Thus, we usually use other, less formal methods to validate the design.

Weighted Matrices

If we are comparing several designs or design decisions, our comparison often involves the use of tables that highlight the characteristics of each design. To begin, we list desirable characteristics, independent of the design. Such a list might include the following characteristics:

1. Modularity
2. Testability
3. Maintainability
4. Efficiency
5. Ease of Understanding

6. Ease of Modification

7. Consistency

Then we associate a degree of importance to each characteristic by assigning a weight to it. For instance, if weights are chosen from 1 through 5 (with 5 being the highest or most desirable), we might rate a design according to the weights in Table 4.4.

Table 4.4   Weighted Design Criteria

Characteristic	Weight
Modularity	5
Testability	4
Maintainability	3
Efficiency	2
Ease of Understanding	3
Ease of Modification	3
Consistency	4

Next, we form a matrix, labeling the rows of the matrix with the characteristics in our table. The first column of the matrix contains the weights assigned in the previous step. In the remaining columns, we rate each design according to the criteria listed. If there are n designs to be compared, columns 2 through $n+1$ correspond to the designs. In each of these columns, we place a rating from 1 through 10, with 10 being the highest, so that the entry in the cell in the ith row and the jth column rates the design represented by column j in terms of how it satisfies the characteristic described by row i. For example, suppose Table 4.5 shows the matrix for comparing three designs according to the weights specified in Table 4.4. If the system described by design 2 is quite easy to understand, we may rate it an 8. Then, we place an 8 in the cell at the intersection of column 3 (corresponding to design 2) and row 5 (corresponding to the "Ease of Understanding" characteristic).

Table 4.5   Weighted Design Matrix

Characteristic	Weight	Design 1	Design 2	Design 3
Modularity	5	8	6	7
Testability	4	7	7	10
Maintainability	3	9	10	8
Efficiency	2	4	6	9
Ease of Understanding	3	10	8	8
Ease of Modification	3	9	9	8
Consistency	4	6	6	7

From this matrix, it is not obvious which is the best design. However, since some characteristics have higher weights than others, we can assign a score to each

Figure 4.27 Computing a Design's Score

Characteristics	Weight		Design 1		Design 2	Design 3
Modularity	⑤ →	㊵ ←	⑧		6	7
		+				
Testability	④ →	㉘ ←	⑦		7	10
		+				
Maintainability	③ →	㉗ ←	⑨		10	8
		+				
Efficiency	② →	⑧ ←	④		6	9
		+				
Ease of Understanding	③ →	㉚ ←	⑩		8	8
		+				
Ease of Modification	③ →	㉗ ←	⑨		9	8
		+				
Consistency	④ →	㉔ ←	⑥		8	7
		=184				

design by multiplying the weight of each characteristic by the rating for each design and summing. Thus, for each column, we multiply the row entry by the weight for that row and sum. Figure 4.27 shows how this calculation is done for design 1. If we sum the scores for the other two designs, what results is Table 4.6.

Table 4.6 Scores for Weighted Design Matrix

Characteristic	Weight	Design 1	Design 2	Design 3
Modularity	5	8	5	7
Testability	4	7	7	10
Maintainability	3	9	10	8
Efficiency	2	4	6	9
Ease of Understanding	3	10	8	8
Ease of Modification	3	9	9	8
Consistency	4	6	6	7
SCORE:		184	170	193

From this analysis, it is clear that the choice is design 3.

Design Reviews

When the design is complete, we meet with our customer to review the design and agree to continue with development. The review process is done in two steps, corresponding to the two parts of the design process. First, a **preliminary design review** occurs, where we examine the conceptual design with the customer. Then, in a **critical design review**, we present the technical design to other system developers to check the details before proceeding with program design. There are several activities involved in each step.

Preliminary Design Review. At a preliminary design review, we meet with the customer to validate the conceptual design. Several key people are invited to the review:

1. The customer(s) who helped to define the system requirements
2. The analyst(s) who helped to define the system requirements
3. The prospective user(s) of the system
4. The system designer(s)
5. A moderator
6. A secretary
7. System developers who are not otherwise involved in this project

The number of people actually at the review depends on the size and complexity of the system under development and the number and kinds of users. Every review team member should have the authority to act as a representative of his or her organization and to make decisions and commitments. The total number is kept small so that discussion and decision making are not hampered.

The moderator leads the discussion but has no vested interest in the project itself. He or she encourages discussion, acts as an intermediary between opposing viewpoints, keeps discussion moving, and maintains objectivity and balance in the process.

Because it is difficult to take part in the discussion and also record the main points and outcome, an individual is designated as secretary. The secretary does not get involved in the issues that arise; his or her sole job is to act as recorder. However, more than stenographic skills are required; the secretary must have enough technical knowledge to understand the proceedings and record relevant technical information.

There are two functions for the developers present who have not been previously involved with the project. First, they can be objective about the proposed design since they have no personal stake in it. Because they are developers themselves, they may have fresh ideas or a new slant on things. The second function of the "outsiders" is to act as a miniature quality assurance team. In participating in the review, they assume equal responsibility for the design with the designers themselves. This shared responsibility forces all in the review process to scrutinize every detail of the design.

We as system designers present the conceptual design to our audience. In doing so, we demonstrate that the system has the structure and characteristics requested by the customer in the requirements specification. Together, we all verify that the proposed system performs the intended functions. The required hardware, the interfaces with other systems, the input and the output are all checked. Then the customer approves the dialogs and menus, the report formats, and the proposed handling of errors. If the system is to be built in phases, we describe the characteristics and functionality of each phase.

Any discrepancies found are noted by the secretary and discussed by the group as a whole. We resolve minor issues as they appear. However, if major errors or misunderstandings arise, we may agree to revise the design. Another preliminary design review is then scheduled to evaluate the new design. Just as the Ehlers would rather redo the blueprints of their house than tear out the foundation and walls later and start again, we too would rather redesign the system now instead of later.

Critical Design Review. A successful preliminary design review is followed by the critical design review. Once the customer is happy with the proposed product, it is time for us to present the *technical* design to a group of technical people to scrutinize the technical specification. The audience for this design review consists of the following members:

1. The analyst(s) who helped to define the system requirements
2. The system designer(s)
3. A moderator
4. A secretary
5. The program designer(s) for this project
6. System developers who are not otherwise involved in this project

The functions of these team members are similar to those at the preliminary review. However, this audience has a more technical bent. The technical design is discussed, and the "outsiders" again participate to assure the quality of the design. The moderator controls the flow of discussion to insure that the focus of the review is on two major questions: Does the design implement all *requirements*, and is the design of high *quality*? Program designers are present not only to criticize the design but to understand it so that they can then derive their program design from it.

We usually present the design both in written and oral form. Using diagrams, data, or both, we explain how and why we made major design decisions. If we used design tools to generate the design, the output is available for the review team to examine. As before, if major problems are identified, the design is redone; a critical design review or both preliminary and critical reviews are scheduled, as necessary.

Value of Design Reviews. The design review process focuses on the *detection* of errors rather than on their *correction*. It is important to remember that those who participate are investigating the integrity of the *design*, not of the designers. Thus, the review is valuable in emphasizing to all concerned that they are working toward the same goal. The criticism and discussion during the design review is egoless, because comments are directed at the process and the product, not at the participants. Communication among the diverse members of the team is encouraged and enhanced by the review process.

Moreover, the process benefits everyone by finding errors and problems when they are easy and inexpensive to correct. It is far easier to change something in its abstract, conceptual stage than when it is already implemented. Much of the difficulty and expense of fixing errors late in development has to do with tracking the error to its source. If an error is spotted in the design review, we know that the problem is located somewhere in the design. However, if an error is not detected until the system is operational, the root of the problem may be in several places: the hardware, the software, the design, the implementation, or the documentation. The sooner we find a problem, the fewer places we have to look to find its cause and fix it.

4.8

DOCUMENTATION

One product of the design process is a document that describes the system to be built. As we saw, the first part of the description tells the customer in plain English what the system will do; the second part uses technical terminology where necessary to tell the program designers what the system will do. Thus, the kinds of things that the two parts contain will overlap, but the way of expressing them may not.

The system design document contains a section outlining the *critical issues and trade-offs* that were considered in generating the design. This guiding philosophy helps both the customer and the program designers to understand how and why certain parts of the design fit together.

The design also contains *descriptions of the components* of the system. One component addresses how the users interact with the system, including the following:

- Menus and other display screen formats
- Human interfaces: function keys, touch screen descriptions, keyboard layout, use of a mouse or joystick
- Report formats
- Input: where data comes from, how it is formatted, on what medium it is stored
- Output: where data is sent, how it is formatted, on what medium it is stored
- General functional characteristics
- Performance requirements
- Archival procedures
- Error handling requirements

A hierarchical diagram or some other figure exhibits the overall *organization and structure* of the system, including data flow as well as functional modularity. The various levels of module interaction are included.

If the system is distributed, the configuration in the design is detailed enough to show the *topology of the network*, how the the network nodes will access one another, and the allocation of functions to the nodes. If the system requirements include constraints on timing, or if the nodes of the network must be synchronized, the design describes how the *timing* will work. Similarly, control and routing of messages are included. The design may also include prescriptions for the *integrity* of the network: making sure the data is accurate or can be recovered after a failure.

If the customer requires it, elements of the design may address *monitoring system performance*. In addition, there may be a manual override of the system, and the design describes how it will work. Other requirements may include *fault location and isolation*, *reconfiguration* of the system, or special *security* measures. The design explains how these requirements are addressed.

Finally, the design is *cross-referenced with the requirements* to demonstrate how the design components are derived from them. This forces us to check for completeness and consistency. In addition, such a cross-reference will make enhancements or modifications easier to track later. For example, if a requirement changes, the cross-reference points to the corresponding design changes needed.

4.9
RESOURCE TRACKING AND SIMULATION EXAMPLE

As we have seen, design can depend on many things: the requirements, the use of automated tools, the type of system, the type of design discipline used, and so on. We can examine our Weaver Farm example to see how the system design process might work.

If we choose a decomposition approach to design, we begin by trying to describe the system from the top down as a set of modules. We want the modules to differ by function. Thus, our first draft of a design may look like Figure 4.28, where a main module decides which of the basic functions to perform: accessing the data base of resources and facilities, simulating activities, generating a maintenance schedule, or changing user access and security privileges.

Next, we reconsider each module in Figure 4.28 to see what additional information may be needed. For example, the module to generate a maintenance schedule should also determine the range of dates, the types of facilities, and the areas of Weaver Farm to be included. Then the data flow diagram might be amended to look like Figure 4.29.

The second level of decomposition describes each of the boxes of this figure in more detail. For instance, the maintenance function may either add new informa-

Figure 4.28   Weaver Farm Main Module

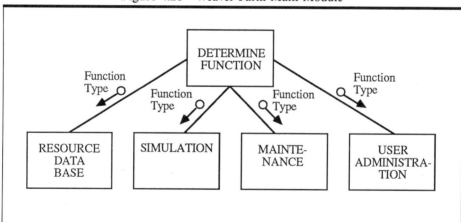

Figure 4.29 Weaver Farm Main and Maintenance Modules in Detail

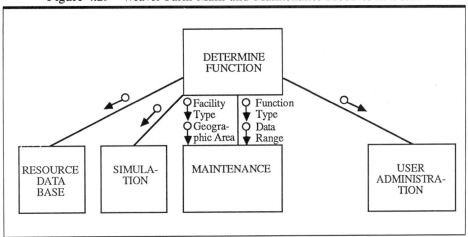

tion to the facilities data base or request information. In Figure 4.30, we see how this detail could be diagrammed. The double bar at the bottom of the figure illustrates a data base that is defined to hold the facilities information. No further detail about the data base is needed on the diagram. A data dictionary accompanies the set of diagrams to define each data element and its component parts. In this case, the entry in the data dictionary defining the facilities information data base might be similar to Table 4.7.

Figure 4.30 Second Level of Weaver Farm Design

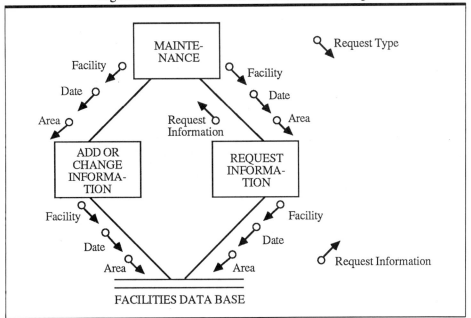

Table 4.7   Data Dictionary Entry

Record: Facility Type		
Key: Facility Type Number		
Fields:		
Facility Type Name	20 characters	Alphabetic
Facility Type Number	9 characters	Numeric
Length	9 characters	Numeric
Width	9 characters	Numeric
Height	9 characters	Numeric
Electricity	1 character	Alphabetic
Water	1 character	Alphabetic
Gas	1 character	Alphabetic
Telephone	1 character	Alphabetic
Record: Facility		
Keys: Facility Type Number, Facility Number		
Fields:		
Facility Name	20 characters	Alphabetic
Facility Type Number	9 characters	Numeric
Facility Number	5 characters	Numeric
Latitude	6 characters	Numeric
Longitude	6 characters	Numeric
Last Maintenance Date	6 characters	Alphabetic

We continue to refine the modules in the design until each describes exactly one function and there are data descriptions for the entire system. As we design, we check our design for the characteristics outlined in this chapter: modularity, cohesion, coupling, information hiding, low fan-in, and so on.

Now we reach an important point in the design process. After reviewing the design as a whole, we decide whether the design is of acceptable quality. Are there aspects of the design that should be different or could be better? Is the design clear enough to be understood by someone else? This is the point in the development process when it is easiest to reconsider and redesign. A poor design decision now will require much time and resources to fix or change later. If necessary, we discard the previous design; then we redesign to construct a set of modules that is "better" than the previous design but performs the same functions.

For example, the design depicted in Figure 4.28 is a transaction-centered system. It has a module with high fan-out. What implications might that have for implementation, testing, and maintenance? Would it be better to redesign with a transform-centered system?

Once we decide on the system's modular structure, we enhance the design by describing its interface with users. To accompany this design, we sketch illustrations of the display screens we will use, the report formats we will generate, and so on. These formats are based on several things:

1. The requirements set forth by the customer

2. Our knowledge of human factors

3. Our experience in designing similar systems

For example, we may choose to place a certain number of fields in a report based on what the customer requests, what is pleasing to the eye, and what can fit on an 8-1/2 × 11-inch piece of paper with a 12-pitch type font.

If we decide to distribute the processing among several computers, the system design should describe which nodes will perform what functions. If our four major modules are independent, then the functional boxes can each be decomposed into separate subsystems. The dependencies among the functions are detailed, and the communication among the nodes of the system must be described.

If we plan to have a phased development of the Weaver Farm system, we must divide the functions of the overall system into groups of functions or subfunctions that will be performed at each phase. For instance, a particular function may need to be implemented only partially in one phase and then fully in a later phase. In effect, then, we are turning one large system into a *series* of several slightly smaller systems. This *may not* reduce the complexity of the design. Often, a phased development is employed so that the users, who are accustomed to a different system, will be able to learn and operate the new system slowly; otherwise, they might be overwhelmed by the automated system in its entirety.

Once the design is complete (that is, it incorporates all the customer requirements), it is presented both as a conceptual and a technical design. The conceptual design includes descriptions of the input screens and output reports but does not explain the modular breakdown of the system; the module definitions are described only in the technical design.

Similarly, the conceptual design explains options available to users at any point in the system's processing, while the technical design describes which modules control what stages of the system's processing. For example, the conceptual design contains a section that reads:

One choice from the main system menu will be a user administration function. It will allow the operator to:

1. Define a user identification code and password for each user (3.4.1).

2. Grant or deny user access to files and libraries (3.4.2).

3. Grant or deny user access to terminals (3.4.4).

4. Grant or deny user access to printers (3.4.6).

5. Grant or deny access to the maintenance function (3.6.1).

6. Grant or deny access to the simulation function (3.7.1).

The numerical references show which requirements generated the design functions.

The technical design describes the same function by describing the modules that perform it. Module descriptions are presented in any way that is consistent with the design technique or tool used. Thus, the user administration function can be defined by displaying a set of data flow diagrams, similar to those shown in Figures 4.28, 4.29, and 4.30 for maintenance.

4.10

CHAPTER SUMMARY

Noting that design is both a process and a product, we have seen how the design of a system generates a product for two audiences: the customer and the program designers. First, the conceptual design tells the customer how the requirements have been translated into a system. Second, a technical design explains the system to the program designers. The resulting design can be judged by several criteria, including the modularity of the design, the amount of information-hiding and abstraction, the cohesion and coupling of the modules, and the completeness of the specification. Several techniques have been presented for simplifying the problem and then generating the design as a proposed solution. We have seen how to compare several designs and pick the most desirable in terms of characteristics and customer satisfaction. Then the review process allows us to scrutinize the proposed design, revise it if necessary, and obtain the approval of both the customer and the program designers. Without this approval, we cannot proceed to the program design stage; we cannot implement a solution until we have solved the problem to the customer's satisfaction.

In the next chapter, we will examine how the program designers transform the system design into descriptions of modules that can then be coded and implemented.

4.11

EXERCISES

1. For each type of cohesion, write a description of a module exhibiting that kind of cohesion.

2. For each type of coupling, give an example of two modules coupled in that way.

3. For a project that you have already developed for another class, draw a system diagram of your software using multiple levels of interconnected modules. How modular was your system? What kind of coupling did it exhibit? Were the modules cohesive? Can your system be restructured to increase the cohesion and decrease the coupling of the modules?

4. Can a system ever be completely "decoupled"? That is, can the degree of coupling be reduced so much that there is no coupling between modules?

5. Are there some systems that cannot be made completely functionally cohesive? Why or why not?

6. Boolean algebra tells us that the sum of a variable and its complement is 1. Use this property to verify that the formulae for the decision table variables in Table 4.2 are equivalent to the simpler formulae in Table 4.3.

7. Draw data flow and structure diagrams for a full-screen editor on a video display terminal. The editor allows text to be inserted, deleted, and modified. Sections of text can be "cut" from one part of the file and "pasted" to another part of the file. The user can specify a text string, and the editor can find the next occurrence of that string. Through the editor, the user can specify margin settings, page length, and tab settings.

8. Draw data flow and structure diagrams for a BASIC interpreter. Thus, your system will accept a string of characters, and determine if it is a valid command in the BASIC language. Write an error message if it is not valid, and execute the command if it is.

9. Draw data flow and structure diagrams for a system that controls building temperature based on thermostat readings in various rooms.

10. Draw data flow and structure diagrams for a grocery store check-out counter system that prints the bill and updates the inventory. Thus, as a customer makes a purchase, the system queries a data base to determine the price of the item, prints the price on the bill, and updates the inventory data base to show that one less item is in stock.

11. A **recursive module** is one that calls itself or in some way refers to itself. Given the design guidelines presented in this chapter, is a recursive module a good or a bad idea? Why?

12. Give an example of a transaction-centered system. Give an example of a transform-centered system. In terms of the characteristics of a good system design, is a transform-centered system better than a transaction-centered system? Why or why not?

13. Give an example of a system for which developing a prototype would not result in saving significant amounts of development time.

14. List the characteristics of a system for which prototyping is most appropriate.

15. Explain why modularity and application generators are inseparable concepts. Give an example of an application generator with which you have worked.

16. Can a spreadsheet package be considered a prototype or an application generator for a system? Why or why not?

17. List the characteristics that you might put in a design evaluation matrix. For each of the following systems, identify the weights you might use: an operating system, a word processing system, a satellite tracking system.

18. Many of your class projects require you to develop your programs by your-self. Assemble a small group of students to perform a design review for the design of one such project. Have several students play the role of the customer and users. Be sure to express all requirements and system charac-teristics in nontechnical terms for the preliminary design review. Then hold a critical design review. List all changes that are suggested by the review process. Compare the time required to make the changes at the design stage to that of changing your existing programs.

19. You have been hired by a computer consulting firm to develop an income tax calculation package for an accounting firm. You have designed a system according to the customer's requirements, and you are presenting your design at a design review. Which of the following questions might be asked at the preliminary design review? at the critical design review? at both? Explain your answers.

    a. What computer will it run on?
    b. What will the input screens look like?
    c. What reports will be produced?
    d. How many concurrent users will there be?
    e. Will you use a multi-user operating system?
    f. What are the details of the depreciation algorithm?

CHAPTER 5

PROGRAM DESIGN

We noted in chapter 1 that system development is both an art and a science. In keeping with development's "scientific" aspect, the next few chapters will investigate ways of planning and structuring the analysis and design processes to improve the quality of the final product. As we can see in Figure 5.1, we are about to translate a carefully planned and well-structured design into specifications for programs that will actually perform the work.

We begin by discussing the nature of program design and how it differs from system design. Next, we list several guidelines to be followed when creating a program design. We look not only at the way in which modules are related to one another but also at the characteristics of the modules themselves. Once we are able to recognize a good design, we examine a variety of design tools that can be useful in documenting the design and in checking for consistency.

Design quality is extremely important; the better the design, the less likely we are to require major changes later in development. Thus, we investigate techniques for evaluating and improving a design. One way to improve a design is to subject it to a design review. We explain what is involved in such reviews and why they are important. Finally we apply design techniques and tools to the resource tracking and simulation system we have been developing.

5.1

WHAT IS PROGRAM DESIGN?

The system design explains exactly how the system will work in terms of data flow and transformation. However, its module descriptions are not written so that programmers can write code directly from the design. There is one more step before the coding can begin. **Program design** defines modules and intermodular interfaces so that each module of the system design corresponds to a new set of modules containing *program specifications*. In turn, the **program specifications** for a module are instructions to a programmer that describe the input, output, and processing to be performed by the module. The specifications are technical and detailed. They reference specific data formats and describe the steps of any algorithms to be used.

The modules of the system design can be traced back to the requirements that generated the description of the system. By relating the program design to the

185

Figure 5.1   The System Development Process

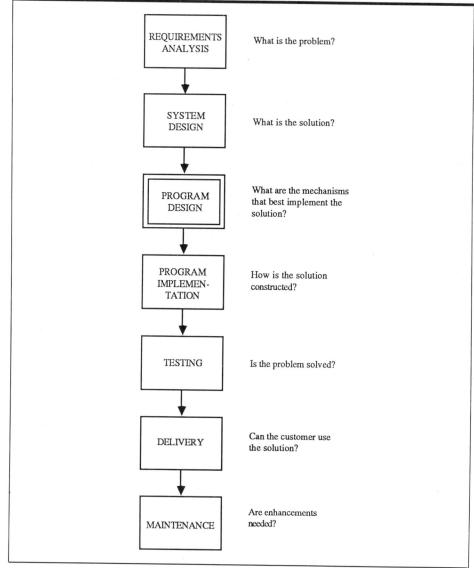

system design, the correspondence between function and requirements is maintained. We show this relationship in Figure 5.2.

We saw in chapter 4 that a modular system design isolates the areas of complexity involved in the problem to be solved. In other words, some parts of the system perform routine functions: reading a tape, sorting a list, or printing a report. However, there are always *pockets of difficulty* in a system that make the solution to this problem different from solutions to other problems. These inherent knots of complexity demand the creativity of designers and programmers; this creativity is what distinguishes the "art" of system building from the "science."

Figure 5.2 Relationship among Requirements, System Design, and Program Design

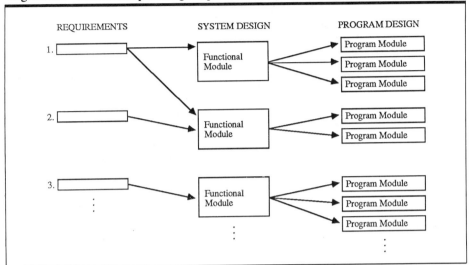

Program design expands on the system design but differs significantly from it. In the system design, data items and structures are described in a relatively *abstract* way. For example, the system design may specify that a certain set of values be represented conceptually in a matrix. The program designers decide what data structure to use to implement the matrix; for instance, special sparse matrix techniques may be most appropriate. (A sparse matrix is one where most of the entries of the matrix are zero. If the matrix is large, it is often desirable to keep track of only the non-zero entries, thus saving space.)

The program design also provides more detail about algorithms. For example, the system design may specify that a module is to sort a list; the program design identifies what sorting algorithm is to be used. The *increased level of detail* in the program design presents enough information about each module so that programmers can code the module in a fairly straightforward manner.

Thus program design modules contain descriptions of the processing logic needed to implement the corresponding system design module, including

- Detailed algorithms
- Data representations and structures
- Relationships among the functions performed and the data used

Each module can then be coded as a procedure, a subroutine, a function, or some other type of nameable object.

Program design is a necessary step in development because it allows a final refinement of the ideas behind the system's structure before construction of a working system begins. Thus, program design allows us to fine-tune *what* we plan to do before we consider *how* to do it. The program design focuses on the *semantics* of the system (that is, the meanings of the parts of the system); the implementation then turns to questions of *syntax* (that is, the arrangement of the parts).

5.2

DESIGN GUIDELINES

Program design involves creativity, so we follow a set of design *guidelines*, rather than a set of hard and fast rules. These guidelines allow us some flexibility in creating and documenting the resulting design modules.

Our first consideration is whether to examine the system modules from most general to more detailed, to begin with the detailed modules and work up to the more general, or use some combination of both. As with system design, no approach is better than another; each has its merits.

Top-down Approach

There are many advantages to approaching the program design from the highest or most general level. In other words, a *top-down* analysis examines all modules but first translates higher levels to more concrete program specifications before descending to lower levels. At any point, only data and control information and structures necessary for a module are defined. The details of the design at lower levels remain hidden. In particular, data structures and algorithms need not be known to the highest level modules.

Bottom-up Approach

Sometimes we prefer to design using the *bottom-up* approach, beginning with the lowest levels of the design, rather than the highest. We may prefer working from the detailed to the general when our system design was generated by a composition technique such as data abstraction, rather than decomposition. By starting with the lowest levels, we identify common functions that can be used by many of the higher level modules. Then, one utility function can be shared by several higher level functions. For example, a bottom-up design may reveal that several modules must sort a list. As program designers we may decide to define a sort procedure that can be called from the other modules. Similarly, we can define common routines to perform syntax checking, encryption, stack manipulation, or other functions.

Our goal in "pooling resources" this way is to make the system more efficient. However, there is often a trade-off: by allowing several modules to control a common module, we may lose many of the desirable design characteristics described in chapter 4. Coupling among modules usually increases, since more control mechanisms are needed and since more data may be passed or shared by modules. This increased coupling makes detecting and correcting an error or changing a function later in the life of the system much more difficult. In addition, it is sometimes hard to maintain the degree of information hiding originally designed into the system. Consequently, bottom-up program design is employed only when its advantages outweigh these disadvantages.

Modularity and Functional Independence

Modularity is a key factor in good program design, just as it was in a system design. The working of the system was broken into modules so that distinct functions could be isolated from one another. This isolation should be maintained in the program design. The advantage to this approach is that removing a module deletes exactly one function from the system. This characteristic makes testing and maintenance much easier. For example, we can test one component at a time, adding a function to the system as each test is completed. If the customer requests that the system change in some way, the modularity allows us to identify quickly the affected modules; functional independence assures us that revising only those modules will implement the change.

We rely on modularity to isolate those system parts that depend on hardware or packaged software mandated by the customer's requirements. If the system is to be moved to a different hardware configuration or to be supported by a different software package, the impact of the changes can be minimized. Often a system is developed initially on one kind of computer system and then moved to or duplicated on another. For example, a payroll system may be built initially on a large mainframe computer; later, the customer wants a similar system to run on a set of microcomputers. Or, a data acquisition system is implemented on a particular vendor's minicomputer; later, when more functions are needed, the customer wants the system moved to another vendor's superminicomputer. We will consider the effects of testing and change in more detail in chapters 7, 8, and 10.

Examination of Algorithms

In generating a program design, we refine the algorithms specified by the system design. First, we determine whether the algorithm is always *correct*. This step may sound strange, but some algorithms work for data satisfying a certain condition but do not work otherwise. Second, we consider the *efficiency* of the algorithm by investigating the system resources it requires. Finally, we determine whether the algorithm is *appropriate* for the particular hardware and software specified in the system design.

Correctness of the Algorithm. Let us look at an example of an algorithm to see when it is correct. You may be familiar with an array of numbers known as a *magic square*, a set of positive integers arranged in n rows and n columns so that the sum of the numbers in any row or any column or on any diagonal is the same. A sample magic square with three rows and three columns is shown in Figure 5.3. As you can see, any row, column, or diagonal sums to 30. Magic squares can be used in a variety of ways. For instance, suppose each number in the grid signifies the allocation of a particular kind of resource. The numbers are arranged in the grid so that the sum of a row or the sum of a column signifies a measure of the total allocation of resources. A manufacturing system may be assigning resources to the production of products, for example, so building a magic square may represent a required or optional allocation of resources.

Figure 5.3   3 × 3 Magic Square

16	2	12
6	10	14
8	18	4

Here is an algorithm to build a magic square of n rows and n columns where n is any odd positive integer.

1. Draw a grid of n rows and n columns.

2. Determine the set of numbers that is to fill the grid. It can be any set of positive integers as long as it forms a sequence that increases by a uniform amount. (In other words, the sequence must be of the form $a, a + s, a + 2s, a + 3s, \ldots, a + (n^2 - 1)s$.)

3. Place the lowest number in the sequence in the center cell of the top row of the grid.

4. Enter the next number of the sequence in the cell that is one row above and one cell to the right. Consider the bottom rows to be the row "above" the top row, and the leftmost column to be the one to the "right" of the rightmost. Thus, if a move leaves the top of the grid, make the entry in the bottom cell of the column to the right. If a move leaves the rightmost column of the grid, make the entry in the leftmost cell of the row above.

5. If the move in step 4 is impossible because that cell is already occupied, make the entry in the cell immediately below the previous entry, thus beginning a new diagonal. Consider the top row to be "below" the bottom row.

6. Repeat steps 4 and 5 until every cell contains a number.

Figure 5.4 shows how a magic square can be constructed using this algorithm and the numbers 1 through 9. This algorithm works only when n is odd and when the entries in the cells of the grid satisfy the condition described in step 2. The algorithm must be changed to apply to magic squares where n is even since step 3 cannot be followed in that case. (Exercise 5.1 investigates the algorithm to see how it can be expanded to other cases.)

If an algorithm such as this one were proposed in our system design, we would note that it is correct only under certain conditions. Once we determine the conditions for which the algorithm is correct, we decide whether the algorithm works for all instances that might occur when the system is functioning. We may

Figure 5.4 Construction of a Magic Square

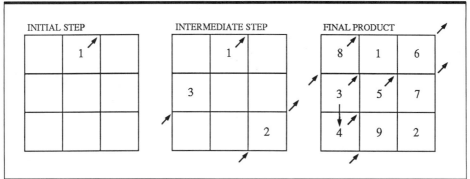

include a check on data before it is used with this algorithm. Thus, in this case, the program design notes that the algorithm is correct only for odd values of n. In addition, the design indicates that the program module should test n and report an error if n is not odd.

Efficiency of the Algorithm. After having determined when and whether an algorithm is sufficient for the purposes of the module, we consider the amount of time or memory required by the algorithm. For example, the system design may specify that a list of length n is to be sorted into alphabetical order. A procedure known as a *bubble sort* can be used to sort the list. Let the elements of the list be labeled $A(1), A(2), \ldots, A(n)$. Then the bubble sort can be described in the following way:

1. Set POINTER $= n - 1$.

2. If POINTER < 1, stop.

3. Set SWITCH = FALSE.

4. For I = 1 to POINTER, if $A(I)$ and $A(I+1)$ are out of order, exchange them and set SWITCH to TRUE.

5. Decrement POINTER by 1.

6. If SWITCH is FALSE, stop; otherwise, go to step 2.

This process compares successive pairs of elements, exchanging them when they are out of order. The process is repeated until the entire list is scanned and no change is made. Each execution of step 4 involves an average of $n/2$ comparisons. On the average, steps 3 through 5 are executed $n/2$ times. This means that the expected total number of comparisons is $n^2/4$. Thus, we say that the complexity of this algorithm is of *order* n^2. For example, if a list has one thousand entries, we expect one million comparisons.

By knowing how many comparisons to expect, we can compare two algorithms to determine which one is likely to use fewer machine resources. This measure of algorithm efficiency is a property of the *algorithm itself*, not of the programming of the algorithm. Therefore, to improve the system efficiency, we may want to specify a more efficient algorithm in our program design.

One of many sort algorithms that are more efficient is the *Quicksort* ([HOA71]). Much of the bubble sort's inefficiency rests with the fact that large elements "bubble" to the end only one position at a time. However, the Quicksort avoids adjacent exchanges. Instead, it designates an element as a dividing point in such a way that all elements above the dividing point are less than the dividing point and all elements below are greater. Thus, the original list is divided into two smaller lists (neither of which is ordered itself); then, the two smaller lists are sorted independently. To sort a list $A(1)$, $A(2)$, . . . , $A(n)$ into ascending order, the Quicksort algorithm works in the following way ([HUG78]):

1. Define a stack called LISTS_TO_SORT. The stack contains pairs of elements of A. Place the pair $(A(1), A(n))$ on the stack.

2. Do steps 3 through 7 while LISTS_TO_SORT is not empty.

3. Remove last pair from LISTS_TO_SORT stack.

4. Set LEFT_POINTER to the first element of that pair and RIGHT_END be the second element of the pair.

5. Do steps 5 and 6 while LEFT_POINTER < RIGHT_POINTER.

6. {Move the left pointer as far as possible:}
   Do while (A(LEFT−POINTER) <= A(RIGHT_POINTER))
      LEFT_POINTER = LEFT_POINTER + 1
      If (LEFT_POINTER >= RIGHT_POINTER) go to step 7.
   End
   {Have found an element out of order: move the left element to the right side.}
   Exchange A(LEFT_POINTER) with A(RIGHT_POINTER).

7. {Now move the right pointer as far as possible:}
   Do while (A(LEFT−POINTER) <= A(RIGHT_POINTER))
      RIGHT_POINTER = RIGHT_POINTER − 1
      If (LEFT_POINTER >= RIGHT_POINTER) go to step 7.
   End
   {Have found an element out of order: move the left element to the right side.}
   Exchange A(LEFT_POINTER) with A(RIGHT_POINTER).

8. {Now RIGHT_POINTER is the dividing point. Split the list into two and sort each independently (but avoid sorting empty lists):}
   If (RIGHT_POINTER − 1) > LEFT_END, put the pair
      (A(LEFT_END), A(RIGHT_POINTER − 1)) on
      LISTS_TO_SORT.
   If (RIGHT_POINTER + 1) < RIGHT_END, put the pair
      (A(RIGHT_POINTER + 1), A(RIGHT_END)) on
      LISTS_TO_SORT.

Knuth ([KNU73]) demonstrates that the number of comparisons made in this algorithm is proportional to $n \log_2 n$. Thus, in a list of one thousand elements we can expect ten thousand comparisons: a substantial savings over the one million of the bubble sort.

These efficiency calculations assume that the algorithms are operating on arbitrary lists. However, the system design may provide us with additional information that may affect the algorithm's efficiency. For example, the list of 1,000 elements may be formed by appending several out-of-order records to an existing sorted file. If there are k out-of-order elements appended to sorted list of $n-k$ elements (for a total list of n elements), a bubble sort will terminate with at most $(k+1)n$ comparisons. Thus, if ten out-of-order elements head a list of 1,000, the bubble sort requires *at most* 11,000 comparisons (but probably fewer). In the extreme case, Quicksort on a list of n elements that already are in order will require n^2 comparisons to terminate, while the bubble sort requires only n. Thus, even though the bubble sort algorithm is inherently slower than Quicksort *on the average*, in specific applications the bubble sort may be preferable.

In general, after determining the efficiency of an algorithm, we then improve the efficiency in several ways. The most powerful method is to find another algorithm with a *lower order of complexity*. We can also *restrict the problem* so that some calculations are eliminated (for cases that will never occur). Sometimes, some calculations can be made in advance of the actual use of the algorithm so that those calculations are done once instead of on every iteration of a loop in the algorithm.

A wise choice of *data structures* may also reduce the time or memory required to implement a particular algorithm. For example, a system design for an encryption module may call for determining whether or not a particular number is prime. (A positive integer is **prime** if its only integer divisors are 1 and itself.) One algorithm for testing whether a number n is prime is to successively divide n by all integers less than or equal to the square root of n. If n is greater than 2, we can reduce the number of calculations by dividing n only by odd numbers less than or equal to the square root of n. However, an algorithm known as the Sieve of Eratosthenes reduces the number of calculations even more. (Exercise 2, page 234, investigates this algorithm.) The sieve method keeps track of primes in a data array. One way of increasing the efficiency of the algorithm, then, is to structure the data array so that search time is minimized.

The analysis of algorithms and the determination of their complexity are explored more fully in other texts. For more information, see Bentley's *Programming Pearls* ([BEN86]).

Interpretation of the Algorithm. In many cases, an algorithm can be implemented in several ways with radically different results. For instance, two types of computers might perform calculations in different ways and with differing levels of precision. The word length of the computer or the existence of a floating-point co-processor can affect execution time and degree of precision. We want to construct algorithms whose interpretation is unambiguous and whose correctness is assured.

In addition, we want our program design to be as free as possible from hardware and software-package constraints. In other words, we do not want to include any compiler-specific algorithms at this stage of development. (In this way, our program design can be implemented easily on other hardware and software configurations.) It may not be possible to verify that our design is free of these constraints. Nevertheless, we try to scrutinize algorithms carefully. We do not want constraints to trap us when our program design is interpreted by the programmers.

For example, suppose a design specifies that a module is to use a variable I to calculate the number of the current week (between 1 and 52) and print out the result. The algorithm refers to I in the calculation, and the design states that I is to be printed. This specification would be clearer to the programmers if the design explains that the algorithm should print the current week, rather than the value of I.

Examination of the Data Types

Often, the way in which we define types of data in the system leads not only to clarity but also to consistency and higher reliability. For example, we may declare that numbers be partitioned into discrete and real numbers.

```
NUMBER = (DISCRETE, REAL)
```

Then, the data types can be further divided.

```
DISCRETE = (ENUMERATION, INTEGER)
REAL = (FIXED, FLOAT)
```

We can use data types to group together similar objects. For example, we may define a new type by listing its values:

```
type DAY is (MONDAY, TUESDAY, WEDNESDAY, THURSDAY, FRIDAY, SATURDAY, SUNDAY)
```

This definition is easier to follow than an encoding of the type characteristics, such as MONDAY = 1, TUESDAY = 2 and WEDNESDAY = 3, and so on. Using types allows us to concentrate on the application, rather than on data representation. Typing data also enhances modification and correction, since data definitions occur in one place and make the design more readable.

We can declare subtypes of a given type in a similar way. A **subtype** does not define a new type; instead, it places constraints on an existing type. Constraints can be checked to insure that an object always contains permissible values. For example, we can define subtypes of the type DAY as follows:

```
subtype WEEKDAY is DAY range MONDAY . . . FRIDAY
subtype WEEKEND is DAY range SATURDAY, SUNDAY
```

Another way to define a type is to declare it to be equal to an existing type. These types are called **derived types**, and the existing type is the **parent type**. For example, if INTEGER is the parent type, we can derive TEMPERATURE from it.

```
type TEMPERATURE is new INTEGER
```

The two types are logically distinct. The distinction allows us to keep types of data separate but to perform similar operations on them (such as addition and subtraction).

Once these data categories are developed, rules for checking the various types can be defined. In this way, *abstraction* is built into the design. Not only are the design and code more readable, but many errors are avoided. Finally, data typing results in a *portable* design. The components of the design are kept separate from their representation or implementation as data, so a change of environment does not require a redesign of the system.

Module Characteristics

Until now, we have discussed general guidelines for program design. Now, we turn to characteristics of the modules themselves, investigating first the content of each module and then the structure.

Module Types. As program designers, we consider each module in light of several factors. The first is the way in which the module is activated. Some modules follow each other in an unvarying sequence; every time the system is used, the modules are invoked in the same sequence. For example, the billing system for a company reads a list of sales for the week and prints the corresponding invoices for its customers. This system runs the same way each week, requires no interaction with the computer operator after the tape of weekly sales is mounted, and runs overnight.

However, a hospital has a computer-based system to monitor its nuclear medicine treatment facility. The system receives information every thirty seconds from hundreds of radiation sensors placed around the hospital. The sensor data are analyzed, and reports are printed daily. However, if analysis of the sensor data indicates that certain levels of radiation are exceeded, the normal running of the hospital is interrupted and special modules are invoked to isolate the area and do whatever is required to respond to the emergency quickly. In this case, the modules of the emergency system do not run the same way each week. They are invoked by *interrupts* from the system. These interrupts are events that are sensitive to a condition or threshold and can occur at any time.

A real-time system always uses interrupts. For instance, much of a computer's operating system is interrupt-driven. We should examine the system we are building to see which modules are invoked by interrupts; those modules are then scrutinized to see if the data they manipulate are structured to allow irregular access. The operating system can be interrupted by a module of the system or by the operating system itself.

We then consider the *degree* to which a module can be interrupted. Most modules begin by executing their first statement. However, when processing is interrupted by another module, we generally want to return eventually to the point of interruption (as with a subprocedure call). For example, the tasks running on the hospital system may be interrupted by a controlling module so that an emergency may be handled. When the modules dealing with emergency functions are complete, the module returns control to the nonemergency task. A module that can be interrupted prior to the completion of its processing and restarted later at the point at which it was interrupted is called an **incremental module**. This kind of module is useful for the hospital's monitoring system; after the emergency is over, normal processing continues where it left off. It would be inappropriate to interrupt a task and then restart the task from the beginning; such a situation would waste enormous amounts of processing time and resources. Furthermore, the previously-executed code may include statements whose reexecution can cause errors (such as incrementing a field).

In some cases, several modules invoke the same module at the same time. For instance, a time-shared system may have a set of modules to perform word processing and edit text. Rather than have a copy of the text editing software for each user, the system can be designed so that the text editing modules can execute simultaneously for several users. A module that works in this way is called a **reentrant** or **parallel module**.

A reentrant module is often found in time-sharing or multiprogramming systems. It must be designed so that it can be invoked by one module, interrupted without having completed its processing, invoked by another module (and perhaps not completing its processing), and then returned to the first point of interruption without losing any information. Associated with each interrupting module is information about where the processing stopped when the interruption occurred.

Figure 5.5 shows how module A might be invoked at time T1 and interrupted at time T2. The data file associated with A is updated to show where processing stopped, while module B begins its processing at the top at time T3. Then module B is interrupted at T4 (and appropriate information is stored in a data file) while A

Figure 5.5   A Reentrant Module

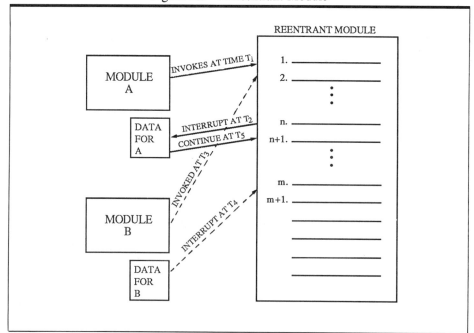

resumes processing at T5. It is not necessary that the times be distinct; A and B may be executing the same reentrant module at the same time.

Special techniques are used in designing and implementing reentrant modules; however, a discussion of the techniques is beyond the scope of this book. For more information, see Bray and Pokrass ([BRA85]).

Single Entry–Single Exit. Each module in the system design was organized to have a single entry point and a single exit. Where possible,the single entry-single exit approach should be carried over to the program design. Since modularization divides the system into small pieces that perform only one function, a single entry-single exit structure makes it easier for us to:

- Consider all possibilities in testing the module
- Trace errors
- Modify the module later during the life of the system

If we find a particular module so complex that multiple entries and exits are needed, we should reevaluate the overall design and perhaps create additional modules to perform smaller pieces of the original task.

Sometimes it is difficult to preserve single entry-single exit. Exception handling is often done by one module, where different conditions enter or exit a module at different places. It is often desirable to handle exceptions within one such module or to structure modules with several early exits for exceptions. By trying to preserve single entry-single exit, we may need extra control mechanisms; this can increase coupling among modules and make the result difficult to understand. As designers, we must balance the advantages of single entry-single exit with the need for a clearly defined exception handling policy.

Packaging

An abstract design must be enhanced or modified to incorporate constraints placed on it by the physical environment in which the system will operate. **Packaging** is the refinement of a design to allow the system to work in a proposed environment. This environment can involve a particular computer; special hardware; a specified operating system, software package, or programming language; storage limitations; time constraints; and a host of other items. When considering packaging, we move from the general to the particular and lose the abstraction we have achieved. Thus, the later in the design process we consider packaging, the easier it is to build a quality design. For instance, maximizing cohesion in each module and minimizing coupling are best accomplished before the modules are evaluated to determine how they might be implemented on a VAX computer.

Therefore, program design is done in two steps. First, we translate the system design into a set of specifications for the programmers, building into the design the characteristics of quality: modularity, functional independence, efficient algorithms, appropriate data types, and single entry-single exit modules. Second, we evaluate each module to make sure that its implementation is feasible, given the system's environment constraints. In other words, we build a quality design first and then package it for a specified environment.

5.3

DESIGN TOOLS

Tools and design aids are available to help us with our design. Some of the tools described in previous chapters can be used throughout all of system development. For example, the Structured Analysis and Design Technique (SADT) described in chapter 4 can also be used to specify a program design. In this chapter, we introduce other design tools and techniques for generating and specifying a program design.

Flow Diagrams

Years ago, a programmer learned first to describe the logic of a program by drawing a **flowchart**. Such a chart depicted the various kinds of processing in a program by using a standardized set of geometrical shapes, combined with arrows tracing logic flow. For example, a diamond shape indicated that the processing was a decision point, while a rectangle with vertical bars was used to show subprocedure processing. When processing logic was complex, the corresponding flowcharts could be enormous and difficult to follow. Although the flow charts depicted the structure of the program, they did not encourage the programmer to modularize or organize the processing logic in any particular way.

Many of today's design methods use diagrams to show the design, but the methods force modularity and structure on the design. The flow diagrams of today borrow the geometric shapes of flowcharts; Figure 5.6 shows the building blocks used to construct flow diagrams. We used similar diagrams in previous chapters when we introduced structure and data flow diagrams. In any flow diagram, each process block or decision point is accompanied by a written description of the

Figure 5.6   Flow Diagram Building Blocks

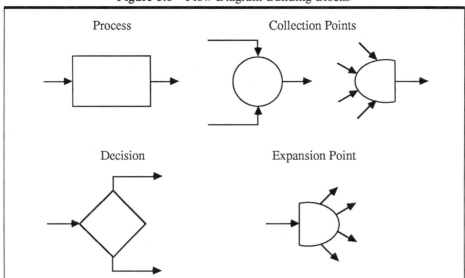

Figure 5.7 A Sequence Structure

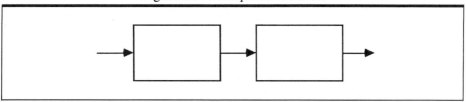

process or decision. For instance, a design may have a process block labeled "Calculate record number" or "Find mean, median and standard deviation." A decision point may ask, "Is SALARY greater than or equal to $45,000?" or "Is this the end of the file?"

In depicting a design, the building blocks of the diagrams form design structures to indicate the data and processing of data. For example, process blocks may follow one another in *sequence*. The illustration in Figure 5.7 might be appear in a file update program, where the first rectangle says "Calculate record key" and the second "Update next record."

When the design requires a decision or selection, the question can be contained in *selection* structures, depicted in Figure 5.8. In a selection, the question is placed in

Figure 5.8 Selection Structures

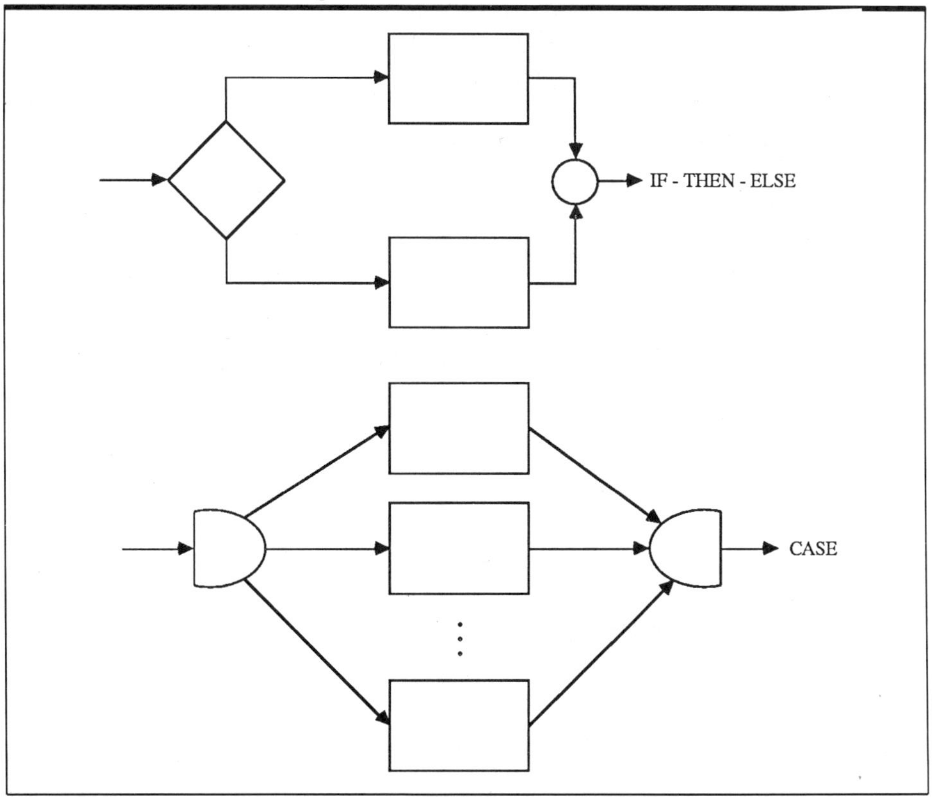

a diamond or expansion point and, depending on the answer, the program branches to one or another process block. Figure 5.9 shows how we might depict a design where the process performed depends on whether or not the value of K is greater than some maximum value. If K is greater than the maximum, we perform process A; otherwise, we perform process B. We can describe this by saying IF K is greater than the maximum, THEN perform A; ELSE perform B.

Often, the design calls for the invocation of one of a series of processes, with the chosen process depending on a particular condition. We can describe this flow by breaking the conditions into *cases*:

Case 1: Invoke process 1.
Case 2: Invoke process 2.
  .
  .
  .
Case n: Invoke process n.

We process our federal income tax forms in this fashion each year. We calculate the amount of taxable income; then, different cases send us to different tables for calculation of the tax. Figure 5.10 shows how an income tax system might be divided into processing modules using a case selection structure.

Sometimes a module is to be repeated as long as a particular relationship stays the same. One of the *repetition* structures shown in Figure 5.11 is used in such a situation. The diamond represents a test of the relationship, and a decision is made about repeating the process or not. The relationship is expressed as an equality or inequality, and the structure is often called a *loop* because control usually loops through the processing block until the relationship no longer holds. For example, the *do-while* structure in Figure 5.12 use a relationship comparing K to the value of MAX. The process B is performed while K stays above the maximum value. In this case, we DO invoke the process block performing process B WHILE K is greater than the maximum. Similarly, we may want to repeat process B until K no longer exceeds the maximum, so we use the *repeat-until* structure shown in Figure 5.13.

Figure 5.9   IF-THEN-ELSE Selection

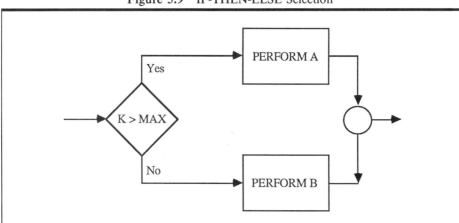

Figure 5.10   CASE Selection

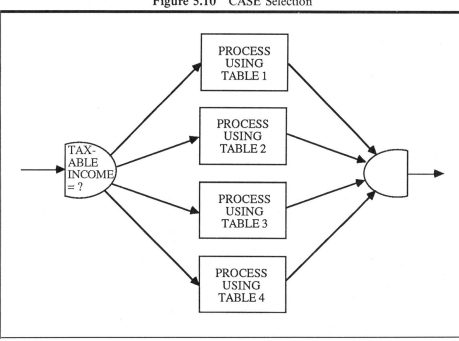

Figure 5.11   Repetition Structures

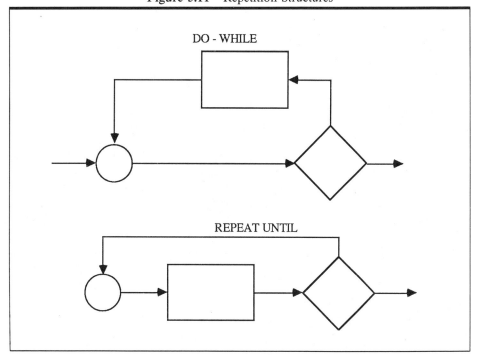

Figure 5.12   DO-WHILE Structure

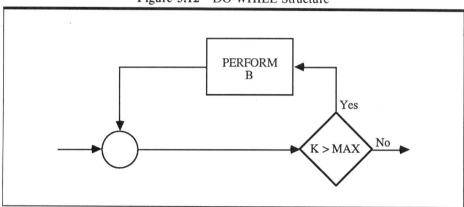

Figure 5.13   REPEAT-UNTIL Structure

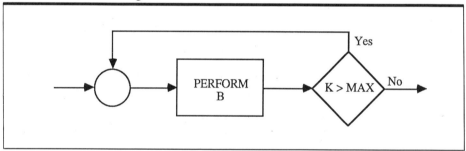

Pseudocode

Some of us prefer to write our design in words, rather than as a set of diagrams. Often we have a programming background and feel more comfortable presenting a design as a set of statements that resemble a programming language. This set of program-like statements, called **pseudocode**, uses a syntax like a programming language to describe the processing each module is to do. When packaging of the design is held off until the end of the design process, we usually want the pseudo-code to be independent of a particular programming language. However, the pseudocode should contain constructs that describe our design philosophy. For instance, if we are composing a design from data abstractions, we can use pseudo-code that resembles a language such as Ada and incorporates types, derived types, objects, and other structures.

An example shows us how a design might look in pseudocode. First, we describe the hierarchy of the modules, often using diagrams. Then the processing of each module is described by using design constructs. For instance, a sequence of actions defined to be a process can be delimited with BEGIN and END statements, as in the following example:

```
BEGIN FLOW_STRENGTH
    Get coordinates of measuring device.
    Signal device to up-load file.
    Record measurement.
    Check measurement for within range.
    Signal device to end transmission.
END FLOW_STRENGTH
```

Selections can be described using if-then-else or case constructs. An if-then-else construct is formed by denoting the IF, THEN and ELSE sections:

```
IF measurement in acceptable range
    THEN update data tape
    ELSE ask for retransmission
ENDIF
```

A case statement in pseudocode describes the conditions for each case and what action is to be taken.

```
CASE of STREAM_HEIGHT
    WHEN STREAM_HEIGHT < N1 call RESERVOIR_LOW
    WHEN STREAM_HEIGHT = N1 call ADEQUATE_SUPPLY
    WHEN STREAM_HEIGHT > N1 call FLOOD_ALERT
ENDCASE
```

We can represent a repetition using a do-while:

```
WHILE hours worked this week > 0
    DO tax computations
ENDDO
```

or a repeat-until:

```
REPEAT data translation
    UNTIL end-of-file is reached
    ENDREPEAT
```

Structured English. There are many kinds of pseudocode, some more formal than others. The examples above use English sentences accompanied by indications of the processing structure. By constraining the way in which English can be used, the resulting program descriptions have a careful, precise structure. For these reasons, this kind of pseudocode is known as **structured English**. Structured English often uses universal constructs; that is, it does not always use constructs specific to a particular programming language. You may find that the company or agency that you will be working with may have its own rules for structuring English to describe a program design.

PDL. A very formally structured pseudocode has been presented by Caine and Gordon as a Program Design Language ([CAI75]). PDL is a marriage of English with the IF and DO programming language constructs. The PDL processor accepts as input a set of control information plus designs for procedures (called *segments* in PDL). The output is a design document, including the following items.

1. A cover page including the date of the run

2. A source listing of the design

3. A design cover page

4. A table of contents listing each group and segment with corresponding page number

5. A design summary, including title pages for each group (a collection of segments), text segments, flow segments, data segments, and external segments (segments not included in this design)

6. Trees showing how the flow segments are referenced

7. An index of the data items

8. An index of the segments

9. Processing statistics

As an example (adapted from [CAI75]), we examine a design for a program to read a set of input lines and produce a set of key words in context. The input lines contain words separated by delimiter characters. The program performs circular shifts of line by moving all words to the left and putting the first word at the end of the line. All resulting lines beginning with key words are sorted and printed. The design is submitted to the PDL processor in a carefully prescribed structured English. Each segment begins with a percent sign (%) and a letter indicating the type of segment (G for group, T for text, S for flow, D for data and E for external). For instance, part of our program design may look like the following commands.

```
 5   %T FILE FORMATS
 6   THE INPUT CONSISTS OF FIXED LENGTH RECORDS OF CHARACTERS. THE
 7   INPUT RECORDS WILL BE REFERRED TO AS LINES.
 8
 9   THE INTERMEDIATE FILE CONSISTS OF FIXED LENGTH RECORDS TWO CHAR-
10   ACTERS LONGER THAN THE INPUT LINES. THE TWO EXTRA CHARACTERS
11   WILL BE AN END LINE CHARACTER ('*') AND A BLANK.
      .
      .
      .
16   %G THE INPUT PHASE
17   %S BUILD A FILE OF THE CIRCULAR SHIFTS OF THE LINES
18   OPEN THE INPUT FILE
19   OPEN THE INTERMEDIATE FILE
```

```
20   DO FOR EACH INPUT LINE
21   READ A LINE
22   IF END OF FILE ON INPUT
23   UNDO
24   ENDIF
25   WRITE ALL OF THE CIRCULAR SHIFTS OF ONE LINE
26   ENDDO
27   CLOSE THE INPUT FILE
28   CLOSE THE INTERMEDIATE FILE
29   %S WRITE ALL OF THE CIRCULAR SHIFTS OF ONE LINE
30   INITIALIZE CURRENT_CHARACTER_POSITION TO THE FIRST CHARACTER OF LINE
31   PUT AN END_OF_LINE CHARACTER AND A BLANK AFTER THE LINE
32   RESET LINE_END
33   LOOP:
34   DO FOR EACH WORD IN THE LINE
35   DO WHILE CURRENT_CHARACTER IS NOT ALPHABETIC
36   GET NEXT CHARACTER
37   IF LINE_END IS SET
38   UNDO LOOP
39   ENDIF
40   ENDDO
41   SAVE CURRENT_CHARACTER_POSITION
42   COLLECT A WORD
43   CHECK FOR WORD IN EXCLUSION TABLE
44   IF IT IS NOT AN EXCLUDED WORD
45   BUILD THE CIRCULAR SHIFT OF THE LINE (SAVED POSITION)
46   WRITE THE SHIFTED LINE IN THE INTERMEDIATE FILE
47   ENDIF
48   ENDDO
      .
      .
      .
```

The line numbers are generated by the PDL processor. Then a table of contents for the processor output is printed:

CHAPTER 5

Each segment is displayed with a cross-reference to other pages that contain more detail. For instance, the processor prints a page for the writing of circular shifts in the following manner:

```
                   WRITE ALL OF THE CIRCULAR SHIFTS OF ONE LINE

REF
PAGE ****************************************************
     *
     * 1     INITIALIZE CURRENT_CHARACTER_POSITION TO THE FIRST CHARACTER OF LINE
     * 2     PUT AN END_OF_LINE CHARACTER AND A BLANK AFTER THE LINE
     * 3     RESET LINE_END
     * 4  LOOP:
     * 5        DO FOR EACH WORD IN THE LINE
     * 6        DO WHILE CURRENT_CHARACTER IS NOT ALPHABETIC
  9  * 7        GET NEXT CHARACTER
     * 8          IF LINE_END IS SET
     * 9             UNDO LOOP
     * 10         ENDIF
     * 11       ENDDO
     * 12       SAVE CURRENT_CHARACTER_POSITION
  8  * 13       COLLECT A WORD
 11  * 14       CHECK FOR WORD IN EXCLUSION TABLE
     * 15         IF IT IS NOT AN EXCLUDED WORD
 12  * 16         BUILD THE CIRCULAR SHIFT OF THE LINE (SAVED POSITION)
     * 17         WRITE THE SHIFTED LINE IN THE INTERMEDIATE FILE
     * 18         ENDIF
     * 19       ENDDO
     *
     ****************************************************
```

The processor checks the syntax of the design, indents to make the procedure easier to understand, and underlines the key construct words. The references on the left of the page point to other pages with more detail.

A segment reference tree includes a column showing the page on which the segment is defined. Each level of indentation indicates a new level of call nesting.

```
PERFORM INDEXING
LN DEF    SEGMENT
  1   4   PERFORM INDEXING
  2   6       BUILD A FILE OF THE CIRCULAR SHIFTS OF THE LINES
  3   7           WRITE ALL OF THE CIRCULAR SHIFTS OF ONE LINE
  4   9               GET NEXT CHARACTER
  5   8               COLLECT A WORD
  6   9                   GET NEXT CHARACTER
  7  11               CHECK FOR WORD IN EXCLUSION TABLE
  8  12               BUILD THE CIRCULAR SHIFT OF THE LINE
  9  14       SORT THE FILE
 10  16       PRINT ALL OF THE CIRCULAR SHIFTS
 11  17           PREPARE TO PRINT A LINE
```

The index to the data items contains entries such as this one:

```
DI    LINE_COUNT
          16    PRINT OF THE CIRCULAR SHIFTS
                 4
          17    PREPARE TO PRINT A LINE
                 1    2    9
```

The data type (DI in our example) is followed by the name of the data element. Beneath are the names of the routines referencing the data item (here there are two) with the page and line numbers. For example, LINE__COUNT is referenced on line 4 of page 16 and on lines 1, 2 and 9 of page 17. Similar entries are made in the index to the flow segments:

```
FS    GET NEXT CHARACTER
          7    WRITE ALL OF THE CIRCULAR SHIFTS OF ONE LINE
                7
          8    COLLECT A WORD
                8
```

PDL is useful in several ways. First, its structured English forces us to organize the design carefully. Second, the evaluation of the PDL processor can point to inconsistencies in the design (such as a DO without an ENDDO). Third, a design written in PDL is far easier to evaluate and modify than a design drawn with diagrams.

The advantages of a structured design language are evident in the improvement of production rates for software development. The developers of PDL compared two projects, the first produced using widely accepted programming techniques, and the second using PDL. The production rates for the second project were fifty percent better than the first. Moreover, the amount of computer time used in developing the first project was approximately four times that of developing the second project.

The use of a programming design language has become so popular that the term PDL is usually used to mean *any* programming design language, rather than just Caine and Gordon's. However, the advantages of the Caine and Gordon language carry over to any other design language that has the same characteristics.

Nassi-Shneiderman Charts

For many years, flowcharting was a manual process, so the charts were difficult to enhance or maintain. More adequate design methods were sought, and a move to develop another pictorial tool for program design was made in the early 1970s. The result was a **Nassi-Shneiderman chart** or **Chapin chart**, proposed by Nassi and Shneiderman ([NAS73]) and extended by Chapin ([CHA74]). We can easily follow the functional flow of a module using such a chart. Because of the chart's construction, the transfer of control from one process to another is strictly regulated.

Every Nassi-Shneiderman chart begins with a large rectangle representing the module being diagrammed. The interior of the rectangle is partitioned into sections that illustrate the processing involved. To see how Nassi-Shneiderman charts are used, we look at how they depict the structures we explored earlier in this chapter.

A process is illustrated by drawing a line from the left side to the right side of the rectangle, forming a smaller rectangle. In general, we show a sequence of tasks or processes in a Nassi-Shneiderman chart, such as the rectangle in Figure 5.14.

Figure 5.14   Nassi-Shneiderman Sequence

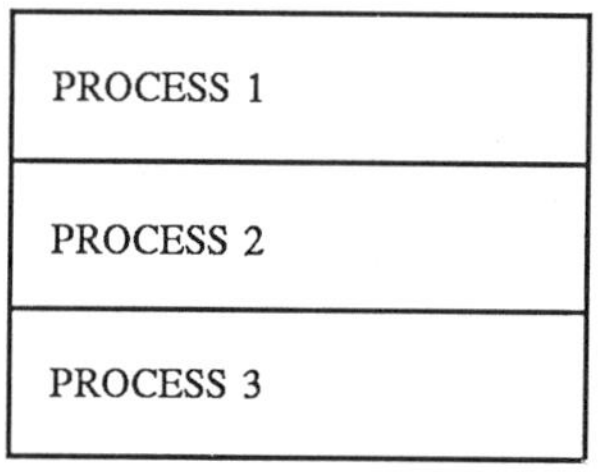

Representing a decision point is more complex. We can represent a decision in various ways: as an if-then-else structure, as a do-while, a repeat-until, or as a case condition. Each type of decision structure is handled in a slightly different way on the chart. As you can see in Figure 5.15, the do-while and repeat-until structures are similar in that they represent the repetition of a process while or until some condition is true. In an if-then-else or case structure, the type of process is selected (rather than repeated) according to whether or not a condition is met. Figure 5.16 shows how a selection process looks in a Nassi-Shneiderman chart.

For example, suppose a module in a program design calls for the following processing:

```
BEGIN process P1
END
BEGIN process P2
END
REPEAT
    IF condition C2 is TRUE
        THEN WHILE condition C4 is true
            DO BEGIN process P7
            END
            ENDDO
        ELSE test for condition C3
            FOR CASE 1 of C3
                BEGIN process P3
                END
                BEGIN process P4
                END
            FOR CASE 2 of C3
                BEGIN process P5
                END
            FOR CASE 3 of C3
                BEGIN process P6
                END
            ENDCASE
    ENDIF
UNTIL condition C1 is met
ENDREPEAT
```

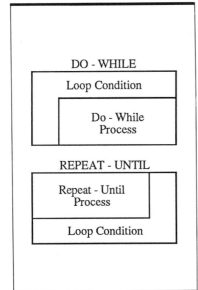

Figure 5.15
Repetition Structures for a
Nassi-Shneiderman Chart

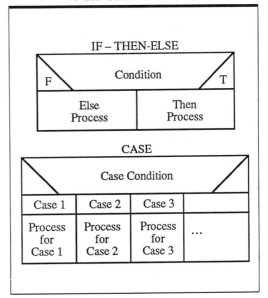

Figure 5.16
Selection Structures for a
Nassi-Shneiderman Chart

The equivalent processing is depicted as the Nassi-Shneiderman chart in Figure 5.17. The rectangle at the top represents process P1. It is followed by a rectangle below for process P2. All remaining processing is shown by the large rectangle whose right and bottom sides form the "until" condition of a repeat-until structure. Thus, the remaining processing is repeated until condition C1 is met. First, condition C2 is tested; if true, then a do-while structure as the right half of the remaining space shows that P7 is performed while C4 is true. The left half represents the processing when C2 is false. Here, we use a case structure to depict the testing of condition C3. Because there are three cases, the remaining space is divided in thirds to represent the appropriate processing.

Figure 5.17   Sample Nassi-Shneiderman Chart

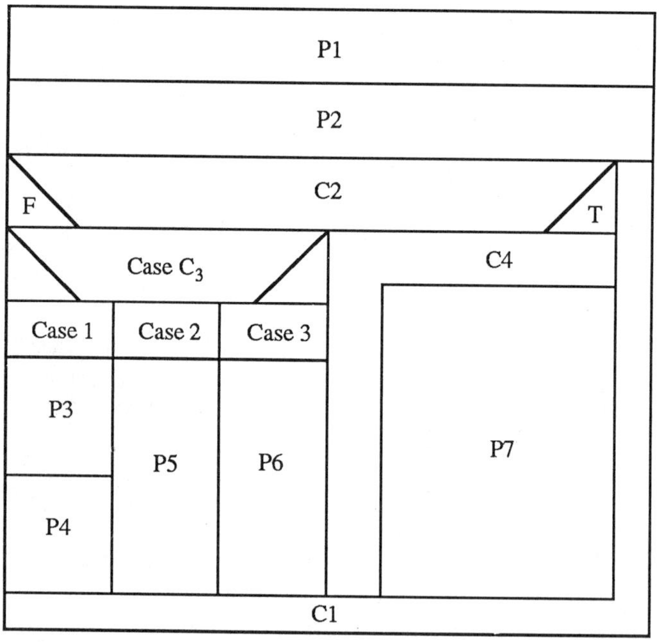

A Nassi-Shneiderman chart represents each operation with a block. That operation is represented by one of the control structures. In turn, each block can contain one or more blocks; *nesting* is automatically built into the design. In particular, using Nassi-Shneiderman charts makes it impossible to transfer control out of a subprocess prematurely. Thus, these charts are well suited for representing recursion. One advantage is that the charts enable us to see clearly the scope of a process or a variable.

Automated Design Tools

As we saw in chapter 3, systems such as PSL/PSA and SREM automate part of the requirements analysis process. Some software engineers believe that, given enough rigor in the requirements specification and given the proper automated tools, a design can be generated automatically from the requirements. Similarly, it would be ideal if a computer-based system could produce code from the design that satisfies the original requirements. These considerations have prompted the development of several automated tools to help us in a variety of ways.

We have seen how the PDL processor evaluates a design and produces cross-referencing documents. Other tools allow us to draw and modify data flow diagrams on a video display terminal and to build the data dictionary at the same time. For example, the Excelerator program from Index Technology Corporation, Cambridge, Massachusetts, runs on the IBM PC to support design activities. Data diagrams of various kinds can be drawn on the screen and stored in a data base. Figure 5.18 shows a sample diagram depicting data flow. After we draw a diagram, we fill in screens such as those in Figure 5.19 to describe files and those in Figure 5.20 to describe data elements. Then Excelerator builds a data dictionary linked automatically to the diagrams.

Figure 5.18 Graphics Menu

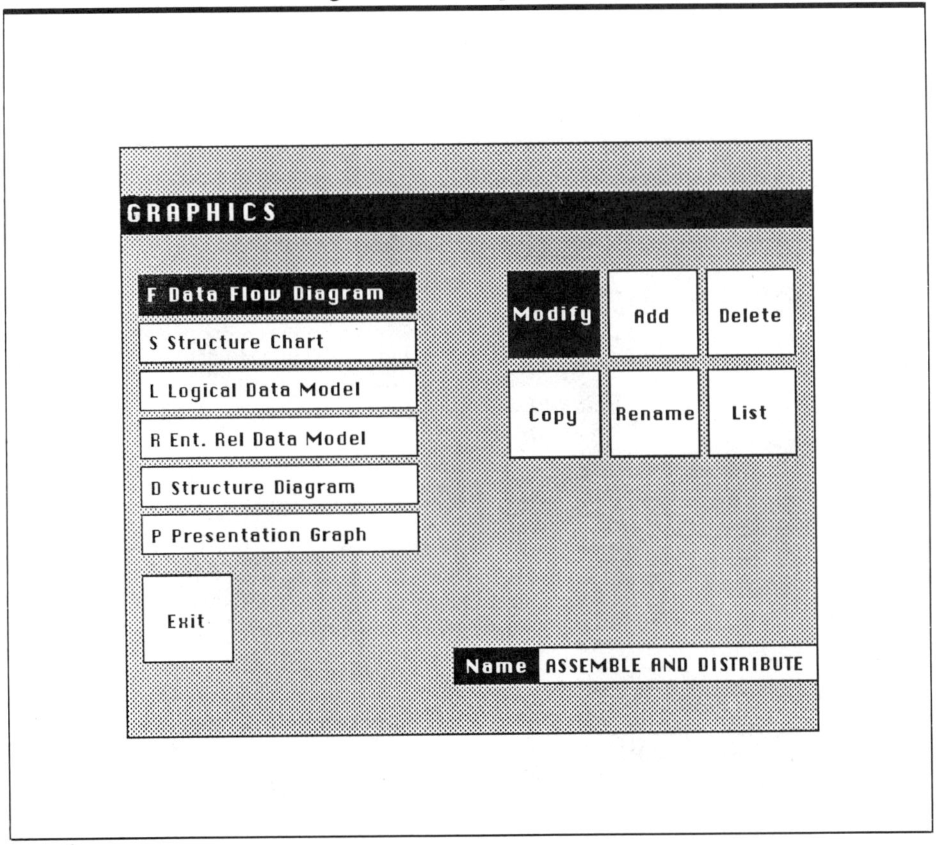

Figure 5.19   Describing a Data Store to the Dictionary

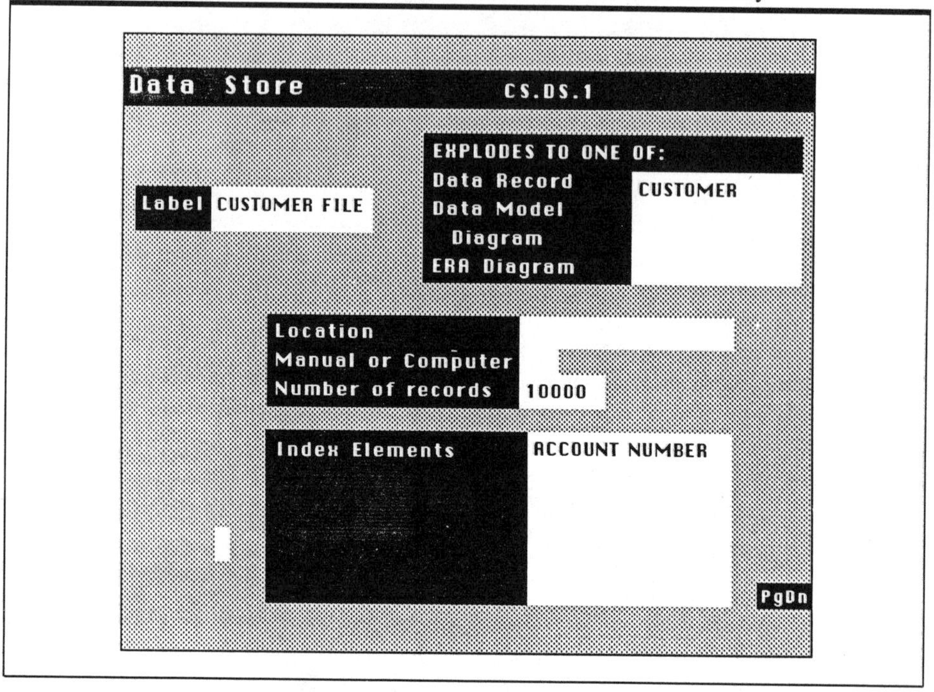

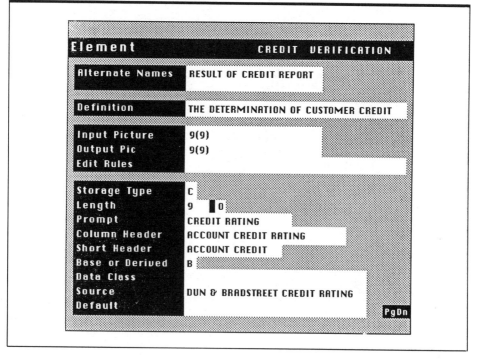

Figure 5.20   A Dictionary Entry for a Data Element

Other automated packages integrate graphics and text by allowing data flow diagrams and the data dictionary to be created simultaneously. Figure 5.21 illustrates a typical screen allowing the data dictionary to be updated interactively as new data structures are diagrammed. When the design is complete, summary reports can be produced (Figure 5.22) and errors noted (Figure 5.23).

Some automated tools permit us to generate a prototype system quickly (as we saw in chapter 4) so that we can make choices about the way in which the system will work when it is completed. Application generators let us specify the way in

Figure 5.21 Screen for Updating Data Dictionary

FIELDS	
Object Name	ITEM-PRICE
Object Type	DATA-ELEMENT
Alias	PRICE/UNIT-PRICE
Data Type	NUMERIC
Data Length	12 DIGITS; 2 DECIMAL
Initial Value	0.0
Description	UNIT PRICE
PROTECTION	NONE
OWNER	G.M. HOPPER
DATE DEFINED	09/19/86
LAST MODIFIED	02/07/87

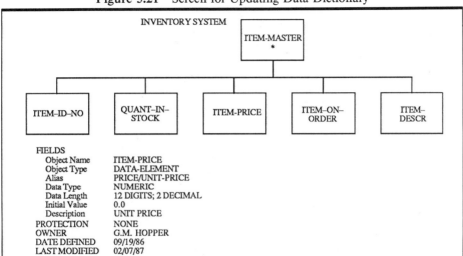

Figure 5.22 Summary Screen

INVENTORY SYSTEM

OCCURRENCE REPORT:

OBJECTS	PAGE	LINE
ITEM-MASTER	3	8
CREATE-REPORT	5	12
ADMINISTRATION	6	15
INPUT-DATA	7	8
PRINT-REPORT	9	15

* * * * * * *

Figure 5.23   Error Report Screen

```
ERROR REPORT               22 FEB 1987
INVENTORY SYSTEM
* * * * * * * *


OBJECT/RELATION        LOCATION            ERROR
                       PAGE  LINE


ITEM-UPDATE              3    15            DEFINED TYPE
                                           DISAGREES WITH USAGE
REPORT-TYPE             21    10            UNDEFINED


* * * * * * * * *


GRAPHIC                LOCATION            ERROR
                       PAGE  LINE


ARROW                    3    21            CONFLICT
ARROW                    4    21            CONFLICT
```

which parts of the system will work, and the generator builds the result from pieces that already exist. For example, we can use the dBase Assistant to describe what is in a set of tables, how data are to be accessed, and how reports should be formatted. Then, the Assistant generates a set of data base applications written in dBase III. We work only with the high-level Assistant language; no low-level code is needed.

Nevertheless, no automated tool has yet been designed that can tackle the most complex parts of a system. Our creativity and originality can be enhanced by tools but cannot be replaced by automation. Automation may enable us to perceive things more clearly or quickly, but it cannot do the entire job for us. Thus the system's complexities must still be addressed by other than automated means. Although tools help us generate it, the resulting design is only one of perhaps many solutions to the given problem; the heart of any solution must come from the combined expertise of the people addressing the problem.

Other Design Methods and Tools

The methods and tools described here and in previous chapters are examples of those available for use in designing programs. Your choice depends to a great degree on the size and type of application you are developing, the standards and procedures of your employer, and your personal preferences and those of your co-workers. For example, a real-time system may require many reentrant modules. To design such a system, you will want to choose design methods that can specify such modules. Or, to design a data-strong system, you may use an automated tool for drawing data flow diagrams and cross-referencing the data.

Any tool or method is acceptable as long as it generates a high-quality design. To compare one with another, we evaluate the following characteristics:

1. What is the fundamental *idea* behind it?
2. How easy is it to *use*? How easy is it to *learn*?
3. How does its *complexity* affect the design? How does the complexity of the design affect the tool or method?
4. Does it promote *modularity*? How is the system separated into modules?
5. Is it best for a particular phase of development? How well does the result *integrate* with the other phases?
6. How easily is the result *modified*?
7. How can it be used in the *phased development* of a project?
8. Does it require the use of *automated equipment*? If so, are the costs justified for a project of this size?
9. Does it produce a *portable* product? In other words, if the same system were to be implemented on a different hardware configuration, would redesign be necessary?

5.4

DESIGN QUALITY

Accompanying any design tool or method is a set of rules about how to use it to generate a high-quality design. Just as a map does you little good unless you know where you want to go, the use of diagrams, pseudocode, or charts in and of themselves are of limited value without knowing how to get the most out of them.

Structured Design

The design guidelines expressed at the beginning of this chapter help us to increase a design's quality. In general, the more structured a design, the easier it is to understand, to implement, and to maintain. Positive results have been noted many times in various writings. In one study, for instance, "programmers following structured designs worked 60 percent to 90 percent faster than those who had used the earlier, unstructured methods." ([KUL85]) A well-structured design has the following characteristics:

1. It is composed of modules that are highly cohesive.
2. There is a low degree of coupling among the modules.
3. Each module has a single entry point and a single exit.

Structure is only one aspect of a design that can be improved. There are other actions we can take to insure that our design is of high quality.

Error Prevention and Correction

A structured design helps us to avoid errors, since it encourages us to consider all cases, reduces complexity where it can, and makes the tracking and eventual elimination of errors easier. However, additional techniques are necessary to make our product as *error free* as possible. We must guard not only against errors built into each module but also against errors introduced to a module from other modules or from outside the system.

Error Detection. Errors can come from several sources: users, the hardware, or the software. In order to correct an error, we must find it first. Thus, **error detection** is the discovery of an error within a system. In developing programs for your courses, you are certain to have had experience in isolating errors before turning the program in for a grade. Finding an error is often difficult. Nevertheless, we want to find an error before it affects the functioning of a system. For example, if a bank's reporting system prints a report mistakenly showing assets to be ten times their actual value, the bank can make disastrous decisions based on that information. Or, if a missile carrying a warhead is launched because of an error in its controlling software, the consequences could destroy lives. The detection of an error during a system's execution is known as **passive error detection**. However, rather than waiting for an error to appear, the system can check itself periodically for symptoms of an error; this form of detection is known as **active error detection**.

One way we can find errors is to practice a policy of **mutual suspicion** ([MYE76]), by which each component of the system assumes that other components contain errors. We build steps into the system to make sure that any data flowing into a component from another are correct.

For example, a module may test its input data to verify that expected relationships hold. Thus, a payroll program may check the number of hours worked to assure that it is a nonnegative number. Moreover, we insure that an error's presence is noted and handled as soon as it is discovered, rather than after the component in which it occurs has finished its processing. It is usually easier to correct an error at its *source* than after its effects have traveled within the system, possibly generating more errors. By doing something about the error as soon as possible, the amount of damage that can be caused by the error is minimized. If the error is repaired at its source, there is no need to follow the "trail of destruction" left by the error.

Another convenient way for us to detect errors is to build *redundancy* into the system. If an outcome can be reached in two different ways, the results can be compared; inequality signals the system that an error has occurred. For example, accounting systems often sum rows first, then add up the row sums to obtain the total of entries in a table in one way; then they sum columns and add the column sums to derive what should be the same answer in a second way. Another simple example of redundancy is the inclusion of a check-sum or guard digit or parity bit in a data stream. Some systems may even require identical computers to perform the same calculations; a comparison is done periodically to guarantee that the results are identical. The space shuttle operates with redundant computers in this way. Sometimes, the redundant computers are designed and developed separately to perform the same tasks. In theory, if two functionally equivalent systems are designed by two different design teams at two different times, the chance of the same error occurring simultaneously is very small.

When active error detection is needed, a system often incorporates a second computer running in parallel with the first. The second system interrogates the first system and examines the system's data, looking for signs that might indicate something has gone awry. For example, the second system may find a process that has not been scheduled for a long period of time. This discovery may indicate that the first system is "stuck" somewhere, looping through a process, for example. Or the second system may find a block of storage that was allocated and is no longer in use but is not yet on the list of available storage blocks. Similarly, the second system may discover a communication line that has not been released at the end of a transmission. This technique is used in some "never-fail" transaction processing systems, where two processors perform the same work in parallel and continually compare results.

If the second of two redundant systems cannot detect certain errors merely by examining related data, it can initiate *diagnostic transactions*. By generating false but benign transmissions in the first system, the second system can determine if the first system is working properly. For example, the second system can dial the communication line of the first system to see if it is answering properly.

Defensive Designing. When learning to drive a car, you learn not only to avoid committing mistakes yourself but also to watch for and protect yourself from other drivers' mistakes. Just as you drive defensively, you must also *design defensively* by checking for errors that may be committed or overlooked by others. The earlier in the design process the checks are specified the better, since the structure of the design can then accommodate the error structures rather than be weakened by adding them later. Many of these error checks involve insuring that the data are in the proper range or have the correct attributes. For instance, your design may specify that data from a peripheral device be compared with data in a table. The size of a list, the number of records passed from another module, the possibility of zero as a divisor, the date of an update, or the width of a table may be candidates for validation.

Error Correction. Once an error is detected, it must be handled. **Error correction** is the system's compensation for the presence of an error. Error correction does not usually correct the *cause* of the error; it only fixes the *damage* done by the error. When designing, we should give consideration to how the system will react to errors; then we develop a consistent *strategy* to handle the errors. Usually, we choose between either stopping the system's activity when the error occurs or merely recording the error and returning to undo the damage later. Certainly, the criticality of the system plays a big part in the strategy we choose. System maintenance is another factor. It is much easier to find the source of the error if activity ceases abruptly than if the system continues its processing; continued processing may produce other effects that hide the error's source.

Error Tolerance. Sometimes correcting an error is too expensive, risky, or inconvenient. Instead, we design the system to minimize the damage done by the error and then carry on. We say that **error tolerance** is the isolation of damage caused by an error. Error tolerance is acceptable or even desirable in some circumstances. For instance, suppose a computer system controls several equivalent conveyor belts on an assembly line. If an error is detected on one of the belts, we may want the system to sound a bell and reroute to other belts the material headed for that one. When the defective belt is fixed, the system can again accommodate it. Certainly, tolerating the error is better than stopping production completely until the offending belt is fixed.

However, the major problem with error tolerance is the need to predict errors. In order to build "work-arounds" into the system, we must be able to guess what might go wrong. As with the conveyor belt example, some errors may be relatively easy to anticipate. However, the more complex a system, the more likely it is that the system will have errors. More importantly, the use of techniques to tolerate certain errors may mask other, unexpected errors whose presence may cause irreparable damage.

Module Complexity

As we have seen, modularity helps make a complex system more manageable. By breaking the system into pieces that can be investigated individually, the complexity of the system is isolated in several knots rather than twisted throughout the entire system. Once we have reduced the overall system complexity by using a modular approach, there are several ways we can determine just how complex each module is.

One method uses a graph derived from a flow diagram to depict the flow of control through the module ([MCC76]). To draw the graph, we first examine the module's structure. Each process (represented by a rectangle on a flow diagram) becomes a node in the graph. If control can flow from one process to another, we draw an arrow on the graph from one process node to another. For example, consider the module represented by the flow diagram in Figure 5.24, which shows part of an insurance system. First, we assign a node to each process rectangle in the diagram. Then, we place an arrow from one node to another in the graph if control can flow from one process to another in the diagram. We have represented this in dashed lines in Figure 5.25, and the result is the graph in Figure 5.26. The control graph divides the page into several regions. By a **region**, we mean an area bounded by arrows or the area outside the module. For example, in Figure 5.27 we identify the four regions into which the graph divides the page.

In the same way, for each module of a system, we can draw the *control flow graph* G for that module. The **cyclomatic complexity metric** for the module, denoted V(G), is the number of regions into which G divides the page. (The metric is independent of the way in which the graph is drawn; equivalent control flows yield the same metric.) McCabe has shown that V(G) is equivalent to one more than the number of decisions in the flow diagram. The larger the number of decision paths and loops in the module, the larger V(G) grows. Thus, we can think of V(G) as a measure of how difficult it is to test the module. Similarly, the more difficult it is to test the module, the greater the chance that errors will remain after testing. Studies have shown that as the value of V(G) increases, so too do the number of errors in the source code for the module ([GRE76], [CUR79]). Because of this relationship, it has been suggested that a module be limited in size. Some software engineers feel that if V(G) exceeds 10 for a particular module, then the program design should be revised to reduce V(G).

Unconditional Branching

In 1966, Bohm and Jacopini ([BOH66]) demonstrated that every logical structure in a design can be expressed using a combination of the sequence, do-while and

Figure 5.24 Flow Diagram for Example Module

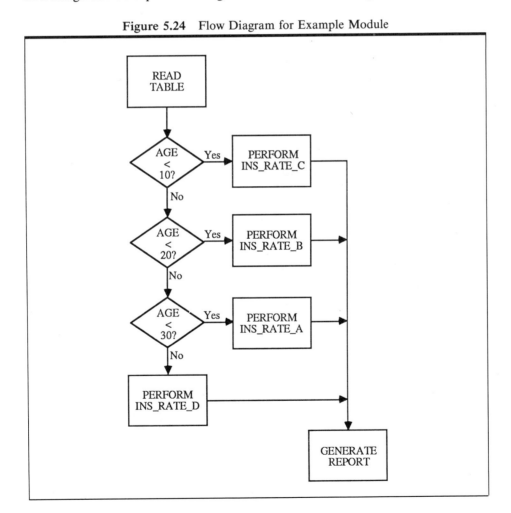

if-then-else structures. Therefore, unconditional branches are not necessary in a program design since such branches can be rewritten in other ways. Subsequent to the publication of the paper, an argument ensued among computer scientists about whether programmers should use unconditional branches (sometimes called "go to" statements) at all. Indeed, some software engineers define a program to be "structured" if and only if it contains no unconditional branching.

The original intention of those advocating the avoidance of "go to" statements was to make the program's flow of control more manageable. As described by Dijkstra, "the unbridled use of the go to statement has an immediate consequence that it becomes terribly hard to find a meaningful set of coordinates in which to describe the process' progress." ([DIJ68]) However, in the same letter, Dijkstra notes that "the exercise to translate an arbitrary flow diagram more or less mechanically into a jumpless one...is not to be recommended. Then the resulting flow diagram cannot be expected to be more transparent than the original one."

For program designers, the battle about "go to" statements calls for judicious use of unconditional branching. Certainly, a high-quality design does not contain

Figure 5.25   Creating a Control Graph

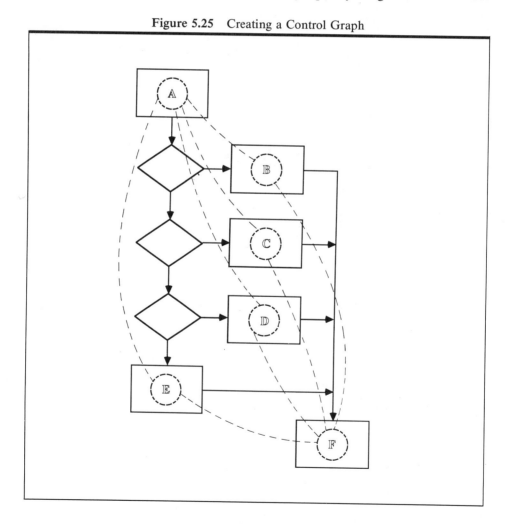

a great deal of unrestrained unconditional branching. However, there are several cases in which such branching is desirable or necessary. For those programming languages with no high-level control structures, low-level structures must be used in their place. FORTRAN has no testing loop, so GOTOs are used instead. Pascal has no exception handling and Ada has no selection, so unconditional branches are used to mimic these constructs. In avoiding unconditional branching completely, a program design may end up being complex and difficult to follow. Thus, for clarity and readability, a "go to" statement may be the structure of choice.

Unconditional branching may also be desirable if a system has storage space and execution time constraints. Peterson et al. ([PET73]) indicate that a program can increase in length and execution time if it is rewritten so that its control structures contain only the sequence, if-then-else and do-while.

Increasing the Structure

After we have eliminated as much unconditional branching as is reasonable, what else can we do to make our program design more structured? One aspect we can

Figure 5.26   The Control Graph

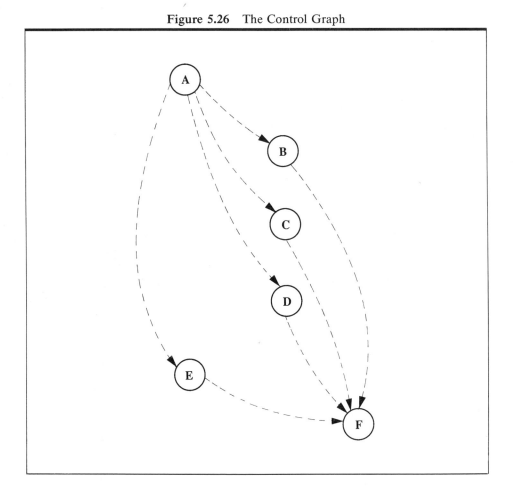

Figure 5.27   Regions of the Control Graph

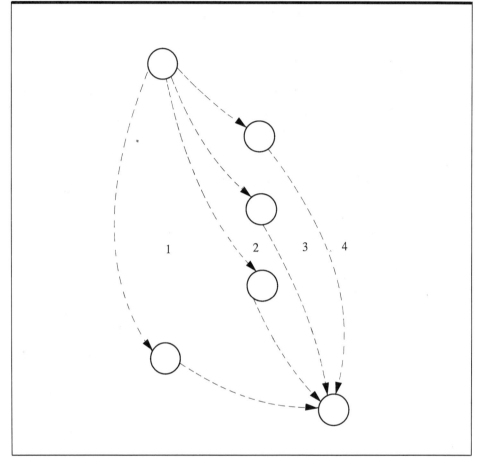

examine is the requirement that the modules each have a single entry point and a single exit. If we find a module that has several exits, we can restructure the design by duplicating some of the modules. Let us look at an example to see how this duplication works.

Figure 5.28 is a diagram of the modules of a system. As you can see, modules A, B and C each have two exits, and module E can be entered from two modules. Note in particular the entry points in E. The double entry points may mean that the processing done by module E depends on the results of processing in modules B and C. However, this dependency also means that a problem occuring in module E can be the perpetuation of a problem that began in module B, module C, or both modules. Clearly, this situation can create a large headache when making changes to or tracking errors through the modules.

The original module E is called **context-sensitive** because its processing depends on which module invokes it. In other words, we cannot tell what E will do unless we know the context in which it was invoked. By reducing the context-sensitivity of a module or process, we make the flow of control and data easier to follow. Thus, reducing context-sensitivity makes the design more well structured than the original one.

To redesign the structure, we could duplicate module E. However, the processing in E when entered from B may be different from that required when it is entered from C. Thus, we create two new modules, E1 and E2, whose processing is similar but not the same. E1 performs all the processing that E would perform if E were entered only from B. Likewise, E2 performs all of E's processing if E were entered only from C. Figure 5.29 shows the resulting new and larger structure. Sometimes we say that the procedure shown *increases the structure* of the design.

These structural problems usually arise in systems that are decomposed into modules. Data abstraction can eliminate the problems by building modules from the bottom up, insuring that each level is well-defined and that the level above abstracts more general notions. Thus, a structural analysis of our design may suggest that we redesign using abstraction rather than decomposition.

Testing the Modules for Structure

The program design resulting from the approaches suggested in this chapter can be evaluated in two ways. First, we can examine the *system* itself for modularity and the associated characteristics that signify a high-quality design. Second, we can examine the module specifications to see whether the *processing* within each

Figure 5.28 Violation of "Single Exit-Single Entry"

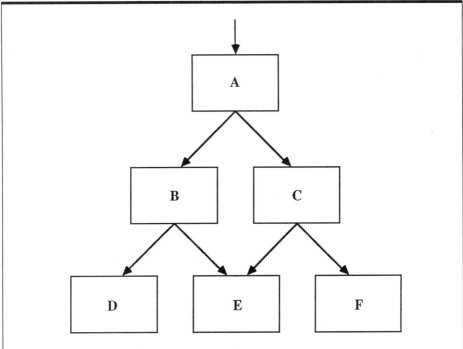

Figure 5.29   Duplicating Module to Increase Structure

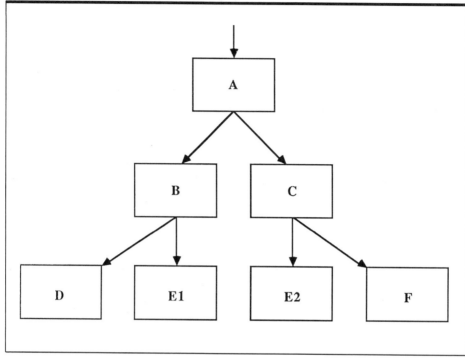

module conforms to the standards we have suggested: single entry point and single exit, limited use of unconditional branching, and use of three basic logical constructs (sequence, selection, and repetition). The closer the design is to this ideal, the easier it will be to understand and maintain.

DeMarco ([DEM78]) proposes that we evaluate modules by examining the flow diagram of each one. Whenever we can, we replace one of the three logical constructs shown in Figure 5.30 by a single sequence construct. In addition, every time one sequence construct directly follows another, we replace the pair by a single sequence construct. If the module's design is ideal, then when we can no longer make any replacements, the entire flow diagram will be a single sequence construct. Figure 5.31 shows how the substitutions are to be made.

We can describe this process in algorithmic form:

1. Draw a flow diagram for the module.

2. REPEAT the following UNTIL no further replacements are possible:
        IF there is a complete selection construct
            THEN replace it with a sequence construct
        IF there is a complete repetition construct
            THEN replace it with a sequence construct
        IF there are two adjacent sequence constructs
            THEN replace them with a single sequence construct

Figure 5.30 Logical Constructs

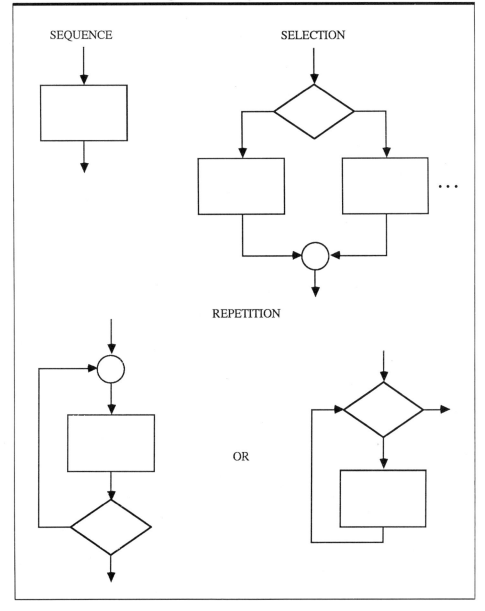

3. If the resulting flow diagram is a single sequence construct, the module has an ideal structure.

Notice that our evaluation involves only the flow of *control* in the design. The replacement of constraints with sequence blocks does not affect the *processing* done by the modules.

Figure 5.31   Substituting Sequence Constructs

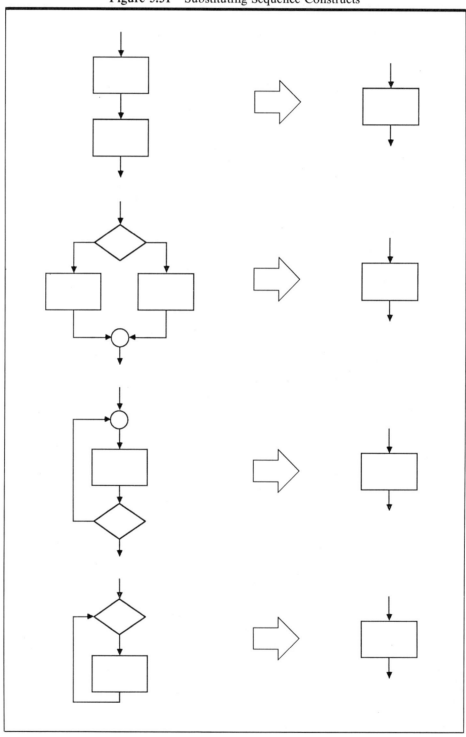

5.5

DESIGN REVIEWS

When we are satisfied that our design is what we want to propose for the project, it is time for the design to be scrutinized in a design review. Just as the system design was reviewed by a group of members of the system development team, a **program design review** is a presentation of the program design to other designers, analysts, and programmers for comment and suggestions. As with the review of the system design, several key people should participate in the review:

- The analyst(s) who helped to define system requirements
- The system designers
- The program designers
- A moderator
- A secretary
- Several analysts and designers who are not otherwise involved in this project.

The number of people attending the review depends on the size and complexity of the project. The members of the review team represent their organizations and must have the authority to make binding decisions. The moderator balances and encourages discussion, and the secretary documents the technical discussion and the decisions made. The outside observers lend objectivity to the review. At the same time, they scrutinize the design and act as a quality assurance group.

We present the details of our design to the entire review team. The review team then checks the design for the following characteristics:

1. Is this design a *solution* to the problem?
2. Is the design *modular* and *well-structured*?
3. Can anything be done to *improve* the modularity and structure?
4. Is the design *portable*?
5. Is the design easy for the programmers to *understand*?
6. Are the *algorithms* appropriate, or can they be improved?
7. If this is a phased development, are the phases interfaced sufficiently to make an easy *transition from one phase to another*?
8. Is the design *well documented*?
9. Does the design contain a *cross-reference* of the modules with the *requirements*?
10. Does the design contain a *cross-reference* of the *data* with the requirements?

Design Rationale

One of the most important parts of a design review is the *justification* for using certain algorithms, structures, and strategies. During the review, we explain to the reviewers why certain modules are fashioned in certain ways. Such a justification is known as **design rationale**; it documents and reviews the options that were available to us and the reasons why we made certain choices. ([FRE75]) An example will show us how the rationalization process works.

Suppose the system being developed requires users to enter commands at a video display terminal. As a designer, you explain to the review team that the system requires a module to check the command string and insure that it is an acceptable command. If an error is found in the string entered by a user, you explain that the designers considered three ways to handle the error. In the first scenario, the system halts when the error is discovered and the screen prints the message:

```
ILLEGAL COMMAND
EXIT
$
```

In the second case, the user is told that the command is in error and is asked to enter the command again:

```
SYNTAX ERROR
PLEASE TRY AGAIN
```

In the third case, the system tries to guess which command the user meant to type and asks the user to verify the guess.

```
SYNTAX ERROR
NAME_ADDR_FMT FOR ZIP < '99999'
AND ZIP > '0'
CORRECT LINE AND PRESS ENTER TO
REEXECUTE; ESCAPE TO ABANDON
```

Once the three possibilities are laid out, you explain the pros and cons of each choice. For instance, the first choice is easy to design and program. However, it does not give the user any chance to correct the error, forcing him or her to waste time. The second choice is more difficult to design and code because it requires the system to reexecute the command checker module. However, the system makes life easier for users by giving them a second chance. The third case is the easiest for users but the hardest for the designers. Much coding would be needed to handle all the possible commands users might try. Given the size of the rest of the system, you may conclude that this case requires too much time and resources. In addition, this case may lead to errors if the system guesses incorrectly and invokes the wrong command. Thus, you present the second alternative as a good choice; it combines aid to users with a simplified design.

Similarly, the remaining system design is rationalized by explaining to the reviewers how each module design was developed. The design review proceeds in this fashion until the review team is satisfied with the functionality and quality of the design.

If major problems are discovered, the review team may recommend one or more design changes. The review is adjourned, you consider the recommendations, and prepare a new or revised design. A second design review is held, and the review team evaluates the new design completely. The *recommendation-and-review process* is repeated until the review team approves the design. In the next chapter, we will see how to translate the approved design into high quality code.

5.6

RESOURCE TRACKING
AND SIMULATION EXAMPLE

We return to the Weaver Farm example to see how a program design might be generated for the resource tracking and simulation system. We begin by reviewing the system design from the top down and noting that the system is divided into several distinct functions:

1. Data Base Functions
2. Maintenance Schedule Functions
3. Simulation Functions
4. User Administration Functions

Each set of functions is further divided into process modules. The system design generated in chapter 4 specifies the modules shown in Figure 5.32. Let us expand

Figure 5.32   Top-Level Design for Weaver Farm

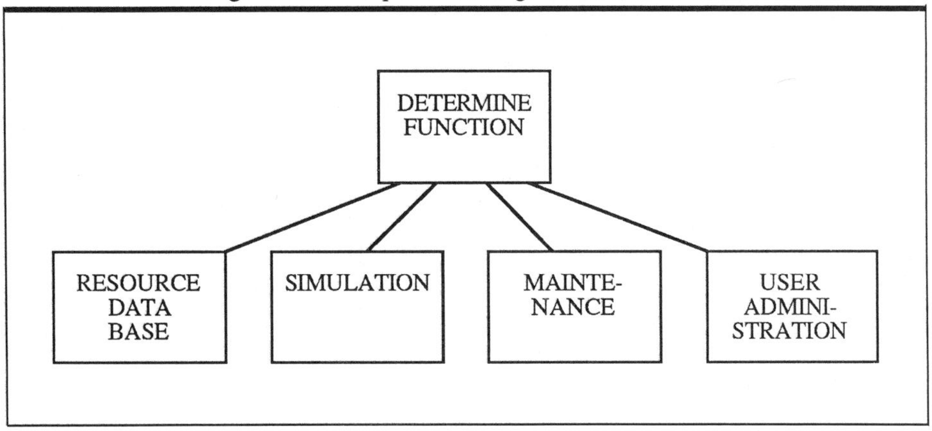

Figure 5.33   Weaver Farm User Administration

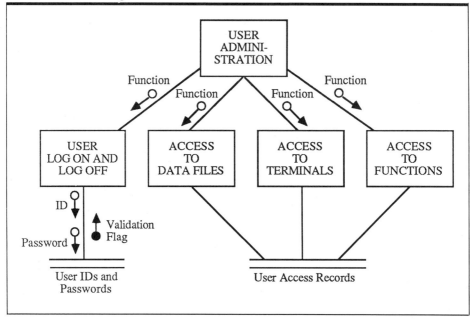

the design for the user administration functions. Figure 5.33 illustrates how we may further divide user administration into smaller functions. Our guidelines for good design suggest that we continue to subdivide modules until each module at the lowest level has a single function. Thus, we may want to divide the "User Log On and Log Off" module into two: "User Log On" and "User Log Off." Our new data flow diagram becomes that of Figure 5.34.

We can continue and subdivide the access modules, too. However, for this example, we concentrate only on user log on and log off.

The next step involves working with the module hierarchy and data base specifications to generate the details of each module's design. For example, a Nassi-Shneiderman chart for the log on and log off modules of Figure 5.34 may look like the ones depicted in Figure 5.35. Notice that the Nassi-Shneiderman chart adds design decisions to those made at the system design stage. As program designers, we detail the use of function keys and menus that are mentioned only briefly in the system design. At the same time, we include enough detail so that programmers can write their code from our program design specifications.

By mentioning function keys and specifying menus, the program design relates the system to specific hardware and software to be used on the Weaver Farm project. Until the program design stage of development, the design has not specified terminal types, function key values, or other such details. Thus, the system design has been portable—to any computer or terminal—but the program design is not. The program design can direct the programmers to take advantage of specific hardware or software characteristics. For example, the system design may refer to a data base management system. The program design may acknowledge the use of a

Figure 5.34 Subdividing "Log on/Log off" Function

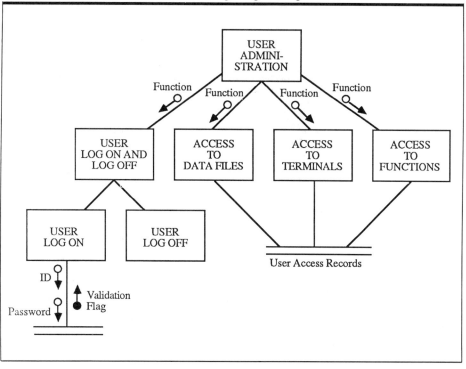

particular data base management system and may reference its utility programs by name.

Other design decisions are reflected in the Nassi-Shneiderman charts. For instance, function keys are used for logging on and off. If the user has not chosen the log on key from the log on/off menu, a second check is made to be sure that the function key is in fact the log off key. If it is *not* the log off key, the error is *tolerated* and the menu displayed again.

Accompanying the design are data definitions and screen formats. Many of these will be the same as or embellishments of those defined in the system design.

When the first draft of the design is complete, it is reviewed by the design team. Each level of the design examined for errors and for areas that can be improved. For example, should the "User Log Off" module redisplay the log on menu for an erroneous function key or merely call the "User Log On" module? Should a limit be placed on the number of consecutive unsuccessful log on attempts (to thwart an unauthorized user attempting to break into the system)?

After the design team is satisfied, the design is presented at a design review. Again the design is analyzed for corrections or improvements. In particular, the review team insures that a *correspondence* is evident between the requirements and the design. Thus, if the director of Weaver Farm requests a change, it will be easy for the system and program designers to isolate the modules affected and implement the change.

Figure 5.35 Nassi-Shneiderman Charts for Log on/off

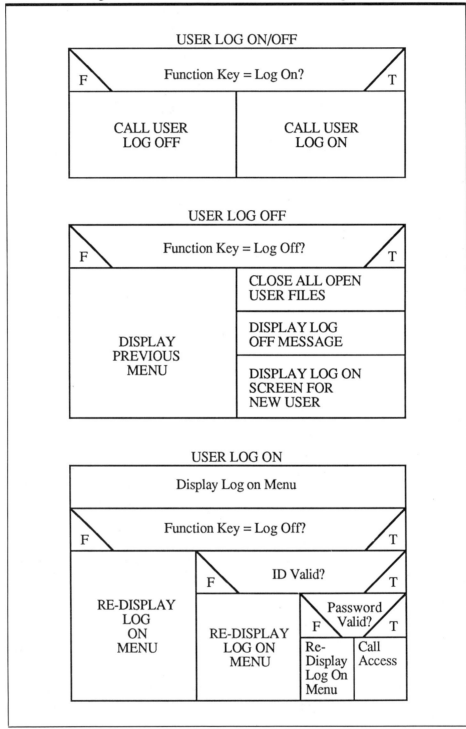

5.7

CHAPTER SUMMARY

In this chapter, we have examined many ways to specify a set of process modules and intermodular interfaces so that a set of process modules containing program specifications corresponds to each module in the system design. This program design tells the programmers what data must flow through the system, how control is managed, and which algorithms should be used to solve the problems encountered. Some designers prefer to generate a program design from the top down, while others like to work from the bottom up. In either case, the resulting design must have the characteristics of a high-quality design, including modularity and functional independence.

We have seen how to determine whether algorithms are correct, efficient, and unambiguous. Similarly, we have divided types of data into subtypes so that we can minimize errors manipulating different types individually. Modules, too, can be classified in a variety of ways; those that are subject to interrupts are treated differently from those that are not. Special techniques can be used for incremental and reentrant modules.

If possible, each module should have a single entry and a single exit. Unconditional branching should be minimized. The designers also ensure that the design will produce a system capable of detecting and handling errors. The design is to be well-structured, and any packaging that is required to conform to hardware constraints should be done as late in the design process as possible.

Many techniques are available for use in designing the program modules: flow diagrams, pseudocode, Nassi-Shneiderman charts, and others, both manual and automated. Any or all are good candidates as long as they are appropriate to the size and complexity of the project and can produce a quality design. The designers can improve the structure of the design by testing each module to see if it can be reduced to a series of sequence constructs. When the designers are happy with their product, they present it to a design review team. The team investigates whether any parts of the design can be enhanced before being turned over to the programmers for implementation. In the next chapter, we will see how the programmers translate the design into a working system.

5.8

EXERCISES

1. Consider the magic square algorithm presented on page 190. Will it work for sequences of numbers other than those described in step 2 of the algorithm? Find an algorithm to generate magic squares where n is even. Is there a general algorithm that will work no matter whether n is even or odd?

2. In discussing the improvement of the efficiency of algorithms, we noted
   that the straightforward way of determining whether a positive integer *n* is
   prime is to divide *n* by all positive numbers less than or equal to the square
   root of *n*. A more efficient algorithm is the Sieve of Eratosthenes:

```
BEGIN: Set LIST_LENGTH = 1000.
       Set ARRAY to be of size LIST_LENGTH.
       Set MARKER = square root of LIST_LENGTH.
       Do for I from 2 to LIST_LENGTH
           If ARRAY(I) = 0, go to SKIP.
           Print I.
           If I <= MARKER, then do J = 1 to (LIST_LENGTH)/I
                       ARRAY (I*J) = 0
SKIP: RETURN
```

Explain in plain, conversational English what this algorithm does. Why is
it called a sieve? How many operations are involved in the straightforward
algorithm; that is, what is the order of magnitude of the efficiency of the
algorithm? Do you know of any way of improving the efficiency still
further?

3. You are designing a program to display data on an automobile dashboard
   as a motorist is driving. Your data include output from several sources,
   including the odometer, the speedometer, the clock, the tachometer, and a
   monitor that tracks the levels of fluids, including their temperature and
   volume. Define a set of data types that will enhance the error-checking
   capabilities of your program.

4. Give an example of a system that requires an incremental module. Give
   another example of a system that requires a reentrant module. Sketch how
   the data might be stored for the reentrant module to enable it to be
   reentered.

5. Give an example of a system where packaging might change the original
   system design substantially.

6. Consider the design logic represented by Figure 5.36. Its equivalent pseudocode description might look like this:

```
LOOP:   IF P THEN GO TO HERE
            ELSE BEGIN
                    INCREMENT A
                    IF Q THEN GO TO HERE
                    ELSE GO TO LOOP
                    ENDIF
            END
HERE:   RETURN
        ENDIF
```

Draw a control flow diagram. Explain why this program is not well structured. Then, redo the design to improve the structure. When you are done,

Figure 5.36   Flow Diagram for Exercise 5.6

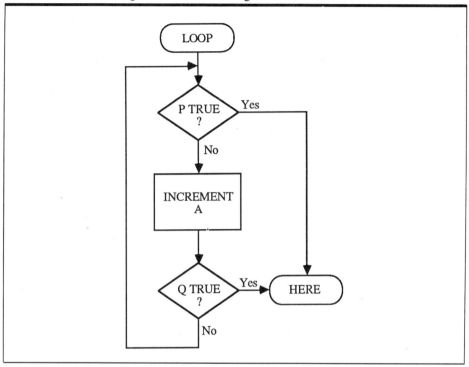

examine your new design. If it uses flags to control the processing, redesign again so that your design has no flags.

7. Consider the following pseudocode for a program design:

```
LOOP:  SET I TO (START + STOP)/2.
       IF ARRAY(I) = TARGET, GO TO NEXT
       IF ARRAY(I) < TARGET, SET START = I + 1
       IF ARRAY(I) > TARGET, SET STOP = I - 1
       IF (STOP - START) > 1, GO TO LOOP
       IF ARRAY(START) = TARGET, GO TO NEXT
       IF ARRAY(STOP) = TARGET, GO TO NEXT
       SET AFLAG = 0
       GO TO EXIT
NEXT:  SET AFLAG = 1
EXIT: RETURN
```

Draw a control flow diagram. Is this program well structured? If not, redesign it. What does this program do?

8. Draw a Nassi-Shneiderman chart for the original program in the previous example. Then draw one for your redesigned one. Comment on the differences.

Figure 5.37   Flow Diagram for Exercise 5.9

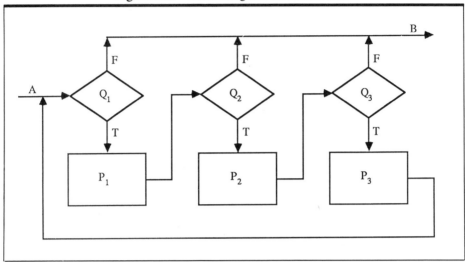

9. Figure 5.37 is a flow diagram for a program design. Redesign it so that its structure is improved.

10. Should error checking be performed within modules or as separate modules? Give examples to support your answer.

11. Draw a program graph G for one of your programs. What is V(G)? If V(G) is high, redesign your program to lower V(G). Is your new design "better" than the old, in the sense described in chapter 4? For example, is your new design more modular with lower coupling and more information hiding? Why or why not?

12. A module in a word processing system is to hyphenate text when a word is too long to fit within the set margin. Develop an algorithm for hyphenating a word. Examine your algorithm in terms of implementation constraints: can it be improved to make it more efficient?

13. Two program designers are comparing notes about their designs. Designer A has interpreted "find the mean of X and Y" as algorithm X/2 + Y/2. However, Designer B has directed the programmers to use (X+Y)/2. Are these algorithms equivalent? If not, explain the differences that may result during the implementation of the designs.

14. The module hierarchy of a design is shown in Figure 5.38. Explain why this hierarchy is not well structured. Rewrite it as a structured set of modules.

15. Explain why data abstraction is useful in designing embedded systems.

16. Ada is a programming language that allows you to define data types, subtypes, and derived types. Learn about Ada constructs and explain why they make a design portable.

Figure 5.38 Module Hierarchy for Exercise 5.14

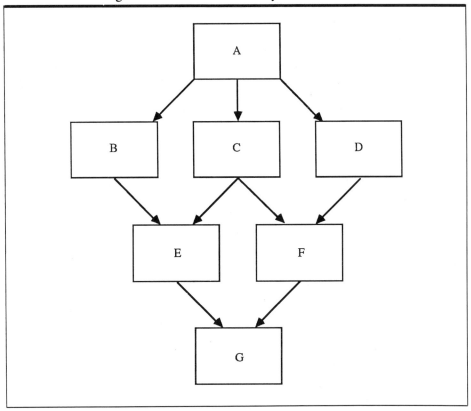

C H A P T E R 6

PROGRAM IMPLEMENTATION

In previous chapters, we looked at how to transform a customer's problem into a solution on a computer-based system. Then, we considered the importance of designing the solution so that it is modular, modifiable, has a low degree of coupling among modules, and has other characteristics of a high-quality design. Finally, we saw the need for specifying a detailed design so that a programmer can translate the design into computer code that functions properly and preserves the desirable design characteristics.

Now, as noted in Fig. 6.1, we turn to the actual writing of computer programs. We assume that you have had a reasonable amount of experience in writing and testing programs for your classes. Consequently, the purpose of this chapter is not to tell you how to program; rather, it is to explain how the software engineering principles of previous chapters can be reflected in code you write from the program design.

6.1
PROGRAMMING STANDARDS AND PROCEDURES

If the software engineering practices described in chapters 1 through 5 have been followed, you, as programmer, understand the design and have little difficulty partitioning the system into clearly defined modules. However, before beginning to write the actual program code, you must know the standards and procedures of the organization in which you are working. Many companies insist on code that conforms in terms of style, format, and content to the programs of others. There are several reasons why such standards are necessary.

Figure 6.1   The System Development Process

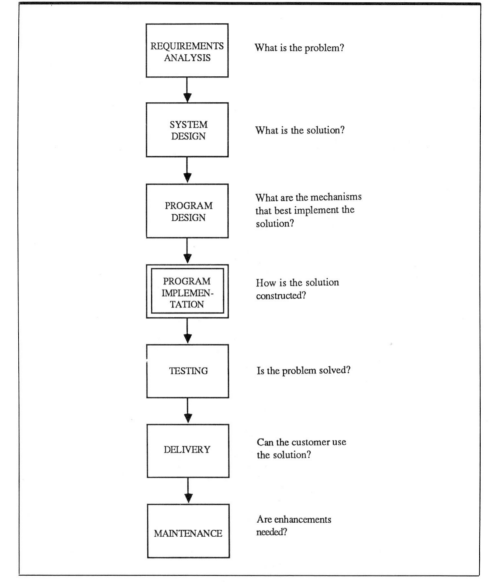

Need for Standards and Procedures

You are likely to work on many different software projects during your career. Some will involve evaluating existing code to replace or modify it. Others will require participation in both formal and informal reviews of code to help the other members of your team. In still others, you will convert designs to actual programs.

Most of the programs you have written in your classes have been done independently so that your instructor could judge the quality of and suggest improvements to your work. However, most software development projects outside of the classroom involve a team of people. As we have seen in studying the software development cycle, a variety of jobs is required to produce a quality product. Even in writing the actual code for the programs, several people may be involved. Thus, writing a program is not done in a vacuum. Others must be able to understand easily what you have written and why.

Standards for You. Standards and procedures can help you to *organize* your thoughts and avoid mistakes. Some of the procedures involve methods of documenting your code so that it is clear and easy to follow. Such documentation allows you to leave and return to your work without losing track of what you had been doing. Standardized documentation also helps in locating errors and in making changes because it clarifies which sections of your program perform which functions.

Standards and procedures also help in *translating* designs to code. By structuring code according to standards, the correspondence from design modules to code modules is maintained. Consequently, changes in design are easy to implement in the code. Similarly, modifications to code that result from changes in hardware or interface specifications are straightforward, and the possibility of error is minimized.

Standards for Others. Once your code is complete, others are likely to use it in a variety of ways. For example, as we shall see in later chapters, a separate team may test the code. Or, another set of people may integrate your software with other programs to build and test subsystems and finally the whole system. Even after the system is up and running, changes may be needed, either because of an error or because the customer wants to change the way the system performs its functions. You may not be part of the maintenance or test teams, so it is essential that you organize, format, and document your code to make it easy for others to understand what it does and how it works.

For example, suppose every program produced by your company begins with a section describing the program's functions and interfaces with other programs. The opening section may look like this:

```
****************************************************************
*
* MODULE TO FIND INTERSECTION OF TWO LINES
*
* MODULE NAME: FINDPT
* PROGRAMMER: K. MERTZ
* VERSION: 1.0 (12 FEB 87)
*
* PROCEDURE INVOCATION:
*    CALL FINDPT (A1, B1, C1, A2, B2, C2, XS, YS, FLAG)
*
* INPUT PARAMETERS:
*    INPUT LINES ARE OF THE FORM
*      A1*X + B1*Y + C1 = 0 AND
```

```
*      A2*X + B2*Y + C2 = 0
*    SO INPUT IS COEFFICIENTS A1,B1,C1 AND
*    A2, B2, C2
* OUTPUT PARAMETERS:
*    IF LINES ARE PARALLEL, FLAG SET TO 1.
*    ELSE FLAG = 0 AND POINT OF INTERSECTION
*    IS (XS, YS).
*
* PROCEDURE CALLED BY:
*    DRAW1
*    FINDNEXT
*
* PROCEDURE CALLS:
*    ERRMSG
*
**************************************************************
```

Notice that the documentation points *up* to the modules that may invoke it and *down* to those modules called by the procedure. With information such as this, making a change to the system is relatively straightforward.

A maintenance programmer will more easily find the module that needs to be changed. Once that module is located, if the data names are clear and the interfaces well-defined, the maintenance programmer can be sure that the change needed will not have any unexpected effects on other parts of the code. At the end of this chapter, we will examine an example of standards and procedures to see how they may direct our programming efforts.

Matching Design With Implementation

The most critical standard is the need for a *direct correspondence* from the program design modules to the program code modules. The entire system design and program design process is of little value if the modularity of the design is not carried forward into the code. The characteristics introduced in the system design and enhanced in the program design (such as low coupling, high cohesion, well-defined interfaces) should not only be the basis of the programs written but also be transferred so that algorithms, functions, and interfaces can be traced easily from system design to implementation and back again.

Remember that the *general purpose* of the system being built is likely to remain the same throughout the software development cycle and for several years thereafter. However, the *nature* of the system may change over time as customer enhancements and modifications are identified. Suppose you are part of a team building a computer-aided design system for automobiles. The system you build will always design automobiles or their parts, but as the customer works with the system, enhancements may be identified. The system menus may change, one type of digitizing tablet may be replaced by another, or new features may be added to the system. These changes to the system are made first at the system design level; then, the design changes are traced through the program design to the program to determine what actual lines of code must be altered.

Thus, a direct correspondence between design and code is essential. We will see in later chapters that testing, maintenance, and configuration management would be almost impossible without the links established through software engineering principles.

6.2

PROGRAMMING GUIDELINES

Programming involves a great deal of creativity. Remember that the program design is a guide to the function of each module. However, the programmer has great flexibility in implementing the program design as lines of code in program modules. The design or the requirements specification may suggest a programming language to be used for implementation, either directly or indirectly because of the constructs and data structures used. Sometimes, the choice of language is left to the programming. Language-specific guidelines are not addressed here since there are many good books on the subject (such as [KER74], [KER76], [HUG78], [FRI81], [BAR84]). Instead, we discuss several guidelines that apply to programming in a procedural language, regardless of which one is used.

No matter what language is chosen, each program module involves three major components: logic control structures, algorithms, and data structures. Let us look more closely at how each is implemented in the corresponding program modules.

Control Structures

Many of the control structures for a module are suggested in the program design specifications. However, the program design is written in a design language or as a set of diagrams with accompanying documentation. The control structures must now be implemented in a particular programming language as actual lines of code. We want to preserve the organization and quality of the design as we translate the design to code.

Using Fundamental Constructs. We noted in chapter 5 that a program is considered to be *structured* if it satisfies several conditions, one of which is that it uses these fundamental control constructs:

```
Sequence:
    BEGIN - END
Selection:
    IF - THEN - ELSE
    CASE
Repetition:
    WHILE - DO
    REPEAT - UNTIL
```

Ideally, the program design is written using only these constructs. You should maintain the use of these control structures in the program code you write. Use of these control mechanisms makes programs easy to read and follow, helps to minimize uncontrolled branching (the infamous GOTO), and even helps you organize your thoughts while writing the program.

However, many programming languages do not have such structures readily available. For instance, there is no CASE statement in LISP, BASIC, FORTRAN, COBOL, or some PL/I dialects. In such situations, as with many other standards and guidelines, it is best to follow the *spirit* of the suggestion if the *letter* is not appropriate.

In some instances, you may implement a construct by writing a function or macro to mirror the use of the construct. For example, in an assembler language, the use of a DO macro may make the program much easier to read. Clearly the method in which the fundamental constructs are used depends both on the language used and your preferences.

Some organizations have guidelines or standards for simulating the control features in languages that do not contain them. These standards often suggest efficient and easy-to-follow methods for creating a structure.

Top-down Flow. Readers of a program should not have to jump wildly through the code, marking sections to which to return, and wondering whether they have followed the right path. They should concentrate on what is being done by a program, not on figuring out the control flow. Thus, it is best to arrange your code so that, as much as is practical, the program can be read from the top down. Let us look at an example. Control in the following PL/I program skips around among the program's statements, making it difficult to follow.

```
    BENEFIT = MINIMUM;
    IF (AGE < 75) THEN GO TO A;
    BENEFIT = MAXIMUM;
    GO TO C;
    IF (AGE < 65) THEN GO TO B;
    IF (AGE < 55) THEN GO TO C;
A:  IF (AGE < 65) THEN GO TO B;
    BENEFIT = BENEFIT * 1.5 + BONUS;
    GO TO C;
B:  IF (AGE < 55) THEN GO TO C;
    BENEFIT = BENEFIT * 1.5;
C:  Next statement
```

We can accomplish the same thing in a format that is easier to follow by rearranging the code.

```
    IF (AGE < 55) THEN BENEFIT = MINIMUM;
    ELSE IF (AGE < 65) THEN BENEFIT = MINIMUM + BONUS;
    ELSE IF (AGE < 75) THEN BENEFIT = MINIMUM * 1.5 + BONUS;
    ELSE BENEFIT = MAXIMUM;
```

Of course, it is not always possible or practical to have exactly a top-down flow. Clearly, reaching the end of a loop may disrupt the top-down flow. However, a general guideline is that the required action should follow each decision as closely as possible.

Use of Submodules. We have seen how modularization introduces many positive characteristics in a software system. The advantages of modularity continue to help us as we write code now and support it later. By building a program from modular building blocks, we can hide some implementation details at various levels so that the entire system is easier to understand, test, and maintain. Similarly, a program module may be enhanced by the use of functions, macros, procedures, or subroutines that perform some of the elemental functions with the details hidden from view.

You can build a modular program from small, general-purpose modules, usable again in many other programs. To be sure that they are general enough to be reusable, program modules should do only one thing. In writing the code, keep in mind that *generality* is often a virtue; make sure that your code is not more specialized than it needs to be. For instance, a program module to search a string of eighty characters of text for a period could be written so that among the input parameters are the length of the string and the character to be found. Then the module can be used to search any length string for any character.

At the same time, do not make your modules more general than they need to be. Your code should follow the design, and the design should follow the specifications. More generality than that is unnecessary and can be confusing.

When one module depends on another in some way, the two modules are *coupled*, just as we described when designing the system. Remember to use parameter names and comments in the code to exhibit the coupling among modules when writing your programs. For example, suppose your module is estimating income tax. It uses the values of gross income (GROSS_INC) and deductions (DEDUCTS) provided by other modules. Instead of commenting a line of code with

```
Reestimate TAX
```

it is better to comment your code with

```
Reestimate TAX based on values of GROSS_INC and DEDUCTS
```

The second comment explains how the calculation is tied to data items in other modules.

In your code, it must be easy to discern what parameters are being passed down to a module and back again. Otherwise, testing and maintenance will be extremely difficult. In other words, the dependence among modules must be visible to a reader of the programs. By the same token, just as the modules of the system were designed to hide some information from each other, the pieces of your program should hide the details of the actual calculation from one another. This *information hiding* has the same function in coding that it had on the design level. Consider again a module to search for a character in a string. It is clear that the text searching module itself must contain information about how the specified character is sought. However, the calling program does not need to know *how* the character is found, only *that* it is found and where it is. In this way, the searching module hides implementation details from the calling programs. This hiding allows you to change the searching algorithm without disturbing the rest of the code.

Algorithms

The program design often specifies a class of algorithms or even a particular algorithm to be used in coding a module. For example, the design may instruct you to use a Quicksort or may list the logical steps of a Quicksort algorithm. However, you have a great deal of flexibility in converting the algorithm to actual lines of code. You must consider the algorithm in light of the implementation language and hardware and write your code accordingly.

Efficiency. Sometimes, programmers try to write code that will run as fast as possible to keep computing costs down. However, these costs must be viewed in the context of other costs:

1. The cost of time to write the code
2. The cost of time to test the code
3. The cost of time for users to understand the code
4. The cost of time to modify the code, if necessary

Execution time is only a small part of the costs involved. That is not to say that a good design or understandable code force the programmer to sacrifice execution time. You must balance execution time considerations with those of design quality, standards, and customer requirements.

It is therefore important to be sure that your code functions *correctly* before you concentrate on improving its speed. When trying to improve efficiency, do not give up clarity and ease of understanding. Most importantly, realize that most of the compilers in use today do a very good job of optimizing code. In fact, if you do not know how your compiler performs its optimization, your attempts at improving efficiency may actually work against the compiler.

To see how this may happen, suppose you are to implement a three-dimensional array in your code. You try to increase efficiency by creating instead a one-dimensional array and peforming all indexing computations yourself. Thus your code contains a computation such as

```
INDEX = 3*I + 2*J + K
```

to calculate the position of an entry. However, the compiler for your programming language may perform its array indexing computations in *registers*, so that execution time is small. The compiler may use an additive increment technique in the registers, rather than actually adding and multiplying for each position calculation. Your one-dimensional array technique may actually result in increased execution time because register calculations are not used and the amount of computation involves more storage and retrieval.

Data Structures

Program flow of control is intimately connected with the data being manipulated by the program. In writing your programs, you should think about how to format and store the data involved so that data management and manipulation are straightforward.

Keeping the Program Simple. The program design for a module may specify some of the data structures to be used in the functioning of the module. Often, these structures are chosen because they fit into an overall scheme that promotes information hiding and control of module interfaces. Data manipulations within a module can influence your choice of data structures in a similar way. For example, restructuring data can simplify a program's calculations. Suppose you are writing a program to determine the amount of federal income tax due. As input, you are given the amount of taxable income and are told the following:

1. For the first $10,000 of income, the tax is 10%.
2. For the next $10,000 of income above $10,000, the tax is 12%.
3. For the next $10,000 of income above $20,000, the tax is 15%.
4. For the next $10,000 of income above $30,000, the tax is 18%.
5. For any income above $40,000, the tax is 20%.

Thus, someone who has a taxable income of $35,000 pays ten percent of the first $10,000 (or $1,000), twelve percent of the next $10,000 (or $1,200), 15% of the next $10,000 (or $1,500) and 18% of the remaining $5,000 (or $900), for a total of $4,600. To calculate the tax, you can include code in your module that reads in the taxable income and follows this algorithm:

```
TAX = 0.
IF TAXABLE_INCOME = 0, GO TO EXIT
IF TAXABLE_INCOME > 10,000, TAX = TAX + 1000.
    ELSE TAX = TAX + .10 * TAXABLE_INCOME
    GO TO EXIT
IF TAXABLE_INCOME > 20,000, TAX = TAX + 1200.
    ELSE TAX = TAX + .12 * (TAXABLE_INCOME - 10000.)
    GO TO EXIT
IF TAXABLE_INCOME > 30,000, TAX = TAX + 1500.
    ELSE TAX = TAX + .15 * (TAXABLE_INCOME - 20000.)
    GO TO EXIT
IF TAXABLE_INCOME < 40,000, TAX = TAX + .18 * (TAXABLE_INCOME - 30000.)
    GO TO EXIT
ELSE TAX = TAX + 1800. + .20 * (TAXABLE_INCOME - 40000.)
    EXIT: END
```

However, we can define a tax table for each "bracket" of tax liability. Table 6.1 includes a base figure and a percentage for each bracket:

Table 6.1   Sample Tax Table

Bracket	Base	Percent
0	0.	.10
10000	1000.	.12
20000	2200.	.15
30000	3700.	.18
40000	5500.	.20

Then, using the table, our program algorithm becomes much simpler:

```
I = 1
LEVEL = 1
FOR I = 2 TO 5 DO
    IF TAXABLE INCOME > BRACKET(I)
    THEN LEVEL = LEVEL + 1
TAX = BASE(LEVEL) + PERCENT(LEVEL)*(TAXABLE_INCOME - BRACKET(LEVEL))
```

Notice how the calculations have been simplified just by changing the way the data are defined. This simplification makes the program easier to understand, easier to test, and easier to modify.

Using Structure of Data to Determine Structure of Program.   In the tax table example, the way we define the data dictates how we perform the necessary calculations. In general, data structures can influence the organization and flow of a program. In some cases, the data structures can influence the *choice of language* used to code a module. For example, LISP is designed to be a list processor, and it contains structures that make it much more attractive than some other languages for handling lists. You should consider the data structures involved when you are choosing a language for a module and implementing a design.

For example, a data structure is said to be a **recursive structure** if it is defined by identifying an initial component and then generating successive components as a function of previously-defined components. For example, recall that a **rooted tree** is a graph composed of nodes and lines so that the following conditions exist:

1. Exactly one node of the tree is designated as the root.
2. If the lines emanating from the root are erased, the resulting graph is a set of non-intersecting graphs, each of which is a rooted tree.

Figure 6.2 illustrates a rooted tree, and Figure 6.3 shows how removing the root results in a set of smaller rooted trees. The root of each smaller tree is the node that had previously been connected to the original root of the larger tree. Thus, the rooted tree is defined in terms of its root and subtrees: a recursive definition.

Programming languages such as Pascal allow recursive procedures in dealing with recursive data structures. You may prefer to use recursive procedures for these data structures, since their use forces the burden of managing the data structure to be borne by the compiler rather than your program. The use of recursion may make the actual programming easier or may result in a program that is easier to undertand.

Localizing Input and Output in Separate Modules. Those parts of a program that read input or generate output are highly specialized and must reflect the characteristics of the underlying hardware and software. Because of this dependence, the program sections performing input and output functions are sometimes difficult to test and are the most likely to change if the hardware or software changes. Therefore, it is desirable to localize these sections in modules separate from the rest of the code.

An added benefit of localization was discussed earlier in this chapter. By coding an input module in a general way, you can use the module for any input needed by the system. Other system-wide functions to be performed on the input (such as reformatting or type checking) can be coded in the general module. This general code eliminates repetition of the same functions in many other, more specific, modules. Hence implementation and testing are much more straightforward. Putting output functions in one place makes flow easier to follow in the calling

Figure 6.2 A Rooted Tree	Figure 6.3 Sub-Trees of Rooted Tree

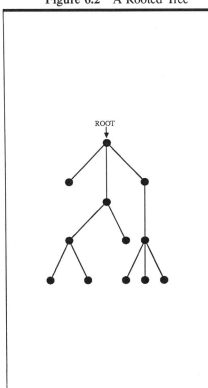 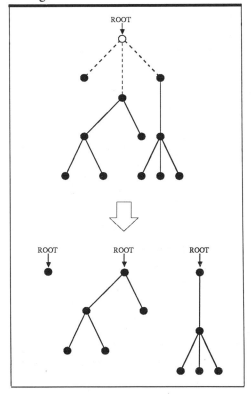

modules, allows the programmer to perform system-wide formatting, and makes testing and maintenance much faster and easier.

General Guidelines

There are several overall design strategies useful in generating high-quality code from a program design. Next we discuss two such approaches that help to preserve good design characteristics in the implementation.

Using Pseudocode. The program design lays out a framework for each program module. Then you add your *creativity* and *expertise* to build the lines of code that implement the design. For example, the program design may be relatively language-free, giving you many choices about the particular language constructs to use, how to use them, how the data will be represented, and so on. Since the program design can be considered an outline of what is to be done in a module, it is useful to move in stages from the program design specification to the program code, rather than to translate the design immediately into a set of code.

Pseudocode can be used to adapt the design to your chosen language. By adopting constructs and data representations without becoming involved immediately in the specifics of each command, you can experiment and decide which implementation is most desirable. In this way, code can be rearranged and restructured with a minimum of rewriting. For instance, suppose the program design for a module in a text processing system states the following:

```
MODULE PARSE_LINE:
    Read next eighty characters.
        IF this is a continuation of the previous line,
            Call CONTINUE
        ELSE determine command type.
        ENDIF
    CASE of COMMAND_TYPE
        COMMAND_TYPE is paragraph: Call PARAGRAPH.
        COMMAND_TYPE is indent: Call INDENT.
        COMMAND_TYPE is skip line: Call SKIP_LINE.
        COMMAND_TYPE is margin: Call MARGIN.
        COMMAND_TYPE is new page: Call PAGE.
        COMMAND_TYPE is double space: Call DOUBLE_SPACE.
        COMMAND_TYPE is single space: Call SINGLE_SPACE.
        COMMAND_TYPE is break: Call BREAK.
        COMMAND_TYPE is anything else: Call ERROR.
    ENDCASE
```

Depending on the chosen language and on your preference as a programmer, this design can be implemented in many ways. As the first stage in our translation of the design into code, we might examine each type of command to see what is involved. Using an intermediate pseudocode first, we can write the following commands:

```
PARAGRAPH:
    Break line, flush line buffer. Advance one line between paragraphs. If
    fewer than 2 lines left on page, eject. Set line pointer to paragraph
    indent.
INDENT:
    Break line, flush line buffer. Get indent parameter. Set line pointer to
    indent parameter, set left margin to indent.
SKIP_LINE:
    Break line, flush line buffer. Get line parameter. Advance (parameter)
    lines or eject if not enough space left on current page.
MARGIN:
    Break line, flush line buffer. Get margin parameter. Set line pointer to
    left margin. Set right margin to margin.
PAGE:
    Break line, flush line buffer. Eject page. Set line pointer to left
    margin.
DOUBLE_SPACE:
    Set interline space to 2.
SINGLE_SPACE:
    Set interline space to 1.
BREAK:
    Break line, flush line buffer. Set line pointer to left margin.
```

However, by reviewing the pseudocode, we see that we can regroup the steps involved so that certain common functions follow one another:

```
FIRST:
    PARAGRAPH, INDENT, SKIP_LINE, MARGIN, BREAK, PAGE:
        Break line, flush line buffer
    DOUBLE_SPACE, SINGLE_SPACE:
        No break line, no flush line buffer
SECOND:
    INDENT, SKIP_LINE, MARGIN:
        Get parameter
    PARAGRAPH, BREAK, PAGE, DOUBLE_SPACE, SINGLE_SPACE:
        No parameter needed
THIRD:
    PARAGRAPH, INDENT, SKIP_LINE, MARGIN, BREAK, PAGE:
        Set new line pointer
    DOUBLE_SPACE, SINGLE_SPACE:
        New line pointer unchanged
FOURTH:
    Individual actions taken
```

Having described the commands in this way, we recognize that the FIRST and THIRD set of actions apply to the same group of commands. In addition, we notice that the line pointer depends on the left margin in all cases except when the command is PARAGRAPH. Using this information, we can write pseudocode in more detail.

```
INITIAL:
    Get parameter for indent, line skip, margin.
    Set left margin to parameter for indent.
    Set temporary line pointer to left margin for all but paragraph; for
    paragraph, set it to paragraph indent.
LINE_BREAKS:
    If not (DOUBLE_SPACE or SINGLE_SPACE), break line and flush line buffer
    and set line pointer to temporary line pointer.
    If 0 lines left on page, eject page and print page header.
INDIVIDUAL_CASES:
    INDENT, BREAK: do nothing.
    SKIP-LINE: skip parameter lines or eject.
    PARAGRAPH: advance 1 line; if < 2 lines on page, eject.
    MARGIN: right_margin = parameter.
    DOUBLE_SPACE: interline_space = 2.
    SINGLE_SPACE: interline_space = 1.
    PAGE: eject page, print page header.
```

Finally, we can write PASCAL code to implement this design:

```
{initial: get parameters}
if (command_type in [indent, line_skip, margin])
    then parm_value:=get_parm(input_line);
if (command_type = indent)
    then left_margin:=parm_value;
if (command_type = paragraph)
    then temp_line_pointer:=paragraph_indent;
    else temp_line_pointer:=left_margin
{break current line, begin new line}
if (not((command_type=dbl_spc) or (command_type=sngl_spc)))
    then begin
        call break_and_flush_line;
        if (lines_left = 0)
            then call begin_new_page
        line_pointer:=temp_line_pointer;
    end;
{actions for individual commands}
case (command_type) of
    line_skip: if (lines_left > parm_value) then
        for i:=1 to parm_value do
            call advance_line
        else call begin_new_page;
    paragraph: begin
        call advance_line;
```

```
        if (lines_left < 2) then
            call begin_new_page
    end;
margin: right_margin:=parm_value;
dbl_spc: interline_space:=2;
sngl_spc: interline_space:=1;
page: call begin_new_page
end; {case of command_type}
```

Thus, pseudocode has acted as a framework on which to construct the code. In briefing the code from the design, notice that several organizational changes have been made to the design. Such changes must be reported to and approved by the program designers; the links among requirements, design, and code must be documented and maintained.

Revising and Rewriting Rather Than Patching. When writing code, as when preparing a term paper or creating a work of art, you often prepare a rough draft and carefully revise and rewrite until you are satisfied with the result. Such an approach is preferable to manipulating an existing piece of code to fit a new system, or to making extensive patches to a program full of errors. In writing a program, if you find that the control flow is convoluted, or the decision processes are difficult to understand, or the unconditional branches are hard to eliminate, it may be time to return to the design. *Reexamine the design* to see whether the problems you are encountering are inherent in the design. Look again at the data structures and representation, at the algorithms chosen, and at the modularization of the program. In many cases, changes to the basic design will make the writing of the code much easier and will result in a clear, understandable program.

Sometimes a programmer likes to adapt to the problem at hand a module from another system or project. If the module has been written in a completely general way, this approach can be useful. However, if the existing module is so specialized that extensive changes are required, it is usually better to write the required module from scratch. In rewriting, the design is free of restrictions imposed from an unrelated problem; the resulting code can be cleaner and more directly applicable to the new problem.

6.3

DOCUMENTATION

Many corporate or organizational standards and procedures focus on the descriptions accompanying a collection of programs. We consider **program documentation** to be the set of written descriptions that accompany programs in order to explain to a reader what the programs do and how they do it. **Internal documentation** is descriptive material written directly within the program; all other documentation is **external documentation**.

Internal Documentation

The internal documentation contains information directed at someone who will be reading the source code of your program. Thus, *summary information* is provided to a reader to identify the program and describe its data structures, algorithms, and control flow. This summary information is placed at the beginning of the program module in a set of comments called the **header comment block**.

Header Comment Block. Just as a good newspaper reporter must include the who, what, where, when, why, and how in a story, you must include the following information in the header comment block:

1. *What* your program is
2. *Who* wrote the program
3. *Where* the program fits in the general system design
4. *When* the program was written and revised
5. *Why* the program exists
6. *How* your program uses its data structures, algorithms and control

We will examine each of these pieces of information in more depth.

First, the name of the program must figure prominently in the documentation. If the program is invoked at some point in the system, the program name in the documentation makes the program easily identifiable.

Next, the writer of the program must be identified. This information explains who is responsible for the program and tells the test and maintenance members of the project team to whom to turn with questions, comments, or problems.

Because the program or module is part of an overall system, it is important for the documentation to indicate how the module fits in the general system scheme. This information can be conveyed in several ways. You can include a diagram of module hierarchy. Alternatively, you can list the modules called and calling modules, as we saw on page 242. Your header block should explain the sequence or procedure for invoking the module, and any modules invoked by this module are also listed.

During the life of a system, program modules are sometimes updated and revised, either because error correction is needed or because customer requirements change over a period of time. As we will see in chapter 10, it is important to keep track of the revisions of each part of the system. Thus, the program documentation includes a notation about when the original program was written and a log of revisions that were made. Often an entry is made to the internal documentation for each revision so that the documentation contains a dated list of each revision type.

A statement of the general purpose of the program module tells a reader what the module is trying to do. This statement summarizes the program so that by scanning the header comment block, someone can quickly see why this program was written.

The way in which the program accomplishes its goal is also summarized in the header comment block. Usually this part of the block includes the following information:

1. Name, type, and purpose of each major data structure and variable
2. Brief description of the logic flow of the module, including major algorithms
3. Description of error handling
4. Expected input, possible output
5. Description of aids to testing and how to use them
6. Description of expected extensions or revisions

Although the order in which the elements of the header comment block are listed can vary, it is usually subject to any formal standards that apply to the project. No matter what the standard for your particular project, it is important to include all of the above information in your header comment block. Here is how a typical header comment block for a text processing module might look:

```
PROGRAM SCAN - Program to scan a line of text for a given character
PROGRAMMER: Beatrice Clarman (718)345-6789
CALLING SEQUENCE: CALL SCAN(LENGTH,CHAR)
    where 'LENGTH' is the length of the line to be scanned, 'CHAR' is the
    character to be sought, line of text passed as array 'NTEXT'.
VERSION 1: written 1-12-86
REVISION 1.1: 2-3-86 improve searching algorithm.
PURPOSE: General-purpose scanning module to be used for each new line of
    text, no matter the length.
DATA STRUCTURES: Variable LENGTH - INTEGER
    Variable CHAR - CHARACTER
    ARRAY NTEXT - CHARACTER array of length 'LENGTH'
ALGORITHM: Reads array NTEXT one character at a time; if CHAR is found, posi-
    tion in NTEXT returned in variable 'LENGTH'; else variable 'LENGTH' set to 0
```

Other Program Comments. The header comment block acts as an introduction to your program, much as an introduction to a book explains its purpose. Additional comments enlighten readers along their way through your program. If the organization of the code reflects a well-structured design, if the statements are formatted clearly, and if the labels, variable, and data names are descriptive and easy to distinguish, then the necessary number of additional comments is small. By following the guidelines in this chapter for code format and structure, the code acts as a source of information about itself.

Comments have a place even in clearly structured and well-written code. Although clarity of code and structure minimize the need for other comments, additional comments are needed wherever useful information can be added to a program module. Comments can play other roles besides providing a line-by-line explanation of what the program is doing. For example, comments can break a program into *phases* that represent major activities. The code for an activity is usually no more than one page in length. Then an individual activity may be separated by comments into smaller *steps*, each only several lines of code in length. Pseudocode from your program design can serve this purpose and remind you of the functions involved.

When code is revised, programmers sometimes forget to update the comments to reflect the change. It is essential that your comments agree with what the code is actually doing. In addition, be sure that every comment adds new information. For example, it is of no use to write

```
I3 = I3 + 1 ; INCREMENT I3
```

when you can add substantially more information by writing

```
I3 = I3 + 1 ; SET COUNTER TO READ NEXT CASE
```

Ideally, the parameter names should help to explain the activity being performed:

```
CASE_COUNTER = CASE_COUNTER + 1
```

Your comments should be written as you write the code itself, not afterward. By beginning with the design and moving to the final code in stages, the design evolves to pseudocode which in turn acts as a framework for your final code and a basis for your comments. As you write in-line comments and explain what the code is doing, beware of code that is difficult to comment. If you are having problems writing understandable comments about complex code, you may need to redesign your code in some way.

Meaningful Variable Names and Statement Labels. Choose names for your variables and statements that reflect use or meaning. Writing

```
WEEKWAGE = (HRRATE * HOURS) + (.5) * (HRRATE) * (HOURS - 40.)
```

makes much more sense to the reader than

```
Z = (A * B) + (.5) * (A) * (B - 40.)
```

In fact, the first example is likely not to need any additional comments. Also, you are less likely to introduce errors into your program when the statement labels and variable names are meaningful.

Similarly alphabetic statement labels should tell readers something about what the labeled section of your program does. If the labels are numeric or incorporate numbers, they should be in ascending order and clustered by related purpose.

Formatting to Enhance Understanding. The format of your comments can help a reader understand what the code is doing and how. Indentation and spacing of statements can reflect the basic control structures. Notice how unindented code like this:

```
IF XCOORD < YCOORD
THEN RESULT = -1;
ELSE IF XCOORD = YCOORD
```

```
THEN IF SLOPE1 > SLOPE2
THEN RESULT = 0;
ELSE RESULT = 1;
ELSE IF SLOPE1 > SLOPE2
THEN RESULT = 2;
ELSE IF SLOPE1 < SLOPE2
THEN RESULT = 3;
ELSE RESULT = 4;
```

can be clarified by using indentation and rearranging the space:

```
IF      XCOORD < YCOORD THEN RESULT = -1;
ELSE IF XCOORD = YCOORD THEN
     IF SLOPE1 > SLOPE2 THEN RESULT = 0;
                        ELSE RESULT = 1;
ELSE IF SLOPE1 > SLOPE2 THEN RESULT = 2;
ELSE IF SLOPE1 < SLOPE2 THEN RESULT = 3;
ELSE                         RESULT = 4;
```

In addition to using format to display the control structure, Weinberg ([WEI71]) recommends formatting your statements so that the comments appear on one side of the page and the statements on the other. In this way, you can cover up the comments when testing your program and not be misled by what may be incorrect documentation. For example, the Pascal code below can be read without comments by looking only at the left side of the page.

```
procedure skipch;                     {updates pointers and skips next single
                                      {character in input }
var
  k: integer;                         {local pointer}
begin
  for k:= iptr+1 to incount do
    ch[k-1] := ch[k];                 {move each char. back one position}
  ch[incount] := " ";
  incount := incount - 1;             {shorten string length by 1}
  iptr := iptr - 1;                   {move input pointer back;will mv ahd}
end;  {skipch}

begin
  incount := endpt;                   {upper bound on chars. to edit}
  iptr := 1;                          {begin with start of ch array}
  cr_last := false;
  while (iptr < incount) do
    begin
      if (ord(ch[iptr]) < ord(" ")) then
        begin                         {is a control character}
```

```
      if (ch[iptr] = chr(cr))
        then                        {character was <CR>}
          if (cr_last) then skipch {repeated <CR>s; keep only one}
            else cr_last := true   {first <CR>; keep it}
          else                      {char was not <CR>}
          if (ch[iptr] = chr(lf))
            then
              if (cr_last)
                then cr_last := false
                  else skipch       {skip repeated <LF>s}
              else                  {neither <CR> nor <LF>}
              skipch                {skip ctrl char.}
        end                         {if (ch < " ")}
    else                            {ch was printable}
      cr_last := false;
    iptr := iptr+1;                 {go to next char}
    end;                            {while iptr < incount}
  ch[0] := chr(incount);
  endpt := incount;
```

Documenting Data. One of the most difficult things for readers of a program to understand is the way in which data are structured and used. A "map" of the data is very useful in interpreting the actions of lines of code, especially when a system handles many files of varying types and purposes, coupled with flags and passed parameters. Thus, internal documentation should include descriptions of the data structures and uses. Be sure to list major variables in the header control block and any default values for each variable. Such a data entry may look like this one.

```
{  DATA STRUCTURES:                    }
{    DAMLOC contains                    }
{      dam locations and height         }
{    DEFAULT VALUES: read from tape     }
{    WATERQUAL to store                 }
{      water quality data from sensors  }
{    DEFAULT VALUES: initialized to 0   }
```

Finally, in the body of the program, indicate when and how the values of the data change:

```
var CURRENT_DAM:DAMLOC;
  .
  .
  .
with CURRENT_DAM do
read (DAMNUM, DAMLAT, DAMLON, DAMHGT); (reset dam record values)
```

External Documentation

Whereas internal documentation is concise and written at a level appropriate for a programmer, external documentation is intended to be read also by those who may never look at the actual code. For instance, system or program designers may review the external documentation when considering modifications or enhancements to the system. In addition, in the external documentation you have a chance to explain things in more detail than might be reasonable within your program's comments. If you consider the header comment block to be an overview or *summary* of your program, then the external documentation can be considered the *full-blown report*. It answers the same questions—who, what, why, when, where, and how—in greater depth.

Because a software system is built from interrelated modules, the external documentation often includes an overview of the modules comprising the system or of several groupings of system modules. Diagrams, accompanied by narrative describing each module, show how data structures are shared and used by one or more modules; in general, the overview describes how information is passed from one module to another.

External program documentation is part of the overall system documentation. At the time the program is written, much of the rationale for the program structure and flow has already been detailed in the system and program design documents. In a sense, the program design is the skeleton of the external documentation; the flesh is supplied by narrative discussing the particulars of the program.

Describing the Problem. In the first section of the external documentation, you explain what *problem* is being addressed by the program. This section sets the stage for describing what options were considered for solutions and why a particular solution was chosen. The problem description is not a repeat of the requirements description that resulted from the requirements analysis. Rather it is a general discussion of the setting: when this program is called and why it is needed.

Describing the Algorithms. Once you make clear why the program exists, you should address the *choice of algorithms*. Each algorithm used by the program is discussed in detail in a narrative form. All formulae are included, and boundary or special conditions discussed. Where appropriate, include the derivation of the algorithm or a reference to it in some other source (such as the program design, a journal article, or a textbook).

If an algorithm deals with *special cases*, be sure to discuss the cases and explain how each special case is derived and handled. If certain cases are not handled because they will never be encountered, the documentation should explain why they will not be encountered. For example, an algorithm may involve a formula where one variable expression is divided by another. The documentation should discuss the possibility that the denominator may be zero. In cases where the denominator is zero, an explanation of how the program handles the formula and subsequent calculation should be included; if it is impossible for the denominator to be zero, then your document addresses why this case will never occur.

Describing the Data.   In the external documentation, users or programmers can see the *data flow* through the system at a program module level. Thus, data flow diagrams accompany any description of a program module. Much of this information may already exist in the program design; the external documentation can refer to the design but should also describe the layout in a narrative form.

6.4
RESOURCE TRACKING AND SIMULATION

We can look at an example of programming and documentation guidelines to see what you can expect. Recall that in chapter 2 we discussed a method for determining if a system has a low, medium, or high degree of difficulty. Some organizations apply different documentation standards, depending on the size, complexity, or difficulty of a proposed system. In general, the more difficult or complex a program, the more detail required by the standards.

For a system of low difficulty or complexity, the guidelines may read as follows:

    DOCUMENTATION:
        Internal documentation:
            Header comment block
            Indentation to exhibit control structure
            Meaningful variable and data names
            Definition of interface requirements
            Description of program invocation
    PROCESSING:
        Error handling:
            Brief error messages
    CONTROL FLOW:
        Use structured techniques
        Keep coupling low
        Keep cohesion high
    LANGUAGE:
        Avoid unconditional branching where possible
        Use language-specific structures to maximize productivity

The Weaver Farm system is more complex. For such systems of medium or high difficulty, we place additional constraints on the programs:

    DOCUMENTATION:
        As above, plus:
        Internal documentation:
            In-line comments
            Blank lines or comment lines of '*' or '=' between major processing
            steps

External documentation:
    Reference manual summarizing each module
PROCESSING:
    As above, plus:
    Validate all input.
    Error handling:
        Identify location of error
        Identify nature of error
        Allow user to override and continue or to terminate processing
CONTROL FLOW:
    As above, plus:
    Establish loop invariants

As you can see, these standards are not constraining. Instead, they direct you to include certain aids in a program or to follow a certain philosophy when writing the code. For example, the error-handling requirements encourage the program to attempt to continue processing when an error is encountered, rather than terminate processing with the display of an error message. The guidelines give you the flexibility of following the usual standards that are applied to the language chosen for implementation. For instance, the organization of processing and comment lines must depend on what the particular language allows.

Other organizations may have more restrictive standards. Often, the standards show a typical block of documentation to be used at the beginning of each program module. Some standards require that certain naming conventions be used. For instance, on a large project, a standard may be set so that all system program names begin with '#', while all input and output module names begin with the letters 'IO'. Whatever standards and procedures are prescribed, they all have the same objective as those preceding; namely, the standards and procedures encourage you to produce correct code that is easy to read and understand.

6.5

CHAPTER SUMMARY

This chapter has presented us with *guidelines* for transforming the program design to its implementation as a computer program. We have seen the need for standards and procedures, as aids not only to programmers but also to others who may have to test or modify the code produced. Implementation follows design in the software development process, and the implementation modules should correspond to the modules already defined in the system and program design steps. Problems in writing code are more likely to be design problems than coding ones. Thus, if you are having difficulty writing a program, it may be better to revise the design and rewrite than to continue to manipulate bad code.

In the previous chapter, we identified several fundamental control structures: sequence, selection (IF-THEN-ELSE and CASE) and repetition (WHILE-DO and REPEAT-UNTIL). These basic constructs can be used to structure each program module. The flow of the program control should begin at the top of the program and continue sequentially, as far as is practicable. By beginning with the program module pseudocode and embellishing each section, a program can be refined and revised while maintaining the same overall flow.

The data structures should be kept simple and understandable. Sometimes, the structure of the data can dictate the structure of the program. Such is the case when recursive data structures are used; recursive procedures can be helpful in manipulating them.

Localization benefits both input and output operations. By placing common services such as input and output in general modules, not only do we make testing easier but also we can enhance or modify particular functions without disturbing the entire system.

Documentation is vital to the life of the system. It helps you as a programmer remember why and how you built your program modules as you did. At the same time, it explains exactly what the code does to others who may be correcting or adapting it. Internal documentation, comprised of a header comment block and in-line comments, enhances the readability of your code. Also, by using clear and meaningful statement labels, formatting your code to reflect its structure, and describing the overall data structures, another programmer will have little trouble understanding your program and its relationship to the others in the system.

External documentation expands upon the internal documentation. It acts as an overview for a programmer, but it also tells an analyst or designer what the components of the system do and how they do it. A program logic manual explains what problem is being solved, what algorithms were chosen to solve the problem, and what data structures have been established to implement the solution.

Writing the code for a system is another aspect of the "art" of computing. The guidelines presented here apply software engineering principles to writing a program so that you can be creative and flexible while preserving the design. Thus, software engineering guidelines encourage the production of high-quality, easy to read, easy to test, easy to maintain code.

Once the code is written, we must determine if it works the way we want and expect it to work. In the next chapter, we will turn to the problem of testing the code modules.

6.6
EXERCISES

1. An unconditional branch in a program, such as a GOTO statement, directs the flow of control of the program to another area, usually by referring to a statement label. Since it is desirable to minimize the use of unconditional branches, is it also desirable to minimize the use of statement labels? Give an example of a program segment where a statement label is used but where an unconditional branch is not involved.

2. We can call a statement in any language a computed case type of statement if it branches to one of several areas in the program depending on the value of a variable. Discuss the positive and negative aspects of this type of statement. In particular, how does it affect the control flow?

3. A data structure that can be defined recursively is a *list*. Give a recursive definition of a list. If you are familiar with a programming language that has recursive procedures (such as LISP or PL/I), explain how elements are added to and deleted from a list in that language.

4. Give an example to show how a language designed for recursion makes the list handling easier to understand than a language without such provision.

5. You are asked to write a program to print out a yearly calendar. The user enters the year desired, and the output is a calendar for that year. Discuss how the representation of internal data will affect the way in which the program is written. Give several examples of data arrays that might be used in such a problem. (**Hint:** Are your arrays cumulative or not? How is a leap year handled?)

6. The common algorithm for calculating the roots of a quadratic equation by the quadratic formula requires considering several special cases in your code. Write appropriate comments for this algorithm so that the comments make it easy to see the different cases and how they are handled. Write accompanying external documentation to explain the algorithm.

7. Find out the paging algorithm for a computer operating system with which you are familiar. Write external documentation for the algorithm, explaining to a user how the paging is handled.

8. Look at a program that you have submitted as a project in another class. Can it be improved by using the suggestions in this chapter? If so, how? Does incorporating these suggestions make your program more or less efficient?

C H A P T E R   7

PROGRAM TESTING

In the previous chapter, we saw how to transform a program's design specification into a programming language implementation of the design. Figure 7.1 shows that we are ready to address the problem of testing the resulting modules to see whether the programs work as intended. First, we look at *defective software* to see what types of errors can occur. Then, we discuss the *purpose* of testing. We see that testing a software project is different from the kind of testing you do for your class projects. The testing process is described in terms of who performs the tests, what steps are involved, and what types of tests can be used.

Next, we examine in depth the *testing of individual modules*. After you, as a programmer, have eliminated errors, your code can be evaluated in several ways. It can be reviewed in a program walkthrough or inspection or proven correct using formal techniques. We note the difference between *testing* and *proving*, and see how tests are designed to be thorough. Finally, we discuss how to generate test data as a set of test cases.

Integration testing involves the merging of tested modules, and several approaches can be taken. We detail each of these and compare their advantages and disadvantages. Once an approach is chosen, we can select among several *automated test tools* to insure a thorough and traceable series of tests.

In general, the testing phase of software development requires careful planning and coordination. We investigate the creation of a *test plan* to direct our testing efforts. Finally, we examine the notions of software *reliability*, *maintainability*, and *availability* to see if testing can demonstrate the quality that we intended to build in.

7.1

DEFECTIVE SOFTWARE

In an ideal situation, we, as programmers, become so good at our craft that every program we produce works properly every time we run it. Unfortunately, this ideal is not reality. We saw in chapter 1 that the inherent differences between software

Figure 7.1   The System Development Process

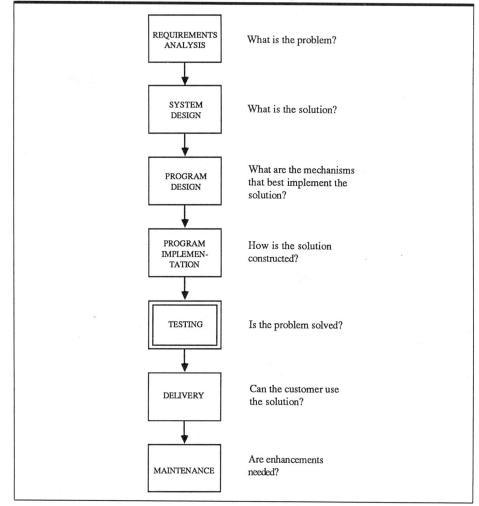

systems and hardware systems lead to software in which we are not 100% confident. This lack of confidence stems from several things. First, many software systems deal with large numbers of states and with complex formulae, activities and algorithms. In addition to that, we use the tools at our disposal to implement a customer's conception of a system when the customer is sometimes uncertain of exactly what is needed. Finally, the size of a project and the number of people involved can add complexity. Thus, the presence of errors in the software we write is a function not only of the software itself but also of user and customer expectations.

Software Errors

What do we mean when we say that there is an error in our software? Usually we mean that the software does not do what the requirements documents describe. For example, the requirements specification may state that the system must respond to a particular query in no more than five seconds. If the program responds in six seconds, we say that the system is not working properly. This may be the result of any of several reasons:

1. The specification may be wrong. It may not be what the customer really wants or needs. Perhaps the customer means that the average response time must be no more than five seconds.

2. The specification may specify something that is physically impossible, given the hardware and software prescribed by the customer.

3. The system design may be at fault. Perhaps the way in which the data base and its query language were designed makes it impossible to respond to the given query in five seconds.

4. The program design may be at fault. The module descriptions may contain a search algorithm that is inherently too slow.

5. The program code may be wrong. The code may implement the search algorithm inefficiently or improperly so that the response to the query takes too long.

By the time we have coded and are testing the program modules, we hope that the specifications are correct. Moreover, having used the software engineering techniques described in previous chapters, we have tried to assure that the design of the system and program modules reflects the requirements and forms a basis for a sound implementation. However, the stages of the software development cycle involve not only our computing skills but also our communication and inter-personal skills. It is entirely possible that an error in a software system can result from a misunderstanding during the development process. We say that a software system contains an **error** if it does not do what the customer expects it to do. A **failure** is an occurrence of an error somewhere in the software system.

Errors are not inherent in software. Bridges, buildings, and other engineered constructions may fail because of shoddy materials or because they wear out after a period of time. However, DO-WHILE statements do not wear out after several hundred iterations, and RETURN statements do not fall off the ends of sub-routines. If a particular piece of code does not work properly and a spurious hardware failure is not the root of the problem, then we can be certain that an error is present in the code. It is for this reason that many software engineers refuse to use the term "bug" to describe a software error; calling an error a "bug" implies that the error wandered into the code from some external source over which the developers have no control.

In previous chapters, we examined the ways in which the system can be specified and designed in order to minimize the introduction of errors during those steps. In this chapter, we examine techniques that can minimize the occurrence of errors in the program code itself.

Types of Errors. After coding the program modules, we usually examine the code to spot errors and to eliminate them right away. When no obvious errors exist, we then test our program to see if we can isolate more errors. Thus, it is important that we know the kinds of errors for which to look. We can catalog the types of errors that occur in the coding of the program modules.

The first kind of error that we usually try to eliminate is an **algorithmic error**. An algorithmic error is one in which program module's algorithm or logic does not produce the proper output for a given input because something is wrong with the processing steps. This kind of error is sometimes easy to spot just by reading through the program. Typical algorithmic errors include:

1. Branching too soon
2. Branching too late
3. Testing for the wrong condition
4. Forgetting to initialize variables or set loop invariants
5. Forgetting to test for a particular condition (such as when division by zero might occur)
6. Comparing variables of inappropriate data types

When checking for algorithmic errors, we may also check for **syntax errors**. Here we want to be sure that we have properly used the constructs of the programming language. Sometimes the presence of a seemingly trivial syntax error can lead to disastrous results. For example, Myers ([MYE76]) points out that the first United States space mission to Venus failed because of a missing comma in a FORTRAN DO loop. Fortunately, compilers catch many of the syntax errors.

Computation and precision errors occur when the implementation of a formula is wrong or does not compute the result to the required degree of accuracy. For example, combining integer and fixed- or floating-point variables in an expression may produce unexpected results. Sometimes, improper use of floating-point data or ordering of operations may result in less than acceptable precision.

When the documentation describes the program's function but does not match what the program actually does, we say that the program has **documentation errors**. Often the documentation is derived from the program design and provides a very clear description of what the programmer would *like* the program to do, but the implementation of those functions is in error. Such errors can lead to a proliferation of errors later in the life of the program since many of us tend to believe the documentation when examining the code to make modifications.

The requirements specification usually details the number of users and devices and the need for communication in a system. Thus, the system design often tailors the system characteristics to handle no more than the maximum load described by the requirements. These characteristics are carried through to the program design as parameters for the lengths of queues, the size of buffers, the dimensions of tables, and so on. **Stress** or **overload errors** occur when these data structures are filled past their specified capacity.

Similarly, **capacity** or **boundary errors** occur when the performance of a system becomes unacceptable as the activity on the system reaches its specified limit. For instance, if the requirements specify that a system must handle thirty-two devices, the programs must be tested to monitor the performance of the system when thirty-two devices are all active. Moreover, the system should also be tested to see what happens when thirty-three devices are active, if such activity is possible. By testing and documenting the system's reaction to a configuration beyond its capacity, the test team helps the maintenance team understand the implications of increasing system capacity in the future. Capacity conditions are also be examined in relation to the number of disk accesses, the number of interrupts, the number of tasks running concurrently, and other system-related measures.

In developing real-time systems, a critical consideration is the coordination of several processes executing simultaneously or in a carefully defined sequence. **Timing** or **coordination errors** occur when the code coordinating these events is inadequate. There are two reasons why this kind of error is very hard to identify and correct. First, it is usually difficult for designers and programmers to anticipate all possible system states. Second, because so many factors are involved with timing and processing, it may be impossible to replicate an error after it has occurred.

Throughput or **performance errors** occur when the system does not perform at the speed prescribed by the requirements. These are timing errors of a different sort: time constraints are placed on the system's performance by the customer's requirements, rather than by the need for coordination.

As we saw in the design stages, care is taken to insure that the system can recover from a variety of error conditions. **Recovery errors** can occur when an error is encountered and the system does not behave as the designers desire or as the customer requires. For example, if a power failure occurs during system processing, the system should recover in an acceptable manner. For some systems, such recovery may mean that the system will continue full processing by using a back-up power system; for others, this recovery means that the system keeps a log of transactions, allowing it to continue its processing whenever the power is restored.

For many systems, a set of hardware and system software is prescribed in the requirements. The software modules are designed according to specifications in the hardware and system software documentation. For example, if a modem is to be used for communications, the modem driver program generates the commands expected by the modem and reads the commands received from the modem. However, **hardware and system software errors** can arise when the documentation for the supplied hardware and software does not match their actual operating conditions and procedures.

Finally, the program modules are reviewed to guarantee that the standards and procedures imposed on the system by the development team have, in fact, been followed. These **standards and procedures errors** may not affect the running of the programs but may foster an environment for the creation of errors as the system is tested and modified. By not having followed the prescribed standards, one programmer may make it difficult for another to understand the programming logic or to find the data descriptions needed to solve a problem.

Purpose of Testing

No matter how capably we write programs, it is clear from the variety of possible errors that we should check to insure that our modules are coded correctly. Many programmers view testing as a demonstration that their programs perform properly. However, the idea of demonstrating correctness is really the reverse of what testing is all about. We **test** a program in order to demonstrate the *existence* of an error. Because our goal is to discover errors, we can consider a test successful only when an error is discovered. Once an error is found, "**debugging**" or **error correction** is the process of determining what *causes* the error and of *making changes* to the system so that the error no longer exists.

Attitudes Toward Testing.   New programmers are not accustomed to viewing testing as a discovery process. As a student, you write programs according to specifications given by your instructor. After having designed a program, you write the lines of code and compile them to determine if any syntax errors are present. When submitting your program for a grade, you usually present your instructor with a program listing and some kind of *test evidence*. The evidence is often a set of input data and the corresponding output from your program; the input data may be chosen to persuade your instructor that the program functions as described in the assignment.

You may have considered your program only as a solution to a problem; you may not have considered the problem itself. If so, your test data may have been chosen to show positive results in certain cases, rather than the absence of errors. Programs written in this way are evidence of your programming skill. Psychologically, a critique of your program is a critique of your ability. Thus, testing by showing that your program works correctly is a way of demonstrating your ability to your instructor.

However, when you are developing a system for a customer, the customer is not interested in knowing that the system works properly under certain conditions but rather in knowing that the system works properly under *all* conditions. Therefore, your goal as a developer should be to eliminate as many errors in the system as possible, no matter where in the system they occur and no matter who created them. There is no room in the development process for feelings to be hurt as errors are discovered.

Hence, many software engineers adopt an attitude known as *egoless programming*, where program modules are viewed as the components of a larger system, not as the property of those who wrote them. When an error is found, the egoless development team is concerned with determining the cause of the error and correcting it, not with placing blame on a particular developer.

Who Performs the Tests?   Even when a system is developed with an egoless approach, it is sometimes difficult for us to remove our personal feelings from the testing process. Thus, we often use an independent test team to test a system. In this way, we avoid conflict between personal responsibility for errors and the need to discover as many errors as possible.

In addition, there are several other factors that justify an independent team. As we have seen earlier in this chapter, there is always the possibility that we have introduced errors when interpreting the program design, determining the program logic, writing the descriptive documentation, or implementing the algorithms. Clearly, we would not have submitted our code for testing if we did not think that the code performs according to the specifications. However, we may be too close to our program to be able to view it objectively and spot some of the more subtle errors.

Furthermore, an independent test team can participate in reviewing the modules throughout development. The team can be part of both the requirements and the design reviews. After having tested each module individually, the team can continue to test as the system is integrated and presented to the customer for acceptance. In this way, testing can proceed concurrently with the coding of programming modules; the test team can test modules and begin to piece them together as the programming staff continues to code other modules.

Stages of Testing. In the development of a large system, testing involves several stages. First, each program module is tested as a single program, usually isolated from the other programs in the system. Such testing, known as **module testing** or **unit testing**, verifies that the module functions properly with the types of input expected from studying the module design. Unit testing is done in a controlled environment whenever possible so that the test team can feed a predetermined set of data to the module being tested and observe what output data are produced. In addition, the test team checks the internal data structures, the logic, and the boundary conditions for the input and output data.

When collections of modules have been unit tested, the next step is to insure that the interfaces among the modules are defined and handled properly. **Integration testing** is the process of verifying that the components of a system work together as described in the program design and system design specifications.

Once we are sure that information is passed among modules according to the design prescriptions, we test the system to assure that it has the desired functionality. A **function test** evaluates the system to determine if the functions described by the requirements specification are actually performed by the integrated system. The result, then, is a functioning system.

Recall that the requirements were specified in two ways: first in the customer's terminology and again as a set of software and hardware requirements. The function test compares the system being built with the functions described in the software and hardware requirements. Then, a **performance test** compares the system with the remainder of the software and hardware requirements. If the test is performed in the customer's actual working environment, a successful test yields a **validated system**. However, if the test must be performed in a simulated environment, the resulting system is a **verified system**.

When the performance test is complete, we as developers are certain that the system functions according to our understanding of the system description. The next step is to confer with the customer to make certain that the system works according to the customer's expectations. We join with the customer to perform an **acceptance test** in which the system is checked against the customer's requirements description. When the acceptance test is complete, the accepted system is installed in the environment in which it will be used; a final **installation test** is performed to make sure that the system still functions as it should.

Figure 7.2 illustrates the several stages of testing. Although systems may differ in size, the type of testing described in each stage is necessary for assuring the proper performance of any system being developed.

In this chapter, we describe the preliminary testing stages: unit and integration testing. These stages deal with the testing of modules and the incorporation of the modules into a cohesive system. In chapter 8, we will investigate the remaining stages of testing, often collectively called **system testing**. In these later stages, the system is tested as one large entity, rather than as separate pieces.

Figure 7.2   Stages of Testing

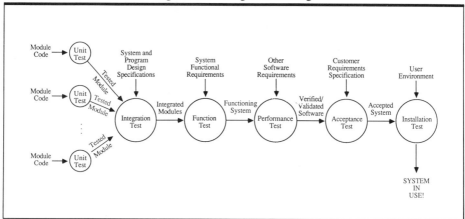

Types of Testing.   Before we discuss unit testing, let us consider the philosophy behind our testing. As you test a module, group of modules, subsystem, or system, your view of the object being tested can affect the way in which the testing proceeds. If you view the test object from the outside as a *closed box* whose contents are unknown, your testing consists of feeding input to the closed box and of noting what output results are produced. In this case, the test's goal is to be sure that every possible kind of input is submitted and that the output observed matches the output expected.

There are advantages and disadvantages to this kind of testing. The obvious advantage is that closed box testing is free of the constraints imposed by the internal structure and logic of the test object. However, it is not always possible to run a complete test in this manner. For example, suppose a simple module accepts as input three real numbers A, B, and C and produces as output the roots of the equation

$$Ax^2 + Bx + C = 0$$

or the message "NO REAL ROOTS." It is impossible to test the module by submitting to it every possible triple of real numbers (A, B, C). In this case, the test team may be able to choose representative test data to show that all possible combinations are handled properly. For instance, test data may be chosen so that the discriminant, B^2-4AC, is in each of three classes: positive, zero, or negative. However, if a test in each of the three classes reveals no error, we have no guarantee that the module is error free. The module may still fail for a particular case.

For some test objects, it is impossible for the test team to generate a set of representative test cases that demonstrate correct functionality for all cases. Recall from chapter 6 the example of the module that accepted an adjusted gross income as input and produced the amount of federal income tax owed as output. We might have a tax table showing expected output for certain given inputs, but we may not know in general how the tax is calculated. The algorithm for computing the tax depends on tax brackets, and both the bracket limits and associated percentages are part of the internal processing of the module. By viewing this module as a closed box, we could not choose representative test cases because we would not know enough about the brackets.

Figure 7.3   Module with Iteration

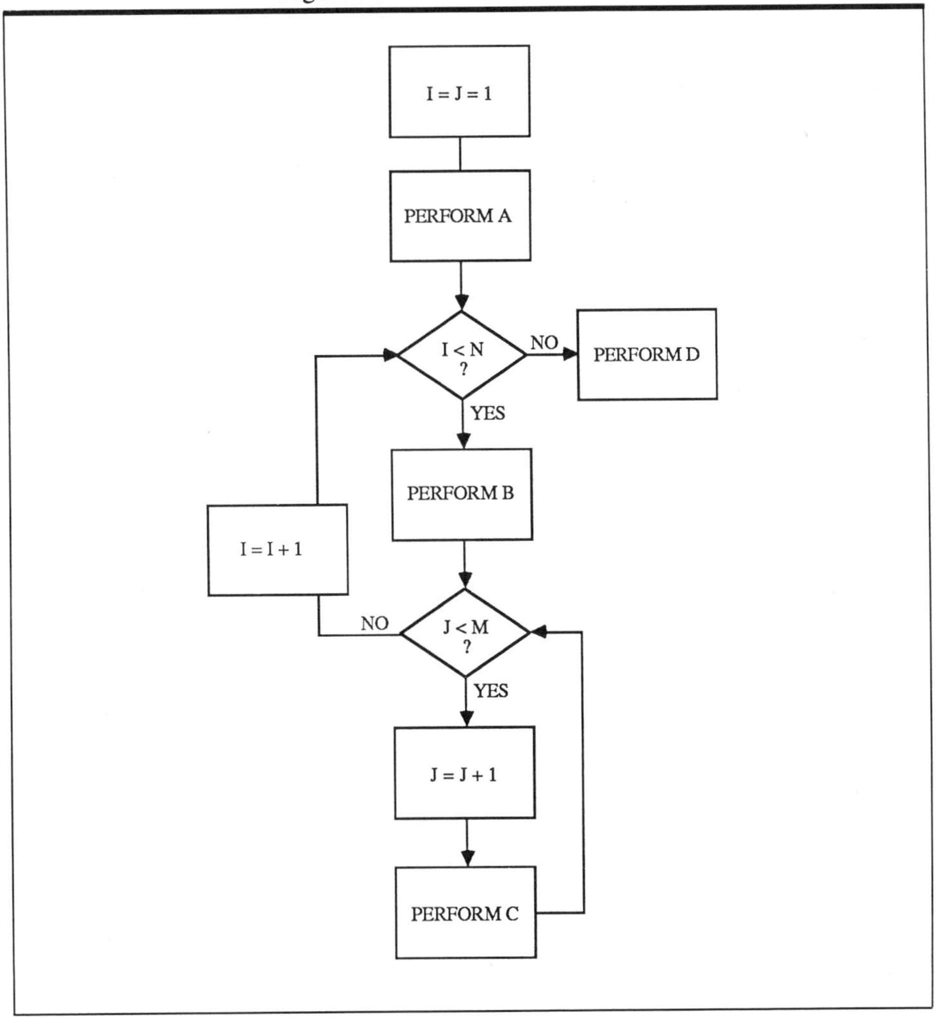

To overcome this problem, we can instead view the test object as an *open box* with whose internal structure and logic we are completely familiar. Then we can devise test cases that execute all the statements or all the control paths within the module or modules to be sure that the test object is working properly. However, as we will see later in this chapter, it may be impractical to take this approach. A module with a large number of branches and loops has many paths to check.

Even with a fairly simple logical structure, a module with substantial iteration or recursion is difficult to test thoroughly. For example, suppose a module's logic is structured so that the module loops NM times as shown in Figure 7.3. If N and M are each equal to 100,000, a test case would have to loop ten billion times to exercise all the logic paths.

When deciding how to test, we need not choose either open or closed box testing exclusively. We can think of closed box testing on one end of a *testing continuum* and open box testing on the other end. Any test philosophy can lie somewhere in between. The choice of test philosophy depends on a number of things, including the following:

1. The number of possible logical paths

2. The nature of the input data

3. The amount of computation involved

4. The complexity of the algorithms

7.2

UNIT TESTING

Now we examine the problem of testing individual modules after they have been coded. Given our goal of finding errors in the modules, how do we start? The process used is similar to the way you test a program assigned in class. First, you probably examine your program by reading through the code and trying to spot algorithm and syntax errors. You may even compare the code with the specifications and with your design to make sure that you have considered all necessary cases. Next, you compile the code and eliminate any remaining syntax errors. Finally, you develop test cases to show that the input is properly converted to the output desired.

Unit testing of a program module is done in the same way. First, you and your peers examine the code for errors. When you find no more errors in this manner, the module is compiled and run with test data to search for other errors. Let us consider each step in turn.

Program Reviews

You work with a program design description to code and document each program module. The program reflects your *interpretation* of the module design, and the documentation explains *in words* what the program is supposed to do *in code*. It is helpful to ask an objective group of experts to review both your code and its documentation for errors. A second opinion from such a review team often can recognize errors caused by your particular biases or interpretations.

This process, known as a **program review**, is similar to the ones in which the system and program design descriptions are reviewed prior to implementation. A team, composed of you as programmer and three or four other technical experts, studies the program. The technical experts can be other programmers, technical writers, designers, or project supervisors. Whereas the design review teams included customer representatives, a program review team contains no one from the customer's organization. In addition to not understanding the technical details of a program module, customers are not concerned with the implementation at this level. They express their requirements and approve the proposed design; they are interested in implementation only when we can demonstrate that the system as a whole works according to their description.

Program Walk-throughs. There are two types of program review: a walk-through and an inspection. In a **program walk-through**, you present your code and the accompanying documentation to the review team, and the team comments on the correctness of the program. During a walk-through, *you* lead the session and control the discussion. The atmosphere is informal, and the focus of attention is on the program, not the programmer. Although supervisory personnel may be present, the walk-through has no influence on your performance appraisal. This approach is consistent with the intent of testing in general: to find errors, not to correct them.

Program Inspections. A program inspection is similar to a walk-through. Whereas a walk-through is an informal presentation to a review team, a **program inspection** is a formal review in which the review team checks the program against a prepared list of concerns. For example, the review team may examine the definition and use of data structures and data types to see if their use is consistent with the program design and with the system standards and procedures. The team can review the algorithms and computation for correctness and efficiency. Comments accompanying the code can be compared with the code itself to insure that the comments are accurate and complete. The interfaces between this module and others can be checked for correctness. The team may even choose to estimate the program's performance characteristics in terms of processing speed or memory usage; this estimate may be necessary for a system in which performance constraints are outlined in the system requirements.

The candidates for members of the inspection team are the same as those for a walk-through. The composition of the team will be determined by the goals of the inspection. For example, an inspection to insure proper communication interfaces may have on its team the system designer who wrote the original communication design plans. Because the list of items to inspect determines what is reviewed, the *inspection team*—not the programmer—controls the review. Rather than having you lead the discussion (as in a walk-through), the review team questions you using the list as a guide. As with walk-throughs, inspections are meant to criticize the program, not the programmer; the inspection results are not part of your performance evaluation.

Success of Program Reviews.   You may feel uncomfortable with the idea of a review team examining your code. However, program reviews have proven to be extraordinarily successful at detecting errors. Remember that the sooner in the system development process an error is spotted, the easier and less expensive it is to correct. The same principle holds true for program errors. It is better to find an error at the module level than to discover it in a later testing phase when it can be much more difficult to determine the error's source.

Several researchers have investigated the extent to which program reviews have identified errors. Fagan ([FAG76]) performed an experiment in which 67% of the errors eventually detected in a system were found before unit testing by using code inspections. In this experiment, a second group of programmers wrote a similar system using informal walk-throughs rather than inspections. The inspection group had 38% fewer errors during the first seven months of operation than did the walk-through group. In another Fagan experiment, of the total number of errors discovered during a system's development, 82% were found during design and code inspections. The early detection of the errors led to large savings in programmer time.

Jones ([JON77]) has done extensive studies of programmer productivity, including investigations of the nature of programmer errors and of the methods for discovering and removing the errors. Examining the history of the errors in ten million lines of program code, he found that code inspections removed as many as 85% of the total errors found. No other technique studied by Jones was as successful; in fact, none could remove even half of the errors known to be present.

Proving Programs Correct

Suppose your program module has been coded, examined by you, and reviewed by a program review team. The next step in testing is to subject the program to scrutiny in a more structured way. We want to establish somehow that the program is correct. For the purposes of unit testing, a program is **correct** if it implements the functions specified in the program design and interfaces properly with the other modules.

One way to investigate program correctness is to view the program as a statement of logical flow. If we can rewrite the program in terms of a formal logical system (such as a series of statements and implications about data), then we can test this new expression for correctness. Although our interpretation of correctness is in terms of the design specification, we want our new expression to be correct in a formal or precise sense. For example, if we can prove that our new expression is a mathematical theorem, then the truth of the theorem may imply the correctness of the program.

A Formal Logic Proof Technique. Floyd ([FLO67]), Naur ([NAU66]) and others have developed a method to display the logic of a program as a series of **assertions**, that is, a series of statements each of which is either true or false. The conversion of the program to its logical counterpart is performed as a series of steps.

1. You begin by writing assertions to describe the input and output conditions for the program. These statements are combinations of logical variables (each of which is true or false) connected by the logical connective symbols displayed in Table 7.1.

Table 7.1 Logical Connectives

Connective	Example	Meaning
Conjunction	x & y	x AND y
Disjunction	x * y	x OR y
Negation	$\overline{x}$	NOT x
Implication	$x \rightarrow y$	IF x THEN y
Equivalence	$x = y$	x EQUALS y
Universal quantifier	FOR ALL x (P(x))	For all x, condition P(x) is true
Existential quantifier	FOR SOME x(P(x))	For at least one x, P(x) is true

For example, suppose a module accepts as input an array T of size N. As output, the module produces an equivalent array T' consisting of the elements of T in ascending order. We can write the input conditions as the assertion

A1: (T is an array) & (T is of size N)

Similarly, we can write the output as the assertion

Aend: (T' is an array) & (FOR ALL i if $i < N$ then (T'(i) <= T(i+1)))
   & (FOR ALL i if $i <= N$ then FOR SOME j (T'(i) = T(j))
   & (T' is of size N)

2. Next, draw a flow diagram depicting the logical flow of the module. On the diagram, denote points at which a transformation of data takes place.

Figure 7.4 shows such a diagram for an example module in which a bubble sort is used to rearrange the array T into ascending order. In the figure, two points have been highlighted to show where data transformations take place.

The point marked with a single asterisk (*) can be described as an assertion in the following way:

[(NOT(MORE)= TRUE)) & (I < N) & (T(i) > T($i+1$))] →
    [(T(i) is exchanged with T($i+1$)]

Similarly, the point marked with a double asterisk (**) can be written as

[(NOT(MORE) = TRUE)) & (I >= N)] → [T(i) sorted]

Figure 7.4   Flow Diagram for Bubble Sort

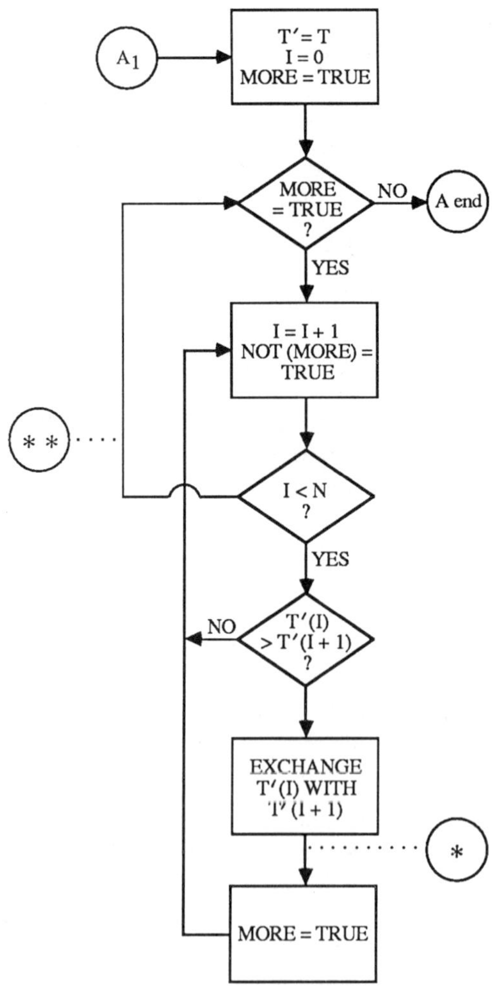

3. From the assertions, generate a series of theorems to be proven. Begin with the input assertion, A1. If the next transformation point is denoted as A2, then the first theorem states that if A1 is true, then A2 is true. In other words, the theorem says that

$$A1 \rightarrow A2$$

Then, proceed to the next transformation point, A3, writing that

$$A2 \rightarrow A3$$

In this way, state theorems

$$Ai \rightarrow Aj$$

where Ai and Aj are adjacent transformation points in the flow diagram. The last theorem states that a condition of TRUE at the last transformation point implies the truth of the output assertion:

$$Ak \rightarrow Aend$$

Alternately, you can work backwards through the transformation points in the flow diagram. Begin at Aend and find a transformation point Ak preceding Aend. Prove that

$$Ak \rightarrow Aend$$

and then that

$$Aj \rightarrow Ak$$

for adjacent pairs of transformation points, and so on, until you have shown that

$$A1 \rightarrow A2$$

The result of this approach is the same.

4. The next step is to locate the loops in the flow diagram. For each one, specify an IF-THEN assertion.

5. At this point, you have identified all possible assertions. To prove the program correct, locate all paths that begin with the input and end with the output. In other words, locate all paths that begin with A1 and end with Aend. By following each of these paths, you are following the ways in which the program shows that the truth of the input condition leads to the truth of the output condition.

6. After identifying all paths, you must verify the truth of each one. Such verification is done by proving rigorously that the input assertion implies the output assertion according to the transformations of the path.

7. Finally, prove that the program terminates.

Advantages and Disadvantages of Logical Correctness Proofs. By constructing a program proof in the preceding manner (either in an automated way or by hand), we can discover algorithmic errors in the module. In addition, the proof technique provides us with a formal understanding of the program, because we examine the formal logical structure underlying the code. Regular use of this demonstration of correctness can force you to be much more rigorous and precise in specifying data, data structures, and algorithmic rules.

However, there is a price to be paid for such rigor. Much work is involved in setting up and carrying out the proof. For example, the code for the bubble sort module is much smaller than the logical description and proof. Thus, it may take more time to prove the code correct than to write the program itself. Moreover, larger and more complex program modules can involve enormous logic diagrams, many transformations, and a large number of paths to verify.

Non-numerical programs may be more difficult to represent logically than numerical ones and, therefore, may be more difficult to prove in this way. Parallel processing is difficult to handle, and complex data structures may result in complex transformation statements.

Notice that the proof technique is based only on how the input assertions are transformed into the output assertions according to logical precepts. Proving the program correct in this logical sense does not mean that there are no software errors in the program code. Indeed, this technique may not spot any errors in the design, in the interfaces with other modules, in interpretation of the specification, in the syntax and semantics of the programming language, or in the documentation.

Finally, we must acknowledge that not all proofs are correct. There have been several times in the history of mathematics when a proof that had been accepted as valid for many years was later shown to have been fallacious. There is always the possibility that an especially complex or intricate proof argument is invalid.

Other Proof Techniques. The logical proof technique ignores the *structure* and *syntax* of the programming language in which the test program is implemented. In a sense, then, this technique proves that the design of the test program is correct but not necessarily the *implementation*. Other techniques take the language characteristics into account.

One such technique is known as **symbolic execution** of the program because the proof involves simulated execution of the test program using symbols instead of data variables. In symbolic execution, the test program is viewed as having an input state determined by the input data and conditions. As each line of the test program is executed, the technique checks to see whether the *state* has changed. Each state change is saved, and the execution of the program can be viewed as a *series of state changes*. Thus, each logical path through the program corresponds to an ordered series of state changes. The final state of each path should be an output state, and the program is correct if each possible input state generates the proper output state.

An example shows us how this technique works. Suppose several lines of a program to be tested read as follows:

```
A = B + C;
IF A > D THEN PERFORM TASKX
ELSE PERFORM TASKY;
```

A symbolic execution module will note that the condition (A > D) can be either true or false. Whereas the conventional execution of a program would involve specific values of A and D, the symbolic execution module records two possible states: (A > D) is FALSE, and (A > D) is TRUE. Instead of testing a large number of possible values for A and D, symbolic execution considers only two cases: when (A > D) is false and when (A > D) is true. In this way, large sets of data are divided into disjoint classes, and the program can be considered only with respect to how it reacts to each *class* of data. Considering only classes of data, represented as symbols, greatly reduces the number of cases to be considered in the proof.

However, this technique has many of the same disadvantages of logical theorem proving. Developing a proof may take longer than writing the program itself, and proof of correctness is not the same as the absence of software errors. Moreover, the technique relies on a careful tracing of changing conditions throughout the paths of the program. The technique can be automated to some extent; but large, complex test programs may still require the checking of many states and paths. It is difficult for an automated symbolic execution system to follow execution flow through loops. In addition, whenever subscripts and pointers are used in the test program, the partitioning of data into disjoint representative classes becomes more complex.

It may be useful to combine the logical flow and symbolic execution approaches to help you to implement the code correctly. First, you write assertions derived from the program design. You can test the assertions and their logical flow using the logical proof technique previously described above. Then, you translate the assertions to lines of code, either manually or with some automated aid.

Automated Theorem Proving. Some software engineers have tried to automate the process of proving programs correct by developing modules that read as input

- the input data and conditions
- the output data and conditions
- the lines of code for the program to be tested.

The output from the test module is either a proof of the program's correctness or a counterexample showing a set of data that the program does not correctly transform to output. The test module must include information about the language in which the input program is written so that the syntax and semantic rules are accessible. Following the outlined steps, the test module identifies the paths of transformations and verifies their validity. Validity can be demonstrated in several ways. If the usual rules of inference and deduction are too cumbersome to be used, a heuristic solution can be found.

Such a theorem-proving module is nontrivial. For example, the module must be able to verify the correct use of unary and binary operations (such as addition, subtraction, and negation) as well as the use of comparisons involving equalities and inequalities. More complex laws such as commutativity, distributivity, and associativity must be incorporated in checking the test program. Expressing the programming language as a set of postulates from which to derive the theorems is very difficult.

Suppose these difficulties can be overcome. Using trial and error to construct the theorems is far too time consuming for any but the most trivial of test programs. Thus, some amount of human interaction is desirable to guide the automated theorem prover. Using methods frequently employed when developing an expert system, an interactive theorem prover works with you to choose transformation points and trace paths. The theorem prover does not really generate the proof; rather, it checks the proof outlined by the person working with it. Using a symbolic execution approach, several experimental programs have been developed to evaluate the code in small FORTRAN, PL/I and LISP programs. However, there is no general-purpose automated symbolic execution system available.

Can the ideal theorem prover ever be built, assuming the existence of a machine that is fast enough and an implementation language that can handle the complexities of the problem? The ideal theorem prover would read in any program and produce as its output either a statement confirming the program correctness or the location of an error. The theorem prover would have to determine if an arbitrary statement in the test program is executed for arbitrary input data. Unfortunately, this kind of theorem prover can never be built. It can be shown (in [PFL85], for example) that the construction of such a program is the equivalent of the *halting problem* for Turing machines. The halting problem is an unsolvable problem, which means not only that there is no solution to the problem but also that it is impossible to ever find a solution to the problem. We can make our theorem prover solvable by applying it only to programs having no branches, but with this limitation the theorem prover is no longer universal. Thus, although highly desirable, any automated theorem prover will have to approximate the ideal.

Testing Programs

Proving programs correct is a goal to which software engineers aspire; consequently, much related research is being done to develop methods and automated tools. However, in the near future, development teams are more likely to be concerned with testing their software, rather than with proving their programs correct.

Difference Between Testing and Proving. In proving a program correct, the test team or programmer considers only the code and input and output conditions of a program. The program is viewed in terms of the classes of data and conditions described in the program design. Thus, the proof of the test program may not involve actual direct program execution, but rather understanding what is going on *inside* the program.

However, customers have a different point of view. To demonstrate to them that a program is working properly, you must show them how the program performs from *outside* the program. In this sense, testing becomes a series of experiments, the results of which become a basis for deciding how the program will behave in a given situation. Whereas a proof tells us how a program will work in the hypothetical environment described by the design and requirements, testing gives us information about how a program works in its actual operating environment.

Figure 7.5   Logic Flow in a Sample Program

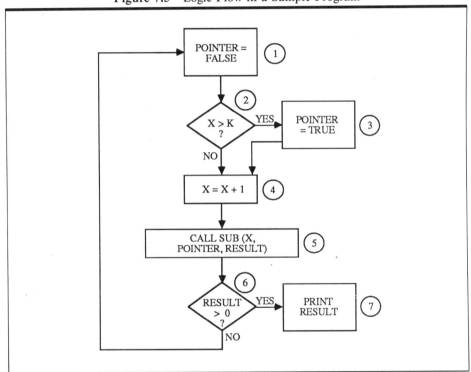

Test Thoroughness.   To perform a test, then, we decide how to demonstrate in a convincing way that the test data exhibits all possible behaviors of the program being tested. Let us look at an example to see what choices we have.

Figure 7.5 illustrates the logic flow in a program to be tested. Each statement, represented by a diamond or rectangle, has been numbered. To test this program thoroughly, we can choose test cases through one of three approaches:

1. **Statement testing**: Every statement in the program is executed at least once.

2. **Branch testing**: For every decision point in the program, each branch is chosen at least once.

3. **Path testing**: Every distinct path through the program is executed at least once.

To perform statement testing on our example program requires a test case that executes statements 1 through 7. By choosing an X larger than K that produces a positive RESULT, we can execute statements

1-2-3-4-5-6-7

in order; thus, one test case suffices.

To perform branch testing, however, we must first find all decision points. The decision points are represented by diamonds in Figure 7.5. We have a decision about the relationship of X to K and another about whether or not RESULT is positive. We can choose two test cases to exercise the paths

1-2-3-4-5-6-7

and

1-2-4-5-6-1

and thereby traverse each possible outcome at least once. The first path uses the yes branch of the first decision point, while the second path uses the no branch. Likewise, the first path uses the yes branch of the second decision point, while the second path uses the no.

If we want our test to exercise each possible path throughout the program, we need more test cases. The paths

1-2-3-4-5-6-7
1-2-3-4-5-6-1
1-2-4-5-6-7
1-2-4-5-6-1

cover all the possibilities: two decision points with two choices at each branch.

In our example, statement testing requires fewer test cases than branch testing, which in turn requires fewer cases than path testing. This relationship is true in general; the more complex a program, the more path test cases required. Exercise 4 (page 307) investigates whether the structure and order of the decision points affect the number of paths through a program.

Usually, path testing is the most desirable since it tests a program more completely than the other two types. However, for complex programs, path testing can take unreasonable amounts of time. As we will see in a later section, time, resources, and other variables are considered when deciding how to test and what test cases to use.

Generating Test Data

To test a module, we choose input data and conditions, allow the program to manipulate that data, and observe the output from the program. We select the input data so that the output demonstrates something about the behavior of the program.

A **test point** or **test case** is a particular choice of input data to be used in testing a program. A **test** is therefore a finite collection of test points. How do we choose test cases and define tests in order to convince ourselves and our customers that the program works correctly not only for the test cases but for all input?

Choosing Test Cases.   We begin by determining the objective of our test. Then we select test cases and define a test in order to meet that specific objective. Our objective may be to demonstrate that all statements execute properly. Or, we may want to show that every function performed by this program is done correctly. The objective determines how we classify the input in order to choose our test points.

We can view the program being tested as a closed box or as an open box, with the choice depending on our test objectives. If the program is a closed box, we supply the box with all possible input and compare the output with what is expected according to the requirements definition. However, if the program is viewed as an open box, we can examine the internal logical of the program. Our test objective can then be related to the assurance that all possible paths execute correctly.

Recall our example of a program that, given the coefficients of the variables, calculates the two roots of a quadratic equation. If our test objective is to demonstrate that the program functions properly, we might choose test points where the coefficients A, B, and C range through representative combinations of negative numbers, positive numbers, and zero. For example, we may choose combinations so that

1. A is greater than B and C

2. B is greater than C and A

3. C is greater than B and A

However, if our test acknowledges the *inner* workings of the program, we can see that the logical flow of the program depends on the value of the discriminant, $B^2 - 4AC$. Then, we can choose our test points so that we represent three cases, namely, when the discriminant is positive, negative, and zero.

Thus, keeping in mind our test objective, we can separate the possible input into classes. Ideally, these classes should meet the following criteria:

1. Every possible input belongs to one of the classes. (That is, the classes *cover* the entire set of input data.)

2. No input data set belongs to more than one class. (That is, the classes are *disjoint*.)

3. If the execution of the program demonstrates an error when a particular member of a class is used as input, then the same error can be detected by using any other member of the class as input. That is, any element of a class *represents all* elements of that class.

It is not always easy or feasible to tell if the third restriction on the classes can be met. We can loosen the third requirement so that if a data set belongs to a class and causes an error, then the probability is high that every other data set in that class causes the error.

Closed box testing suffers from uncertainty about whether the test cases selected will uncover a particular error. On the other hand, open box testing always admits the danger of paying too much attention to the code's internal processing. You may end up testing what the program *does* instead of what it *should* do.

We can combine open and closed box testing to generate test data. First, by considering the program as a closed box, we can use the *external specifications* of the program to generate initial test cases. These cases should incorporate not only the expected input data but also boundary conditions for the input and output, as well as several cases of invalid data. For instance, if the module is coded to expect an input variable that is supposed to be positive, a test case may be included for each of the following:

1. A very large positive integer

2. A positive integer

3. A positive fixed point decimal

4. A number between zero and one

4. Zero

5. A negative number

Some of the data are purposely chosen to be improper input points; we test them to insure that the program handles erroneous input gracefully.

Next, by viewing the *internal structure* of the program, we can add other cases. For example, we can add data to test all branches of decision points and to exercise as many paths as possible through the test program. If there are loops involved, we may want test cases that pass through the loop many times, one time and not at all.

We also examine the *implementation of algorithms*, where appropriate. For example, if we know that the program does trigonometric calculations, we may include cases that test the extremities of the trigonometric functions. Or, we may include data points that exercise functions where division by zero may occur so that we can test how the program handles such illegal divisions.

For some systems, *sequences* of test cases are needed. Sometimes a system "remembers" conditions from the previous case. For instance, recall of a previous state is needed when a system implements a finite state machine; the previous state and a current action determine the next state. Similarly, real-time systems are often interrupt-driven; tests are required for sets of cases, rather than for single ones.

7.3

INTEGRATION TESTING

When we are satisfied that individual program modules are working correctly and meet our established objectives, we combine the modules into a working system. This integration is planned and coordinated so that when an error occurs, we have some idea of what caused it. In addition, the order in which modules are tested affects our choice of test cases and the types of tools used. For large systems, some modules may be in the coding phase; others may be in the unit testing phase, while still other module collections are being tested together. Our *testing philosophy* explains why and how modules are combined to test the working system. This philosophy not only affects the timing of the integration and the order in which the program modules are coded, but it can also affect the cost and the thoroughness of the testing.

For testing, the entire system is again viewed as a hierarchy of modules, consistent with its modular design. As we have seen, each module belongs to a layer of the design. In integration testing, we begin with the modules at the highest levels of the design and work down, begin at the bottom with the lowest level and work up, or use some combination of these approaches.

Bottom-up Approach

One popular philosophy for merging modules to test the larger system is called the **bottom-up testing** approach. Using this method, each module at the lowest level of the system hierarchy is tested individually. Then, the next modules to be tested are those that call the previously tested modules. This approach is followed repeatedly until all modules are included in the testing. The bottom-up method is useful when many of the low-level modules are general purpose utility routines that are invoked often by others.

For an example of bottom-up testing, consider the system modules illustrated in Figure 7.6. To test this system from the bottom up, we first test the modules in the lowest level: modules E, F, and G. Because we have no modules ready to call these lowest level programs, we write special programs to aid us in the integration tests. A **module driver** is a routine that calls a particular module and passes a test case to it. A module driver is not difficult to code, since it rarely requires complex processing. However, care is taken to be sure that the driver's interface with the test module is defined properly. Sometimes, test data can be supplied automatically in a special-purpose language that facilitates the defining of the test data. This automated test data definition program is called a **module tester**.

In our example, we need a module driver for each of modules E, F, and G. When we are satisfied that E, F, and G work correctly, we move to the next higher level. Unlike the modules in the lowest level, the modules in this next level are not tested

Figure 7.6   Sample Modular Heirarchy

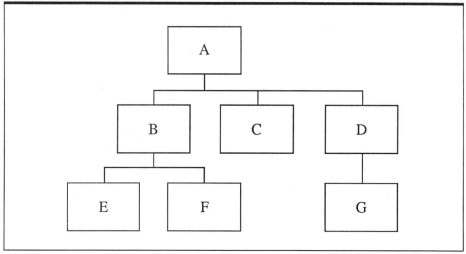

by themselves. Instead, they are combined with the modules that they call (which have already been tested). Thus, the next step is to test B, E, and F together. If an error occurs, we know that its cause is probably in module B or in the interface between B and E or B and F, since E and F functioned properly on their own. Had we tested B, E, and F without having tested E and F separately, we might not be able to isolate the error's cause as easily.

Similarly, we test module D with module G. Because C calls no module, we test it by itself. Finally, we test all modules of the system together. Figure 7.7 shows us the sequence of the tests and their dependencies on one another.

Figure 7.7   Bottom-up Testing Strategy

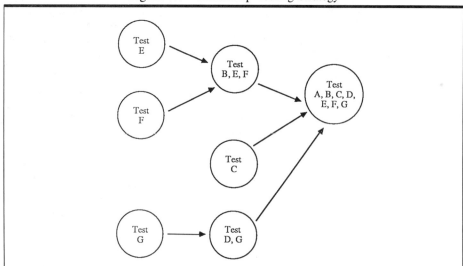

A frequent complaint about bottom-up testing is that the top level of modules in a system are usually the most important but are tested last. The top level directs the major activities of the system, whereas the bottom level often performs the more mundane tasks, such as input and output functions or repetitive calculations. The top levels are more general, while the lower levels are more specific. Thus, some developers feel that by testing the bottom levels first, the discovery of the major errors is postponed until the end of testing. Moreover, sometimes errors in the top levels reflect errors in design; obviously, these errors should be corrected as soon as possible in development. Finally, top-level modules often control or influence timing. It is difficult to test a system from the bottom up when much of the system's processing depends on timing.

Top-down Approach

Thus, many developers prefer to test using a **top-down approach**. In many ways, top-down is the reverse of bottom-up. The top level, usually one controlling module, is tested by itself. Then, all modules called by tested module(s) are combined and tested as a larger unit. This approach is reapplied until all modules are incorporated.

A module being tested may call another that is not yet tested. When this situation occurs, a special-purpose program is written to simulate the activity of the missing module. A **stub** is a program that simulates the activity of a missing module by answering to the identical calling sequence of the module and passing back output data that allows the testing process to continue. For example, if a module is called to calculate the next available record number but that module is not yet integrated into the collection being tested, a stub for that module may pass back a fixed record number only to allow testing to proceed. As with drivers, stubs need not be complex nor logically complete.

Figure 7.8 shows how top-down testing works with our example system. Only the top module is tested by itself. Once tested, it is combined with the next level; and A, B, C, and D are tested together. Stubs may be needed for modules E, F, and G at this stage of testing. Finally, the entire system is tested.

Figure 7.8 Top-down Testing Strategy

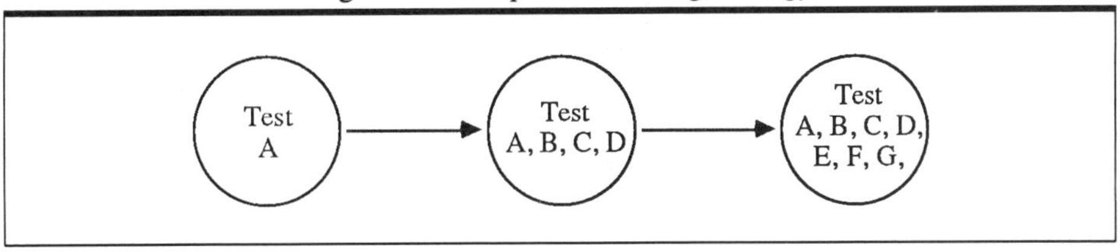

If the lowest level of modules performs the input and output operations, stubs for these modules may be almost identical to the actual programs. In this case, the integration sequence may be altered so that input and output modules are incorporated earlier in the testing sequence.

Many of the advantages of performing top-down design and coding also apply to the test process. Having localized functions in particular modules by using top-down design, testing from the top down allows the test team to exercise one function at a time, following its command sequence from the highest levels of control down through appropriate modules. Thus, test cases can be defined in terms of the functions to be examined. Moreover, any design defects or major questions about the feasibility of the functioning of the system can be addressed at the beginning of testing, rather than at the end.

Notice, too, that driver programs are not needed in top-down testing. On the other hand, writing stubs can be difficult. Stubs must allow all possible conditions to be tested. For example, suppose module Z of a map-drawing system performs a calculation using latitude and longtitude output by module Y. The design specifications state that the output from Y is always in the northern hemisphere. Since Z calls Y, when Z is part of a top-down test, Y may not yet be coded. A stub is written that generates a number between 0 and 180, allowing the testing of Z to continue. However, suppose a design change allows the output of Y to be in the southern hemisphere. The testing of the higher level may not have checked for output in this wider range of −180 to 180. Thus, coding the stub is an important part of the testing, and its correctness may affect the validity of the test.

Figure 7.9   Modified Top-down Testing Strategy

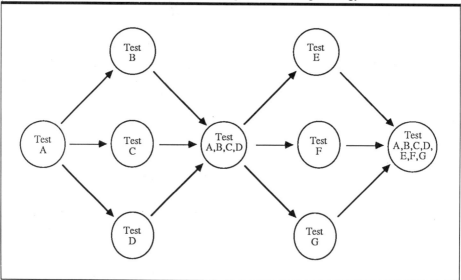

Modified Top-down Testing. A disadvantage to top-down testing is the possibility that a very large number of stubs may be required. This can happen when the lowest level of the system contains many general-purpose routines. One way to avoid this problem is to alter the strategy slightly. Rather than incorporate an entire level at a time, a modified top-down approach tests each level's modules individually before the merger takes place. For instance, our sample system can be tested with the modified approach by first testing module A; then testing modules B, C, and D; and then merging the four modules for a test of the first and second levels. Then modules E, F, and G are tested by themselves. Finally, the entire system is combined for a test. Figure 7.9 shows this integration sequence.

Testing each level's modules individually, however, introduces another difficulty. Both stubs and drivers are needed for each module so that each module can be tested individually. As we have seen before, the use of stubs and drivers can lead to additional problems.

Figure 7.10 Big-Bang Testing Strategy

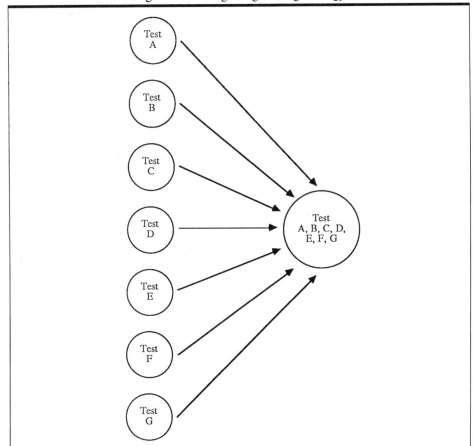

Big-bang Testing

When all modules are tested in isolation, it is tempting to mix all of them together as the final system and see if it works the first time. Myers ([MYE76]) calls this **big-bang testing**. Figure 7.10 shows how modules are integrated using big-bang testing on our example system. Many programmers use the big-bang approach for small systems, but this approach is not practical for large systems. In fact, since big-bang has several major disadvantages, there is little to recommend it for *any* system. First, it requires both stubs and drivers for each module, since each module is tested by itself. Second, because all modules are merged at once, it is difficult to find the cause of any error that appears. Finally, interface errors cannot easily be distinguished from other errors. Thus, although widely used, big-bang testing is not recommended.

Figure 7.11   Sandwich Testing Strategy

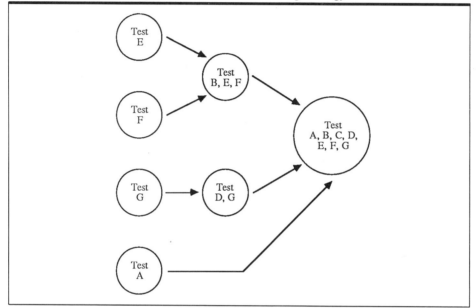

Sandwich Testing

Myers combines a top-down strategy with a bottom-up one to form a **sandwich testing** approach. The system is viewed as having three layers just as a sandwich does: a target layer in the middle, the levels above the target, and the levels below the target. A top-down approach is used in the top layer and a bottom-up approach in the lower layer. Testing converges on the target layer, chosen on the basis of system characteristics and the structure of the module hierarchy. For example, if the bottom layer contains many general-purpose utility programs, the target layer may be the one below which lie most of the modules using the utilities. This allows bottom-up testing to verify the correctness of the utilities at the beginning of testing. Then stubs for the utilities need not be written, since the actual utilities are available for use in further testing. Figure 7.11 depicts a possible integration sequence for sandwich testing our example, whose target layer is the middle level composed of modules B, C, and D.

Sandwich testing allows integration testing to begin early in the testing process. It also combines the advantages of top-down and bottom-up by testing the controlling module and the utility modules at the very beginning. However, it does not test all individual modules thoroughly before integration. A variation **modified sandwich testing**, allows upper level modules to be tested individually before merging them with others for testing. Figure 7.12 illustrates this procedure with our example.

Figure 7.12   Modified Sandwich Testing Strategy

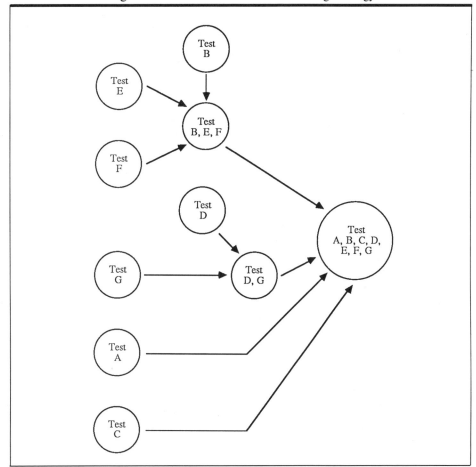

Comparison of Integration Strategies

The choice of integration strategy depends not only on system characteristics but also on customer expectations. For instance, the customer may want to see a working version of the system as soon as possible, so you may adopt an integration schedule that produces a basic working system early in the process. In this way, programmers are coding while others are testing so that the test and code phases can occur concurrently. Myers has composed a matrix, shown in Table 7.2, that compares the several types of testing strategies according to the characteristics of the system and the project and the expectations of the customer.

Table 7.2 Comparison of Integration Strategies

	Bottom-Up	Top-Down	Modified Top-Down	Big-Bang	Sandwich	Modified Sandwich
Integration	Early	Early	Early	Late	Early	Early
Time to basic working program	Late	Early	Early	Late	Early	Early
Module drivers needed	Yes	No	Yes	Yes	In part	Yes
Stubs needed	No	Yes	Yes	Yes	In part	In part
Work parallelism at beginning	Medium	Low	Medium	High	Medium	High
Ability to test particular paths	Easy	Hard	Easy	Easy	Medium	Easy
Ability to plan and control sequence	Easy	Hard	Hard	Easy	Hard	Hard

No matter what strategy is chosen, each module is merged only once for testing with the system. Furthermore, at no time is a module modified to simplify testing. Stubs and drivers are separate new programs, not temporary modifications of existing programs.

7.4

AUTOMATED TESTING TOOLS AND TECHNIQUES

Our discussion of unit testing described several kinds of automated tools to aid in testing program modules. Similar tools and techniques are available to help integration testing as well. They can be distinguished from one another in an important way. **Static analysis** of a program or module is performed when the program is not actually executing; **dynamic analysis** is performed while the program is running.

Static Analysis

Several tools can analyze a source program before it is run. Tools that investigate the correctness of a program or set of modules can be grouped into four types:

1. *Code Analyzers*: The test modules are evaluated automatically for proper syntax. Statements can be highlighted if the syntax is wrong, if a construction is prone to error, or if an item has not been defined.

2. *Structure Checkers*: A graph is generated from the modules submitted as input. The graph depicts the hierarchy of the module or set of modules, and the automated tool checks for structural flaws.

3. *Data Analyzers*: An automated tool reviews the data structures, data declarations and module interfaces and then notes improper linkage between modules, conflicting data definitions, and illegal data usage.

4. *Sequence Checkers*: The sequence of events is checked; if coded in the wrong sequence, they are marked.

For example, a code analyzer can generate a symbol table to record where a variable is first defined and when it is used. Similarly, a structure checker can read a program and determine the location of all loops, mark statements that are never executed, note the presence of branches from the middle of a loop, and so on. A data analyzer can notify us when a denominator may be set to zero; it can also check to see that subroutine arguments are passed properly. The input and output modules of a system may be submitted to a sequence checker to determine if the events are coded in the proper sequence. For example, a sequence checker can insure that all files are opened before they are modified.

Dynamic Analysis

Many times, systems are difficult to test because several parallel operations are being performed concurrently. This is especially true for real-time systems. In these cases, it is difficult to anticipate conditions and generate representative test points. Automated tools enable the test team to capture the state of events during the execution of a program by preserving a "snapshot" of conditions. These tools are sometimes called **program monitors** because they "watch" and report the behavior of the program.

A monitor can list the number of times a submodule is called or a line of code is executed. These statistics tell the testers if their test cases have statement coverage. Similarly, a monitor can report on whether a decision point has branched in all directions, thus providing information about branch coverage.

Additional information may help the test team evaluate the system's performance. Statistics can be generated about particular variables: their first value, last value, minimum value, and maximum value, for example. Breakpoints can be defined within the system so that when a variable attains or exceeds a certain value, the test tool reports the occurrence. Some tools stop when breakpoints are reached, allowing the tester to examine the contents of memory or values of specific data items; sometimes it is possible to change values as the test progresses.

For real-time systems, capturing as much information as possible about a particular state or condition during execution can be used after execution to provide additional information about the test. Control flow can be traced forward or backward from a breakpoint, and the accompanying data changes can be examined.

Other Automated Aids

In addition to analyzing code, automated tools can aid the testing itself. For example; *data bases* can be developed to track test cases. These data bases store the input data for each test case and describe the expected output. The test team can also use this data base to record the actual output. Associated with such tools are *nonprocedural languages* that are used to define and generate the test case descriptions. Several of these testing aids are sometimes combined into one automated tool. A **test harness** is an automated monitoring system that tracks test input data, passes it to the program or system being tested, and records the resulting output. A test harness can also compare actual with expected output and report any discrepancies.

7.5

THE TEST LIFE CYCLE

As we have seen, much is involved in testing a program and integrating it with other programs to build a system. The test process has a *life cycle* of its own within the development cycle. The steps in the test process include:

1. Establishing the test objectives
2. Designing the test cases
3. Writing the test cases
4. Testing the test cases
5. Executing the tests
6. Evaluating the test results

The test objective is essential in deciding what kinds of test cases to generate. Moreover, the design of test cases is the key to the success all testing. If the test cases are not representative and do not thoroughly exercise those functions that demonstrate the correctness and validity of the system, then the remainder of the testing process is useless.

Therefore, running a test begins with a review of the test cases to verify that

1. They are correct.
2. They are feasible
3. They provide the desired degree of coverage
4. They demonstrate the desired functionality

When we have validated the test cases according to these criteria, we can proceed with the actual test.

Test Plans

We use a plan to organize the activities of testing. The test plan takes into account the objectives of the testing process and incorporates any scheduling mandated by the type of testing strategy used. Let us investigate test plans in more detail.

Purpose of Test Plan. The system development cycle requires several levels of testing, beginning with unit and integration testing and proceeding to demonstrate the functionality of the full system. The **test plan** describes the way in which we will demonstrate to our customer that the software works correctly (that is, that the software is free of technical errors and performs the functions as specified). Thus, a test plan addresses not only unit and integration testing but also system testing. The test plan is a guide to the entire testing activity. It explains *who* does the testing, *why* the tests are performed, *how* tests are conducted, and *when* the tests are scheduled.

To develop the system's test plan, we must know the requirements, functional specifications, and the modular hierarchy of the system's software. As we develop each of these aspects of a system, we can apply what we know to choosing a test objective, defining a test strategy, and generating a set of test cases. Consequently, the test plan for a system is developed *as the system itself is developed*.

Contents of Test Plan. A test plan begins with the *test objectives*. As we saw earlier in this chapter, there are several stages in the testing process, from unit testing through functional testing and acceptance testing to installation testing. The test plan for a system addresses each kind of testing and explains the objectives of each. Thus, a system test plan is really a series of test plans, one for each kind of testing to be performed: each stage is addressed in turn, elaborating on the objectives of each test.

Next, the test plan describes *how the tests will be administered* and what criteria will be used to judge when the test is complete. In other words, this part of the test plan explains when the tester knows that the test objectives have been met. Knowing when the test is over and that the objectives have been satisfied is not always easy. We have seen examples of code where it is impossible or impractical to test every possible set of input data. By choosing a subset of all possible data, we admit the possibility that an error might occur. This trade-off between completeness of testing and the realities of cost and time often involves a compromise with our objectives. Later in this chapter, we will discuss methods for estimating how many of the existing errors we have found.

Knowledge of the test objectives is a critical part of the test plan. The writers of the test plan (usually the members of the test team) work with the system and program designers to determine completion criteria for the early stages of testing and with the customer to define the criteria for the later stages.

When a test team can recognize that a test has met its objectives, we say that the test objectives are well-defined. It is then that we decide how to *integrate* the program modules into a working system. At this point, we consider statement, branch, and path coverage at the module level and top-down, bottom-up, and other *integration strategies* at the integration level. The result is a plan for merging the modules into a whole, sometimes referred to separately as a **system integration plan**.

For each stage of testing, the test plan describes in detail the *methods* to be used to perform the tests. For example, unit testing may be composed of informal walk-throughs or formal inspections followed by static analysis of the code and then dynamic analysis of each module's performance. If an automated test tool or special techniques are to be used, the plan lists them and the conditions for their use. The explanation helps the test team plan its activities and schedule the tests.

A detailed list of *test cases* accompanies each test method or technique. The reasons for choosing test cases are provided to explain how the test cases address the test objectives. The test cases include:

- The *input data* to be used
- The *conditions* under which each test point is to be submitted to the module or system being tested
- A description of the *expected output*

The plan also describes the use of automated tools to generate the test cases or capture the output. If a data base is to track test points and the resultant output, the data base and its use are to be explained, too.

Thus, as you read the test plan, you have a complete picture of testing, from the overall strategy to the particular test data. By writing the test plan as you design the system, you are forced to understand the overall goals of the system. Sometimes the testing perspective forces you to ask questions about the nature of the problem and the appropriateness of the design.

Many customers specify the contents of a test plan in their requirements documentation. For example, the Department of Defense provides a developer with automated data systems documentation standards ([DOD77]) when a system is being built. The standards explain that the test plan

> is a tool for directing the. . . testing, and contains the orderly schedule of events and list of materials necessary to effect a comprehensive test of a complete [automated data system]. Those parts of the document directed toward the staff personnel shall be presented in nontechnical language and those parts of the document directed toward the operations personnel shall be presented in suitable terminology.

We will investigate the details of this test plan example in the next chapter.

7.6

ESTIMATING SOFTWARE QUALITY

In previous chapters, we have discussed the need for quality software. In testing the software we write, we and our customers want to be sure that the promised quality is indeed there. The characteristics often discussed as measurements of overall system quality are *reliability*, *availability* , and *maintainability*, The terms are borrowed from the engineering world, where these criteria are used to judge the quality of a hardware system.

Reliability, Availability and Maintainability

Consider the meaning of these terms as they relate to an automobile. When we think of a car as being *reliable*, we mean that the car functions properly most of the time. We realize that there may be parts that break down, wear out, and need to be fixed or replaced, but a reliable car operates for long periods of time before it requires any kind of maintenance. In general, we can say that something is reliable if it has long periods of consistent behavior between maintenance periods.

Just as reliability reflects the car's condition over a period of time, *availability* reflects the car's condition at a particular point in time. A car is available if you can use it when you need it. Your car may be ten years old and have required maintenance only twice, so we know that the car is highly reliable. However, if it happens to be in the shop when you need it, it is still not available. Thus, something can be highly reliable, but if it is not working when you need it, it may have low availability.

Suppose your car is highly reliable and available but it was manufactured twelve years ago by a foreign manufacturer who is no longer in business. When your car needs a repair (which, admittedly, is infrequently), you have difficulty finding the needed parts. Moreover, your mechanic has difficulty repairing the car because of its unusual construction. Because of these difficulties, repairing your car takes a long time; your car has low *maintainability*. In contrast, if the repair time were short, the car would be considered highly maintainable.

The same concepts carry over to software systems. We can judge software in terms of its reliability, availability, and maintainability. We want it to function consistently and correctly over long periods of time, to be available when we need it, and to be quickly and easily repaired if it does fail. A program's performance is **successful** if the program performs according to the customer's requirements. **Software reliability** is the probability that the program is successful for a given period of time. Since we use probability for our measure, reliability is expressed as a number between 0 (not reliable at all) and 1 (completely reliable).

Another measure of reliability is the time between failures. Often represented as the mean time between failures (in hours, abbreviated MTBF), the reliability R of a system is

$$R = \frac{MTBF}{1 + MTBF}$$

Thus, if the mean time between failures is very small, R is close to 0; as the mean time between failures grows large, R approaches 1.

Similarly, **software availability** is the probability that a program is performing successfully according to specifications at a given point in time. If we denote the mean time (in hours) to repair a software error by MTTR, then the availability A of a system is related to MTTR and MTBF in the following way:

$$A = \frac{MTBF}{MTBF + MTTR}$$

Software maintainability is the probability that a software error can be fixed right away and is related to the mean time to repair:

$$M = \frac{1}{1 + MTTR}$$

The remainder of this chapter examines reliability in more detail. For more information about other measures of software quality, see Shooman ([SHO83]).

Software Reliability

Software reliability cannot be added to a program at the last minute. To make software reliable, quality must be built into the system by basing the code on complete and accurate specifications followed by a well-engineered design. How do we measure reliability once we begin testing? We know that the measurement of reliability involves the mean time between failures. The fewer errors are in a system or program, the fewer failures will result. Thus, an estimate of the *number of errors* in a program helps us determine if the program is reliable.

Estimating Number of Errors. It seems natural to assume that the software defects that are the most difficult to find are also the most difficult to correct. It also seems reasonable to believe that the most easily fixed errors are detected when the program is first examined, and the more difficult defects are located later in the testing process. However, Shooman and Bolsky ([SHO75]) have found that this is not the case. Sometimes it takes a great deal of time to find trivial errors, and many such errors are overlooked or don't appear until well into the testing process. Moreover,

Figure 7.13   Relationship Between Errors Found and Undetected

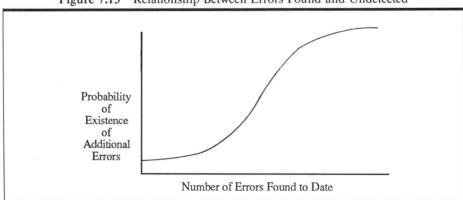

Probability
of
Existence
of
Additional
Errors

Number of Errors Found to Date

Myers (MYE76]) reports that as the number of detected errors increases, the probability of the existence of more undetected errors increases, as shown in Figure 7.13. If there are many errors in a program, we want to find them as early as possible in the testing process. However, this graph tells us that if we find a large number of errors at the beginning of testing, we are likely to have a large number left undetected.

In addition to being contrary to our intuition, these results also make it difficult to know when to stop looking for errors during testing. We have to estimate the number of errors remaining, not only to know when to stop our search for more errors but also to give us some degree of confidence in the programs we are producing. The number of errors also indicates the maintenance effort we can expect if errors are left to be detected after the system has been installed.

Mills ([MIL72]) developed a technique known as **error seeding** to estimate the number of errors in a program. It is based on an intentionally placed known number of errors, called *seeded errors*. A member of the test team seeds a program with errors. Then, the other team members test the program and locate as many of any kind of error as possible. The underlying assumption is that the ratio of seeded errors detected to total seeded errors should be the same as the ratio of non-seeded errors detected to the total number of non-seeded errors:

$$\frac{\text{detected seeded errors}}{\text{total seeded errors}} = \frac{\text{detected non-seeded errors}}{\text{total non-seeded errors}}$$

Thus, if 70 of 100 seeded errors are found, it is logical to assume that seventy percent of the non-seeded errors have also been found.

We can express the ratio more formally. Let S be the number of seeded errors placed in a program, and let N be the number of actual (non-seeded) errors. If n is the number of actual errors detected during testing and s the number of seeded errors detected during testing, then an estimate of the total number of actual errors is

$$N = \frac{Sn}{s}$$

Although simple and useful, this approach assumes that the seeded errors are of the *same kind* and *complexity* as the actual errors in the program. We do not know what the typical errors are before all the errors are found; consequently, it is difficult to make the seeded errors representative of the actual ones.

To overcome this obstacle, we can use two independent groups to test the same program, Test Group 1 and Test Group 2. Let x be the number of errors detected by Test Group 1 and y be the number of errors detected by Test Group 2. Some of the errors detected by the groups will be the same; that is, there will be some errors detected by both by Group 1 and Group 2. Let q be the number of these errors. Finally, let n be the total number of all errors in the program. We want to estimate n.

The *effectiveness* of each group's testing can be measured by calculating the fraction of errors found by each group. Thus, the effectiveness $E(1)$ of Group 1 can be expressed as

$$E(1) = \frac{x}{n}$$

and the effectiveness $E(2)$ of Group 2 as

$$E(2) = \frac{y}{n}$$

The *effectiveness of a group* measures the group's ability to detect errors from among a set of existing errors. Thus, if a group can find half of all errors in a program, its effectiveness should be 0.5. Consider errors detected by both Group 1 and Group 2. If we assume that Group 1 is just as effective in finding errors in any part of the program as in any other part, we can look at the *ratio* of errors Group 1 found from the set of errors found by Group 2. Group 1 found q of the y errors that Group 2 found, so Group 1's effectiveness should be the same; that is,

$$E(1) = \frac{x}{n} = \frac{q}{y}$$

However, we know that E(2) is y/n, so we can derive the following formula for n:

$$n = \frac{q}{E(1)*E(2)}$$

We have a known value for q, and we can use estimates of q/y for $E(1)$ and q/x for $E(2)$; this enables us to estimate n.

To see how this method works, suppose two groups test a program. Group 1 finds 25 errors. Group 2 finds 30 errors, and 15 of those errors are duplicates of those found by Group 1. Thus, we have

$$x = 25$$
$$y = 30$$
$$q = 15$$

The estimate $E(1)$ of Group 1's effectiveness is q/y, or .5, since Group 1 found 15 of the 30 errors found by Group 2. Similarly, the estimate $E(2)$ of Group 2's effectiveness is q/x, or .6. Thus, our estimate of n, the total number of errors in the program is

$$\frac{15}{.5*.6} = 50 \text{ errors}$$

The test *strategy* defined in the test plan directs the test team in deciding when to stop testing. The strategy can use this estimating technique to tell us when testing is complete. If n is our estimate of the number of errors in a program, we can assume that our testing is thorough when we find approximately n errors. In the example above, Group 1 has found 25 errors and Group 2 30. Since we have found 40 errors and the estimate for n is 50, testing should continue.

Confidence in the Software. We can use estimates of program errors to give us some idea of the confidence we can have in the software. Confidence is usually expressed as a percentage. We say that we have a **n% level of confidence** in the truth of an assertion if there is an $n/100$ probability that the assertion is true. For example, if we say that a program is error free with a 95% level of confidence, then the probability that the program is error free is .95. Sometimes the reliability requirements for a system are stated in terms of a confidence level for freedom from errors.

Suppose we have seeded a program with S errors and we claim that the program has only N actual errors. We test the program until we have found all S of the seeded errors. If, as before, n is the number of actual errors detected during testing, the confidence level can be calculated as

$$C = \begin{cases} 1 & \text{if } n > N \\[2ex] \dfrac{S}{S - N + 1} & \text{if } n <= N \end{cases}$$

For example, suppose we claim a program is error free. Then, our claim means that N is zero. If we seed the program with ten errors and find all ten without finding an unseeded error, we can use the confidence formula with $S = 10, N = 0$. This tells us that C is 10/11, so we have a confidence level of 91%. Suppose our contract with the customer requires all programs to be tested to a level of 98% confidence. To achieve that level of confidence, we would need S seeded errors, where

$$\frac{S}{S - 0 + 1} = \frac{98}{100}$$

Solving this equation, we find that S must be 49. In other words, to guarantee 98% confidence in an error-free program, we must seed the program with 49 errors and continue the testing process until all seeded errors are found.

The problem with this approach is that we cannot predict the level of confidence until all seeded errors are detected in the program. Richards ([RIC74]) has modified this technique so that the confidence level can be estimated using the number of detected seed errors, whether or not all have been located. In this case, C is

$$C = \begin{cases} 1 & \text{if } n > N \\[2ex] \dbinom{S}{s-1} \Big/ \dbinom{S + N + 1}{N + s} & \text{if } n <= N \end{cases}$$

These estimates assume that all errors have an equal probability of being detected, an assumption which is not likely to be true. However, many other estimates take these factors into account. Such estimation techniques not only give us some idea of the confidence we may have in our programs but also provide a side benefit. Many programmers are tempted to conclude that each error is the last one.

If we estimate the number of errors left or if we know how many errors we must find in order to satisfy a confidence requirement, we have incentive to keep testing for one more error.

Module Complexity and Reliability.   Some errors are more difficult to detect than others because some modules are more complex than others. Thus, modeling the *complexity* of system modules can enhance our estimation techniques. The complexity of a system and its modules depends largely on the modules' characteristics. In particular, the amount of coupling among modules and cohesion within modules can be modeled. If we number the modules of the system from 1 through n, we can define a matrix C, where each entry c_{ij} of the matrix is a measure of the coupling between module i and module j. At the same time, we define a vector D of size n, where D_i is a measure of the cohesion within module i. Using the information in the matrix and the array thus formed, we can form a new matrix, A, where entry a_{ij} is the probability that module i will have to change when module j is changed in some way. The methods for quantifying these characteristics and working with the matrices can be found in works of DeMarco ([DEM82]) and Myers ([MYE75], [MYE86]). The matrices can be useful in pointing out those modules that are most prone to contain errors. For example, we can look at the entries of matrix A that indicate a *high degree of change*. These entries correspond to modules that are probably complex and *most likely to develop new errors* when errors are detected elsewhere.

7.7

TESTING THE RESOURCE TRACKING AND SIMULATION SYSTEM

We can apply the concepts introduced in this chapter to the Weaver Farm example with which we have been working. Suppose we have decided to implement and test the simulation subsystem first. If Figure 7.14 is the modular hierarchy for the subsystem, we examine the relationships among the modules and the characteristics of each module to decide on a testing strategy. For example, because the lowest level modules are utility routines, we may want to incorporate some bottom-up testing in our plan. When we have decided on an ordering of tests, we can depict the test cycle by drawing a diagram of the test schedule, as shown in Figure 7.15.

The test schedule tells us exactly how the modules will be unit tested and integrated with one another. If coding and testing are being done simultaneously, the test schedule tells you when your code must be written and unit tested.

After the tests are scheduled, test cases are defined. Because the simulation system is to simulate all possible combinations of resources and timing constraints, the test team decides to use an automated tool to evaluate the test coverage. They use a tool to identify the paths in a module and report on the degree to which a test case covers all paths.

The tool notes the paths on a source code listing. As you can see from the sample that follows, each decision path is assigned a number.

Figure 7.14   Module Heirarchy for Simulation Subsystem

Figure 7.15   Test Schedule for Weaver Farm

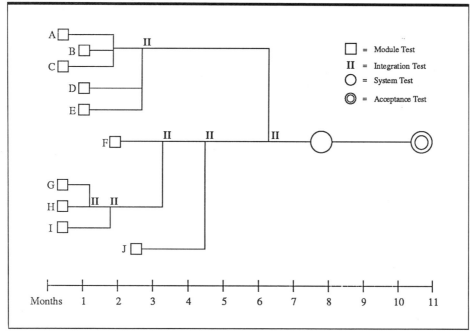

```
Statement    Listing                                      Decision Paths

   1  begin
   2      incount := endpt;
   3      cr_last := false;
   4      while (iptr < incount) do
   5        begin
   6          if (ord(ch[iptr]) < ord(" ")) then              1 - 2
   7            begin
   8              if (ch[iptr] = chr(cr))                      3 - 4
   9                then
  10                  if (cr_last) then skipch                 5 - 6
  11                    else cr_last := true
  12                else
  13                  if (ch[iptr] = chr(lf))                  7 - 8
  14                    then
  15                      if (cr_last)                         9 - 10
  16                        then cr_last := false
  17                        else skipch
  18                    else
  19                        skipch
  20            end
  21          else                                            11
  22            cr_last := false;
  23          iptr := iptr+1;
  24        end;
  25      ch[0] := chr(incount);
  26      endpt := incount;
```

Accompanying the listing is more information about each decision path.

```
Path Number        Statement Number    Branch Description

     1                    6             PATH IS FALSE BRANCH
     2                    6             PATH IS TRUE BRANCH
     3                    8             PATH IS FALSE BRANCH
     4                    8             PATH IS TRUE BRANCH
     5                   10             PATH IS FALSE BRANCH
     6                   10             PATH IS TRUE BRANCH
     7                   13             PATH IS FALSE BRANCH
     8                   13             PATH IS TRUE BRANCH
     9                   15             PATH IS FALSE BRANCH
    10                   15             PATH IS TRUE BRANCH
    11                   21             PATH IS LOOP ESCAPE
```

As each test case is executed, the tool prints out a summary of the paths traversed during the test. The report for test case 6 may look like the one below.

TEST CASE	MODULE	NBR OF PATHS	THIS TEST			CUMULATIVE		
			INVO-CATIONS	PATHS TRAV.	% COVER	INVO-CATIONS	PATHS TRAV.	% COVER
6	SIMPARM	4	1	3	75.	6	4	100.
	INDATA	7	1	2	29.	6	6	89.
	DBSRCH	6	1	3	50.	5	5	83.
	SIMRUN	9	1	4	44.	6	8	88.
	OUTDATA	5	1	3	60.	6	4	80.
	FORMAT	4	0	0	00.	5	3	75.

Corresponding to this analysis, a list is printed of the decision paths not executed after six test cases:

MODULE	TEST	PATHS MISSED	TOTAL
SIMPARM	6	2	1
INDATA	6	3 4 5 6 7	5
DBSRCH	6	2 4 5	3
SIMRUN	6	2 3 4 5 9	5
OUTDATA	6	3 5	2
FORMAT	6	1 2 3 4	4

Clearly, the test tool tells the team whether it has met its test coverage objectives as specified in the test plan.

7.8

CHAPTER SUMMARY

This chapter has introduced the idea of testing a software system. Rather than viewing testing as a demonstration that a program or system works properly, the test team tries to detect errors. The testing phase of development is composed of a life cycle of its own—beginning with unit testing of each module, followed by integration of the software modules, and leading to a demonstration for the customer of the system's functionality and performance at the system's final destination.

Testing philosophies at various stages are based on test objectives set for each stage. Once the objectives are established, we select a set of test data that covers as many cases as possible. The testing of modules and their integration can include static analysis (evaluating programs before they are executed) and dynamic analysis (monitoring performance while the program is running). Many of the tools for testing programs have been automated, and tools are available for all stages of the test cycle.

We have seen the need to measure the quality of the resulting software system. Quality can be determined by how reliable, available, and maintainable the software is. By counting the number of errors found as we test, we can estimate the total number of errors present in our programs and judge, from the number found, how many are left undetected.

In the next chapter, we will continue our discussion of testing with an investigation of the remainder of the test life cycle: function testing, performance testing, acceptance testing, and installation testing.

7.9

EXERCISES

1. Let P be a program module that reads in a list of N records and a range condition on the record key. The first seven characters of the record form the record key. The module P reads the key and produces an output file that contains only those records whose key falls in the prescribed range. For example, if the range is "JONES" to "SMITH," then the output file consists of all records whose keys are lexicographically between "JONES" and "SMITH." Write the input and output conditions as assertions to be used in proving P correct. Write a flow diagram of what P's logical flow might be, and identify the transformation points.

2. Complete the proof of the example in the text illustrated by Figure 7.4. In other words, write assertions to correspond to the flow diagram. Then, find the paths from input condition to output. Prove that the paths are theorems.

3. Suppose a program contains N decision points, each of which has 2 branches. How many test cases are needed to perform path testing on such a program? If there are M choices at each decision point, how many test cases are needed for path testing? Can the structure of the program reduce this number? Give an example to support your answer.

Figure 7.16   Graph of Program in Figure 7.5

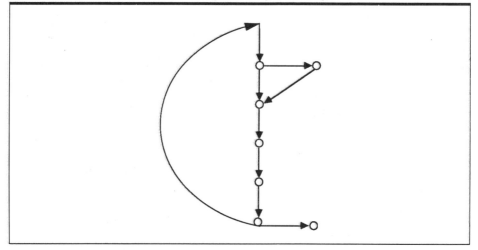

4. Consider a program flow diagram as a directed graph in which the diamonds and boxes of the program are nodes of the graph and the logic flow arrows between them are directed edges. For example, the program in Figure 7.5 can be graphed as shown in Figure 7.16. Prove that statement testing of a program is equivalent to finding a path in the graph that contains all nodes of the graph. Prove that branch testing of a program is equivalent to finding a set of paths whose union covers the edges of the graph. Finally, prove that path testing of a program is equivalent to finding all possible paths through the graph.

5. Programmable Problem: Write a program that accepts as input the nodes and edges of a directed graph and prints as output all possible paths through the graph. What are the major design considerations for your program? How does the complexity of the graph (in terms of the number of branches and cycles) affect the algorithm you use?

6. Figure 7.17 illustrates the hierarchy of modules in a software system. Describe the sequence of module tests for integrating the modules using a bottom-up approach; a top-down approach; a modified top-down approach; a big-bang approach; a sandwich approach; a modified sandwich approach.

7. Measurements of reliability, maintainability, and availability are often placed in the system requirements document. Give examples of systems that might be able to tolerate low levels of these qualities. Give examples of systems that can tolerate only high levels of these qualities.

Figure 7.17   System Module Heirarchy for Exercise 7.6

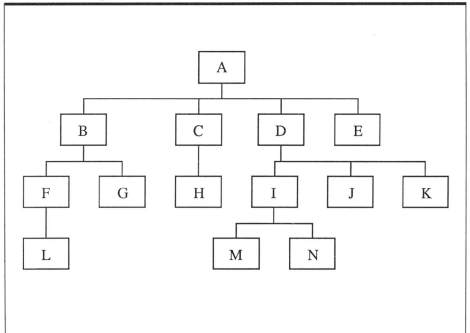

8. Explain why the graph of Figure 7.13 can be interpreted to mean that if you find many errors in your code at compile time, you should throw away your code and implement it again.

9. What are some possible reasons to explain the behavior of the graph of Figure 7.13?

10. A program is seeded with 25 errors. During testing, 18 errors are detected, 13 of which are seeded errors and 5 of which are indigenous errors. What is the Mills estimate of the number of indigenous errors remaining undetected in the program?

11. You claim that your program is error free at a 95% confidence level. Your test plan calls for you to test until you find all seeded errors. With how many errors must you seed the program before testing in order to substantiate your claim? If for some reason you do not intend to find all seeded errors, how many seed errors does the Richards formula require?

CHAPTER 8

SYSTEM TESTING

In Chapters 3, 4, 5, and 6, we discussed the use of reviews and walk-throughs to guarantee the quality of a system, and we emphasized the need for documentation to establish a common understanding of the requirements, design, and code. In the last chapter, we began to examine the testing phase of software development. We concentrated on finding errors within the program modules and in the interfaces among the modules. As shown in Figure 8.1, testing can be viewed as a two-step process. First, we must be sure that the implementation works as the programmers intend. Then, when the modules are combined into a working system, we insure that the system functions according to the prescriptions of the requirements documents.

Now we turn from a program-level view of testing to a system-level view. To test the software from a systems perspective, we verify that the software developed satisfies both our customers and ourselves. *System testing* verifies that a system solves the problem as defined by the requirements documents.

We begin our investigation of system testing by looking at the differences between system testing and program testing. We discover where system errors originate and use that information to outline the steps of system testing. As with program testing, we need test objectives and an integration plan. To tie system testing back to previous development and ahead to maintenance, we include tests to support configuration management.

Next, we discuss each step of system testing in detail: function testing, performance testing, acceptance testing, and installation testing. The test team is described in terms of its members and their roles, and we look at tools that aid test administration.

Several types of test documents are useful during testing, and we return to our Weaver Farm example to see what they look like.

8.1

PRINCIPLES OF SYSTEM TESTING

System testing is different from program testing (that is, from unit and integration testing). Let us see how.

311

Figure 8.1   The System Development Process

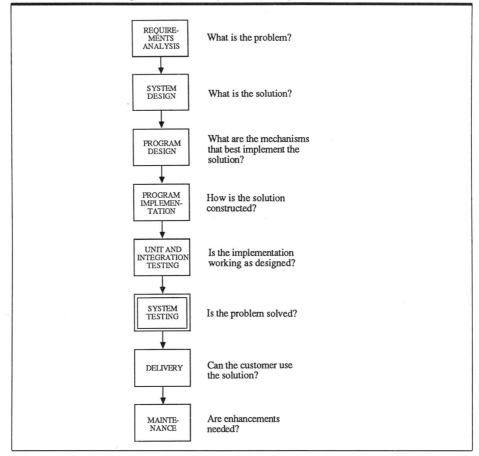

Where System Errors Originate

Errors can occur at any point during development. Figure 8.2 illustrates the likely causes of errors in each stage. Although we would like to find and correct errors as early as possible in development, system testing acknowledges that errors may still be present after integration testing.

Errors may have been introduced to the system early in development or recently, such as when correcting a previously found error. For example, defective software can result from errors made when determining requirements. Whether a requirement was ambiguous because the customer was unsure of a need or because we misinterpreted the customer's meaning, the result is the same: a system that does not work the way the customer wishes.

The same kind of communication mishaps can occur during system design. We may misinterpret a requirement and write an incorrect design specification. Or, we understand the requirement but may word the specification so poorly that those who subsequently read and use the design misunderstand it.

Similar events can lead to errors in the program design. Misinterpretations are common when the system design is translated into lower level descriptions for program design specifications. Programmers are several levels removed from the initial discussions with customers about system goals and functionality. Having responsibility for one "tree" but not the "forest," programmers cannot be expected to spot design errors that have been perpetuated through the first steps of the development cycle. For this reason, requirements and design reviews are essential to assuring the quality of the resulting system.

The programmers and designers on our development team may also fail to use the proper syntax and semantics for recording their work. A compiler or assembler can catch some of these errors before a program is run, but they will not find errors where the form of a statement is correct but does not match the intention of the programmer or designer.

Figure 8.2   Where Errors May Occur

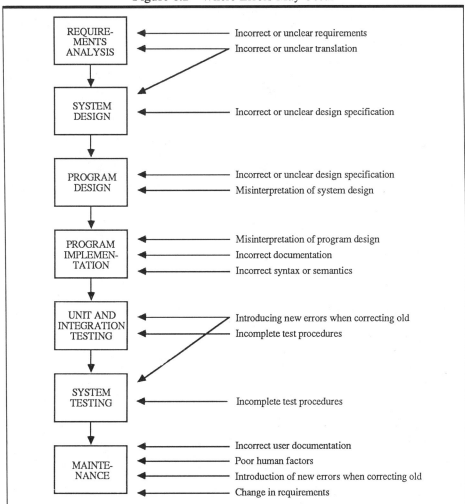

Once program module testing begins, errors may be added unintentionally in changes to correct other errors. These errors are often very difficult to detect, because they may appear only when certain functions are exercised. If those functions have already been tested when a new error is inadvertently added, the new error may not be noticed until much later when the source of the new error may not be clear.

For example, suppose you are testing modules A, B, and C. You test each separately. When you test all three together, you find that A passes a parameter to C incorrectly. In repairing A, you insure that the parameter pass is correct, but you add code that sets a pointer incorrectly. Because you may not go back and test A independently again, you may not find evidence of the error until much later in testing—when it is not clear that A is the culprit.

In the same manner, errors may be introduced during maintenance. Enhancements to the original system require changes to the requirements, the system design, the program design, and the implementation itself, so that all of the errors discussed above can occur during maintenance. In addition, the system may not function properly because users do not understand how the system was designed to work. If the documentation is unclear or incorrect, an error may occur. Human factors, including user perception, play a large role in understanding the system and interpreting its messages and required input. Users who are not comfortable with the system may not exercise the functions of the system properly or to greatest advantage.

Test procedures should be thorough enough to exercise the system functions to everyone's satisfaction: user, customer, and developer. If the tests are incomplete, errors may remain undetected. As we have seen, the sooner we detect an error, the better; errors detected early on are easier and cheaper to fix. Thus, complete and early testing can help not only to detect errors quickly but also to isolate the causes more easily.

Figure 8.2 shows reasons for error, not evidence of them. Because testing aims to uncover as many errors as possible, it is concerned with where they may exist. Knowing how errors are created can give us clues about where to look when testing a system.

Steps In System Testing

There are several steps in testing a system:

1. Function testing
2. Performance testing
3. Acceptance testing
4. Installation testing

The steps are illustrated in Figure 8.3. Each step has a different focus, and the success of a step depends on whether its goal or objective has been met. Thus, it is helpful to review the purpose of each part of system testing.

Figure 8.3   Steps in System Testing

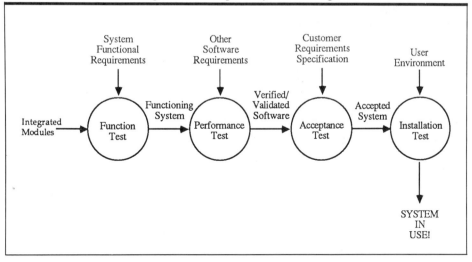

Objectives of Testing Steps.   Initially, we test the functions performed by the system. We begin with a set of modules that have been tested individually and then together. The *function test* checks that the integrated system performs its functional requirements as specified in the requirements. For example, a function test of a bank account package verifies that the package can correctly credit a deposit, enter a withdrawal, calculate interest, print the balance, and so on.

Once the test team is convinced that the functions work as specified, the *performance test* compares the integrated modules with the nonfunctional system requirements. These requirements include security, accuracy, speed, and reliability; they constrain the way in which the system functions are performed. For instance, a performance test of the bank account package evaluates the speed with which calculations are made, the precision of the computation, the security precautions required, and the response time to user inquiry. A *validated system* is the result of a performance test in the customer's actual working environment; if the testing is done in a simulated environment, the performance test results in a *verified system*.

At this point, the validated or verified system operates the way the *designers* intend; it is their interpretation of the requirements specification. Next, we compare the system's performance with the *customer's* expectations by reviewing the requirements definition document. The *acceptance test* checks the system's characteristics to assure that they are in compliance with the defined requirements. If the system has not yet been installed in the user's environment, a final *installation test* is done to allow users to exercise system functions and document additional errors. For example, if a system is being designed for the Navy, all initial testing (that is, up to and including acceptance testing) may be performed at a headquarters site configured exactly as a ship might be. However, installation tests are performed at sea on the actual ship or ships that will use the system.

Build or Integration Plan.   Ideally, after program testing, you can view the collection of modules as a single entity. Then, during the first steps of system testing, the integrated collection is evaluated from a variety of perspectives, as previously described. However, large systems are sometimes unwieldy when tested as one enormous collection of modules. In fact, such systems are often candidates for phased development simply because they are much easier to build and test in smaller pieces. Thus, you may choose to perform *phased system testing.* We saw in chapter 1 that a system can be viewed as a nested set of levels or subsystems. Each level is responsible for performing at least the functions of those subsystems it contains. Similarly, we can divide the test system into a nested sequence of subsystems and perform the system test on one subsystem at a time.

The subsystem definitions are based on predetermined criteria. Usually, the basis for division is *functionality*. For example, a system that routes telephone calls might be divided into subsystems in the following way (as illustrated in Figure 8.4):

System A: Routing calls within a single exchange

System B: Routing calls within a single city

System C: Routing calls within a single area code

System D: Routing calls within a single state

System E: Routing any calls

Figure 8.4   Example of Nexted Phone Systems

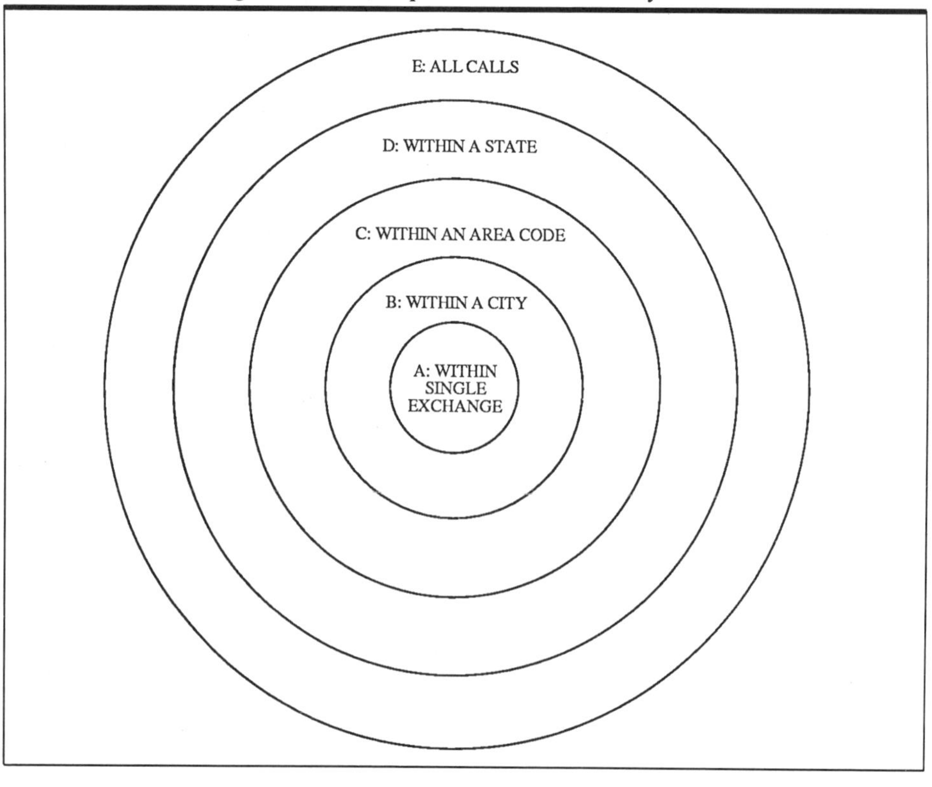

Each larger system contains all the systems preceding it. We begin our system testing by testing system A. When we have met the objectives of the function test step for system A, we proceed to a function test of system B. After a successful test of B, we continue to test systems C, D, and E in the same way. The result is a successful function test of the entire system, but incremental testing may have made error detection and correction much easier than having tested only system E. For example, an error discovered in the testing of system C is likely to be the result of something other than those modules dealing with state-related characteristics. Had the error been discovered only when testing system E, we could not eliminate the functions or modules that reside in systems E and D but not in system C.

Incremental testing requires careful planning. The test team must create a **build plan** or **integration plan** to define the subsystems to be tested and to describe how, where, when, and by whom the tests will be conducted. Sometimes, a level or subsystem of a build plan is called a **spin** or **driver**. The spins are numbered, with the lowest level of spin called spin 0. For large systems, spin 0 is often a minimal system; it can even be only the operating system on a host computer.

For example, the build plan for the system depicted in Figure 8.4 may contain a schedule similar to Table 8.1.

Table 8.1 Build Plan for Phone System

Spin	Function	Test Start	Test End
0	Calls within exchange	1 Sep 87	15 Sept 87
1	Calls within city	30 Sep 87	15 Oct 87
2	Calls within area code	25 Oct 87	5 Nov 87
3	Calls within state	10 Nov 87	20 Nov 87
4	All possible calls	1 Dec 87	15 Dec 87

The build plan describes each spin by number, functional content, and testing schedule. Thus, as shown in Table 8.1, the first system to be tested will handle only those phone calls on a single exchange. The test will begin on September 1 and should end by September 15. After a successful test of spin 0, the next system to be tested has more functionality than the previous one. It is better to have a large number of spins so that the amount of change from one spin to the next is small; this gives the test team a greater amount of control over the testing process. If a test of spin N succeeds and an error arises in spin $N+1$, then the most likely source of the error is related to the difference between spin N and spin $N+1$: namely, the added functionality from one spin to the next. If the difference between two successive spins is small, then we have relatively few places to look for the defect's source.

The number of spins and their definitions depend primarily on our resources and those of the customer. These resources include not only hardware and software but also time and personnel availability. A minimal system is placed in the earliest spin, and subsequent spins are defined by integrating the most important or the most critical functions as early as feasible. For example, suppose a system involves a network of computers arranged in a star-like fashion as shown in Figure 8.5. The center of the star is a large computer that receives messages from a set of smaller

Figure 8.5   Message Processing System

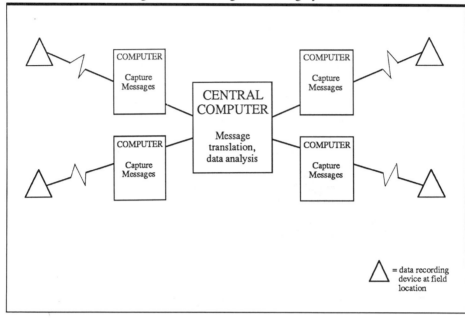

computers whose main purpose is to capture and transmit data for processing. One of the major functions of the central computer is to translate and assimilate the messages from the outlying computers. Since this function is critical to the other functions of the system, it should be included in an early spin. In fact, we may begin to define the spins in the following way:

Spin 0: Test the central computer general functions

Spin 1: Test the message translation function on the central computer

Spin 2: Test the message assimilation function on the central computer

Spin 3: Test each outlying computer in stand-alone mode

Spin 4: Test each outlying computer's message-sending function

Spin 5: Test the central computer's message-receiving function

and so on.

The spin definitions also depend on the ability of the system components to operate in stand-alone mode. It may be harder to simulate a missing piece of a system than to incorporate the piece in a spin, since interdependencies among parts of the system sometimes require as much simulation code as actual code. Remember that our goal is to test the system. Time and effort needed to build and use test tools might be better spent in testing the actual system. This trade-off is similar to the one involved in choosing a test philosophy during program testing: developing many stubs and drivers may require as much time during program testing as testing the original modules they simulate.

Configuration Management

As we saw in the last chapter, the purpose of testing is to identify errors, not to correct them. However, it is natural to want to find the source of and then correct errors as soon as possible after discovery. Otherwise, the test team is unable to judge if the system is functioning properly, and the presence of some errors might halt further testing. Thus, any test plan must include a set of *guidelines* for error correction.

Defects may result from causes in any phase of system development. Correcting an error may mean modifying several lines of code, updating program documentation, revising the program or system design, or altering requirements. The configuration management team is responsible for assuring that these changes are made accurately and promptly. Accuracy is critical because we want to avoid generating new errors while correcting existing ones. Similarly, promptness is important because error correction is proceeding at the same time that the test team is searching for new errors. Therefore, those who are trying to repair defects in the system should work with documentation that reflects the current state of the system.

Regression Testing. Regression testing identifies new errors that may be introduced as current ones are being corrected. A **regression test** is a test applied to a new version of a system to verify that it still performs the same functions in the same manner as an older version.

For example, suppose that the functional test for system C was successful, and testing is proceeding on system D, where D has all the functionality of C plus some new functions. You request that several lines of code be changed in system D to repair an error located in an earlier test; the code must be changed now so that the testing of system D can continue. If the test team is following a policy of regression testing, the testing will include these steps:

1. Insertion of your new code
2. Testing of the functions known to be affected by the new code
3. Testing of the essential functions of system C to verify that they still work properly
4. Continuation of the function testing of system D

These steps insure that adding new code has not negated the effects of the previous tests.

Often the regression test involves the reuse of the most important test cases from the previous level's test; if you specify regression testing in your test plan, you should also explain which test cases are to be used again.

The Issue of Control. The configuration management team works closely with the test team to control all aspects of testing. Any change proposed to any part of the system is approved first by the configuration management team. The change is entered in all appropriate *documentation*, and the team notifies all who may be affected. For example, if a test results in modification of a requirement, changes are also likely to be needed in the requirements specification, the system design, the program design, the code, all relevant documentation, and even the test plan itself. Thus, altering one part of the system may affect everyone who is working on the system's development.

One method for insuring that all project members are working with the most up-to-date documentation is to keep documents online. By viewing documents on a screen and updating them immediately, we avoid the time lag usually caused by having to print and distribute new or revised pages. However, the configuration management team still maintains some degree of control to make sure that changes to documents mirror changes to design and code.

Libraries of documentation are not the only aspects of the system that must be controlled. If system development is *phased*, a production system runs in parallel with a development system. A **production system** is a version of the system that has been tested and performs according to only a subset of the customer's requirements. The next version with more features is developed while users operate the production system. This **development system** is built and tested; when testing is complete, the development system replaces the production system to become the new production system.

For example, suppose a power plant is automating the functions performed in the control room. The power plant operators have been trained to do everything manually and are uneasy about working with the computer, so we decide to build a phased system. The first phase is almost identical to the manual system but allows the plant operators to do some automated record keeping. The second phase adds several automated functions to the first phase, but half of the control room functions are still manual. Successive phases continue to automate selected functions, building on the previous phase until all functions are automated. By building up the automated system in this way, we allow the plant operators to slowly become accustomed to and feel comfortable with the new system.

At any point during the phased development, the plant operators are using the fully tested production system. At the same time, we are working on the next phase, testing the *development* system. When the development system is completely tested and ready for use by the plant operators, it becomes the production system (that is, it is used by the plant operators) and we move on to the next phase. We add functions to the current production or operational system, and the copy of the system we work with is our new development system.

While a system is in production, errors may occur and be reported to us. Thus, a development system often serves two purposes: it *adds the functionality* of the next phase, and *corrects the errors* found in previous versions. A development system can therefore involve adding new modules as well as changing existing ones. However, this procedure allows errors to be introduced in modules that have already been tested. When we write build and test plans, we should address this problem and consider the need for controlling changes implemented from one version to the next. Regression testing can make sure that the development system performs at least as well as the current production system. However, records must be kept of the exact changes made to the code from one version to the next so that we can trace problems to their source. For example, if a user on the production system reports a problem, you must know what version of code is being used. The code may differ dramatically from one version to another. If you work with the wrong listing, you may never locate the source of the error. Worse yet, you may think you have located the source and make a change that introduces a new error while not fixing the old error.

When a new production system is ready for operation, users are trained to exercise the new functions or change the way they worked with the previous version. Should an error be discovered, we may decide to return to a previous version until the error is corrected. The configuration management team must be able to "roll back" the changes and present the users with their old system.

Similar issues arise when the final system is being maintained for the customer. We will address these issues in more depth in chapter 10.

8.2

FUNCTION TESTING

We begin system testing with function testing. While previous steps concentrated on modules and their interactions, this step of testing ignores system structure and focuses on *functionality*. Our approach from now on is more a closed box than an open one. We need not know what modules are being exercised; rather, we need to know what the system is *supposed* to do. Thus, to perform function testing, we must know the system functional requirements.

Each function can be associated with those system components that accomplish it. For some functions, the parts may comprise the entire system. The set of module actions associated with a function is called a **thread**; hence, function testing is sometimes referred to as **thread testing**.

Logically, it should be easier to find the cause of an error in a small set of modules than in a large one. Thus, ease of testing calls for choosing carefully the order in which functions are tested. Functions may be defined in a *nested* manner, just as spins are defined in levels. For example, suppose a requirement specifies that a water monitoring system is to identify large changes in four characteristics: dissolved oxygen, temperature, acidity, and radioactivity. The requirements specification may treat change acknowledgment as one of many functions of the overall system. However, for testing, we may want to view the monitoring as four separate functions:

- Acknowledging change in dissolved oxygen
- Acknowledging change in temperature
- Acknowledging change in acidity
- Acknowledging change in radioactivity

Then, we test each one individually.

Effective function tests should have a high probability of detecting an error. We use the same guidelines for function testing that we discussed in chapter 7 for unit testing. We can summarize the guidelines as:

1. Having a high probability of detecting errors
2. Using a test team independent of the designers and programmers
3. Knowing what the expected actions and output are
4. Testing both valid and invalid input
5. Never modifying the system being tested just to make testing easier
6. Knowing when the tests should stop

Function testing is performed in a carefully controlled situation. Moreover, since we are testing one function at a time, function testing can actually begin before the entire system is constructed, if need be.

Function testing compares the actual performance of the system with its requirements, so the test cases for function testing are developed from the requirements document. In the next section, we examine a method for analyzing the requirements to generate the set of test cases.

Cause and Effect Graphs

Testing would be easier if we could automatically generate test cases from the requirements. Work has been done at IBM ([ELM73] and [ELM74]) to convert the natural language specifications of a requirements definition document to a formal specification that can be used to enumerate test cases for functional testing. The test cases that result are not redundant; that is, one test case does not repeat the testing of functions that have already been tested by another case. In addition, the process finds incomplete and ambiguous aspects of the requirements definition if any still exist.

The process examines the semantics of the requirements definition and restates the requirements as logical relationships between inputs and outputs or between inputs and transformations. The inputs are called *causes*, and the outputs and transformations are *effects*. The result is a Boolean graph reflecting these relationships called a **cause and effect graph**.

We add information to the initial graph to indicate rules of syntax and to reflect environmental constraints. Then we convert the graph to a decision table. Each column of the decision table corresponds to a test case for functional testing.

There are several steps in the creation of a cause and effect graph. First, the requirements are separated so that each requirement describes a single function. Then all causes and effects are described. The numbered causes and effects become nodes of the graph. Placing causes on the left-hand side of the drawing and effects on the right, we draw the logical relationships depicted in the graph by using the notation shown in Figure 8.6. Extra nodes can be defined to simplify the graph.

Figure 8.6   Cause and Effect Relationships

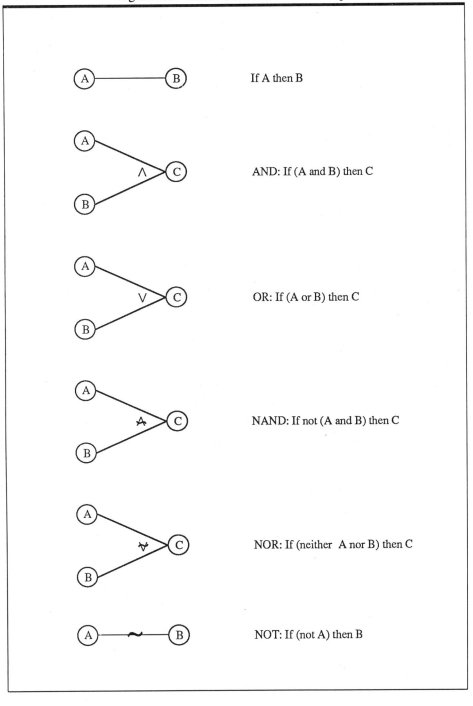

An example will show us how such a graph is built. Suppose we are testing a water level monitoring system. The requirements definition for one of the system functions reads as follows:

The system sends a message to the dam operator about the safety of the lake level.

Corresponding to this requirement is a design description.

INPUT: The syntax of the function is

LEVEL(*A*, *B*)

where *A* is the height in feet of the water behind the dam, and *B* is the number of inches of rain in the last twenty-four-hour period.

PROCESSING: The function calculates whether the water level is within a safe range, is too high, or is too low.

OUTPUT: The screen shows one of the following messages:
1. "LEVEL = SAFE" when result is safe or low
2. "LEVEL = HIGH" when result is high
3. "INVALID SYNTAX"
depending on the result of the calculation.

We can separate these requirements into five causes:

Cause 1. The first five characters of the command are 'LEVEL'.
Cause 2. The command contains exactly two parameters separated by a comma and enclosed in parentheses.
Cause 3. The parameters A and B are real numbers such that the water level is calculated to be LOW.
Cause 4. The parameters A and B are real numbers such that the water level is calculated to be SAFE.
Cause 5. The parameters A and B are real numbers such that the water level is calculated to be HIGH.

We can also describe three effects.

Effect E1. The message "LEVEL = SAFE" is displayed on the screen.
Effect E2. The message "LEVEL = HIGH" is displayed on the screen.
Effect E3. The message "INVALID SYNTAX" is printed out.

These become the nodes of our graph. However, the function includes a check on the parameters to be sure that they are passed properly. To reflect this, we establish two intermediate nodes:

Node 10. The command is syntactically valid.
Node 11. The operands are syntactically valid.

Figure 8.7   Cause and Effect Graph for LEVEL Function

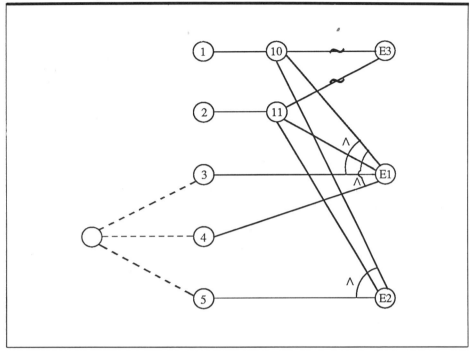

We can draw the relationships between cause and effect as shown in Figure 8.7. Notice that there are dashed lines to the left of the effects. These lines mean that exactly one effect can result. Other notations can be made on cause and effect graphs to provide additional information. Figure 8.8 illustrates some of the possibilities. By looking at the graph, we can tell if

- At most one of a set of conditions can be invoked
- At least one of a set of conditions must be invoked
- Exactly one of a set of conditions can be invoked
- One effect masks the observance of another effect
- Invocation of one effect requires the invocation of another

At this point, we are ready to define a decision table using the information from the cause and effect graph. We put a row in the table for each cause or effect. Thus, in our example, our decision table needs five rows for the causes and three rows for the effects. The columns of the decision table correspond to the test cases. We define the columns by examining each effect and listing all combinations of causes that can lead to that effect.

In our LEVEL example, we can determine the number of columns in the decision table by examining the lines flowing into the effect nodes of the cause and effect graph. We see in Figure 8.7 that there are two separate lines flowing into E3; each corresponds to a column. There are four lines flowing into E1, but only two

Figure 8.8   Additional Cause and Effect Notation

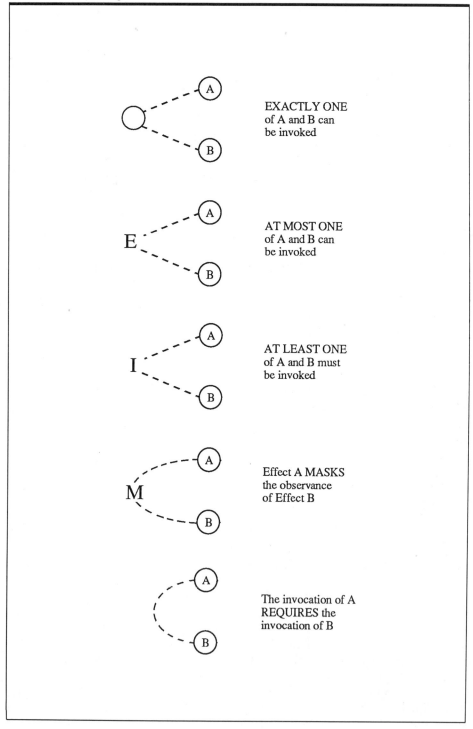

EXACTLY ONE
of A and B can
be invoked

AT MOST ONE
of A and B can
be invoked

AT LEAST ONE
of A and B must
be invoked

Effect A MASKS
the observance
of Effect B

The invocation of A
REQUIRES the
invocation of B

combinations yield the effect. Each of the combinations is a column in the table. Finally, only one combination of lines results in effect E2, so we have our fifth column.

Each column of the decision table represents a set of *states* of causes and effects. We keep track of the states of other conditions when a particular combination is invoked. We indicate the condition of the cause by placing an I in the table when the cause is invoked or true, or an S if the cause is suppressed or false. If we do not care whether the cause is invoked or suppressed, we can use an X to mark the "don't-care" state. Finally, we indicate whether a particular effect is absent (A) or present (P).

For testing the LEVEL function, the five columns in Table 8.2 display the relationship between invocation of causes and the resultant effects. If causes 1 and 2 are true (that is, the command and parameters are valid), then effect depends on whether causes 3, 4, or 5 are true. If cause 1 is true but cause 2 is false, the effect is already determined, and we don't care about the state of causes 3, 4, or 5. Similarly, if cause 1 is false, we no longer care about the states of other causes.

Note that theoretically we could have generated 32 test cases: five causes in each of two states yield 2^5 possibilities. Thus, the use of a cause and effect graph substantially decreases the number of test cases we must consider.

Table 8.2   Decision Table for Cause and Effect Graph

		Tests				
		1	2	3	4	5
	1	I	I	I	I	S
	2	I	I	I	X	I
Causes	3	I	S	S	X	X
	4	S	I	S	X	X
	5	S	S	I	X	X
	E1	P	P	A	A	A
Effects	E2	A	A	P	A	A
	E3	A	A	A	P	P

S = Suppressed   I = Invoked   A = Absent   P = Present   X = Don't Care

In general, we can reduce the number of test cases even more by using our knowledge of the causes to eliminate certain other combinations. For example, if the number of test cases is high, we may assign a priority to each combination of causes. Then, we can eliminate the combinations of low priority. Similarly, we can eliminate those combinations that are unlikely to occur or for which testing is not economically justifiable.

In addition to reducing the number of test cases to consider, cause and effect graphs help us predict the possible outcomes of exercising the system. At the same time, the graphs find unintended side effects for certain combinations of causes. However, cause and effect graphing has several limitations. The graphs are not practical for systems that include time delays, iterations, or loops where the system reacts to feedback from some of its processes to perform other processes.

8.3

PERFORMANCE TESTING

When the system performs the functions required by the requirements definition, we turn to the way in which those functions are performed. Thus, system performance is measured against the *objectives* set by the customer. For example, function testing may have demonstrated that a test system can calculate the mean and standard deviation of a set of numbers. *Performance testing* examines how well the calculation is done; response to user commands, accuracy of the result, and accessibility of the data are checked against the customer's performance prescriptions.

Test Case Coverage

Performance testing is based on the requirements, so the types of performance tests used are determined by the requirements. The test team chooses from among several kinds of tests.

1. **Stress tests** evaluate the system when stressed to its limits over a short period of time. If the requirements state that a system is to handle up to a specified number of devices or users, a stress test evaluates how the system performs when all of those devices or users are active simultaneously. This is especially important for systems that usually operate below maximum but are severely stressed at certain times of peak demand.

2. **Volume tests** address the handling of large amounts of data in the system. For example, the system should handle large data sets according to the requirements. In a volume test, we look at whether data structures (such as queues and stacks) have been defined to be large enough to handle all possible situations. In addition, fields, records, and files are checked to see if their sizes can accommodate all expected data. The team investigates the system's response to filled data sets, too.

3. **Configuration tests** analyze the various software and hardware configurations specified in the requirements. Sometimes a system is built to serve a variety of audiences, and the system is really a spectrum of configurations. For instance, a minimal system may be defined to serve a single user, and other configurations build on the minimal configuration to serve additional users. A configuration test evaluates all possible configurations to make sure that each satisfies the requirements.

4. **Compatibility tests** are needed when a system interfaces with other systems. We find out whether the interface functions perform according to the requirements. For instance, if the system is to communicate with a large data base system to retrieve information, a compatibility test examines the speed and accuracy of data retrieval.

5. **Regression tests** are required when the system being tested is replacing an existing system. The regression tests guarantee that the new system's performance is at least as good as that of the old. Regression tests are always used during a phased development.

6. **Security tests** insure that the security requirements are met. We test access to the system itself, to functions and to data, to see if requested restrictions have been implemented properly.

7. **Timing tests** evaluate the requirements dealing with time to respond to a user and time to perform a function. If a transaction must take place within a specified time, the test performs that transaction and verifies that the requirements are met. Timing tests are usually done in concert with stress tests to see if the timing requirements are met even when the system is extremely active.

8. **Environmental tests** look at the system's ability to perform at the installation site. If the requirements include tolerances for heat, humidity, motion, chemical presence, moisture, portability, electrical or magnetic fields, disruption of power, or any other environmental characteristic of the site, then our tests guarantee the system's proper performance under these conditions.

9. **Quality tests** evaluate the reliability, maintainability, and availability of the system. These tests address the characteristics described in chapter 7 and include requirements for mean time between failures and mean time to repair. In addition, we investigate requirements relating to detecting and correcting errors. Quality tests are sometimes very difficult to administer. For example, if a requirement specifies a long mean time between failures, it may be infeasible to let the system run long enough to verify the mean.

10. **Recovery tests** address response to the presence of errors or to the loss of data, devices, or power. We subject the system to a loss of system resources and see if it recovers properly.

11. **Maintenance tests** address the need for diagnostic tools and procedures to help in finding the source of errors. We may be required to supply diagnostic programs, memory maps, traces of transactions, diagrams of circuitry, and other aids. We verify that the aids exist and that they function properly.

12. **Documentation tests** insure that we have written the required documents. If user manuals, maintenance guides, and technical documents are needed, we verify that these materials exist and that the information they contain is consistent, accurate, and easy to read. Moreover, sometimes requirements specify the format and audience of the documentation; we evaluate the documents for compliance.

13. **Human factors tests** investigate requirements dealing with the user interface to the system. We examine display screens, messages, report formats, and other aspects that may relate to ease of use. In addition, operator and user procedures are checked to see if they conform to ease of use requirements.

Many of these tests are much more difficult to administer than the function tests. We stressed in chapter 3 the need for requirements to be explicit and detailed. The quality of the requirements is often reflected in the ease of performance testing. Unless a requirement is clear, it is hard for the test team to know when the requirement is satisfied. Indeed, it may even be difficult to know *how* to administer a test because it may not be clear when the test is successful.

8.4

ACCEPTANCE TESTING

When function and performance tests are complete, we are convinced that the system meets all requirements specified during the initial stages of system development. The next step is to ask the customer and users if they concur. Until now, we as developers have designed the test cases and administered all tests. Now the customer leads testing and defines the cases to be tested.

Types of Acceptance Tests

There are three ways the customer can evaluate the system. In a **benchmark test**, the customer prepares a set of test cases that represent typical conditions under which the system will operate when actually installed. The customer submits the test cases and evaluates the system's performance for each. Benchmark tests are performed with actual users or a special test team exercising system functions. In either case, the testers are familiar with the requirements and able to evaluate the actual performance.

Benchmark tests are commonly used when a customer has special requirements. Two or more development teams are asked to produce systems according to specification; one system will be chosen for purchase, based on the success of the benchmark tests. For example, a customer may ask two communications companies to install a voice and data network. Each system is "benchmarked." Both systems may meet a requirement, but one may be faster or easier to use than the other. The customer decides to purchase one rather than the other based on how the systems met the benchmark criteria.

A **pilot test** installs the system on an experimental basis. Users exercise the system as if it had been permanently installed. Whereas benchmark tests include a set of *special test cases* that the users apply, pilot tests rely on the *everyday working* of the system to test all functions. The customer often prepares a suggested list of functions that each user tries to incorporate in typical daily procedures. However, a pilot test is much less formal and structured than a benchmark.

Sometimes we test a system with users from within our own organization or company before releasing the system to the customer; that is, we "pilot" the system before the customer runs the real pilot test. Our in-house test is called an **alpha test** and the customer's pilot a **beta test**. This approach is common when systems are to be released to a wide variety of customers. For example, an office automation system or a new version of an operating system may be alpha tested at our own office and then beta tested using a specially selected group of customer sites. We try to choose as beta test sites customers who represent all kinds of customer organizations.

Even if a system is being developed for just one customer, a pilot test usually involves only a small subset of the customer's potential users. We choose the users for the pilot so that their activities represent those of most others who will use the system later. One location or one organization may be chosen to test the system, rather than allowing all intended users to have access.

If a new system is replacing an existing one or is part of a phased development, a third kind of testing can be used for acceptance. In **parallel testing**, the new system operates in parallel with the previous version. The users gradually become accustomed to the new system but continue to use the old one to duplicate the new system's functions. This gradual transition allows users to compare and contrast the new system with the old. It also allows skeptical users to build their confidence in the new system by comparing the results obtained by both. In a sense, parallel testing incorporates a user-administered combination of compatibility and function testing.

Results of Acceptance Tests

The type of system being tested and the preferences of the customer determine the choice of acceptance test. In fact, a combination of some or all of the approaches can be used. Allowing users to test sometimes finds places where the customer's expectations, as stated in the requirements, do not match what we have implemented. In other words, acceptance testing is the customer's chance to verify that what was wanted is what was built. If the customer is satisfied, the system is then accepted as stated in the contract.

In reality, acceptance testing uncovers more than requirements discrepancies. The acceptance test also allows the customer to determine what is really wanted, whether specified in the requirements or not. Remember that the requirements analysis stage of development gives the customer an opportunity to explain to us what problem needs a solution. The system design is our proposed solution to the customer's problem. Until the customer and the users actually work with a system as a proposed solution, they may not really know whether the problem is indeed solved.

We have seen in previous chapters that rapid prototyping may be used to help the customer understand more about the solution before the entire system is implemented. However, prototypes are often impractical or too expensive to build. Moreover, when building large systems, there is sometimes a long time between the initial specification of requirements and the first viewing of even part of a system. During this time, the customer's needs may change in some way. For instance, the nature of the customer's business may change, affecting the nature of the original problem. Thus, changes in requirements may be needed not only because they were improperly specified at the beginning of development; the customer may decide that a different solution is needed.

After acceptance testing, the customer tells us which requirements are not satisfied and which must be deleted, amended, or added because of changing needs. We will see in chapter 10 how the configuration management team identifies these changes in requirements and records the resulting modifications to design, implementation, and testing.

8.5

INSTALLATION TESTING

The final round of testing involves installing the system at user sites. If acceptance testing has been performed on site, installation testing may not be needed. However, if acceptance testing conditions were not the same as actual site conditions, additional testing is necessary. To begin installation testing, we configure the system to the user environment. We attach the proper number and kind of devices to the main processor and establish communications with other systems. We allocate files and assign access to appropriate functions and data.

Unlike acceptance tests, installation tests require us to work with the customer to determine what tests are needed on site. Regression tests may be administered to verify that the system has been installed properly and works "in the field" as it did when tested previously. The test cases assure the customer that the system is complete and that all necessary files and devices are present. The tests focus on two things: *completeness* of the installed system, and *verification* of any functional or nonfunctional characteristics that may be affected by site conditions. We can conduct the tests ourselves, or we can allow the customer to do so. In either case, when the customer is satisfied with the results, testing is complete and the system is formally delivered.

8.6

TEST TOOLS

Several tools are available to help us administer the variety of tests involved in system testing. Most are automated and capture data that can be of use in evaluating a system's performance.

Simulation allows us to concentrate on evaluating one part of a system while portraying the characteristics of other parts. A **simulator** presents to a system all characteristics of a device or system without actually having the device or system available. Just as a flight simulator allows you to learn to fly without an actual airplane, a device simulator allows you to control a device even when the device is not present. Thus, if a communications controller is part of your system but is being developed by another company, you can simulate the behavior of the controller and continue your testing.

A device simulator is particularly useful if a special device is located on-site but testing is being done at another location. For example, if the system you are building controls a ship's navigation system, you need not have a ship to perform the actual tests. Sometimes a device simulator is more helpful than the device itself, since the simulator can store data indicating the device's state during the various stages of a test. Then the simulator reports on its state when an error occurs, possibly helping you find the source of the error.

Simulators are also used to look like other systems with which the test system must interface. If messages are communicated or a data base accessed, a simulator provides the necessary information for testing without duplicating the entire other system. The simulator also helps with stress and volume testing, since it can be programmed to load the system with substantial amounts of data, requests, or users.

In general, simulators give you control over the test conditions. This control allows you to perform tests that might otherwise be dangerous or impossible. For example, the test of a missile guidance system can be made much simpler and safer by using simulators.

A **monitor** is a device that captures data passing from one device or process to another. For example, an input/output monitor can be placed between two processors to store any data flowing between them. Additional information (such as interrupts) can also be stored. We can use a monitor to save a "snapshot" of the conditions before and after an error occurs. Again, the snapshot helps track down the source of the error and verifies proper performance.

An **analyzer** goes one step beyond a monitor; it not only captures data but also evaluates them according to some prescribed criteria. For example, a *test coverage analyzer* records the number of each statement executed during a test step and notifies us if certain routines or statements are not exercised. Similarly, a *timing analyzer* works with predefined areas of memory or code and tracks the amount of time spent in each area as the system functions are performed. This tracking can be useful during performance testing when timing requirements are checked.

As we shall see later in this chapter, there are also tools for generating test cases and tracking test results.

8.7

TEST TEAM

We have primary responsibility for function and performance testing, while the customer plays a large role in acceptance and installation tests. However, the test team for all tests draws from both staffs, as shown in Figure 8.9. No programmers

Figure 8.9   Test Team Members

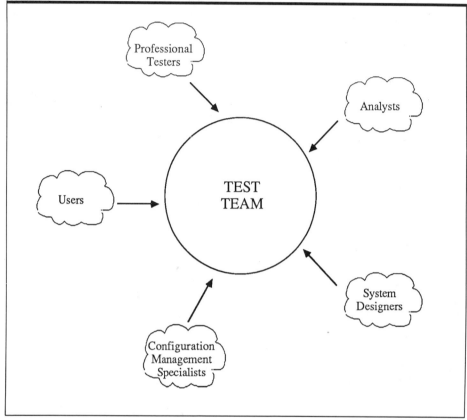

from this project are involved in system testing; they are too familiar with the structure and intention of the implementation, and they may have difficulty recognizing the differences between implementation and required function.

Professional Testers

Thus, the test team is independent of the implementation staff. Ideally, some test team members are already experienced as testers. Usually, these "professional testers" are former analysts, programmers, and designers who now devote all their time to testing systems. The testers are familiar not only with the specification of the system but also with testing methods and tools.

Professional testers *organize and run* the tests. They are involved from the beginning, designing test plans and test cases as the project progresses. The professional testers work with the configuration management team to provide documentation and other mechanisms for tying tests to the requirements, design modules, and implementation modules.

Analysts

The professional testers focus on test development, methods, and procedures. Because the testers may not be as well versed in the particulars of the requirements as those who wrote them, the test team includes additional people who are familiar with the requirements. Analysts who were involved in the original requirements definition and specification are useful in testing because they are *familiar with the problem* as defined by the customer. Much of system testing compares the new system to its original requirements, and the analysts have a good feeling for the needs and goals of the customer. Since they have worked with the designers to define a solution, analysts have some idea of how the system should work to solve the problem.

System Designers

System designers on the test team add the perspective of *intent*. The designers understand what we proposed as a solution to the customer's problem; they know the constraints imposed on the solution by the overall design. The designers also know how the system is divided into functional subsystems and understand how the system is *supposed* to work. When designing test cases and assuring test coverage, the test team calls on the designers for help in listing all possibilities.

Configuration Management Specialists

Because tests and test cases are tied directly to requirements and design, a configuration management representative is on the test team. As errors are discovered and changes requested, the configuration management specialist arranges for the changes to be reflected in the documentation, requirements, design, implementation, or anything else affected by the change. In fact, changes to correct an error may result in modifications to other test cases or to a large part of the test plan. The configuration management specialist implements these changes and coordinates the revision of tests.

Users

Finally, the test team includes users. They are best qualified to evaluate issues dealing with appropriateness of audience, ease of use, and other human factors.

Sometimes, users have little voice in the early stages of the project. Customer representatives who participate during requirements analysis may not plan to use the system but have jobs related to those who will. For instance, the representatives may be managers of those who will use the system or technical representatives who have discovered a problem that indirectly relates to their work. However, these representatives may be so removed from the actual problem that the requirements description is inaccurate or incomplete. The customer may not be aware of the need to redefine or add requirements.

Therefore, users of the proposed system are essential if they were not present when the system requirements were first defined by the customer. A user is likely to be intimately familiar with the customer's problem because of daily exposure to it, and can be invaluable in evaluating the system to verify that it solves the problem.

8.8

TEST DOCUMENTATION

Testing can be complex and difficult. The system's *software* and *hardware* can contribute to the difficulty, as can the *procedures* involved in using the system. In addition, a distributed or real-time system requires great care in *tracing* and *timing* data and processes to draw conclusions about performance. Finally, when systems are large, the large number of people involved in development and testing can make *coordination* difficult. To control the complexity and difficulty of testing, we use complete and carefully designed test documentation.

Several types of documentation are needed. A **test plan** describes the system itself and the plan for exercising all functions and characteristics. A **test specification and evaluation** details each test and defines the criteria for evaluating each feature addressed by the test. Then, a **test description** presents the test data and procedures for the individual test components. Finally, the **test analysis report** describes the results of each test. Figure 8.10 displays the relationship of the documents to the testing process.

Test Plans

In chapter 7, we discussed the role of the test plan in laying out the pattern of testing for the entire testing stage. Now we look at how a test plan can be used to *direct* system testing.

Figure 8.11 illustrates the components of a test plan. The plan begins by stating its *objectives*. These objectives should:

1. Guide the management of testing

2. Guide the technical effort required during testing

3. Establish planning and scheduling of tests, including specification of equipment needed, organizational requirements, test methods, anticipated outcomes, and user orientation

4. Explain the nature and extent of each test

5. Explain the way in which the tests will lead to a complete evaluation of the system function and performance

6. Document test input, specific test procedures, and expected output

Figure 8.10 Test Documentation

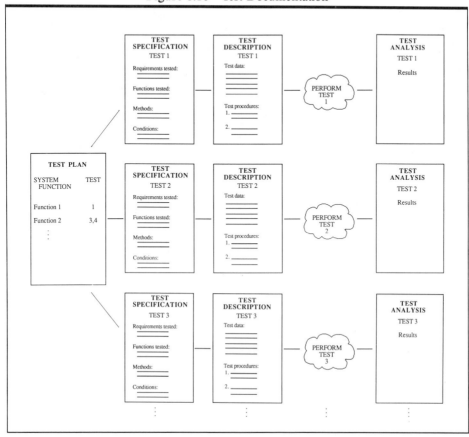

Figure 8.11 Test Plan Components

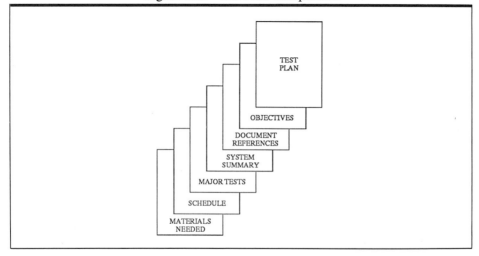

Next, the test plan *references* the other *major documents* produced during project development. In particular, the plan explains the relationships among the requirements documents, the design documents, the implementation documents, and the test procedures. For example, there may be a numbering scheme that ties together all documents; requirement 4.9 may be reflected in module 5.6 of the design and be tested by test procedure 8.1.

Following these preliminary sections is a *system summary*. Since a reader of the plan may not have been involved with the previous stages of development, the system summary puts the testing schedule and events in context. The summary need not be detailed; it can be a drawing depicting the major system inputs and outputs with a description of major transformations.

Once testing is placed in a system context, the plan describes the *major tests and test approaches* to be used. For example, the test plan distinguishes among function tests, performance tests, acceptance tests, and installation tests. If the function tests can be further divided by some criteria (such as subsystem tests), the test plan lays out the overall organization of the testing.

After explaining the component tests, the plan addresses the *schedule of events*. The schedule includes the place of the test as well as the time frame. Often depicted as a milestone chart or activity graph, the test schedule includes the following information:

1. The overall testing period

2. The major subdivisions of testing and their start and stop times

3. Any pretest requirements (such as orientation or familiarization with the system, user training, or generation of test data) and the time necessary for each

4. The time necessary for preparation and review of the test analysis report

If testing is to take place at several locations, the test plan includes a schedule for each location. A chart illustrates the hardware, software, and personnel necessary for the administration of the tests at each location and the duration for which each resource will be needed. Noted are special training or maintenance needs, too.

The plan identifies *test materials* in terms of deliverables (such as user or operator manuals, sample listings, or tapes) and materials supplied by the site (such as special test apparatus, data base tables, or storage media). For example, if a test is to use a data base management system to build a sample data base, the test may require the users at the site to define data elements before the arrival of the test team. Similarly, if any security or privacy precautions are required by the test team, the personnel at the test location may be required to establish passwords or special access for the test team before the test begins.

Test Specification and Evaluation

The test plan describes an overall breakdown of testing into components that test for specific items. For example, if the system being tested has its processing distributed over several computers, the function and performance tests can be further divided into tests for each subsystem.

For each such test component, a test specification and evaluation is written. The specification begins by listing the *requirements* whose satisfaction will be demonstrated by the test. Referring to the requirements definition document, this section explains the purpose of the test.

One way to view the correspondence between the requirements and the tests is to establish a table or chart relating the two. Table 8.3 is an example of such a chart and is appropriate for inclusion in the Weaver Farm Test Plan.

Table 8.3   Test-Requirement Correspondence Chart

Test	Requirement		
	Generate and Maintain Data Base (2.4.1)	Selectively Retrieve Data (2.4.2)	Produce Specialized Reports (2.4.3)
1. Add new record	X		
2. Add field	X		
3. Change field	X		
4. Delete record	X		
5. Delete field	X		
6. Create index		X	
Retrieve record with a requested:			
7. Cell number		X	
8. Water height		X	
9. Canopy height		X	
10. Ground cover		X	
11. Percolation rate		X	
12. Print full data base			X
13. Print directory			X
14. Print keywords			X
15. Print simulation summary			X

Note that the requirements listed across the top of the chart reference the number in the requirements document; the function on the left of the chart is mandated by the requirement in whose column the 'X' is placed.

The *system functions* involved in the test are enumerated in Table 8.3. The performance tests can be described in a similar way. Instead of listing functional requirements, the chart lists requirements relating to the speed of access, to the security of the data base, and so on.

Often, the test component is a collection of smaller tests, the sum of which illustrates the satisfaction of a set of requirements. In this case, the specification shows the relationship between the smaller tests and the requirements.

Each test component is guided by a *test philosophy* and adopts a set of *methods*. However, the philosophy and methods may be constrained by other requirements and by the realities of the test situation. The specification makes these test conditions clear. Among the *conditions* may be some of the following:

1. Is the system using actual input from users or devices, or are special cases generated by a program or device?

2. Will the test cover all paths? all branches? all functions?

3. How will data be recorded?

4. Are there timing, interface, equipment, personnel, data base, or other limitations on testing?

5. If the test is a series of smaller tests, in what order are the tests performed?

If test data is to be processed before being evaluated, the *processing* is discussed. For instance, when large amounts of data are produced by a system, data reduction techniques are sometimes used on the output so that the result is more suitable for evaluation.

Accompanying each test is a way to tell when the test is *complete*. Thus, the specification is followed by a discussion of how we know when the test is over. For example, for the output collected, the plan explains what range will meet the requirement.

The *evaluation method* follows the completion criteria. For example, data produced during testing may be collected and collated manually and then inspected by the test team. Alternately, the team could use an automated tool to evaluate some of the data and then inspect summary reports or do an item-by-item comparison with the expected output.

Test Description

A test description is written for every individual test defined in the test specification. We use the test description document as a guide in performing the test. These documents must be detailed and clear. The test description is composed of several parts:

1. Means of control
2. Data
3. Procedures

A *general description* of the test begins the document. Then, we indicate whether the test will be initiated and controlled by manual or automatic means. For instance, data may be input manually from the keyboard, but then an automated driver may exercise the functions being tested. Alternatively, the entire process could be automated.

The *test data* can be viewed as several parts: input data, input commands, output data, and messages produced by the system. Each is described in detail. For instance, input commands are provided so that the team knows how to initiate the test, halt or suspend it, repeat or resume an unsuccessful or incomplete one, or terminate the test. Similarly, the team must interpret messages to understand the status of the system and to control testing. We explain how the team can distinguish among errors resulting from input data, from improper test procedures, or from hardware malfunction (wherever possible).

For example, the test data description for a test of a SORT routine may be the following:

INPUT DATA:
>Input data is to be provided by the LIST program. This program generates randomly a list of *N* words of alphanumeric characters; each word is of length *M*. The program is invoked by calling

>>RUN LIST (N, M)

>in your test driver. The output is placed in global data area LISTBUF. The test data sets to be used for this test are as follows:

>>Case 1: Use LIST with N = 5, M = 5
>>Case 2: Use LIST with N = 10, M = 5
>>Case 3: Use LIST with N = 15, M = 5
>>Case 4: Use LIST with N = 50, M = 10
>>Case 5: Use LIST with N = 100, M = 10
>>Case 6: USE LIST with N = 150, M = 10

INPUT COMMANDS:
>The SORT routine is invoked by using the command

>>RUN SORT (INBUF, OUTBUF) or
>>RUN SORT (INBUF)

OUTPUT DATA:
>If two parameters are used, the sorted list is placed in OUTBUF. Otherwise, it is placed in INBUF.

SYSTEM MESSAGES:
>During the sorting process, the following message is displayed:

>>"Sorting ... Please wait ..."

>Upon completion, SORT displays the following message on the screen:

>>"SORT completed"

>To halt or terminate the test before the message is displayed, press CTRL-C on the keyboard.

Test procedures are often called a **test script** because they give us a step-by-step description of how to perform the test. A rigidly defined set of steps gives us control over the test. We can duplicate errors or conditions, if necessary. If the test is interrupted for some reason, we must be able to continue the test without having to return to the beginning. In addition, if the interruption is the result of an error, knowing the exact steps that led to the interruption allows us to try to duplicate the error and verify that it is a genuine system problem and not a random event.

For example, part of the test script for testing the "Change Field" function (listed in Table 8.3) might look like the steps in Table 8.4.

The test script steps are numbered, and data associated with each step are referenced. If we have not described them elsewhere, we explain how to prepare the data or the site for the test. For example, the equipment settings needed, the data base definitions, and the communication connections may be detailed. Next, the script explains exactly what is to happen during the test. The keys pressed, the screens displayed, the output produced, the equipment reactions, and any other

Table 8.4   Test Script for Change Field Function

Step *N*:   Press function key 4: Access data file.

Step *N*+1:   Screen will ask for name of data file. Type 'sys:test.text'.

Step *N*+2:   Menu will appear, reading:
   • Delete file
   • Modify file
   • Rename file
   Place cursor next to 'Modify file' and press RETURN key.

Step *N*+3:   Screen will ask for record number. Type '4017'.

Step *N*+4:   Screen will fill with data fields for record 4017:
```
RECORD NUMBER: 4017    CELL X: 0042 CELL Y: 0036
SOIL TYPE: CLAY        PERCOLATION RATE: 4 FT/HR
VEGETATION: KUDZU      CANOPY HEIGHT: 25 FT
WATER TABLE: 12 FT     CONSTRUCT: OUTHOUSE
MAINTENANCE CODE: 3T/4F/9R
```

Step *N*+5:   Press function key 9: Modify.

Step *N*+6:   Entries on screen will be highlighted. Move cursor to VEGETATION field. Type 'GRASS' over 'KUDZU' and press RETURN key.

Step *N*+7:   Entries on screen will no longer be highlighted. VEGETATION field should now read 'GRASS'.

Step *N*+8:   Press function key 16: Return to previous screen.

Step *N*+9:   Menu will appear, reading:
   • Delete file
   • Modify file
   • Rename file
   To verify that modification has been recorded, place cursor next to 'Modify file' and press RETURN key.

Step *N*+10:   Screen will ask for record number. Type '4017'.

Step *N*+11:   Screen will fill with data fields for record 4017:
```
RECORD NUMBER: 4017    CELL X: 0042 CELL Y: 0036
SOIL TYPE: CLAY        PERCOLATION RATE: 4 FT/HR
VEGETATION: GRASS      CANOPY HEIGHT: 25 FT
WATER TABLE: 12 FT     CONSTRUCT: OUTHOUSE
MAINTENANCE CODE: 3T/4F/9R
```

manifestation of activity are reported. We explain the expected outcome or output, and we give instructions to the operator or user about what to do if the outcome differs.

Finally, the test description explains the sequence of *activities required to end the test*. These activities may involve reading or printing critical data, terminating automated procedures, or turning off pieces of equipment.

Test Analysis Report

When a test has been administered, we analyze the results to determine if the function or performance tested meets the requirements. Sometimes the mere *demonstration* of a function is enough. Most of the time, though, there are *performance constraints* on the function. For instance, it is not enough to know that a column can be sorted or summed. The speed of the calculation must be measured and compared with the corresponding constraint. Thus, a test analysis report is necessary for the following reasons:

1. It documents the results of a test.

2. If an error is discovered, the report provides information necessary to locate the source of and correct the error.

3. It provides information necessary to determine if the development project is complete.

4. It establishes confidence in the performance of the system.

The test analysis report may be read by people who were not part of the test process but who are familiar with other aspects of the system and its development. Thus, the report includes a brief *summary of the project* and its objectives and relevant references for this test. For example, the test report mentions those parts of the requirements, design, and implementation documents that describe the functions exercised in this test. The report also indicates those parts of the test plan and specification documents dealing with this test.

Once the stage is set in this way, the test analysis report lists the *functions and performance characteristics* that were to be demonstrated and describes the actual results. The results include function, performance, and data measures, noting whether the target requirements have been met. If an error or deficiency has been discovered, the report discusses its impact. Sometimes, we evaluate the test results in terms of a measure of severity. This measure helps the test team decide whether to continue testing or wait until the error has been corrected. For example, if the error is a spurious character in the upper part of a display screen, testing can continue while we locate and correct the error. However, if an error causes the system to crash or a data file to be deleted, the test team may decide to interrupt testing.

Discrepancy Report Forms.   Since the purpose of testing is to locate errors, not to correct them, the test analysis report discusses only the *existence* of errors and their impact on the system. For each error or deficiency noted in the report, a **discrepancy report form (DRF)** is completed and given to the development team. The DRF includes the following information:

1. The *state* of the system before the error occurred
2. The *evidence* of the error
3. Any *action* or procedure that appears to have led to the error's occurrence
4. A description of how the system *should* work without the error or discrepancy
5. A reference to relevant *requirements*
6. The *impact* of the error's presence on the system
7. The level of *severity*, if available

The developer can use the DRF information to decide what action to take. Customer and developer may consult to determine if the error is severe enough to interrupt testing. Then the DRF is assigned to members of the development team, who locate the *source* of the error. As we shall see in the next two chapters, the location and correction of an error may involve anything from correcting documentation to redesigning the system.

8.9

RESOURCE TRACKING AND
SIMULATION SYSTEM

The testing concepts introduced in this chapter can be applied to the Weaver Farm project. We continue to view the Weaver Farm system as a set of subsystems. Suppose we decide to test it one subsystem at a time. We write a build plan to describe the individual parts to be tested and the way in which the entire system will be constructed from its parts. For instance, we may build the data base management system first, the simulation system next, the reporting system third, and then have a sequence of spins that reflect the combining of the different functions.

The function testing of the Weaver Farm system can focus on each of the subsystems in turn. For example, the subsystem that manages the data base of information about the geographical cells can be tested for a variety of functions. We have seen how the functions and requirements can be related in a table to show how each test will address the testing of which functions.

We have also seen how the tests can be specified and how test scripts detail the steps of each test. For instance, the test script in Table 8.4 asks us to update a record by typing 'GRASS' to replace 'KUDZU'. The steps read as follows:

Step $N+5$: Press function key 9: Modify.

Step $N+6$: Entries on screen will be highlighted. Move cursor to VEGETATION field. Type 'GRASS' over 'KUDZU' and press RETURN key.

Step $N+7$: Entries on screen will no longer be highlighted. VEGETATION field should now read 'GRASS'.

Suppose we run this test and find an error. We perform all steps through step $N+7$, but the VEGETATION field is not updated; it still reads 'KUDZU'.

We complete a discrepancy report form to notify the others on the test team that something has gone wrong. The DRF for the Weaver Farm system is formatted as in Figure 8.12. The DRF number is assigned by the configuration management member of the test team. We describe the error by explaining what was done before the error occurred (an attempt to modify a record) and what keys were pressed. We explain that we expected the updated field to contain the new information ('GRASS') but the old information ('KUDZU') was still displayed.

Figure 8.12 Weaver Farm Discrepancy Report Form

DRF Number: _____   Tester Name: _____

Date: _____   Time: _____

Test Number: _____

Script step executed when error occurred: _____

Description of error:
_____
_____
_____
_____
_____

Activities before occurrence of error:
_____
_____

Expected results:
_____
_____

Requirements affected:
_____

Impact of error on test:
_____
_____

Impact of error on system:
_____
_____

Severity Level: (LOW)   1   2   3   4   5   (HIGH)

We refer to the test specification to see what requirements are affected by the error. The configuration management team can use this information to decide whether other tests will be affected by the failure of this one. For example, any other test that includes a data base update by a user may fail.

The update failure may prevent the rest of this test from being performed if the test depends on the information being placed in the field by the update process. Or, the update may be independent of the remainder of the test, so the test can continue to completion. However, the impact of the error on the *test* may be very different from the effect of the error on the *system*. For example, perhaps the field was updated in the wrong record; another possibility is that the correct record was updated on the disk but the source of the error lies in the module that retrieves the information and displays it on the screen. Errors of this nature may have a much more severe effect on the system than they do on the particular test being run. The group performing this test must rate the error on a scale from 1 (not very severe) to 5 (extremely severe); then, the test team uses this information to decide whether to continue this test, halt this test but allow others to proceed, or halt some or all of the other tests until the source of the error is located and repaired.

8.10

CHAPTER SUMMARY

In this chapter, we have taken a close look at where errors might originate. We saw that there are many places in the system development process that can lead to a proliferation of errors later on. Next, we discussed the testing of a system as a whole, once we were convinced that the implementation modules worked as the program designers intended. System testing can be thought of as a progression of steps, from testing for functional requirements (function testing) and nonfunctional requirements (performance testing) to see if the developer's implementation agrees with the customer's written requirements, to acceptance and installation testing to see if the customer is happy with the result.

Configuration management is an important part of the testing process, because it is necessary for connecting the errors discovered with the requirements and design elements from which they came. Both configuration management and regression testing are techniques that the test team can use to be sure it is in control of the testing process.

Although there are automated test tools that can help the test team to do its job, the test team still has an enormous task. It must plan its tests carefully and coordinate them with the customer, user, and all members of the development team. The blueprint for all testing is written in the form of a test plan. Each major test addressed by the plan is broken into smaller tests in the test specification, and the test description describes each small test as a step-by-step test script. Thus, the members of the test team can enter each step of testing knowing what is needed as input; what procedures should be followed; what to expect on the display screens, in data bases or as printed output; and how to report errors or discrepancies.

Once testing is complete, the system is delivered to the customer. In the next chapter, we will investigate the steps involved in transferring responsibility for the system to the customer.

8.11

EXERCISES

1. Consider the development of a two-pass assembler. Outline the functions of the assembler. Then describe how you might test the assembler so that each function is tested thoroughly before the next function is examined. Suggest a build plan for the development, and explain how the build plan and the testing must be designed together.

2. Certification is an endorsement of the correctness of a system by some outside source. Certification is often granted by comparing the system to a predefined standard of performance. For example, the Department of Defense certifies an Ada compiler after testing the compiler against a long list of functional specifications. In the terminology of this chapter, is a test for certification a function test? a performance test? an acceptance test? an installation test? Explain why or why not for each type of test.

3. The development of a build plan must take into account the resources available to the customer and developer, including time, personnel, and money. Give examples of resource constraints that can affect the number of builds defined for system development. Explain how these constraints affect the build plan.

4. Suppose a mathematician's calculator has a function that computes the slope and intercept of a line. The requirement in the definition document reads "The calculator shall accept as input an equation of the form $Ax + By + C = 0$ and print out the slope and intercept." The system implementation of this requirement is the function LINE whose syntax is 'LINE(A, B, C)', where A and B are the coefficients of x and y and C is the constant in the equation. The result is a printout of 'D; E', where D is the slope and E the intercept. Write this requirement as a set of causes and effects, and draw the corresponding cause and effect graph.

5. In chapter 3, we discussed the need for requirements to be "testable." Explain why testable requirements are essential for performance testing. Use examples to support your explanation.

6. What kinds of performance tests might be required for a word processing system? for an automatic bank teller system? for an office payroll system?

7. A word processing system can be designed so that it serves one user or many. Explain how such a system can have a variety of configurations, and outline how a set of configuration tests might be designed.

8. A navigation system is to be installed in an airplane. What issues must be considered in an installation test?

9. Give an example to illustrate a situation where testing would be impossible without the use of a device simulator. Give another example of a situation where testing would be impossible without a system simulator.

10. A payroll system is designed so there is an employee information record for each employee. Once a week, the employee record is updated with the number of hours worked by the employee that week. Once every two weeks, summary reports are printed to display the number of hours worked since the beginning of the fiscal year. Once a month, paychecks are printed for all employees. For each of the categories of performance tests discussed in this chapter, describe what kinds of tests should be administered to insure that this system performs properly.

11. Willie's Wellies, Inc. has commissioned HMP Systems to develop a computer-based system for testing the strength of its complete line of rubber footwear. Willie's has nine factories in various locations throughout the world, and each system will be configured according to the size of the factory. Explain why HMP and Willie's should conduct installation testing when acceptance testing is complete.

12. Write a test script for testing the LEVEL function described in this chapter.

13. Outline a build plan for testing the Weaver Farm system.

CHAPTER 9

SYSTEM DELIVERY

We are nearing the end of system development. The previous chapters have shown us how to recognize a problem, design a solution, and implement and test it. Figure 9.1 indicates that we are ready to present the customer with the solution (*system delivery*) and make sure that the system continues to work properly (*maintenance*).

Many software engineers assume that system delivery is a formality—a ribbon-cutting ceremony or presentation of the key to the computer room. However, delivery involves more. It is the time during development when we help the users to understand and feel comfortable with the product. If the delivery is not successful, users will not use the system properly or may be unhappy with its performance. In either case, users are not as productive as they could be, and the care taken by all members of the development team has been wasted.

Thus, in this chapter, we investigate two issues in the successful transfer of ownership from developer to user: training and documentation. As the system is designed, we plan and develop aids that help users learn to use the system. Accompanying the system is documentation to which the users refer for problem solving or further information. Delivery is successful if training and documentation enable the user to solve the problem the system was intended to solve.

9.1

TRAINING

Two types of people use a system: *users* and *operators*. We can think of them in the same way that we think of chauffeurs and mechanics. The major function of an automobile is to provide transportation. A chauffeur *uses* a car to go from one location to another. However, a mechanic *services* or *supports* the car to enable the chauffeur to drive. The mechanic may never drive the car (the major function), but without the supplementary functions used by the mechanic, the car would not work at all.

A **user** exercises the main system functions to solve the problem described by the requirements definition document. Thus, a user is a problem-solver for the customer. However, a system often has supplementary tasks that support major system functions. For example, a supplementary function may define who has access to the system. Another creates backup copies of essential data files on a

Figure 9.1   The System Development Process

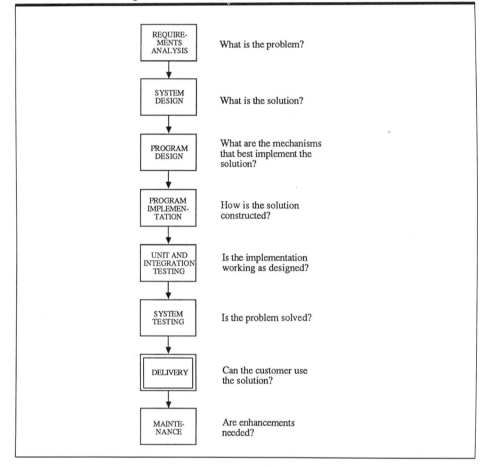

periodic basis to enable recovery from a system failure. These auxiliary functions are usually not performed directly by the users. Instead, an **operator** performs these functions to support the major work. The operator is sometimes called a *computer operator* if the operator's functions include powering up, configuring the devices, or performing other tasks that relate to the equipment rather than to the system operation. Table 9.1 contains examples of user and operator functions.

Table 9.1   User and Operator Functions

User Functions	Operator Functions
Manipulating data files	Granting user access
Simulating activities	Granting file access
Analyzing data	Performing backup
Communicating data	Installing new devices
Drawing graphs and charts	Installing new software
	Recovering damaged files

Types of Training

User and operator tasks have very different goals, so their training emphasizes different aspects of the system.

User Training. Training for users is based primarily on major system functions and the user's need for access to them. For example, if a system manages the records of a law firm, the user must be trained in record management functions: creating and retrieving records, changing and deleting entries, and so on. In addition, users must navigate through the records to access particular ones. If information is to be protected with a password or protected against accidental deletion, users learn special protection functions.

At the same time, users need not be aware of the system's internal operation. They can sort a set of records without knowledge of whether the sort is a Shell sort, a bubble sort, or a Quicksort. A user accessing the system may not need to know who else is accessing the system at the same time or on which disk the requested information is being stored. Because these are support functions, rather than primary ones, only the operator is concerned with them.

User training introduces the primary functions so that users understand what the functions are and how to perform them. Training relates how the functions are performed now (with the existing system) to how they will be performed later with the new system. Doing so is difficult, because users are often forced to block out familiar activities in order to learn the new ones. (Psychological studies call this difficulty "task interference.") The similar but subtle differences between old and new can impede learning.

Operator Training. The focus of operator training is familiarity with the system's *support* functions. Training addresses *how* the system works, rather than *what* the system does. In this type of training, task interference is less likely, unless the system closely resembles another system with which the operator has worked.

Operators are trained on two levels: how to bring up and run the new system, and how to support users. First, operators learn such things as how to configure the system, how to grant or deny access to the system, how to assign task sizes or disk space, and how to monitor and improve system performance. Then operators concentrate on the particulars of the developed system: how to recover lost files or documents, how to communicate with other systems, and how to invoke a variety of support procedures.

Special Training Needs. Users and operators are usually trained in a concentrated and complete course in system use. Often training begins with the basics: how the keyboard is configured, how menu selections are made, and so on; these and other functions are introduced slowly and investigated thoroughly. This complete training is offered during system delivery to those who will be using the system.

However, *new users* may later replace trained users, often because of changing job assignments. Training must be available to show them how the system works.

Sometimes users want to *brush up* on things missed in the original training. Even when initial training is comprehensive, it may be difficult for users or operators to absorb everything taught. Users often like to review some of the functions originally presented in the initial training sessions.

You can appreciate the need for brushing up by remembering what it was like to learn your first programming language. You learned all legal commands, but you remembered the syntax and meaning of some better than others. To master the language, you returned to your notes or textbook to review infrequently used commands.

A similar problem is encountered by *infrequent users* of the system. The knowledge gained in training can easily be forgotten for those functions of a system that are not exercised regularly. For example, consider a word processing system at a large corporation. The system's primary users may be typists who type documents daily and communicate them from one location to another. Using the system often helps the typists remain familiar with most functions. However, the president of the corporation uses the system once or twice a week to create a document or memorandum; the document is then put into final form by a regular typist. Training for an infrequent user is different from standard user training. The president has no need to know all special features of the system; training for users such as he can address only the basic document creation functions.

Operators encounter the same difficulty. If one system function is the semi-annual storage of archival material on a separate disk, the operator may not remember the archive procedure after six months of not having performed it. Without review training, users and operators tend to perform only the functions with which they feel comfortable; they may not use other system functions that can make them more efficient and productive.

Similarly, specialized training courses can be designed for those who have special needs. If a system produces charts and reports, some users may need to know how to *create* the charts and reports, while others only want *access* to existing charts and reports. Training can teach limited system functions or review just part of the total system activity.

Training Aids

Training can be done in many ways. No matter how training is provided, it must offer information to users and operators at all times, not just when the system is first delivered. At some time, if users forget how to access a file or want to exercise a new function, training includes methods to find and learn this information.

Documents.   Formal documentation accompanies every system and supports training. The documents contain all the information needed to use the system properly and efficiently. Existing in separate manuals or online, documents are accessible to users and operators as the system is functioning. The system manuals are often similar to an automobile owner's manual; they are references to be used when a problem or question arises. You may not read your car owner's manual from cover to cover before you put the key in the ignition and go for a drive; likewise, users and operators do not always read training documents before trying to use the system. In fact, one study ([SCH83]) showed that only ten to fifteen percent of the users in an intensive training program actually read the manual at all. Six months later, no one else had read the user manual, and replacement pages with revised information had not been filed in the manual. In this and many other cases, users may prefer demonstrations and classes to learn how the system works.

Demonstrations and Classes. Demonstrations and classes add *individualization* to training, and the users and operators respond positively. Users needs are paramount, and the demonstration or class is focused on a particular aspect of the system. Demonstrations and classes are usually organized as a series of presentations, so that each class in the series teaches one function or aspect of the system.

Demonstrations and classes can be more flexible and dynamic than documents. Users prefer a show-and-tell approach, where users try to exercise a demonstrated function. The demonstration can be a formal classroom presentation. However, computer-based training has been very successful at demonstrating and teaching system concepts and functions.

Some training programs use videodisk or videotape in conjunction with a regular display screen. A teacher demonstrates the concept or function on a television monitor, and the user or operator repeats the function on a live or simulated system. Discworks, Inc. (Cambridge, Massachusetts) has created such a videodisk package for Wang's word processing functions. First, a trainer demonstrates a function on the television monitor. Then, software presents a simulated word processing screen on student workstations, and students can try out the function on their own. Flight simulation programs work in a similar manner, with software controlling the view through a window to simulate the effects of using aircraft navigation devices.

Other training systems split the computer screen into parts or provide a second screen to give the student additional information and guidance. For example, training available from Mentor Resources (Nashua, New Hampshire) teaches operators to run system support functions. As simulated output is displayed at a user workstation, the screen is split and the user sees an explanation of what is happening. Figure 9.2 is an example of a Mentor Taskmaster screen, where the information within the dotted lines is an explanation of the menu presented on the student's screen.

Demonstrations and classes involve a multimedia approach. Hearing, reading, and seeing how a function works reinforce learning, and you as as a student may remember the function more easily. In general, a verbal presentation holds your attention better than a written one.

A key factor in the success of demonstrations and classes is giving the user feedback. The trainer, whether on tape or in person, should offer as much encouragement as possible.

Expert Users. Sometimes, it is not enough to see a demonstration or participate in a class. You need a *role model* to convince you that you can master the system. In this case, it is useful to designate one or more users and operators as "experts." The experts are trained in advance of other users and then used as demonstrators or helpers in a classroom. The other students feel more at ease because they recognize that the experts are users (just like them) who managed to

Figure 9.2   Split Training Screen (Mentor)

```
WORKSTATION  83  —  USER SUN  —  Debra M. Pyatt, 3147

11:38:25 am    Wednesday    July 30, 1986



**********************************************************************************
****        1         2         3         4         5         6         7         8 ****
**** 12345678901234567890123456789012345678901234567890123456789012345678901234567890 ****
**********************************************************************************
* *                                                                              * *
* 1*                              Index                                          * 1*
* 2*                                                                             * 2*
* 3*                  T H E   C O M M A N D   P R O C E S S O R                   * 3*
* 4*                                                                             * 4*
* 5*                                    . . . .. . . .. .. .. . .. . ..          * 5*
* 6*    1+ Introduction                 :                                :       * 6*
* 7*    2  Files                        : This index provides an easy means :    * 7*
* 8*    3  Libraries                    : of locating the information you   :    * 8*
* 9*    4  Volumes                      : want.                             :    * 9*
*10*    5  Printouts                    :                                   :    *10*
* 1*    6  Printers                     : Choose a topic and press the      :    * 1*
* 2*    7  Disks                        : corresponding PF key.             :    * 2*
* 3*    8  Tapes                        :                                   :    * 3*
* 4*    9  Workstations                 : Press PF32 when you want to       :    * 4*
* 5*    10 Programs                     : leave the index.                  :    * 5*
* 6*    11 Procedures                   : . .. . . .. . .. .. .. . .. .. ..  :    * 6*
* 7*    12 Word Processing                                                       * 7*
* 8*    13 Print Screens                                                         * 8*
* 9*    14 Operator Console                                                      * 9*
*20*    15+ Logon and Logoff                                                     *20*
* 1*                                                                             * 1*
* 2*                                                                             * 2*
* 3*                                                                             * 3*
* 4*                                                   PF32: Exit                * 4*
* *                                                                              * *
**********************************************************************************
****        1         2         3         4         5         6         7         8 ****
**** 12345678901234567890123456789012345678901234567890123456789012345678901234567890 ****
**********************************************************************************
```

master the techniques. Experts can point out places where they had difficulty but overcame it. Thus, experts convince the students that the "impossible" is really possible.

Expert users can also be floating instructors after the formal training period is over. They act as consultants, answering questions and making themselves available to others when problems arise. Many users who feel uncomfortable asking a question in class will not hesitate to call a more proficient user to ask the same question.

Expert users give feedback to the system analysts about *user satisfaction* with the system, the need for *additional training*, and the *occurrence of errors*. Users sometimes have trouble explaining to analysts why the system should be changed or enhanced.

The experts learn both the language of the user and of the analysts, so they help to avoid communication problems that often occur between users and analysts.

Guidelines for Training

Training is successful only when it meets your needs and matches your capabilities. Personal preferences, work styles, and organizational pressures play a role in this success. A manager who cannot type or spell may not want the department secretary to know. A worker may be embarrassed or uncomfortable correcting a superior in class. Some students prefer to learn by reading, some by hearing, and others by a combination of techniques.

Individualized systems often accommodate this variation in backgrounds and experience. While one student may be totally unfamiliar with a particular concept and may want to spend a great deal of time studying it, another may be familiar with the concept and skip over it. Even keyboarding skill can play a part: an exercise requiring substantial typing can be completed faster by an experienced typist. Since backgrounds vary, different training modules can address different types of students. Users who know how to keyboard can skip the modules on typing, and operators who are well versed in computer concepts need not study the module on what each peripheral does. Review modules can be developed for those who are already familiar with some functions.

Material in a training class or demonstration should be divided into presentation units, and the scope of each should be limited. Too much material at once can be overwhelming, so many short sessions are preferable to a few long ones.

Finally, the *location* of the students may determine the type of training. Installation at hundreds of locations all over the world may require a computer-based training system that runs on the actual installed system, rather than flying all prospective users to a central site for training.

9.2

DOCUMENTATION

Documentation is part of a comprehensive approach to training. The quality and type of documentation can be critical, not only to training, but also to the success of the system. There are several considerations involved in training and reference documents.

Considering the Audience

A computer-based system is used by a variety of people. In addition to users and operators, other members of the development team and the customer staff read documentation when questions arise or changes are to be made to the system. For example, suppose an analyst is working with a customer to determine whether to build a new system or modify the old one. The analyst reads a system overview to understand what the current system does and how it does it. This overview for the analyst is different from one written for a user; the analyst must know about computing details that are of no interest to a user. Similarly, descriptions needed by operators are of no importance to a user.

Thus, our discussion begins by considering the intended audience. Manuals and guides can be written for users, operators, systems support people, or others.

User Manuals. A user manual is a reference guide for a system user. The manual should be complete and understandable, so sometimes it presents the system to users in layers, beginning with the general purpose and continuing to detailed functional description. First, the manual describes its purpose and refers to other system documents that may have more detailed information. This preliminary information is especially helpful in reassuring users that the document contains the type of information they seek. Special terms, abbreviations, or acronyms used in the manual are listed for easy reference.

Next, the manual describes the system in more detail. A system summary presents the following items:

1. The purpose or objective of the system
2. The capabilities and functions of the system
3. The features, characteristics, and advantages of the system, including a clear picture of what the system accomplishes

The summary need not be more than a few paragraphs. For example, the overview for a MODCOMP® graphics system is displayed as Figure 9.3. Its graphics capabilities are outlined as follows ([MOD 79]).

1.4.2 MIRAGE

MIRAGE provides color graphics capability. . . . In a distributed system, it is a host function, and uses information from the SCALE data base in generated displays.

MIRAGE provides the tools for the creation, display, and storage of color graphics pictures. MIRAGE maintains a library of user created shapes and pictures. User created shapes may contain lines, text, and other shapes. User created pictures may contain lines, text, shapes, dynamic variable fields, and dynamic bars. Dynamic variables and bars which are associated with SCALE data base variables are periodically updated.

During picture creation or modification, a line, text field, shape, etc., can be repositioned, or color changed. Without MIRAGE, the field would have to be erased and redrawn from the beginning to accomplish this. All lines, shapes, text, etcetera, are labeled, and any item may be deleted from the picture by referencing its label.

Every user manual needs illustrations to support the text. For instance, a diagram depicting the inputs and their sources, the outputs and their destinations, and the major functions of the system helps users understand what the system does. Similarly, a diagram accompanies a narrative about the equipment used.

The system design emphasizes a modular approach to problem solving. These modules are described in the user's manual. The description helps the user understand the logical parts of the system and their roles in solving the problem.

Figure 9.3 Hardware and Software Diagram from MODCOMP® User Manual

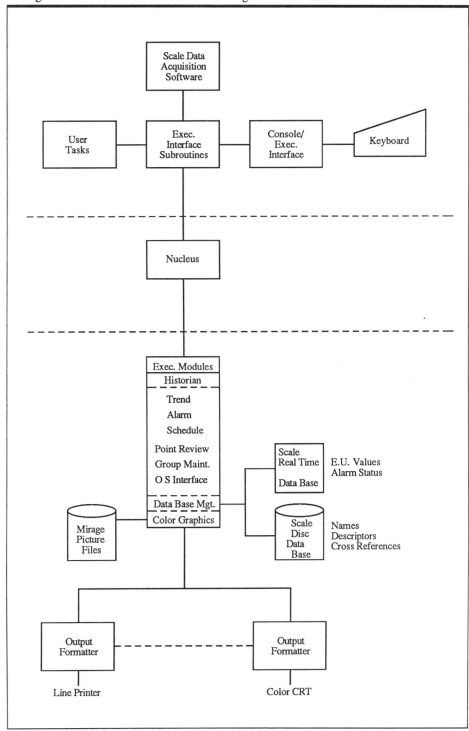

No matter what functions are performed by the system, a user manual functional description includes at least the following elements.

1. A map of the major functions and how they relate to one another
2. A description of each function in terms of the screens the user can expect to see, the purpose of each, and the result of each menu choice or function key selection
3. A description of all input expected by each function
4. A description of all output that can be created by each function
5. A description of the special features that can be invoked for each function

For instance, the major parts of the MIRAGE system are explained in the user manual in the following fashion.

3.2 MIRAGE SOFTWARE ELEMENTS

3.2.1 *Picture Manager*

The Picture Manager is a versatile graphics module that manages the picture files and displays the requested pictures. It communicates with the Picture Generation processor to create, display, and modify pictures in the picture file. Only the Picture Manager alters the physical picture file.

The Picture Manager is required in a system that is to have the capability to generate and modify pictures in the picture file. The Picture Manager will not permit multiple users to modify a specific picture at the same time.

3.2.2 *Picture Generation Processor*

The Picture Generator is an interactive processor with the capability to generate and modify pictures and shapes from a CRT terminal. The picture forms may be: (1) tabular displays, and (2) process flow diagrams. The Picture Generator inputs user's directives from the CRT terminals, decodes the directives, and communicates with the Picture Manager Task to access the physical Picture Files.

3.2.3 *Picture Utility Processor*

The Picture Utility is an interactive processor with the capability to initialize a file to be used for building pictures and shapes. It is also used to SAVE and RESTORE picture files to/from another disc file or magnetic tape.

3.2.4 *Picture Display Processor*

The Picture Display Processor is required in a system that does not have the Picture Manager but needs the capability to display pictures already stored in a picture file. The Picture Display Processor is a subset of the Picture Manager Processor and only has the capability to access, but not alter, picture files.

3.2.5 *Application Data Base*

The Application Data Base is the SCALE Data Base. It contains the dynamic data that is displayed in the pictures. The Application Data Base does not contain the Picture File.

3.2.6 *Picture File*

The Picture File contains all the information concerning the generated picture forms except the current values for the dynamic data. The Picture Files are only accessed directly by the Picture Manager or Picture Display Processor.

Then, each function is expanded so that users understand each one.

3.3 PICTURE GENERATION

To CREATE a PICTURE, the interactive user manipulates picture components until the desired picture is achieved. The picture components available to the user are:

ORIGINS, LINES, BARS, SHAPES, TEXT, and VARIABLES

The manipulation directives available to the user are:

DEFINE, SET, CHANGE, MOVE, and DELETE

The final picture consists of sets of LINES, BARS, SHAPES, TEXT, and VARIABLES with their characteristics, and a set of ORIGINS.

To CREATE a SHAPE, the interactive user may manipulate components as if creating a picture. The final shape consists only of the relocatable image of the information that is read from the screen when the END SHAPE directive is entered. The shape may not contain dynamic VARIABLES or dynamic BARS. NOTE: There is no predefined shape library.

Picture Component CHARACTERISTICS which are available to the SET and CHANGE directives are:

```
COLOR:  (FOREGROUND BACKGROUND)
            BLACK, RED, GREEN, BLUE, YELLOW, MAGENTA,
            CYAN, WHITE
BLINK:  BLINK, NOBLINK
SIZE:   STANDARD, LARGE
INTENSITY:  NORMAL, HIGH
```

Picture Generation MOVE SPECIFICATIONS are as follows:

```
UP: Un where n defines the number of
 character positions to move.
DOWN:   Dn
LEFT:   Ln
RIGHT:  Rn
```

Figure 9.4   Function Key Assignment Diagram

PAGE FOR- WARD	SEARCH	COPY	EXIT TO MAIN	DIREC- TORY	CALEN- DAR	SEND	HELP
PAGE BACK	REPLACE	MOVE	SAVE	MES- SAGE	EDITOR	RECEIVE	PRINT SCREEN

A complete and thorough user manual is useless if you cannot find needed information quickly and easily. A poorly written user manual results in frustrated users who are uncomfortable with the system and may not use it as effectively as possible. Thus, any techniques to enhance *readability* or *access to information* are helpful; glossaries, tabs, numbering and cross-referencing schemes, color coding, diagrams, and multiple indices are some of the techniques used. For example, a diagram of a set of function keys is much easier to understand than narrative describing their placement. A simple chart like Figure 9.4 can do more to help a user locate the proper key than a several-page descriptive list.

Operator Manuals.   **Operator manuals** present material to operators in the same fashion as user manuals. The intended audience is the only difference between the operator manual and the user manual: users want to know the details of system *function and use*, and operators want to know the details of system *perfor- mance and access*. Thus, the operator guide explains hardware and software config- urations, methods for granting and denying access to a user, procedures for adding or removing peripherals from the system, and techniques for duplicating or back- ing up files and documents.

Just as the user is presented with the system in layers, so too is the operator. An overview of the system is described first, followed by a more detailed description of the system's purpose and functions. The operator manual may overlap the user manual somewhat, since operators must be aware of system functions even though they never exercise them. For example, operators may never create a spreadsheet and transform it to graphical form. However, knowing that the system has such functions gives operators a better understanding of how to support the system. In addition, operators may learn the names of software routines that perform the spreadsheet and graph functions and the hardware that is used to print the spread- sheet and draw the graphs. Then, if a user reports a problem with the spreadsheet function, the operators may know whether the problem can be remedied with a support function or whether the maintenance staff should be notified.

General System Guide.   Sometimes you want to learn about what the system does without learning the details of each function. For instance, as head of the audit department of a large company, you may read a system description in order to decide if the system is appropriate for your needs. This system description need not describe every display screen and the choices on it. However, the detail should allow you to decide if the system is complete or accurate enough for your company's needs.

A **general system guide** addresses this need. Its audience is the *customer*, rather than the developer. The general system guide is similar to the system design document; it describes a solution to a problem in terms the customer can understand. In addition, the general system guide depicts the system hardware and software configuration and describes the *philosophy* behind the system's construction.

A general system guide is similar to the glossy, nontechnical brochure given to prospective customers by automobile dealers. The car is described in terms of type and size of engine, type and size of body, performance statistics, standard and optional features, and so on. The customer may not be interested in the exact design of the carburetor, for example, in deciding whether or not to buy. Similarly, the general system guide for an automated system need not describe the algorithm used to compute the address of the next record allocated nor the command used to access that record. Instead, the guide describes only the information needed to create and access a new record.

A good general system guide provides cross-referencing. If readers of the guide want more information about the precise way in which a function is implemented, they find a reference to the appropriate pages of the user manual. On the other hand, if readers want more information about the support of the system, they can turn to the operator manual.

Tutorials and Automated System Overviews. Some users prefer to be guided through actual system functions, rather than to read a written description of how the functions work. For these users, *tutorials* and *automated overviews* can be developed. The user invokes a software program or procedure that explains the major system functions, step by step. Sometimes a document is combined with a special program; the user reads about the function first, then exercises the next step in the program to perform the function. For example, Lotus 1-2-3 (Cambridge, Massachusetts) leads users on a tour of system functions with a tutorial guide and accompanying special program that displays and manipulates sample data. The user can see how a function works, rather than merely read its description. Similarly, Borland's Quick Reflex (Scotts Valley, California) program presents a user with a sample data base to manipulate with Reflex commands.

Other System Documentation. Many other system documents can be supplied during system delivery. Some are products of the intermediate steps of system development. For example, the *requirements documents* are written after requirements analysis and updated as necessary. The system design is recorded in the *system design document*, and the *program design document* describes the program design.

The details of implementation are in the programming documentation that we described in chapter 6. However, additional documents help those who will maintain and enhance the system. A **programmer guide** is the technical counterpart of the user manual. Just as the user manual presents a picture of the system in layers, from a system overview down to a functional description, the programmer guide presents an overview of how the software and hardware are configured. The overview is followed by a detailed description of software modules and how they relate to the functions performed.

To help a programmer locate the code that performs a particular function, either because an error has occurred or because a function must be changed or enhanced, the programmer guide is cross-referenced with the user manual.

A **program maintenance guide** may also be written. The maintenance guide emphasizes those aspects of the system that enable the maintenance staff to locate the source of problems. Thus, the maintenance guide describes system support functions such as the running of diagnostic programs, the display of executed lines of code or segments of memory, the placement of debugging code, and other tools. We will investigate maintenance techniques in more depth in chapter 10.

Maintenance and program guides also help maintenance personnel implement enhancements to the system. For example, suppose a new site is to be added to the communications network. The programmer guide points out those code modules dealing with communications; the maintenance guide explains the tools available for updating the code and corresponding documentation. The paragraph below appears in an actual MODCOMP® maintenance guide ([MOD79]).

4.15.3 Switch-over Initialization

The Switch-over Initialization task is requested only on the secondary processor when primary failure is detected or by explicit task request as an OC directive or from a user task. The actions of switchover are completely table driven and consist of specific configuration dependent items as follows:

- the specific peripherals to be switched with the peripheral switch
- the list of user tasks to be scheduled with all scheduling parameters
- the list of [application] tasks to be scheduled with their scheduling parameters
- the list of user global COMMON blocks to load from disc
- SCALE data base COMMON blocks to be loaded from disc.

User Help and Trouble-shooting

Users and operators refer to documentation to determine the cause of a problem and to call for assistance if necessary. Several types of user help can be provided, including reference documents and online help files.

Error Message Reference Guide. If the system detects an error, the users and operators are notified in a uniform and consistent way. Recall that the system design proposes a philosophy for discovering and reporting errors. The variety of system error messages is included in the design, and user documentation lists all possible error messages and their meanings. Whenever possible, error messages point to the source of the error. However, sometimes the reason for the error is not known or there is not enough room to display a complete message on the screen or in the report where the error is generated. Thus, an **error message reference guide**, being the document of last resort, must describe the error completely. An error message appearing on the screen may include the following information.

1. The name of the code module executing when the error occurred

2. The source code line number in the module that was executing

3. The severity of the error and its impact on the system

4. The contents of any relevant system memory or data pointers, such as registers or stack pointers

5. A brief description of the nature of the error, or an error message number

For example, an error message may appear on a user screen as:

```
ERROR 456A1: STACK OVERFLOW
OCCURRED IN: MODULE DEFRECD
AT LINE:    12300
SEVERITY:    WARNING
REGISTER CONTENTS:
  0000 0000 1100 1010 1100 1010 1111 0000
PRESS FUNCTION KEY 12 TO CONTINUE
```

The user refers to the error reference guide and finds an entry that looks like this:

ERROR 456A1: STACK OVERFLOW
This error occurs when more fields are defined for a record than the system can accommodate. The last field defined will not be included in the record. You can change the record size using the RECMAINT function to prevent this error from occurring in the future.

Notice that this error message reflects a particular philosophy of error handling. An alternate system design might have recovered from such an error automatically, rather than suggesting that the user handle the problem by redefining the record size.

Online Help. Many users prefer to have automated assistance at their fingertips, rather than having to locate a reference guide of some kind to help them. Some systems include an *online help* function. Often, the keyboard has a key labeled 'help'; the user presses the key when assistance is needed. Pressing the help key invokes a program or set of programs that attempt to answer the user's question.

For example, suppose you are using PC-Write™ (Quicksoft™, Seattle, Washington) word processing to prepare an invoice. When the main menu is displayed (Figure 9.5), you do not understand the differences among the several options shown at the top of the screen; so you press the help key. PC-Write™ shows you a screen listing major system functions (Figure 9.6).

More detailed information can be displayed by pressing another key. Some systems also refer you to a page in a supporting document. Thus, you can get information directly from the automated system rather than having to search for the information in a document.

Figure 9.5   Word Processing Screen

```
Esc:cancel.     F1-F1:help.     Alt/Shf/Ctl/Arrow:select.    Fn-key/Letter/Enter:action.
sF1.Fn-keysq                                      sF7.Reformq        sF9.Location
sF2:Merging        sF4:Shareware                  sF8.Center
Turn function key reminder on+ or off-


                                                            17 June 1986



     MUXLAB, Attn:  Jais Cohen


     165 Graveline                           Systems/Software, Inc.


     Ville St. Laurent                       Attn: L. Davis


     P. Q. CANADA   H4T 1R3                  Knoxville, Tennessee   37919
```

Figure 9.6   Help Screen for Word Processing

```
Esc: Help off, cancel. F1: Help off, continue. Arrows: Select a Help topic:
Basics          DOS commands     Footnotes        Merge: input     References
Auto-numbering  Dot lines I      Guide lines      Merge: template  Ruler lines
Auto-reformat   Dot lines II     Headers/footers  Merging steps    Scroll/jump
Char: foreign   Dot lines III    Locate cursor    Misc. stuff      Page breaks
Char: math      Enhance text     Manual reformat  Page breaks      Spaces/hyphens
Copy/move text  Enter text       Margins/tabs     Page layout      System/file
Cursor moves    File management  Mark text        Printing         Windows
Delete text     Find/replace     Merging          Record keys      Glossary


B A S I C S                                         Loading a File and Exiting
ZDDDDDDDDDDDDDDDDDDDDDDDDDDDDDDDDDDDDDDDDDDDDDDDDDDD?
3 FILE OPERATIONS                        3 SEE ALSO:
3 1. Create or load a file   AMED filename  3   CURSOR MOVES: Arrow keys
3                                        3
3 2. Enter text              from keyboard 3   RULER LINES: format (margins)
3                                        3
3 3. Save the text to disk   Press F1 F3  3   DOT LINES: format (printing)
3                                        3
3 4. Edit the text           Bksp, Del, Ins 3   ENTERING TEXT: editing
3                                        3
3 5. Close the file          Press F1 F2  3   MARKING: move, copy, delete
3                                        3
3 6. Print the file          Press F1 F7  3   FIND/REPLACE: text or chars
@DDDDDDDDDDDDDDDDDDDDDDDDDDDDDDDDDDDDDDDDDDDDDDDDDDDDY
```

Quick Reference Guides.   A useful intermediate measure is a **quick reference guide.** This summary of primary system functions and their use is designed to be a one- or two-page reminder that users or operators can keep at the terminal. By referring to the guide, you can find out how to perform functions without having to read a lengthy explanation of how each one works. Such a guide is especially useful when you must remember special function key definitions or use codes and abbreviations. In some systems, the quick reference guide is available on the screen; it can be displayed by touching a function key.

9.3

RESOURCE TRACKING AND SIMULATION EXAMPLE

Preparing a user manual for Weaver Farm can teach us a great deal about methods of presentation. Suppose we are writing the section of the manual explaining how to log on to the system. One way of presenting the material is in *paragraph form*:

> The log on screen for Weaver Farm (Figure 9.7) provides access to the system. Use the arrow keys to move the cursor to the first box of the USER ID field. Type up to three characters for your user identification. Press the TAB key to move to the PASSWORD field. Type up to eight characters as your password and press RETURN. If your identification and password are correct, the system will display the Weaver Farm main menu (Figure 9.8). Otherwise, a blinking message will appear at the bottom of the screen, saying:
>
> "UNAUTHORIZED USER"
>
> The cursor will move back to the first box of the USER ID field, and you may reenter your identification code.

Figure 9.7   Weaver Farm Log on Menu

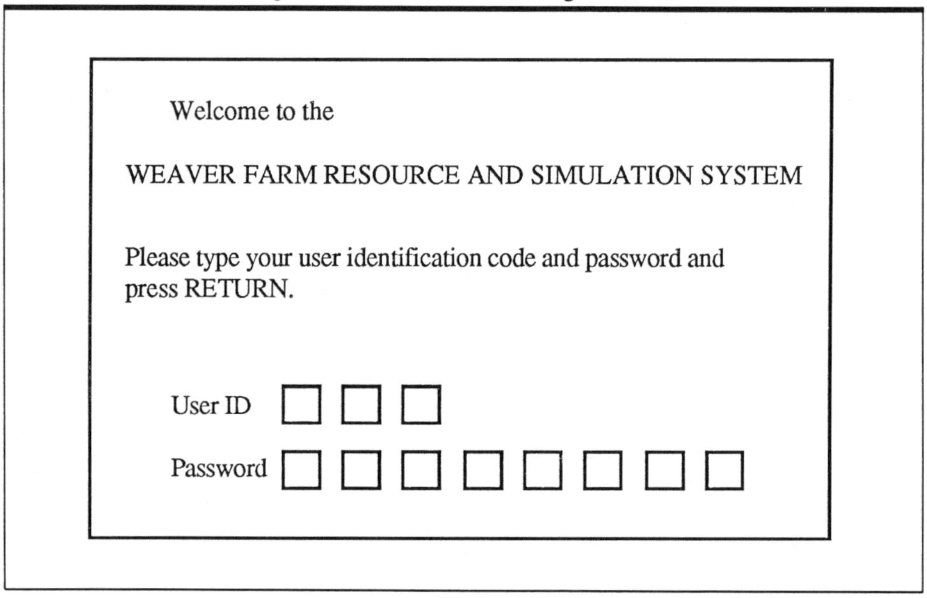

Welcome to the

WEAVER FARM RESOURCE AND SIMULATION SYSTEM

Please type your user identification code and password and press RETURN.

User ID   ☐ ☐ ☐

Password ☐ ☐ ☐ ☐ ☐ ☐ ☐ ☐

Figure 9.8   Weaver Farm Main Menu

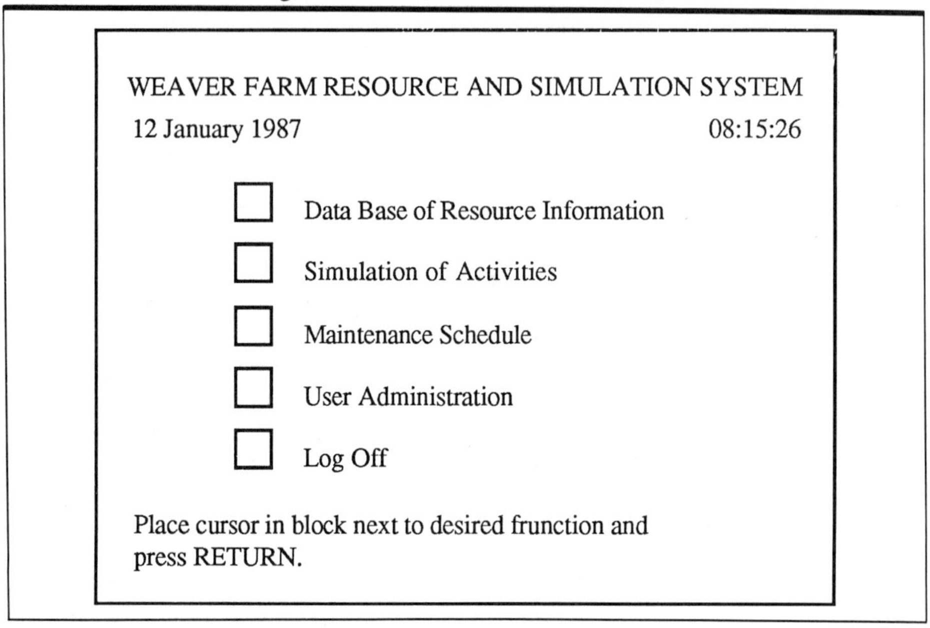

WEAVER FARM RESOURCE AND SIMULATION SYSTEM
12 January 1987   08:15:26

☐   Data Base of Resource Information

☐   Simulation of Activities

☐   Maintenance Schedule

☐   User Administration

☐   Log Off

Place cursor in block next to desired frunction and
press RETURN.

The paragraph contains all information needed by a user to log on. However, the log on procedure is really a series of steps. Users may prefer to read the procedure as a *list* of things to do.

The log on screen for Weaver Farm provides access to the system (Figure 9.7).

1. Use the arrow keys to move the cursor to the first box of the USER ID field.
2. Type up to three characters for your user identification.
3. Press the TAB key to move to the PASSWORD field.
4. Type up to eight characters as your password and press RETURN.
5. If your identification and password are correct, the system will display the Weaver Farm main menu (Figure 9.8). Otherwise, a blinking message will appear at the bottom of the screen, saying:

"UNAUTHORIZED USER"

The cursor will move back to the first box of the USER ID field, and you may reenter your identification code.

A similar approach formats the procedure so that it guides users through the decisions they must make. The *map layout* lets users move from one decision point to the next until they have completed the activity.

1. Is the terminal turned on?
     If YES, go to step 2.
     If NO, return to previous section of manual.

2. Is the cursor at the first box of the USER ID field?

> If YES, go to step 3.
> If NO, use arrow keys to move cursor to first box of USER ID.

3. Type up to three characters for your user identification code and press the TAB key.

4. Type up to eight characters for your password and press the RETURN key.

5. Is the Weaver Farm main menu displayed (Figure 9.8)?

> If YES, you are now logged on to the system.
> If NO, is the message "UNAUTHORIZED USER" displayed?
>> If YES, return to step 2.
>> If NO, notify the system operator.

Likewise, a *flowchart* can depict the procedure. Figure 9.9 is an example of how the log on flowchart might look. The user moves from one block to the next by answering questions and following the arrows. The circled page numbers refer to procedures described on other pages of the user manual.

Finally, this information can be described as a *condition table*. For each step, the condition of the system determines the action taken. Table 9.2 is a condition table for the log on procedure.

Table 9.4   Condition Table for Log On Procedure

Procedure	Step	Condition	Action
LOG ON	1	Terminal on?	
		Y	Go to step 2.
		N	See page 2.
	2	Cursor at User ID?	
		Y	Type user identification code and press TAB. Type password and press RETURN.
		N	Use arrow keys to position cursor. Repeat step 2.
	3	Main menu displayed?	
		Y	See page 4.
		N	If "UN-AUTHORIZED USER", go to step 2. Else, notify operator.

The most appropriate approach depends on the experience and preferences of the users. For instance, the paragraph format tends to be dry and can be difficult to follow. As users execute one step after another, it is hard to find the next step; users can get lost and confused. The list gives users reference points, and it is easy to finish one step and look at instructions for the next.

Figure 9.9   Flowchart for Log On Procedure

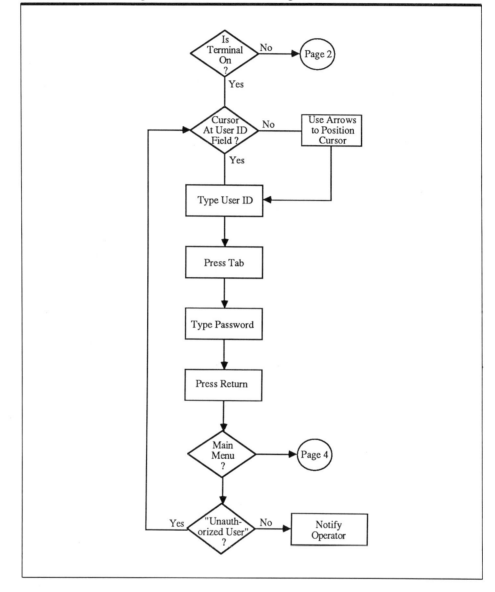

A map adds formality and organization to the description. Users can see that every circumstance is described, so they always know what to do next. The flowchart serves the same purpose. In addition, the graphic depiction of the procedure is clear and concise. It may appeal to those who prefer graphical explanations to textual ones. However, flow charts can intimidate users who are unaccustomed to and fearful of automated systems. The condition table is a compromise between the map and the flow chart. It guides users but does not distract them with graphic representation.

Remember that the user manual is used not only for learning the material initially but also for reference when brushing up. When deciding which method of presentation to use, you should consider how the material will look to someone flipping through the pages of a manual to find information. The paragraph format is the least appealing, since there is nothing to "jump out at you" and grab your attention. Similarly, the information on a flow chart may get lost among the circles and boxes. The condition table can be helpful for this purpose in isolating the important points of each procedure.

These choices for presenting material about the system give you flexibility in writing system documentation. Although our example deals with a user manual, the types of presentation are applicable to any kind of documentation. You can be creative at the same time that you are being instructive.

There are many other factors to consider when writing documentation. For more information about technical writing, see the books by Sides ([SID84]) and Weiss ([WEI85]).

9.4

CHAPTER SUMMARY

The transfer of a system from developer to customer involves much more than a ribbon-cutting ceremony. As we have seen, careful planning is needed. When the project is first planned and scheduled, the development team must consider the need to train users and operators to take over a system. Users learn what the system does and how to do it; operators are trained in how the system is configured and how it functions. Training is also available for infrequent as well as regular users. A variety of training techniques can be used, including documents, demonstrations and classes, and expert users. Automated training aids and help functions should be incorporated in the design of the general system.

Documentation is written with the audience in mind. User manuals describe what the major system activities look like to the user, while operator manuals refer to auxiliary functions. A general system guide is an overview of the system characteristics and functions; its audience includes those who need a general idea of what the system does without learning details of the screen and report formats. Written documentation is often supplemented with automated tutorials and overviews.

More technical documentation is needed for those who deal with the program code. Accompanying the documentation generated throughout development, a programmer guide and a maintenance guide help technical employees understand the nature of a problem or error and trace it to its source.

Additional help is given to users in an error message reference guide. This guide explains more completely the meaning of the short error messages displayed when an error is detected by the system. Online help (usually using a help key) explains to users the options available as users are performing system functions. A quick reference guide is also useful in reminding users of function key meanings and option names.

In the next chapter, we look at the final stage of system development: maintaining the system once it is built. If we build quality systems, maintenance should be the easiest part of development. However, as we shall see, maintenance often requires more time and effort than all other stages of development combined!

9.5

EXERCISES

1. Prototyping allows the users to try out a working model of a system before the actual system is complete. Explain how prototyping can be counterproductive if it creates task interference during training.

2. Give an example of a system for which user training and operator training are the same.

Figure 9.10   Page from P-System User Manual

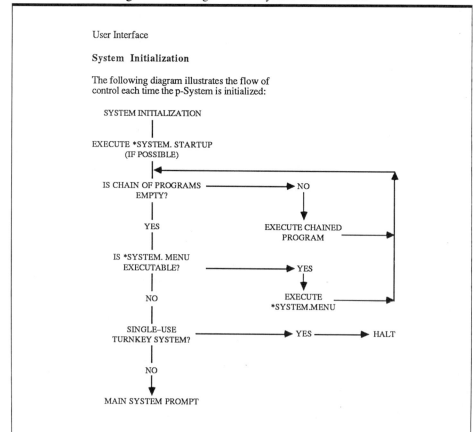

3. The user of an automated system need not be familiar with computer concepts. However, knowledge of computers is beneficial for most operators. In what cases should the user of an automated system be unaware of the underlying computer system? Is this lack of awareness a sign of good system design? Give examples to support your answer.

4. Examine the user documentation for a computer system at your school or job. Is it clear and easy to understand? Would it be understandable to a user who knows little of computers? Are the error messages easy to interpret? Is there a listing of error messages separate from the user manual? Is it easy to look up topics in the documentation? How would you change the documentation to improve it?

5. Table 9.5 contains some of the error messages in a reference guide from an actual BASIC interpreter. Comment on their clarity, amount of information, and appropriateness for a user or operator.

Table 9.5 Basic Error Messages

Number	Message
23	Line buffer overflow An attempt has been made to input a line that has too many characters.
24	Device timeout The device you have specified is not available at this time.
25	Device fault An incorrect device designation has been entered.
26	FOR without NEXT A FOR statement was encountered without a matching NEXT.
27	Out of paper The printer device is out of paper.
28	Unprintable error An error message is not available for the condition which exists.
29	WHILE without WEND A WHILE statement does not have a matching WEND.
30	WEND without WEND A WEND statement was encountered without a matching WHILE.
31–49	Unprintable error An error message is not available for the condition which exists.

6. Figure 9.10 is a page from a Sage computer (Stride Micro, Reno, Nevada) user manual. It is clear and easy to understand. What audience understands the terms used?

C H A P T E R 10

MAINTENANCE

In previous chapters, we have investigated the building of a system. As we can see from Figure 10.1, system-building begins when we work with a customer to define requirements. Then we develop a specification of the system that can be understood by the customer but can also act as a framework for program designers. Once the program designers produce a detailed description from which the programmers write the code, the programs are implemented and tested. Finally, the system is delivered to the actual users.

However, the life of a system does not end with delivery. We saw in the last chapter that the "final system" is subject to continuing change, even after it is built. Thus, now we look at the challenge of maintaining a *continually evolving system*. First, we review those aspects of a system that are likely to change. Then, we study the activities and personnel involved in maintaining a system. The maintenance process can be difficult; therefore, we examine the problems involved, including the nature of costs and how they escalate.

Several techniques and tools are available to help us perform maintenance. A major technique, configuration management, is used to tie together requirements, design, code, and documentation. Strictly speaking, configuration management begins when the system requirements are defined. However, configuration management structures and activities play an especially important role during maintenance and therefore require a second look. Finally, we examine several examples of automated tools that can be used in maintenance and configuration management.

10.1

THE CHANGING SYSTEM

System development is complete when the system is *operational*, that is, the system is being used in its actual environment. Any work done to change the system after it is in operation is considered to be **maintenance**. Many people think of software system maintenance as they do hardware maintenance: repair or prevention of broken or improperly working parts. However, software maintenance cannot be viewed in the same way. Let us see why.

373

Figure 10.1   The System Development Process

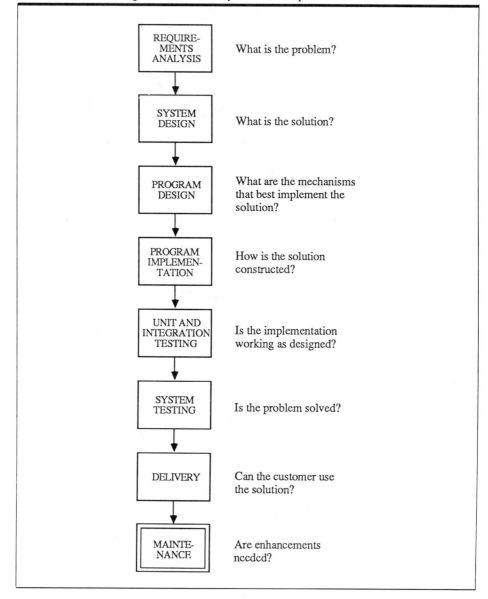

One goal of software engineering is the development of techniques that a developer can use to exactly define a problem, design a system as a solution, implement a correct and efficient set of programs, and test the system for errors. This goal is similar to that of hardware developers: producing a reliable, error-free product that works according to specification. Hardware maintenance in such a system concentrates on replacing parts that wear out or using techniques that prolong the system's life. However, WHILE-DO constructs do not wear out after ten thousand loops, and semicolons do not fall off the end of Pascal statements. Unlike hardware, software does not degrade or require periodic maintenance. Thus, software systems are different from hardware, and we cannot think of their maintenance in the same way.

The biggest difference between hardware and software systems is that software systems are built to incorporate *change*. Except in the simplest cases, the systems we develop are evolutionary. That is, one or more of the system's defining characteristics usually changes during the life of the system. Lehman ([LEH80]) has described a way to categorize programs in terms of how they may change. In the next section, we extend his categories to systems.

Types of Systems

Software systems may change, not just because a customer makes a decision to do something a different way, but because the *nature* of the system itself changes. For example, consider a system that computes payroll deductions and issues paychecks for a company. The system is dependent on the tax laws and regulations of the city, state, and country in which the company is located. If the tax laws change or if the company moves to another location, the system may require modification. Thus, changes to a system may be required even if the system has been working acceptably in the past.

Why are some systems more prone to change than others? In general, we can describe a system in terms of the way it is related to the environment in which it operates. Unlike problems handled in the abstract, the real world contains uncertainties and concepts we do not understand completely. The more dependent is a system on the real world for its requirements, the more likely it is to change.

S-Systems.   Some systems are formally defined by and are derivable from a *specification*. In these systems, a specific problem is stated in terms of the entire set of circumstances to which it applies. For example, we may be asked to build a system to perform matrix addition, multiplication, and inversion on a given set of matrices within certain performance constraints. The problem is completely defined, and there are one or more correct solutions of the problem as stated. The solution is well known, so the developer is concerned not with the *correctness of the solution* but with the *correctness of the implementation* of the solution. A system constructed in this way is called an **S-system**. Such a system is static and does not accommodate a change in the problem that generated it.

As shown in Figure 10.2, the problem solved by an S-system is related to the real world, and the real world is subject to change. However, if the world changes, the result is a completely new problem that must be specified.

P-Systems.   Computer scientists can often define abstract problems using S-systems and develop systems to solve them. However, it is not always easy or possible to describe a real world problem completely. In many cases, the theoretical solution to a problem exists, but the implementation of the solution is impractical or impossible.

Figure 10.2   An S-System

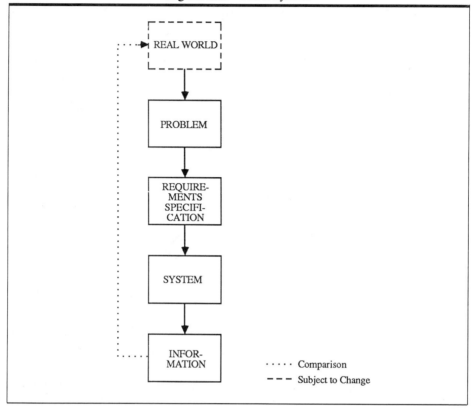

For example, consider a system to play chess. Since the rules of chess are completely defined, the problem can be completely specified. At each step of the game, a solution might involve the calculation of all possible moves and their consequences to determine the best next move. However, the implementation of such a solution is infeasible using today's technology. The number of moves is too large to be evaluated in a practical amount of time. Thus, we must develop an *approximate* solution that is more practical to build and use.

To develop this solution, we describe the problem in an abstract way and then write the requirements specification for the system from our abstract view. A system developed in this way is called a **P-system** because it is based on a *practical* abstraction of the problem, rather than on a completely defined specification. As shown in Figure 10.3, a P-system is more dynamic than an S-system. The solution produces information that is compared with the problem; if the information is unsuitable in any way, the abstraction of the problem may be changed and the requirements modified to try to make the resulting solution more realistic.

Thus, in a P-system, the requirements are based on approximation. The solution depends in part on the interpretation of the analyst who generates the requirements. Even though an exact solution may exist, the solution produced by a P-system is tempered by the environment in which it must be produced. In an

Figure 10.3 A P-System

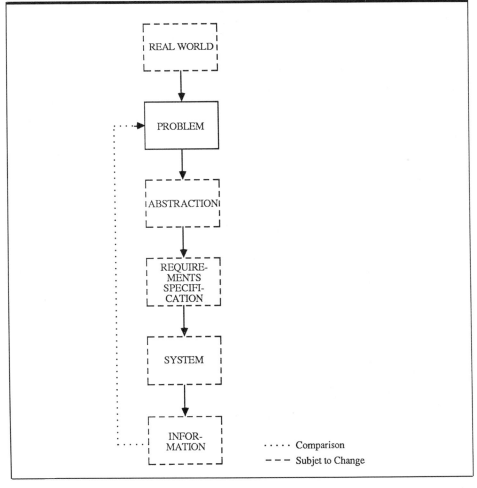

S-system, the solution is acceptable if the specifications are correct. However, in a P-system, the solution is acceptable if the results make sense in the world in which the problem is embedded.

Many things can change a P-system. When the output information is compared with the actual problem, the abstraction may change or the requirements may need to be altered, and the implementation may be affected accordingly. The system resulting from the changes cannot be considered a new solution to a new problem. Rather, it is a modification of the old solution to better fit the existing problem.

E-Systems. In considering S-systems and P-systems, the real world situation remains stable. However, a third class of systems incorporates the changing nature of the real world itself. An **E-system** is one that is *embedded* in the real world and changes as the world does. The solution is based on a model of the abstract processes involved. Thus, the system is an integral part of the world it models.

For instance, a system that predicts the economic health of a country is based on a model of how the economy functions. Changes occur in the world in which the problem is embedded. In turn, the economy is not completely understood, so the model changes as our understanding changes. Finally, our solution changes as the abstract model changes.

Figure 10.4 illustrates the changeability of an E-system and its dependence on its real world context. Whereas S-systems are unlikely to change and P-systems are subject to incremental change, E-systems are likely to undergo almost constant change. Moreover, the success of an E-system depends entirely on the customer's evaluation of system performance. Since the problem addressed by an E-system cannot be completely specified, the system must be judged solely by its behavior under actual operating conditions.

These categories show us the system elements subject to change. The greater the number of changeable elements, the more likely the need for system maintenance. In particular, since the *problem* generating an E-system may change, an E-system

Figure 10.4   An E-System

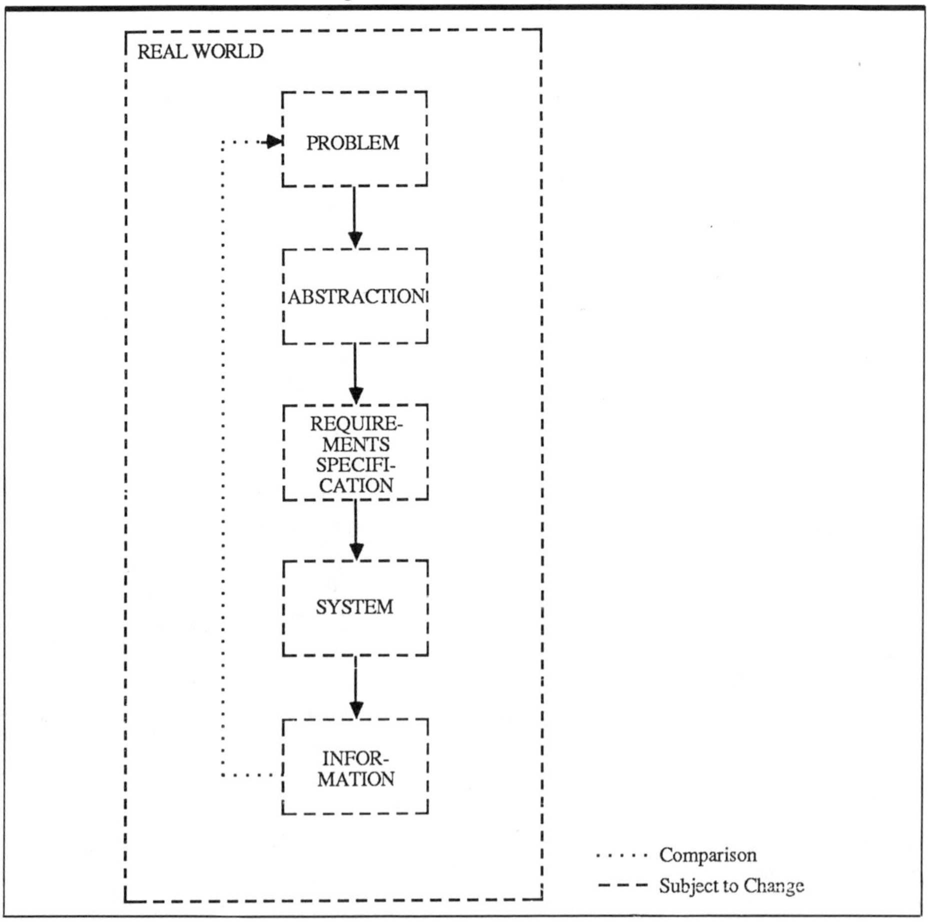

solution will probably undergo constant enhancement. At the end of this chapter, we will categorize the Weaver Farm project to help us predict how much maintenance will be required after system delivery.

Changes During the System Life Cycle

By examining the system in light of its category, we can see where during development change may occur and how it will affect the system. By its nature, an S-system problem is completely defined and unlikely to change. A similar problem may be solved by modifying the S-system, but the result is a completely new problem with solution. If an S-system performs unacceptably, it is usually because it addresses the wrong problem. Dissatisfaction results in a *redefinition* of the problem and generation of a new problem description; then a new solution is developed, not a modification to the old one.

A P-system is an approximate solution to a problem and may require change as discrepancies and omissions are identified. In fact, as the information produced by the system is compared and contrasted with the actual situation being modeled, the P-system may undergo change to insure that the system is economical and effective.

For a P-system, a model approximates a solution to the stated problem, so modification can occur during all stages of development. First, the abstraction may change. In other words, the abstract description is altered, and the requirements specification changes accordingly. Next, the system design is modified, and implementation and testing are redone to incorporate the changes. The appropriate system and program documentation are then modified, and new training may be required.

E-systems use abstractions and models to approximate a situation, so E-systems are subject to at least the kinds of changes that a P-system may undergo. Indeed, their nature is more inconstant because the problem can also change. Being embedded in changing activities, E-systems may require that characteristics be built into the system itself to accommodate change.

The effect of changes to any type of system is summarized by the entries in Table 10.1. For instance, a modification to the requirements during requirements analysis may result in a change to the specification. A modification to the technical design may require a change in the system design and perhaps the original requirements. Thus, a change at any stage of development can also affect the results of previous stages.

The software engineering principles suggested for system development also make change easier during maintenance. For example, having modularized the design and code and cross-referenced the modules with the requirements, you can easily trace a change in the requirements to the modules affected and to the tests that must be redone. Similarly, if an error occurs, the offending module may be identified; then corrections can be made at many levels (design, code, and test) rather than just in the program documentation. Thus, software engineering principles contribute not only to good design and correct code but also to the ability to make changes easily and quickly.

Table 10.1   The Impact of Change During Software Development

Stage of Development	Effect of Changes
Requirements Analysis	Requirements Specification
System Design	Conceptual Design Specification Technical Design Specification
Program Design	Program Design Specification
Program Implementation	Program Code Program Documentation
Unit Testing	Test Plans Test Scripts
System Testing	Test Plans Test Scripts
System Turnover	User Documentation Training Aids Operator Documentation System Guide Programmer Guide Training Classes

The System Lifespan

As software engineers trying to build a maintainable product, the first question we must ask ourselves is whether it is possible to build the system "right" the first time. In other words, if we use highly cohesive modules with low coupling, if the documentation is complete and up-to-date, and if the entire system is cross-referenced, will we need a maintenance phase? Unfortunately, the answer is yes. The reasons lie in the *nature of the systems* themselves. As we have seen, there is no way to guarantee that P-systems and E-systems will not require change. In fact, we must assume that they *will* change and then build them so that they can be changed easily.

The next question is *how much* change can we expect? Again, the answer depends on the nature of the system. S-systems will have little or no change, P-systems much more, and E-systems are likely to change continually. For this reason, many software engineers prefer to call the maintenance stage of development the *evolutionary phase*.

Development Time Versus Maintenance Time.   We can look at the development and maintenance times of other projects to get an idea of how long we can expect the evolutionary phase to be. According to Parikh and Zvegintzov ([PAR83a]), the typical development project takes between one and two years but requires an additional five to six years of maintenance time. In terms of time, more than half of the programming resources devoted to a project are spent on the project's maintenance. A survey by Fjeldstad and Hamlen ([FJE79]) of 25 data processing installations illustrates this fact. Their study showed that 39% of a programmer's work involves development, while the remaining 61% addresses corrections, modifications, and user support. (See Figure 10.5.)

Figure 10.5 Allocation of Programmer Resources (from [FJE79])

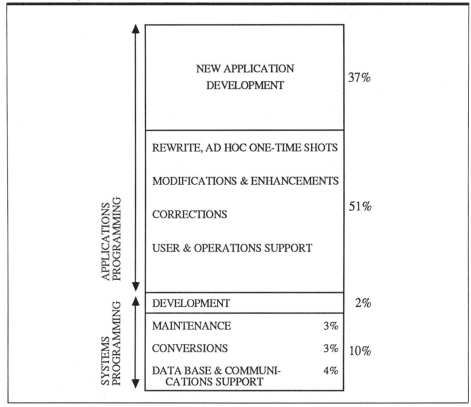

System Evolution vs. System Decline. A large amount of maintenance time indicates that a lot of changes are being made to the systems we build. If a system requires so much change, perhaps it is sometimes better to scrap the system and build a new one instead of modifying the old one. Several questions must be answered in order to make that determination.

1. Is the cost of maintenance too high?
2. Is the reliability of the system unacceptable?
3. Is the system able to adapt to change?
4. Can the system adapt to change within a reasonable amount of time?
5. Is system performance no longer within prescribed constraints?
6. Are the system functions of limited usefulness?
7. Can other systems do the same or better job faster or cheaper?
8. Is the cost of maintaining hardware great enough to justify the rebuilding of the system with new hardware?

A positive answer to all or some of these questions may mean that it is time to consider a new system to replace the old one.

10.2

THE NATURE OF MAINTENANCE

The main focus of development is producing code that implements the requirements and works correctly. At each stage of development, the development team continually refers to earlier stages. The design modules are tied to requirements specifications, the code modules are cross-referenced and reviewed for compliance with design, and the tests are based on finding out whether functions and constraints are working according to requirements and design. Thus, the development involves looking back in a careful, controlled way.

Maintenance support is different. The maintenance staff *looks back* at all development: requirements, design, code, and test. In addition, the maintenance staff *looks at the present* by establishing a working relationship with users and operators to find out how satisfied they are with the way the system works. Finally, the maintenance team *looks forward* to anticipate things that might go wrong and fix them before an error causes difficulty or damage. Because maintenance encompasses more than development, the job is more difficult; there is more to track and control. Let us examine the activities involved in keeping an existing system running smoothly and properly and who performs them.

Maintenance Activities

Maintenance activities are similar to those of development: analyzing requirements, evaluating system and program design, writing or rewriting code, testing changes, and updating documentation. Thus, the people who perform maintenance—analysts, programmers, and designers—have similar roles. However, because changes often require an intimate knowledge of the structure and content of the system's code, programmers play a much larger role in maintenance than they did in development.

Who Performs Maintenance.   The team that develops a system is not always used to maintain the system once it is operational. Often a separate maintenance team is employed to ensure that the system runs properly. There are positive and negative aspects to using a separate maintenance team. The development team is familiar with the program code, the design and philosophy behind it, and the functions of the system. If the developers know that they are building something that they will maintain, they will build the system in a way that makes maintenance easier.

However, developers sometimes feel so confident in their knowledge of the system that they tend not to keep the documentation up-to-date. Their lack of care in writing and revising documentation may result in needing more people or resources to tackle a problem. This situation leads to a long response time from the time a problem is detected to the time it is fixed. Many customers will not tolerate a delay.

Often a separate group of analysts, programmers, and designers (sometimes including one or two members of the development team) is designated as the maintenance team. A fresh, new team may be more objective than the original developers. A separate team may find it easier to distinguish how a system *should* work from how it *does* work. If they know others will work from their documentation, developers tend to be more careful about documentation and programming standards.

Responsibilities of the Maintenance Team. Maintaining a system involves all members of the maintenance team. Typically, users, operators, or customer representatives approach the maintenance team with a comment or problem. The maintenance analysts or programmers determine which parts of the code are affected by the comment or problem, how the design is affected by any resulting change, and how much it will cost (in time or resources) to implement a change. Thus, the maintenance team works with the system to accomplish several purposes:

1. Understand the system
2. Locate information in the system documentation
3. Keep system documentation up to date
4. Extend existing functions to accommodate new or changing requirements
5. Add new functions to the system
6. Find the source of errors in the system
7. Correct errors identified in the system
8. Answer questions about the way the system works
9. Restructure design and code
10. Rewrite design and code
11. Delete design and code modules that are no longer useful
12. Manage changes to the system as they are made

In addition, maintenance team members work with users, operators, and customers. First, they try to understand the problem as expressed in the user's language. Then, the problem is transformed into a request for modification. The change request includes a description of how the system works now, how the user wants the system to work, and what modifications are needed to produce the changes. Once design or code is modified and tested, the maintenance team retrains the user, if necessary. Thus, maintenance involves *interaction with people* as well as with software and hardware.

The Flow of Maintenance

Maintenance focuses on four major problems simultaneously:

1. Maintaining control over the system's day-to-day functions
2. Maintaining control over the modifications made to the system
3. Perfecting existing acceptable functions
4. Preventing system performance from degrading to unacceptable levels

Corrective Maintenance. To control the day-to-day functions of the system, the maintenance team responds to problems resulting from errors in the system. Addressing these problems is known as **corrective maintenance** . As errors are brought to the attention of the team, emergency repairs are made. Long-range changes may be implemented to correct more general problems in design or coding procedure.

For example, a user may show the maintenance staff an example of a report with too many printed lines on a page. The programmers determine that the problem results from an error in the design of the printer driver. As an emergency repair, a member of the team shows the user how to reset the lines per page by setting a parameter on the report menu before printing the report. Eventually, programmers redesign, recode and retest the printer driver so that it works properly without any special user intervention.

Adaptive Maintenance. Sometimes, a change introduced in one part of a system requires changes to other parts of the system. The implementation of these *secondary* changes is known as **adaptive maintenance**. For instance, suppose the existing data base management subsystem of a large hardware and software system is upgraded. In the process, the programmers find that disk access routines require an additional parameter. The changes made to add the extra parameter are adaptive changes. They do not correct errors; they merely allow the system to adapt to a change elsewhere in the system.

Similarly, suppose a compiler is enhanced by the addition of a debugger. The menus or function key definitions are then altered to allow users of the compiler to choose the debugger as an option when compiling a program. These menu and key changes modify the system to accommodate the debugging tool.

Perfective Maintenance. As we have seen, system functions are based on the real-world environment in which they must operate. Changes in the environment can result in changes to the system. Such enhancements are known as **perfective maintenance**. For example, a tax program may require perfective maintenance if a new tax code modifies the deductions or the percent of income subject to tax. An operating system may require perfective maintenance if changes are needed to · allow it to recognize a new type of storage device.

Perfective maintenance also includes changing design or code to *improve the performance* of the system. For example, the system may be functioning satisfactorily, but the maintenance team may redesign the data retrieval modules to speed data access. Similarly, a maintenance programmer may rewrite a sorting algorithm to improve a system's response time for the user. In these cases, there is nothing wrong with the way the system performs; the changes make the system perform better.

Documents also require changes. If documentation is enhanced to allow users and operators to understand more or to allow programmers to find information more easily, the document modifications or additions are also considered to be perfective maintenance.

Preventive Maintenance. The final type of maintenance is similar to that performed on hardware to try to prevent malfunctions. **Preventive maintenance** is work performed on a system in an effort to prevent an error or malfunction from occurring. An example is the addition of typechecking to a data entry system. The typechecking of input data allows the data entry modules to detect input errors before they are passed on to other modules where data in the data base might be corrupted. The maintenance team can also add code to track changes made to a file during an editing session, so that the changes can be re-created if the session ends improperly.

Use of Maintenance Time and Resources. Lientz and Swanson ([LIE80]) have administered a series of surveys to determine how much time each type of maintenance requires. The results, shown in Figure 10.6, indicate that half of the maintenance effort is perfective: improving system quality. Fjeldstad and Hamlen ([FJE79]) have done similar studies to determine how efforts to *correct* errors compare with efforts to *enhance* or *modify* a system. Correction means that an error exists; something is working improperly, and there is often a degree of urgency attached to an assignment to correct an error. The study found that the maintenance team allocates its time differently for correction than for modification or enhancement. In both cases, the team must define and understand the change, review the documentation, trace the program logic, and implement the change. Then they must test the result and modify the documentation to reflect the change. Table 10.2 shows that corrections require more time for understanding the program and tracing the program logic than do enhancements. However, the team spends more time testing enhancements than testing corrections. In both cases, the amount of time needed to actually change the code is small.

Figure 10.6   Distribution of Maintenance Effort

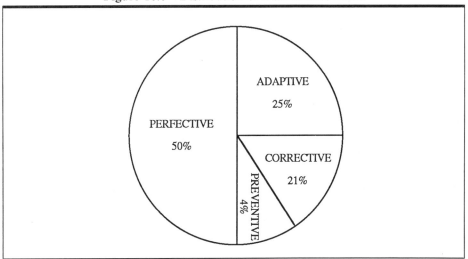

Table 10.2   Time Spent on Maintenance Tasks

Maintenance Task	Enhancements and Modifications	Corrections
Define and understand change	18%	25%
Review documentation	6%	4%
Trace logic	23%	33%
Implement change	19%	15%
Test change	28%	20%
Update documentation	6%	3%

Note that in both columns, the team spends a considerable amount of time reviewing documentation. This review is done, not only because team members want to learn about the system structure and logic, but also because team members often have little confidence in the quality of the documentation. It is not unusual for a maintenance programmer to compare code with documentation to verify that the code does what the documentation says.

Fjeldstad and Hamlen also asked the respondents in their study to identify which *program areas* were affected by maintenance changes. The results (shown in Table 10.3) indicate that business (rather than processing) factors are involved in a quarter of the enhancements implemented, and slightly more than half of the modifications affected the logic of the application. However, processing logic was affected by 87% of the corrections.

Table 10.3   Program Areas Affected by Maintenance

Program Area	Enhancements and Modifications	Corrections
File and data definition	18%	12%
Application logic	57%	75%
Business factors	25%	13%

10.3

THE PROBLEMS OF MAINTENANCE

Maintaining a system is difficult. Because the system is already operational, the maintenance team balances the need for change with the need for keeping a system accessible to users. For example, upgrading a system may require that the system be unavailable to users for several hours. However, if it system is critical to the users' business or operation, there may not be a window of several hours when users can give up the system. The maintenance team must find a way to implement changes without unnecessarily inconveniencing the users.

Factors Contributing to the Difficulty of Maintenance

Lientz and Swanson ([LIE81]) surveyed programmers to determine other factors that contribute to maintenance difficulties. Figure 10.7 illustrates their findings. We can examine some of these factors in more depth.

Limited Understanding. In addition to balancing user needs with software and hardware needs, the maintenance team deals with the limitations of *human understanding*. There is a limit to the rate at which a person can study documentation and extract material relevant to the problem being solved. Furthermore, we usually look for more clues than are really necessary for solving a problem. Adding the daily distractions of the office, we have a prescription for limited productivity. User understanding also presents problems. Lientz and Swanson found that more than half of maintenance programmers' problems derived from users' lack of skill or understanding.

These results illustrate the importance of clear and complete documentation and training. The results also emphasize the need for the maintenance team to have good "people skills." As we saw in chapter 2, there is a variety of work styles. The members of the maintenance team must understand how people with different styles think and work, and team members must be flexible in communication.

Figure 10.7   Maintenance Difficulties

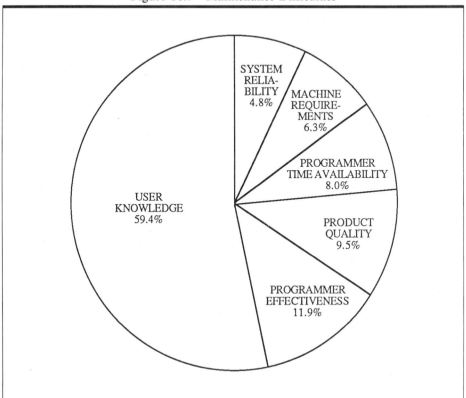

Management Priorities. The maintenance team also weighs the desires of the customer's management with the needs of the system. A survey of 120 organizations ([LIE78]) with a maintenance programming staff indicates that *management priorities* often override technical ones. The study found that maintenance and enhancement activities were viewed by management as being more important than the development of new applications. In other words, companies were more interested in making sure that they could carry on business as usual than in investigating new alternatives. The most important problem area for management was user demand for enhancement of the system. Thus, the maintenance team may be under pressure from management to repair an old system, even though users may be clamoring for new functions or a new system.

Technical Problems. Technical problems also affect maintenance productivity. If the logic of the design or code is not obvious, it may not be clear whether the design can handle the changes required. The design may be flawed or inflexible. For instance, the developers may have included a module for input and output that handles only tape; major modifications must be made for disk or online access. Similarly, the developers may not have anticipated changes that might occur. This technical problem is easy to see in programs whose data records contain exactly five digits for a postal code. The change to a nine-digit postal code might have been relatively easy if the original designers had anticipated a change in the code format.

In general, inadequate design specifications and the poor quality of programs and documentation account for almost ten percent of the time spent on maintenance. A similar amount of time is spent dealing with the requirements of the hardware: obtaining adequate storage and processing time. As a student, you understand the frustration of having a problem to solve but having no access to a terminal or waiting in a queue to log on to the system. Problems also arise when hardware, software, or data are unreliable.

Testing Difficulties. Testing can be a problem when finding time to test is difficult. For example, an airline reservation system must be available around the clock. It may be difficult to convince users to give up the system at midnight for two hours of testing. When a system performs a critical function such as air traffic control or satellite tracking, it may be impossible to test. Tests are run on a duplicate system; then tested changes are transferred to the production system.

In addition to time availability problems, there may not be good or appropriate test data available for testing the changes made. For instance, an earthquake prediction system may be modified to accommodate signals from a sensing device being developed. Test data must be simulated. Because scientists do not yet have a complete understanding of how earthquakes occur, accurate test data may be difficult to generate.

Most important, it is not always easy for testers to predict the effects of design or code changes and to prepare for them. This unpredictability is true especially when different members of the maintenance team are working on different problems at the same time. If Pat makes a change to module ABC to fix problem 1 while Dennis makes a change to the same module to fix problem 2, the combination of changes may be the cause of a new error. We will see shortly that configuration management techniques can help to prevent this situation from generating new errors.

Problems of Morale

The Lientz and Swanson studies indicate that 11.9% of problems during maintenance result from low morale and productivity. A major reason for low morale is the second-class status often accorded the maintenance team. Programmers sometimes think that it takes more skill to design and develop a system than to keep it running. However, as we have seen, maintenance programmers handle problems in addition to those of development. Maintenance programmers are not only skilled in writing code, but also at *working with users*, at *anticipating change*, and at *sleuthing*. Great skill and perseverance are required to track an error to its source, to understand the inner workings of a large system; and to modify that system's structure, code, and documentation.

Some groups rotate programmers among several maintenance and development projects to give the programmers a chance to do a variety of things. This rotation helps to avoid the perceived stigma of maintenance programming. However, programmers are often asked to work on several projects concurrently. Demands on a programmer's time result in conflicting priorities. During maintenance, 8% of the problems result from a programmer's being pulled in too many directions at once and thus being unable to concentrate on one problem long enough to solve it.

Problems of Compromise

The maintenance team is always involved in balancing one set of goals with another. As we saw earlier in this chapter, conflict arises between system availability for users and implementation of modifications, corrections and enhancements. Because errors occur at unpredictable times, the maintenance staff is constantly aware of this conflict.

As computing professionals, another conflict arises whenever a change is necessary. Principles of software engineering compete with expediency and cost. Often, a problem may be fixed in one of two ways: a quick but inelegant way that works but does not fit in with the design or coding strategy of the system, or a more involved but elegant way that is consistent with the guiding principles used to generate the rest of the system. Programmers may be forced to compromise elegance and design principles because a change is needed immediately.

When such compromise is made, several events are likely to make system maintenance more difficult in the future. First, the complaint is usually brought to the attention of the maintenance team by a *user or operator*. This person is not likely to understand the problem in the context of design and code, only in the context of daily operations. Second, solving the problem involves only the *immediate correction* of an error. No allowance is made for revising the system or program design to make the overall system more understandable or to make the change consistent with the rest of the system components. These two factors combine to present the maintenance team with a quick repair as its *limited goal*. The team is forced to concentrate its resources on a problem about which it may have little understanding.

An additional conflict must be resolved by the maintenance team. When a system is developed to solve an initial problem, its developers sometimes try to solve similar problems without change to the design and code. Such systems often run slowly because their general-purpose code must evaluate a large number of cases or possibilities. To improve performance, the system can instead incorporate special-purpose modules that sacrifice generality for speed. The special-purpose modules are often smaller because they need not consider every eventuality. The resulting system can be changed easily, at a cost of the time it takes to modify or enhance the system or program design. The maintenance team must weigh generality versus speed when deciding how and why to make a modification or correction.

Other factors that may affect the approach taken by the maintenance team include

1. The type of error involved
2. The criticality or severity of the error
3. The difficulty of the needed changes
4. The scope of the needed changes
5. The complexity of the modules involved in the changes
6. The number of physical locations at which the changes must be made

All the factors described here tell us that the maintenance staff performs double duty. First, they understand the system's design, code, and test philosophies and structures. Second, they develop a philosophy about the way in which maintenance will be performed and how the resulting system will be structured. They balance short- and long-term goals, and they decide when to sacrifice quality for speed.

The Cost of Maintenance

All the problems of maintaining a system contribute to the *high cost* of maintenance. In the 1970s, most of a software system's budget was spent on development. The ratio of development money to maintenance money reversed in the 1980s, as shown in Figure 10.8. Zelkowitz ([ZEL78]) points out that now only one-third of the money spent on a system is used for developing it; the remaining two-thirds are spent on modification. The trend toward higher maintenance cost is expected to continue, and three-quarters of a system's cost is likely to be devoted to maintenance by the 1990s.

Figure 10.8 Escalating Maintenance Costs

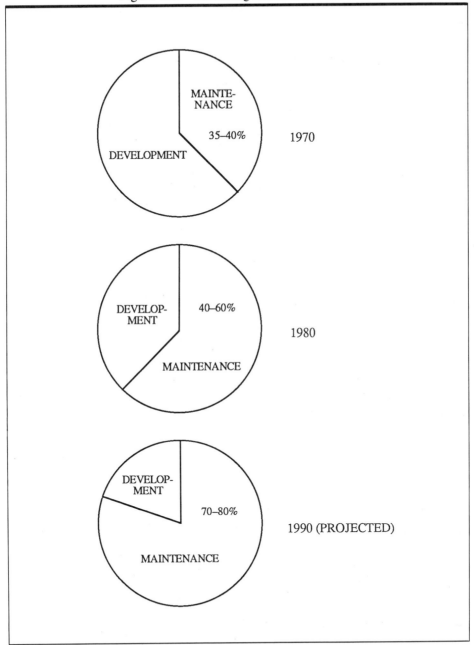

Factors Affecting Cost. In addition to problem areas already discussed, many other factors contribute to the cost of maintaining a system. As shown in Figure 10.9, costs can be generated by several factors:

1. *The type of applications supported by the system.* Systems such as real-time systems and those that require much synchronization are more difficult to change than those for which timing is not important. Great care is taken to insure that a change to one module does not affect the timing of other modules. Similarly, changes to programs with rigidly defined data formats can result in changes to a host of data access routines.

2. *The amount of turnover in the maintenance staff.* Substantial time is required to learn enough about a system to understand it and change it. The maintenance effort will suffer if team members are routinely rotated to other groups, or if employees frequently leave the company to work elsewhere.

3. *The lifespan of the system.* A system that is projected to last many years is likely to require more maintenance than one whose life is short. Quick corrections and lack of care in updating documentation are probable for a system with a short life. In contrast, if the system is to be useful for a long time, the maintenance crew tends to be more careful in using consistent design principles and keeping documentation up-to-date.

4. *Dependence on changing environment.* An S-system will require less maintenance than a P-system, which in turn will need less adaptation and enhancement than an E-system. In particular, a system dependent on the characteristics of its hardware is likely to require many changes if the hardware is modified or replaced.

5. *The characteristics of the hardware.* Unreliable hardware components or unreliable vendor support may make it more difficult to track a problem to its source.

6. *The quality of the design.* If the system is not composed of independent, cohesive modules, finding and fixing the source of an error may be compounded by changes creating unanticipated effects in other modules.

7. *The quality of the code.* If the code is not structured or does not implement the structure and principles of the design, it may be difficult to locate the source of an error. In addition, some programming languages are easier to understand than others. A system written in assembler language will be more difficult to maintain than one written in a higher level language.

8. *The quality of the documentation.* Undocumented design or code makes the search for the solution to a problem almost impossible. Similarly, if the documentation does not describe the code properly, the maintenance team can be thrown off track.

9. *The quality of testing.* If tests are run with incomplete data or do not anticipate all repercussions of a change, the modifications or enhancements to a system can generate other system problems.

Figure 10.9 Factors Affecting Cost of Maintenance

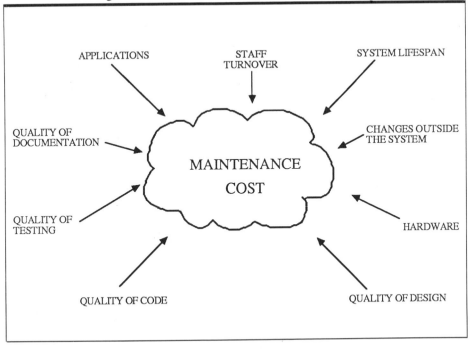

A Model of Maintenance Effort. Belady and Lehman ([BEL71] and [BEL72]) have tied the various maintenance costs together by developing a model of the maintenance process. They have taken into account the deterioration that occurs to a large system over time. A series of repairs and enhancements usually leads to the fragmentation of system activities. In general, the system grows *larger* with each round of maintenance repairs.

On large systems, members of the maintenance team become experts in certain aspects of the system. This specialization sometimes leaves the team without any generalists; that is, there is no one person who has a system-wide perspective of how the system should function and how it relates to its requirements. The specialization of the staff usually leads to an exponential increase in the resources devoted to maintenance. More people are needed to tackle the growing system; machines and time must be made available for their support.

At the same time, the system usually becomes more *complex* as a result of two things. First, as one error is repaired, the additional code required to make the repair often introduces new errors into the system. Second, as repairs are made, the structure of the system is changed. Because many repairs are made within the limited view of solving a particular problem, the coupling and cohesion of modules is changed and often degraded.

The result of Belady and Lehman's studies is an equation that reflects the factors involved in maintenance cost:

$$M = p + K^{c-d}$$

In this equation, M is the total maintenance effort expended for a system. The value of p represents wholly productive efforts: analysis, evaluation, design, coding and testing. Complexity, the value of c, is not a general measure of the complexity of the system, but rather a measure of the complexity caused by the lack of structured design and documentation. The complexity is reduced by d, the degree to which the maintenance team is familiar with the software. Finally, the constant K is to be determined by comparing this model with the cost relationships of actual products; it is called an *empirical constant* because its value is dependent on the environment.

The Belady-Lehman equation expresses a very important relationship among the components of maintenance. If a system is developed without software engineering principles, the value of c will be high. If, in addition, it is maintained without an understanding of the software itself, the value of d will be low. The result is that the cost for maintenance increases *exponentially*. Thus, to economize on maintenance, the best approach is to build the system according to software engineering guidelines and to give the maintenance team time to become thoroughly familiar with the system software.

10.4

TECHNIQUES FOR IMPROVING MAINTENANCE

In the previous section, we saw that one way to lower maintenance cost is to build in the quality from the start. Trying to force good design and structure into a system retroactively is not as successful as building the system correctly in the first place. Consistent with that philosophy is the use of several other techniques that can result in an easily changed system of high quality.

Configuration Management

The maintenance of a software system focuses on change. All aspects of the system are subject to modification, and it is the job of the maintenance team to understand the system, identify needed changes, and implement the changes successfully. Thus, an important aspect of maintenance is the *management of change*. To this end, all or part of the maintenance team is involved with configuration management.

Configuration management is the management and control of all kinds of changes made to a system so that the state of every component is always known. Requirements, design, code, tests, and documents are cross-referenced so that modifications to a module or document can be tracked and reflected in all others that are affected. The development team uses this cross-reference to evaluate the possible impact of a change on other modules in the system. Configuration management begins with the start of the project and continues throughout development. Since configuration management also plays a critical part in maintenance, we focus on maintenance issues here.

Problems of Configuration Management. Configuration management is difficult because software is difficult to work with. Software systems often consist of a large number of interrelating modules. Keeping track of changes to the modules and to their effect on other system components is not an easy task. The more complex the system, the more modules are affected by a change in any one of them. Unlike hardware, it is not always easy to see or understand the relationships among the modules. Further, it is not always easy to examine two similar systems and identify the differences between them.

An added difficulty rests in the perceptions of customer and users. Users often expect the system to be flexible enough to adapt easily to changes in the requirements. They understand neither the complexities of the system nor the coordination required to implement even a minor system modification. For this reason, customer representatives should be involved in configuration management. Their involvement gives them an appreciation for the work required to implement a change.

The Configuration Management Process. Even though customer representatives are involved in configuration management decisions, the actual administration of configuration management *procedures* rests with the maintenance team. Everyone on the maintenance team is involved with configuration management in some way or another. Usually, several people are assigned the task of supervising configuration management and are known as the **configuration management team**. The team includes:

1. Analysts who work with users to identify problems.
2. Programmers who work with the analysts to locate the source of identified problems.
3. Program librarians who work with the analysts and programmers to track modifications to design or code and update documentation that is affected by them.

The team works closely with customer representatives throughout the change process. A **configuration control board** or **change control board**, consisting of customer representatives and members of the configuration management team, handles problems in the following way:

1. A problem is *discovered*, either by a user or operator, a member of the customer's staff, or a member of the configuration management team.

2. The problem is *reported* to the configuration control board using a formal procedure requesting a change. (Figure 10.10 is an example of a change request form that the complainant might use to report the problem.) The change must be described in terms of how the system works now, what the nature of the problem is, and how the system should work after the change.

3. The configuration control board meets to discuss the problem. First, it determines if the problem is a *failure* to meet the requirements or a request for an

Figure 10.10   Change Request Form

Change Number _____

Date _____

Contact Name _____ Phone _____

DESCRIPTION OF PROBLEM:

How System Works Now: _____

Nature of Problem: _____

_____

DESCRIPTION OF NEEDED CHANGE:

_____

_____

_____

- -

TO BE COMPLETED BY CONFIGURATION CONTROL BOARD

SEVERITY: _____

RESPONSIBLE   ANALYST/PROGRAMMER _____

DEADLINE: _____

- -

TO BE COMPLETED BY ANALYST/PROGRAMMER

SYSTEM AFFECTED _____

MODULES AFFECTED _____

CHANGE REPORT REFERENCE _____

enhancement. This decision usually affects who pays for the resources to implement the change.

4. Next, the control board discusses the source of the problem. If the source is understood, programmers and analysts may describe the scope of any needed changes and the length of time needed to implement them. The control board assigns to the problem a *priority* or *severity level* and a programmer or analyst responsible for correcting it.

5. The designated analyst or programmer locates the *source* of the problem and identifies the changes needed to fix it. Working with a test copy rather than the operational version of the system, the programmer or analyst implements changes and tests them to assure that they work.

6. The programmer or analyst works with the program librarian to *control the installation* of the change in the operational system. All relevant documentation is updated.

7. The programmer or analyst files a *change report* that describes in detail all changes made to the system.

The Control of Change. The most critical step in the process is in the *control of change*. At any moment, the configuration management team must know the state of any module or document in the system. Consequently, the emphasis of configuration management should be communication among those whose actions affect the system. Cashman and Holt ([CAS80]) suggest that change be controlled by always knowing the answers to the following questions:

1. *Synchronization*: When was the change made?
2. *Identification*: Who made the change?
3. *Naming*: What components of the system were changed?
4. *Authentication*: Was the change made correctly?
5. *Authorization*: Who authorized that the change be made?
6. *Routing*: Who was notified of the change?
7. *Cancellation*: Who can cancel the request for change?
8. *Delegation*: Who is responsible for the change?
9. *Valuation*: What is the priority of the change?

Notice that these are *management* rather than *technical* questions. Thus, the answer to how to control change is to put in place *procedures* that will carefully manage the change.

Management of change is aided by the use of several *conventions*. First, each working version of the system is assigned an identification code or number. As a version is modified, a revision code or number is assigned to each resulting changed module. A record is kept of the status of each module and version. In addition, a history of all changes is generated. Thus, at any point in the life of the system, the configuration management team can identify the current version of the operational system and the revision number of each module being used. The team can also find out how the various revisions differ, who made the changes, and why they made them.

From your perspective as a student, these configuration management conventions probably sound unnecessary. Your class projects are usually managed alone or by a small group of programmers using verbal communication to track modifications and enhancements. However, imagine the chaos that would result from using the same techniques that you use for your class projects on the development and maintenance of a system of 200 modules. Often large systems are developed by having independent groups work simultaneously on different aspects of the system. Sometimes, these groups are located in different parts of town or in different cities. If Pam in one group is modifying a module that affects the data base at the same time that Nancy modifies another module that affects the data base, the result can be disastrous. Moreover, if the disaster occurs, the maintenance team must be able to "undo" the changes and *restore* the system to its original condition. The restoration can be made only when the team knows who made exactly what changes to which modules and when.

A restoration to a previous version is sometimes needed when you are continually unsuccessful in fixing a problem. You make a small change, and the problem is partially, but not completely, solved. Then you make another change, and the problem is less severe but still not entirely fixed. Your third change causes the system to abort in the middle of performing the function you are trying to fix. Unless you have kept track of your changes, you may not be able to roll the system back to its original state to try a new approach to solving the problem.

Automated Maintenance Tools

Tracking the status of all modules is formidable job. Fortunately, there are many automated tools that can help in performing both the configuration management and maintenance activities.

Text Editors. The simplest type of automated tool is a text editor. It is useful for maintenance in many ways. First, the ability to *copy* a group of lines of code or documentation from one place to another allows a programmer or analyst to avoid errors when duplicating correct material in another part of the system. Second, some text editors are coupled with a feature that *stores the changes* to one file in another, separate file. For example, using a Digital PDP-11, a program called SLP can be invoked to store the changes made to text. For each change desired, the number of the line in the original file and the change are noted in an "SLP" file. To actually implement the change, the SLP program merges the two files to produce a third file updated with the desired changes. (See Figure 10.11.)

This method of tracking changes is especially useful when a development system is being changed at the same time that a production system is being used. The original files are the modules of the production system. The SLP files contain all changes made to the production system for further development. No changes are transferred to production until the development system has been tested completely. Then, the SLP files are merged with the original, and the result becomes the new production system. The SLP files are emptied, and the cycle begins again. (See Figure 10.12.)

Some text editors identify and date each version of a text entry, track the modifications that have been made, and provide a method for rolling the file back to the previous version. In addition, access to files can be restricted to those authorized to change the file. Bell Laboratories' Programmer's Workbench ([IVI77]) is an editor of this type.

File Comparison. A tool similar to a text editor is a program that compares two files and reports on their *differences*. This kind of program is often used to ensure that two systems or programs that are supposedly identical actually are. The program reads both files and prints out a list of the discrepancies.

Figure 10.11 Using SLP Files

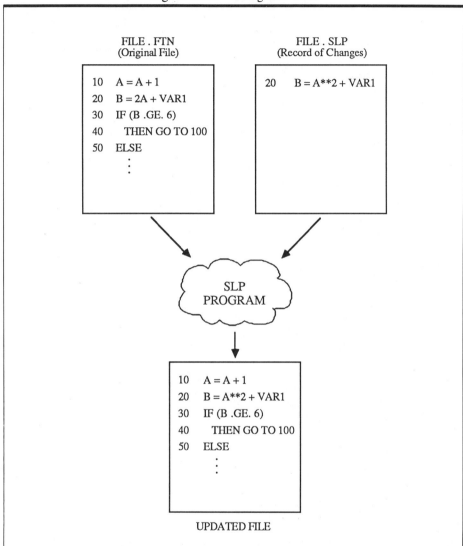

Compilers and Linkage Editors. Compilers and linkage editors often contain features that simplify maintenance and configuration management. A compiler checks the code for syntax errors. In many cases, the compiler points out the location and type of error it has found. Some languages, notably Modula-2 and Ada, have compilers that check for consistency across separately compiled components.

When the code has compiled properly, a linkage editor links the code with the other modules required for running the program. Some linkage editors keep track of the version numbers of the required modules and insure that only correct versions are linked together. This technique helps to eliminate problems caused by using the wrong copy of a system or subsystem to test a change.

Figure 10.12   Using SLP Files for Development and Production

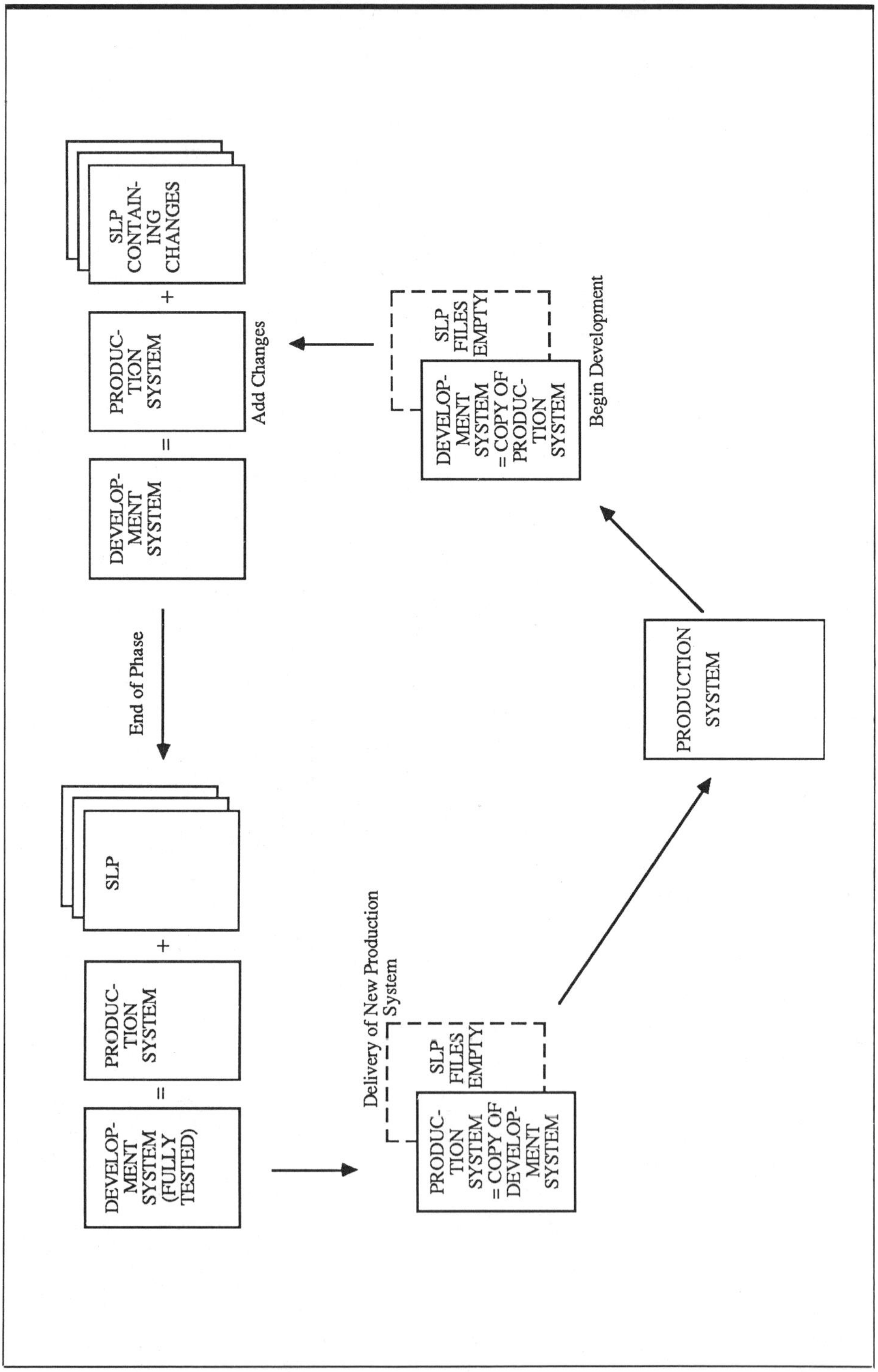

An IBM product called SBS is one such linkage editor. It tracks separate file types for source files, object files, linkage information, data files, and documents. The files are associated as specially designated groups. A group name is assigned to all the materials needed for a program to run, as shown in Figure 10.13. When a group is ready to be compiled, SBS compiles and links the correct versions as identified in the group definition. If the source code for a program is updated, the SBS program automatically deletes the old object code for the source file and for any group containing the source in its group definition. In this way, the system is guaranteed to always use the most current version of a program.

Debugging Tools. Many systems include debugging tools that aid maintenance by tracing through the logic of the program step by step, examining the contents of registers and memory areas, and setting special flags and pointers. The debugging tools, described in detail in chapter 6, play an important part in maintenance.

A major goal of software engineering is to develop more automated debugging tools. The need for a tool is often identified on a large software development project. Manual solutions are eventually replaced by automated ones on the project, making programming much easier. Helpful solutions that are tied to the type of language being used are sometimes incorporated in a new language definition that lessens or eliminates the original problem. The result is that the language itself acts to prevent problems from occurring.

Cross-reference Generators. Throughout this text, we have noted the importance of being able to trace the requirements through the design, code, tests, and documentation. There are automated systems, such as the INTERCOL system

Figure 10.13 SBS Group Designation

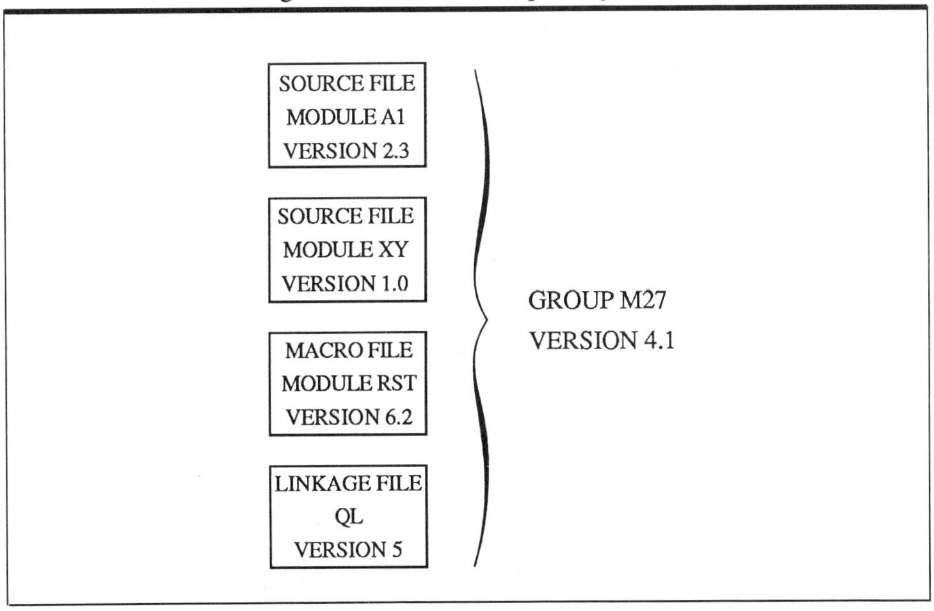

from Carnegie-Mellon University ([TIC79]), that generate and store these cross-references. This cross-referencing gives both the development and maintenance teams tighter control over modifications to the system.

Other systems, such as the Designer/Verifier's Assistant ([MOR79]), cross-reference each module with specifications stating the properties of the module. These specifications can be formulated from the requirements definition of the system. In the Designer/Verifier's Assistant, the result is a set of logical formulae called verification conditions. If all formulae yield a value of "true," then the code satisfies the specifications that generated it. When a programmer modifies an aspect of the system—either the code or the specifications for the code—the Assistant reevaluates the code and related verification conditions. It then reports on whether the new code is consistent with the specifications.

Complexity Calculators. We saw in chapter 5 that we can measure the *complexity* of a module using McCabe's metric. Recall that the metric measures the number of decision points in a module. There are several similar complexity metrics, too. The notion of complexity can be useful in maintenance because it shows us how a change may make a module more difficult to maintain in the future. The Belady-Lehman equation for the cost of maintenance tells us that an increase in complexity results in a drastic increase in the cost of maintenance.

Automatic complexity calculators are available to generate a complexity metric for a specified module. They can be used when programmers are weighing several alternatives for modifying a system. It may be desirable to select the alternative that results in a minimal (if any) increase in complexity.

Control Libraries. Configuration management would be impossible without the use of libraries of information that allow the team to control the change process. One such library system is called MONSTR, the Monitor for Software Trouble Reporting ([CAS80]). It keeps a history of software trouble reports, and it not only includes the problem itself, but also tracks the organizations involved and the communication paths among them. Thus, MONSTR allows a set of interrelated users to keep tabs on the status of reported problems with the system they use.

A library system that is popular on IBM systems is Pansophic Systems' PANVALET. The package incorporates source code, object code, control language (such as IBM job control language), and data files for running the programs. The files can be associated as special file types. PANVALET allows you to alter a string in one file, in all files of a given type, or in an entire library of files.

More than one version of a file is allowed. One version is designated as the production version, and there is no way to alter the production file. To modify something in the file, a new version must be created and a copy of the production version must be moved into this new version. Thus, modifications are strictly controlled.

In addition, a hierarchical structure is imposed on the files, including cross-referencing. Each version of a file is associated with a directory of information about the version: its status with respect to the production version, the dates of the last access and last update, the number of statements contained in the file, and the kind of action last taken with respect to the file. When the file is compiled, PANVALET automatically places the version number and the date of the last change on both the compiler listing and the object module.

To aid maintenance, reports of various kinds are available, and backup and recovery functions are included. If files have not been used in a long time, there are PANVALET routines to archive the files. A final control mechanism is the availability of three levels of security access.

Similarly, SCCS (Source Code Control System) and its successor, RCS, are packages developed at Purdue that are designed to control *changes to source code*. To do so, they provide functions for retrieving, updating, and storing all versions of modules. Several types of updating privileges can be assigned to those who access the system. Load modules are given a version number, and the version number appears in the source code. Each modification is accompanied by information about when, why, and by whom the change was made and where in the code the change is located.

Configuration Management Data Base Management Systems. The most sophisticated of configuration management tools uses its own data base management system to control changes. One such system is the Lifespan system from Yard Systems. Lifespan provides an online data base supporting a controlled environment for making changes to a system. A production copy of software is never accessed directly by programmers or analysts. Instead, a copy of the file is loaned to those who need it. When the file is returned to the Lifespan system, it is automatically checked for consistency.

A component in Lifespan can be a program, a subprocedure, a test case, or a document. Components are assigned version numbers and grouped into packages in a hierarchical way. Other documentation, such as discrepancy reports, is fully cross-referenced with the components and retained and distributed by the data base. This information is shown in a header module that looks like the following example:

```
HEADER-FORMAT-IS
    (2.1)
MODULE-TYPE-IS
    (PACKAGE)
MODULE-NAME-IS
    (EXAMPLEHEADER)
TITLE-IS
    (COBOL ACCESS TO VMS STRING HANDLING ROUTINES STR)
MODIFICATION-RECORDS-ARE
    ISSUE(2.2A)   MOD-BY      (PAE )  ON(24-MAR-87)  COMMENT(New procedure added)
    ISSUE(2.1)    APPROVED-BY(SLP )   ON(30-MAR-87)  IN-PACKAGE(STR  1.2)-
                                                     COMMENT(New package
                                                     for issue to SOLK)
```

Components are managed by tying each one to a *technical manager* responsible for it. All reports of defects relating to the component are duplicated and sent to the manager. In turn, the manager is responsible for authorizing work on the component and for releasing the tested modules to other users.

Every component is also related to an *owner*. The owner can regulate access to the component by other Lifespan users. In addition, the owner is automatically provided with copies of changes authorized by the component's technical manager.

To each request for a change to a component, Lifespan attaches a list of all *other related components* that are necessary to evaluate the problem and make the change. This information eliminates much work for the programmer who is making a change.

Because configuration management is critical to the success of a large software system, many other configuration management data base systems are being developed and used, both at educational institutions and at large corporations interested in holding down the cost of software maintenance.

10.5

RESOURCE TRACKING AND SIMULATION EXAMPLE

Throughout this text, we have followed the development of the Weaver Farm system. We have examined the system with an eye toward good development techniques. Now, let us reexamine the system in terms of how easy or difficult it may be to maintain.

Since it simulates the activities on Weaver Farm, it is clear that the Weaver Farm system includes a model of its real-world environment. It cannot be an S-system; the model represents an abstraction of the problem to be solved. If the model never changes, then we can consider Weaver Farm's system to be a P-system. However, as the system is used, more understanding is gained about the interrelationships of the soil, water, air, physical structures, and traffic patterns. It is likely that the director of Weaver Farm will want to alter the model so that it more closely resembles the reality it mimics. Thus, the Weaver Farm system is an E-system, embedded in a reality that is undergoing continual change.

As with all E-systems, we can expect maintenance costs to be high. However, the use of good software engineering techniques in the original development may defray some of the potential costs. Because the major subsystems of the Weaver Farm system are so different, it may be suitable to assign specialties to the programmers working on maintenance. Complete, up-to-date, and well-written documentation will make the system easier for the maintenance team to understand. Modularization and the use of highly cohesive modules related with low coupling will make the isolation of the source of an error relatively easy.

Let us examine two examples to see how design decisions made during development will affect maintenance. First, suppose the director of Weaver Farm had assured analysts that the number of acres of Weaver Farm would remain the same. Consequently, the system was designed with a fixed number of cells (where each cell represents a 100-square-foot region of the Farm). However, after system delivery, a philanthropist donates an additional seven thousand acres to the Farm. To support this gift, the maintenance team must change the data base design and code.

Since the data base is critical to almost every system function, the entire system must undergo regression testing.

Second, suppose the director of the Farm wants to create and display maps and graphs on the system. The original system was not designed to perform graphics. The maintenance team must first investigate whether the terminal screens can display graphics. Then the team must design a graphics function: determine requirements, develop a system design, create a program design, and implement the code. To preserve the quality of the overall system, the design of the graphics function should be consistent with the design principles of the original system. Testing the graphics functions may involve regression testing to insure that existing system functions have not been affected adversely.

In addition to design considerations, control of change will be an issue for the Weaver Farm system, since problems may be reported simultaneously involving different subsystems. Users accessing the resource data base to produce a facility maintenance schedule will be different from users needing the same data base to graph or simulate activity in the recreation area. It is easy to see that unless changes are controlled, the data base may be corrupted and the functions that rely on them severely degraded.

10.6
CHAPTER SUMMARY

This chapter has examined the activities involved in maintaining a system after it is operational. Although many software engineering techniques concentrate on initial development, most of the resources of software engineers are devoted to maintaining systems. This high degree of maintenance is a result of the very nature of the systems we develop; more P- and E-systems result from our efforts than do S-systems. In addition to the changing nature of the systems we build, we must decide whether it is better to fix an aging system or to build a new one.

We have seen that maintenance involves four distinct types of activities: *correction* of errors, *adaptation* to other changes, *perfection* of acceptable functions, and *prevention* of future errors. The nature of the maintenance determines the kind of work we do to modify the system. Correction requires much time to study how the system works now, while enhancement may require more time in designing new modules than in working with existing ones.

Many factors contribute to the problems associated with maintenance. Management issues make it difficult for the maintenance team to balance user and customer needs with technical and professional expertise. A morale problem among maintenance programmers compounds the problem, even though maintenance programming often requires more skill and insight than development work. Thus, the maintenance team is constantly compromising and working with limited goals, limited resources, and limited understanding.

All these factors combine to yield a large maintenance cost. Not only are more physical and human resources often required to handle a problem, but the resources must be available over the lifespan of the system—often five times as long as the development life.

Efforts are being made to develop automated techniques and tools to aid the maintenance team. Configuration management plays a big part in addressing the control and management difficulties associated with maintenance. Other development and maintenance tools contribute to the increased efficiency of the maintenance team. As software engineers continue their investigation of the system's life cycle, productivity will be increased and costs will be reduced on two fronts. First, software engineering techniques used during the development of a system will make the system easier to understand and maintain once it is operational. Second, configuration management tools will automate the enormous task of always knowing the status of every component of a system and thus controlling changes to it.

10.7

EXERCISES

1. Categorize the following systems as S-, P- or E-systems. For each one, explain why it belongs in that category. Identify those aspects of the system that may change.

   a. An air traffic control system

   b. An operating system for a microcomputer

   c. A floating point acceleration system

   d. A data base management system

   e. A system to find the prime factors of a number

   f. A system to find the first prime number larger than a given number

2. Explain why a high degree of coupling among modules can make maintenance very difficult.

3. Explain why the success of the maintenance of a system depends heavily on the quality of the documentation generated during the system life cycle.

4. Some computer science classes involve the building of a term or semester project that begins as a small system and is continually enhanced until the result is complete. If you have worked on such a project, review your notes. How much time was spent defining and understanding the problem? How much time was spent implementing the code? Compare the categories of Table 10.2 with the time estimates for your project and comment on whether the differences are good or bad.

5. Explain why maintenance programming may be more challenging than development. Why must a maintenance programmer have good "people skills"? What are other desirable characteristics of a maintenance programmer?

6. Examine a large program from one of your class projects. How must you add to the documentation so that someone else can maintain it? Discuss the pros and cons of writing this supplementary documentation as the program is developed.

7. Borrow a copy of a large program (more than 1,000 lines of code) from a friend. Try to choose a program with which you are not at all familiar. How useful is the documentation? Compare the code with the documentation; how accurate is the documentation? If you were assigned to maintain this program, what additional documentation would you like to see? How does the size of the program affect your ability to maintain it?

8. As with the previous problem, examine a friend's program. Suppose you want to make a change to the code, and you must perform regression testing on the result to ensure that the program still runs properly. Are test data and a test script available for your use? Discuss the need for retaining formal test data sets and scripts for maintenance purposes.

9. Explain why low coupling of system modules helps to prevent problems when changes are made simultaneously during maintenance.

10. Explain why single entry, single exit modules make testing easier during maintenance.

11. The following is a list of the version and configuration control functional criteria for configuration management tools for a British agency. Explain how each factor contributes to the ease of maintenance.

   a. Record versions or references to them.
   b. Retrieve any version on demand.
   c. Record relationships.
   d. Record relationships between versions to which the tool controls access and those to which it does not.
   e. Control security and record authorizations.
   f. Record changes to a file.
   g. Record the status of a version.
   h. Assist in the configuring of a version.
   i. Relate to a project control tool.
   j. Produce reports.
   k. Control releases.
   l. Control itself.
   m. Archive and retrieve infrequently used files.

CHAPTER 11

WHAT CAN GO WRONG

As software engineers, we build systems to help people solve problems. We have a variety of skills:

- Interviewing customers and users to determine their needs
- Designing a solution to solve a perceived problem
- Specifying algorithms and data structures to implement a solution
- Writing and testing code that implements a design
- Integrating code modules into a working system
- Writing documents to describe a system
- Training users and operators to work with a system
- Modifying and enhancing a system as necessary or desirable

We learn about people and their styles, about computers and their characteristics, about languages and their use, and about analysis of problems and synthesis of solutions. We create techniques and tools and use them to improve the *quality* and *performance* of the systems we build and maintain. Our software engineering skills are often specialized and address a particular aspect of system development.

However, the activities of development follow one another in an orderly fashion only when what we say is what we mean and when people work with consistent and predictable speed, quality, and style. Unfortunately, this is an ideal situation; reality is quite different. As we have pointed out several times, it is often necessary to return to a stage of development and respecify, redesign, recode or retest because some aspect of the system has changed. We can think of the development process as repeating or iterating, as shown in Figure 11.1; we may return to a previous step and repeat it in whole or in part.

There are many reasons why development steps are repeated, and they can be understood by examining the ways in which a developer can fail to provide a customer with what is needed or wanted. This chapter discusses the realities of system development to see *why* things may not proceed as planned, *where* things can go wrong, and *what* we can do to correct them. We begin by examining our initial estimates of time, money and resources. Then we look at the problems inherent in building a system using a phased approach. Next, we see how requirements can change as the system is being constructed. Personnel preferences and the office environment contribute to the success of a project, too. Finally, we see that the backgrounds of users and operators should be considered in designing and developing training and documentation.

Figure 11.1   Repeating Development Steps

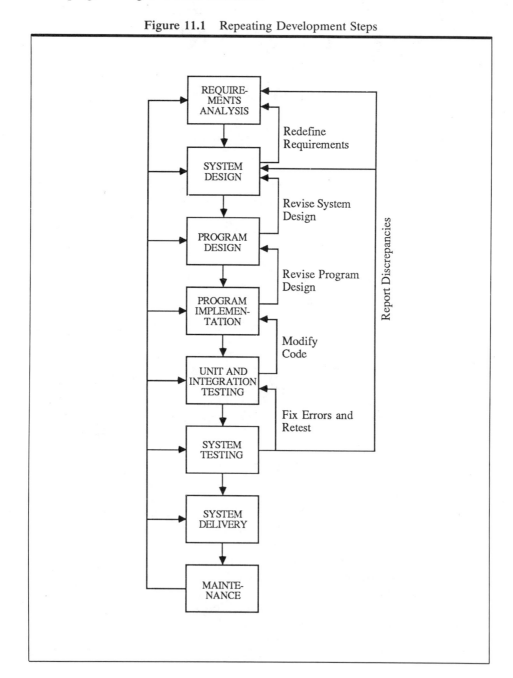

11.1

DIFFICULTIES OF ESTIMATION

The press is often reporting that large software systems are more expensive and have taken longer to build than originally anticipated. In chapter 1, we saw several examples of projects that overran their budgets and schedules. In chapter 2, we examined several techniques for estimating the effort required to build a system. There we saw that software engineers have not been very successful in developing accurate estimates. As software projects become larger and more expensive, customers are more concerned with the accuracy of estimates. Consequently, we have been reexamining our estimating techniques in an effort to make them more accurate and reliable. In this section, we look at the aspects of estimation that may be creating difficulty.

When a customer commissions a developer to build a system, it is because a need exists that is not being met. Usually the sooner the system is available for use, the better. In addition, a customer often has a limited amount of money to pay for the system. For these reasons, a customer is concerned with the cost and schedule of development in initial discussions about the system.

Estimation Before System Design

If you are negotiating with a contractor for the construction of a new roof on your house, you have every right to ask for a written estimate of time and expenses. Indeed, it might be foolish to agree to such a project without having some idea of what it will cost and how long it will take. Similarly, defining a schedule and setting a price for a project before the system is actually built are not unreasonable customer expectations. If a developer is unsure of an exact price, a customer may agree to pay a fixed base price plus actual expenses. (This agreement is known as a *cost plus fixed fee* contract.) However, even if a customer is willing to open the corporate pocketbook in this manner, delays in the project schedule can lead to customer dissatisfaction.

There are several obvious problems in trying to estimate the required human and machine resources and schedule for a project before the project has even begun. First, without having worked with the customer to determine the exact requirements of the system, it seems unreasonable to try to estimate a characteristic such as the number of lines of code. Second, even if that estimate could be made, some lines of code cost more per line than others. For example, a straightforward sort routine may have the same number of lines of code as a fast Fourier transform algorithm, but the design and test of the first may take much less time than the second; consequently, the lines of code for the sort are less expensive than those for the Fourier transform.

In addition to difficulties in estimating size and complexity, it may be impossible for the developer and customer to anticipate changes during the development cycle in the following areas:

1. System requirements
2. Available hardware and software
3. Available hardware and software support
4. Available personnel with the needed skill and expertise

There may be problems with design and implementation that cannot be antici- pated. For example, the design of a system may seem acceptable to all who review it, but the testing stage of development may show that the system does not perform as fast as is required. Implementing the consequent new design may require a great deal of additional time and effort and possibly a new set of hardware and software.

Even though the idea of making an initial estimate with any reasonable degree of accuracy may seem impossible to you, we must do something to address the problem. Our estimating techniques in the past have been so inadequate that we must try to develop new ones that, poor as they may be, are closer to the actual usage of people and equipment. If we can estimate with an acceptable level of confidence, then we have at least a range in which we think the actual number will fall.

The Way We Estimate

One problem with our estimates is the way we think about them. If your professor asks you to estimate how long it will take you to code and test a particular program, you may answer "ten hours." What you really mean is that if conditions are optimal (that is, if you have access to the computer when you want it and if you make no major mistakes), then you can probably finish in ten hours. In other words, the probability of the work's actually taking less than ten hours is nil, and the probability of its taking more than ten hours is high.

However, a value is an **estimate** if the probability of its being higher than the actual result is the same as the probability of its being lower. In Figure 11.2, the dashed line separating area A from area B represents the estimate. The dotted line represents the minimum value, which we sometimes mistakenly call an estimate. By "estimating" with minimum values, we build a schedule that has no tolerance for mistakes or unusual circumstances.

Since conditions are rarely optimal, we sometimes amend our usual way of estimating (that is, of suggesting minimum values rather than true estimates). Having learned from experience, we may pad our initial "estimate" with extra hours to allow for unanticipated events. However, the way in which we pad is often based on intuition, not on an analysis of likely events. Thus, deriving "estimates" in this way usually results in a schedule that is almost impossible to meet. More- over, when we are estimating our own work, we are more likely to *underestimate* than when we are estimating someone else's.

Models and Metrics

Clearly, a more objective method for estimating is needed. One way to approach estimation is to model the system and somehow *measure* what and how it performs.

A **metric** is a measurable characteristic of a system. Thus, we would like our system model to include metrics to indicate characteristics that help estimate human and machine resource requirements. Perhaps by looking at past experience in combination with projected characteristics of a system, we can make a more accurate estimate.

This is not a new or unusual concept. When a building contractor is asked to estimate how much it will cost to construct a new office building, the contractor's estimator evaluates a variety of characteristics of the building: number of square feet of floor space, windows, plumbing, wiring, and so on. Approximate amounts of materials are calculated using published guidelines that are based on the experiences of contractors in building other projects. The estimator can calculate cost and schedule with a reasonable degree of accuracy. In the same way, we would like to isolate the characteristics of a system that play a major role in determining the cost or schedule. Then we want to use metrics to indicate the magnitude of these characteristics.

Every metric measures the *result* of something or *predicts* something that will happen. For example, we saw in the chapters on testing that we can measure the number of seeded errors found during testing. Not only is this an absolute measurement, but it also predicts how many errors are left to be found in the system.

Establishing metrics ultimately gives us control over the development process. Measurement of several characteristics may tell us how fast we are progressing, in terms of how much of the system is complete. If requirements or resources change during the life cycle, having metrics in place can help to reestimate and repredict the developer's new resource requirements.

In 1974, Weinberg and Schulman ([WEI74]) demonstrated that when metrics are available, people can use them to measure progress against a single goal. Five different development teams were given the same assignment with different but measurable goals. The result of each team's efforts was a system with the team's goal optimized. Since most projects do not have built-in metrics but are measured solely against a schedule, it is logical to assume that most development teams work against the clock, rather than toward a measurable quality goal. Thus, in addition

Figure 11.2   The Difference Between a Minimum and an Estimate

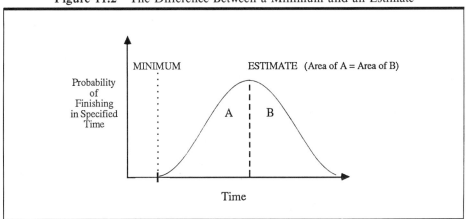

to allowing members of the development team to measure their adherence to a schedule, metrics can be used to help the development team build the required *quality* into a new system.

To develop metrics for a system, we must *model* the system and describe the way the metrics correspond to each other and to the system as a whole. The model tells us how the system will change if one or more parts do. The information from the model shows us how to interpret a change in a metric; if the value of a metric increases, we see how the system as a whole is affected, and we know how to revise our estimates of resources needed.

We begin modelling a system by examining its requirements. Recall that a system has both functional and nonfunctional requirements. The functional requirements describe what the system does, and the nonfunctional the way the system does them. Thus, a system can be thought of as a collection of interacting functions, where a *function* is a transformation of some kind of input to some kind of output. We can model the system by describing it in terms of these functional components.

For instance, we can define a model of Weaver Farm in terms of its major functional components: the simulation function, the data base management function, the reporting function, and so on. Because each major function is complex, we can break major functions into a collection of smaller ones and model the relationships among them. The data base management function is composed of a data retrieval function, a data storage function, an inquiry function, a sorting function, and others. A model describes how the functions are related to one another. The model is presented as a series of equations that relate the functions to each other. For example, an equation such as

$$I = aR + bS$$

may exhibit the relationship among the data retrieval function (R), the data storage function (S) and the inquiry function (I).

Using a functional system model, we can assign a value to each kind of function in the system. This value can be a measure of the difficulty or cost (in the sense of human and machine resource usage) of the function. Thus, a sorting function may have a lower value than a simulation function, because the sorting function requires less time to write and test. The equations of the model are combined with the functional estimates to generate a total amount of resources needed.

We use a model and its associated function metrics to evaluate the size and complexity of a system. Because we are modelling the functions that a system performs, the measures that we use tell us how much *functionality* the system contains. From the customer's point of view, the goal is to maximize the amount of functionality delivered for each dollar spent on the system. DeMarco ([DEM82]) calls the total amount of functionality delivered by a system the system *bang*, and he tries to maximize bang per buck.

We can track the schedule of development by identifying the amount of functionality or bang delivered at a given point in time. Estimating functionality informs *us* as well as our customers. We can track the amount of functionality developed as we build the system; if requirements or designs are modified, we can note which functions are affected and understand how the system's functionality as a whole has changed. This information gives us a basis on which to estimate changes to cost and schedule in the middle of development; it also tells us what resources we will need to address the changes.

Use of a Measurement Team

DeMarco suggests that one of the reasons we as software engineers are such poor estimators is that we do not get enough practice. He recommends the establishment of a *measurement team* or group whose sole purpose is to collect data about the system. The measurement group's first efforts are devoted to the study of other projects to establish standards for performance.

When the standards are established, the measurement team can distinguish a high-quality system from one of low quality. Suppose X is a characteristic of quality, such as reliability. The measurement team examines other systems and collects data on characteristics of the system that may be predictors of the value of X. By establishing correlations between these characteristics and X, the measurement team can estimate how long the project should take and what degree of confidence they have in their estimates. After the project has begun, the predictor characteristics can be measured again to see if the project is ahead of or behind schedule. With experience, the measurement team can be as proficient in estimating software projects as construction team estimators are in estimating the cost of building a physical structure.

11.2
DEALING WITH PHASED DEVELOPMENT

When you build a system for one of your classes, the development time is usually measured in terms of weeks. However, many development projects for large companies or government agencies measure the development time in *years*. On a project that takes such a long time to complete, a customer is not willing to wait several years to see the first results. Instead, the development is *phased*, and users begin working with the first phase of the system early in the development process.

As we have noted in previous chapters, phased development offers many advantages. It allows users and operators to become familiar with the system slowly, one function or level at a time. This gradual familiarization is especially useful when the new system is replacing an old one with which users and operators are very familiar; the phases allow a smooth, slow transition. In addition, a phased approach permits customer to begin to solve their problems as soon as possible, although a step at a time.

However, phased development adds complexity to the development process. Additional planning and tracking must be incorporated in development, and additional staff is needed.

Configuration Management

Phased development puts an extra burden on configuration management. Each requirement and design constraint must be tied to the phase in which it is implemented. As each development or test system becomes a production system, the configuration management staff knows exactly where changes have been made. Regression tests are designed and administered to insure that the functions and performance of one phase are not degraded with installation of the next phase.

Testing requires additional effort. Each phase needs its own test plan, test cases, and scripts; when errors are discovered, error correction activities are needed. Errors detected in one phase must be corrected before the next phase is installed. The test team works with the programmers and the configuration management team to locate the error and correct it; change any documentation to reflect the change; and alter any future test plans, data, or scripts that are affected by the error and its resultant change.

User Comfort

When a new system is an automated version of a manual one, users may feel uncomfortable with it. Although users may trust the new technology, underlying feelings of resentment or loss of control in allowing the computer to "make decisions" may prevent users from accepting and using the system effectively. For instance, users have been discovered checking the totals from a computer printout by adding them again on an adding machine or electronic calculator; the users were uncomfortable allowing the computer system to perform the calculations.

To lessen user discomfort, phases can be designed to present one automated function at a time. As users become comfortable with one function, the next one is introduced. Sometimes intermediate phases of development provide a manual backup or override for a function; skeptical users are assured that the old method is available if something goes wrong with the new one. This technique is especially helpful when users have been employing manual equipment for many years. Air traffic control, power plant operation, and telephone communication have been automated slowly so that users are not threatened by computer assistance. In some cases, a manual override still exists. In others, such as telephone switching, the function is completely automated now but was phased in while operators were retrained for a completely different activity.

11.3

CHANGING SCHEDULE

When a developer agrees to build a system, certain resources are devoted to development. People, facilities, and equipment are made available to the project for the amount of time estimated by the project schedule. If the schedule changes, the product may change, too. For example, the project programmers may be very familiar with the application and the implementation language. We saw in chapter 2 that this familiarity can speed the project schedule. Suppose the schedule for a one-year project is lengthened by six months (for reasons we will discuss below). The chief programmer may be committed to starting a new project and may not be able to stay on the initial one. If the chief programmer is replaced by a competent software engineer who is unfamiliar with the project and the language, the replacement will need time just to learn enough to take over. If the rest of the development team is then pushed to complete the project in haste, the resulting product may be short on documentation and may not be tested as thoroughly as it might otherwise have been.

Many things can affect the project schedule. The delays that follow have actually happened on large development efforts of which the author has been a part.

1. The computer was to be delivered mid-week, and the vendor reported that the computer had been placed on a truck and was on its way to the developer site. The day before the scheduled delivery, the vendor phoned to say that a higher-priority customer needed that type of computer, and the truck was redirected to the other customer. Another computer was delivered three months later, so the project schedule slipped by three months before the project had even begun.

2. The building in which cable was to be pulled was on the National Register of Historic Places. Permission to pull the cable was granted by the National Register, but the required paperwork took six weeks to produce.

3. A computer was delivered with a 5¼″ disk drive, but the system software was provided on 8″ disks. It took ten months for the vendor to acknowledge the error, resubmit the paperwork, and ship the software on the correct disks.

4. The customer was a government agency, and federal regulations required that the customer request proposals and prices for the equipment. Proposals were submitted and evaluated, and a vendor was chosen. The project proceeded: requirements were analyzed and systems were designed and configured for each of the twenty-three nodes in the network that was to be built. In the meantime, the government agency determined that the functionality of the vendor's equipment was not sufficient to meet the requirements of the project. The contract with the vendor was cancelled, and another contract was awarded to a new vendor. The first vendor's equipment used stand-alone functions, and the second used shared logic. This difference meant that the project's network design was no longer appropriate; the project team was forced to redesign the system and reconfigure each node.

Notice that all of the incidents described have two characteristics. First, they *could not be anticipated*. Second, each one *delayed the schedule significantly*. The lessons to be learned from such delays are that customers must be flexible enough to understand the delays, and developers must try to be thorough in their initial investigation of the constraints on a project before a schedule is defined.

11.4

CHANGING REQUIREMENTS

Customer requirements and their interpretation by a developer form the backbone of development. Every step of development is tied back to the requirements; indeed, the overall purpose of configuration management is maintaining the links from requirement to design module to code to test. Thus, a change in requirements after the initial stages of development can have a devastating impact on the success of the project. Because of the importance of requirements, both developer and customer must do whatever they can to insure that the initial requirements are correct and that future changes can be accommodated with as little impact as possible to the resulting system.

Prototyping

Prototyping is a popular method for generating and testing requirements. As we have seen earlier, a developer can work with a customer to build a system that resembles or simulates the final product. This process allows the customer and developer to change the design or implementation before the final system is complete. Because the cost of a change increases drastically the further into development it is made, the best time to make a change is during requirements analysis; the next best is during design.

There are many automated tools available to help the developer build a prototype. For example, TOM Software's SpeedII allows stubs and drivers to be written quickly for some minor system functions, so that options for major functions can be explored.

However, developing a prototype for a large and complex system can become a project in itself. The developer may not be able to have a prototype ready very early in development. Even automated tools do not always help when a system is based on a new concept or technique. Constructing a prototype can require almost as many human and nonhuman resources as the actual system, and the customer may not want to pay for a prototype. Thus, the use of prototyping must be weighed against the project cost and schedule requirements. Although time may be saved by identifying system changes earlier than with standard development, this time difference may be less than the time it takes to develop the prototype.

Communication Problems

Requirements sometimes change when misunderstandings exist among members of the development team or with the customer. Although precautionary measures such as reviews try to prevent such problems, sometimes faulty communication results in a misunderstanding.

Figure 11.3 illustrates the amount of communication involved in development. The arrows indicate the direction of communication, and a reverse arrow shows that information is passed in both directions. First, the customer (sometimes

Figure 11.3   Communication Required to Produce a System

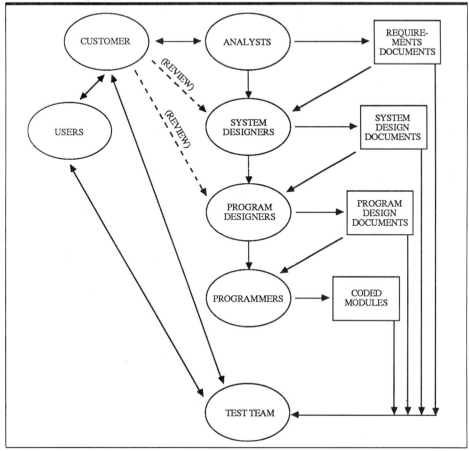

consulting with prospective users of the system) explains needs and desires to analysts. The result is documentation of the requirements. Then, the designers produce a system design based on their understanding of the customer's problem, and the customer reviews the design. Similarly, the program designers write a program design that is subject to the customer's review. The programmers implement the design and give the modules of code to the test team for testing. In the later stages of testing, users work with the test team to discover errors. If requirements change for any reason, more communication is needed, and the number of arrows in the diagram increases.

The success of the project, dependent on successful communication of ideas, rests on the interaction represented by the arrows of Figure 11.3. If communication fails at any point, a change in requirements may be needed. Developers and customers can work to avoid these mishaps by understanding the factors that promote effective communication. As we have seen in previous chapters, effective communication depends on many things: work style, experience, expertise, personal preference, organizational dynamics, and others.

Technological Change

Advances in technology are always viewed positively, and technology has been advancing at incredible speed in the last decade. However, technological change can negate some of the positive aspects of development. When the development schedule spans a year or more, the resulting system may be technologically out of date before it is even complete.

Some development projects try to avoid this situation by using design or program modules that are as *independent* of each other and of the technology as possible. When hardware changes, only those modules that define the hardware interface need revision. Similarly, the system can be designed so that it is independent of the particular computer system on which it runs. For example, if a system is *portable* (i.e., can easily be moved from one computer system to another), then a newer and better computer does not threaten the existing system with obsolescence. One method for insuring the portability of a system is to code it in a *standard high-level language*, making no use of machine-specific features available on the chosen hardware. Of course, the drawback to this approach is that the special features may enhance the functionality or performance of the system or speed the project schedule (by using application generators, for example).

Even use of a standard language or interface is not always successful, since standards change periodically. Consider the number of versions of FORTRAN or COBOL or the number of incarnations of the UNIX operating system, and you will see that even standards are revised. Thus, developers sometimes try another approach: by using phased development and a flexible design, the developer can sometimes create a "living system," in the sense that a new phase can be designed and integrated with the existing phase. Techniques for creating such a system depend a great deal on successful configuration management. Because the problem of changing technology is a relatively new one, only time and research will show us the best routes to a flexible system design.

Vendor Promises

Automated systems depend in part on the proper functioning of computer hardware and software for their success. In addition to the basic computer, a system usually incorporates an operating system and special hardware and software. Thus, a developer must not only understand the functions and performance characteristics of these purchased items but also be sure that they work properly.

Many times, what the vendors promise is very different from what they deliver. For example, a vendor may promote a computer system with a feature that is under development but will be available when the project begins. Or, a vendor assures a developer that a particular product will interface with another or perform according to a specification or standard. However, when the project actually begins, sometimes the vendor's product is not ready for release or does not work as originally described. In some cases, the requirements cannot be implemented using the product actually available.

Problems often arise when a vendor claims that a compiler implements a standard or that code from one machine can be transferred directly to another. For example, when Digital Equipment Corporation announced its VAX line of computers, the company included a PDP-11 mode to allow users of the PDP computers to transfer assembler language applications to a VAX. However, the PDP-11 code must be modified somewhat before it will run successfully on a VAX.

Sometimes, the specifications in vendor documentation do not match the performance of the hardware or software being described. The author worked on a networking project where a communications controller was being supplied by a separate company. The system and program designs were based on the descriptions contained in the documentation, but the actual device was not available until the testing stage. After all programs had been coded and testing had begun, it was discovered that the controller did not function the way the documentation had described. The project team revised requirements, redesigned, and redeveloped the system. The delays caused by the poorly documented controller added eight months to the project schedule.

Holding the vendor accountable may be the obvious remedy, but that may not always help the project. If the vendor cannot deliver a product that performs as needed, the project schedule may be set back for months while a new approach is taken by the developer. Sometimes, to save time and effort, the customer rather than the vendor will agree to change the requirements. Although this change is not always the most logical solution, it is often the most expedient one.

11.5

PERSONNEL PROBLEMS

A major consideration in building a system is the number and kinds of people working on it. The interaction among project personnel can impede the schedule or can cause unanticipated results. Let us see what factors are involved.

Difficulties of Peer Review

As we saw in previous chapters, peer review plays an important role in finding errors as early as possible in development. Both customer and developer review the requirements documents to insure that what the customer wants is what the developer intends to build. Next, the system design is reviewed by the developer and then with the customer to make sure that everyone understands the proposed solution to the problem. When the program design is complete, it is reviewed by members of the developer's staff for completeness, consistency, and other characteristics of good design. Similarly, the programs themselves are reviewed by the programmer's peers to guarantee that the design has been implemented properly and according to good programming principles.

The success of peer review has been verified by much research. However, a problem remains. No matter how often we assure ourselves that peer review criticizes the *product* of our work, rather than ourselves *personally*, it is still very difficult to divorce personal feelings from professional criticism. You may unintentionally allow your feelings and sensitivities to disrupt a peer review.

Another problem with peer review is its attempt to be objective. When outside professionals are invited to a review, it is often very difficult for them to understand enough of the system characteristics to be able to give any beneficial advice. For example, if you are invited to review another programmer's code, you may not be able to understand the intricacies of a particular algorithm or its importance to the entire module or system without having been involved in the processes that led to the program design. Well-qualified reviewers are professionals who have followed the development from the beginning. However, in doing so, they may lose their objectivity. Thus, inviting reviewers involves a decision weighing objectivity against understanding.

A final difficulty with peer review is its need for strong management support. Managers are concerned about the project schedule and the need to deliver the final product on time. Sometimes, they do not like to devote time to peer reviews because they see no tangible results. However, support for a policy of peer reviews throughout the life of the project should be made clear at the beginning of the project. Examples from professional literature confirm that the use of peer reviews can actually shorten development time by catching errors early in the process. If your managers are skeptical, you can present them with the examples we studied in previous chapters.

Inflexible Work Styles

We saw in chapter 2 that workers have different work styles, depending on whether they base their decisions on intuition or logic and on whether they prefer to gather or give information. Each style has its advantages and disadvantages, and no one style is better than another. However, work styles can lead to problems when a worker having one style has difficulty interacting with a worker of another style.

This inflexibility in dealing with others can impede the development process. Consequently, members of a team must understand how and why other members make their decisions. Otherwise, discussions become defensive, and decisions are the result of wearing each other down, rather than of reason and logic.

Peer Preferences

Just as you have a preferred work style, you also prefer some types of work to others. Some project team members like to perform testing, while others would rather write programs. While you may look forward to meetings and interaction with other people, others may prefer to work alone and uninterrupted. These preferences must be considered when assigning people to jobs on the project team. Often a disregard for preferences leads to inefficient use of human resources. For example, a highly skilled programmer is sometimes rewarded with promotion to the managerial ranks. While the employee as programmer was superb at working alone and unsupervised, the employee as manager is now uncomfortable having to direct peers and being scrutinized by the managers above. What was a stellar programmer is now a mediocre manager, and the project suffers.

The Learning Curve

The variation in backgrounds of employees is frequently overlooked but can have an impact on the success of a project. Some members of the team come to the project with experience on similar or related projects. Other members are highly skilled but unfamiliar with the particular characteristics of this project. Still others must join the project well after its beginning (when, for example, one member of the team leaves the project); these employees cannot be expected to work immediately at the same level as those who have been involved with the project for a long time. Time must be allowed for building confidence and respect and for understanding the work styles of others.

Each team member has an individual "learning curve"; that is, the team members take varying amounts of time to learn about the different aspects of the system and feel comfortable in performing their jobs. A project schedule must take into account these learning curves. Often those projecting a schedule assume the best conditions: complete familiarity with the project and a high degree of expertise in the required skills. The reality of the situation is usually quite different. For example, a large project often has a host of new programmers working on it. The program designer may be a proficient programmer who has just been moved to the program design team. The head of the test team may leave the company in the middle of testing.

Such considerations do not imply that the schedule should predict the worst in every case. However, some flexibility should be built into the schedule and made clear to the customer; otherwise, the project may become driven by the schedule and suffer a resulting decrease in quality.

11.6

PRODUCTIVITY

The most expensive part of a project's development cost can be the cost of the people who are doing the development. Thus, increasing productivity can save a great deal of money. We have seen previously that individual productivity can vary, depending on experience, education, work style, and other factors. Many factors cannot be changed easily, if at all. However, there have been some attempts to improve productivity not by changing the people working on the project but by changing the environment in which they work.

Use of Automated Tools

Much attention has been paid to the use of automated tools to help developers be more productive. As we have mentioned in earlier chapters, tools are available to perform many functions. For example, there are tools to

1. Track and check requirements
2. Track and cross-reference data definitions and relationships
3. Draw and manipulate design diagrams
4. Input design specifications
5. Check for certain design characteristics
6. Generate applications automatically
7. Check code for syntax and structure
8. Track updates to requirements, design, code and documentation

These tools require additional effort to learn and use. Often they also require additional software and hardware resources. However, by using them, the development team can hope to avoid making mistakes that might otherwise have cost a great deal of time later in development. For example, chapter 2's COCOMO example using Before You Leap showed us that the Weaver Farm Project can be completed faster and with fewer people by using automated tools and good software engineering techniques.

Office Environment

Most development takes place in an office, but the working conditions for the development team are often overlooked as a way to improve the productivity of the development team. As a student, you are probably familiar with working in an unsatisfactory office environment. You may have worked on a class project where your development schedule slipped because you had to wait for an available terminal or because the computer was down. You may have tried to write a program from a dormitory room or student office shared with several other people; visitors and telephones cause distractions that make it difficult for you to concentrate. As we saw in chapter 7, the size of the *work space*, the *noise* level in the office, and the number and kind of *interruptions* can affect the quantity and quality of work that is done. Productivity tools and advanced methods are useless in a noisy, crowded office with inadequate access to computer resources.

The relationship between management and staff also affects the quality of work produced. Managers have to act as buffers between the developers and the customer. This relationship allows designers, programmers, and testers to concentrate on the system rather than the schedule, the budget, or the political and logistical problems relating to the project.

Members of the development team should be free to do what they do best. Unfortunately, this freedom does not always exist. In many organizations, technically proficient employees are promoted to managerial positions. However, as noted earlier, technical excellence does not always indicate capability or interest in management. If a manager is more interested in technical problems than managerial ones, the distinction between the technical and managerial aspects of the project becomes blurred. Soon, all members of the project team are involved in all aspects of the project, not just the ones for which they are most capable or in which they have the most interest. This involvement can slow the project or distract the developers.

11.7

THE CONTEXT OF TRAINING

Training users and operators is difficult, because the training addresses the *context* in which it is done as well as the system for which the user or operator is being trained. You approach the system with a background from which to judge and use it. Thus, you interpret the words and ideas of a trainer and training materials in terms of your individual experience and expertise.

In this sense, we can view understanding an automated system as the combination of many things, each of which affects the others. As shown in Figure 11.4, you begin with the software itself and add to it the information obtained by reading the official system documentation. However, there is also a great deal of unofficial documentation: notes from a class or demonstration, memoranda about tips and shortcuts, jottings in the margin of official papers, and other user-generated aids to help explain how the system works.

Figure 11.4 The Context of Training

ORGANIZATIONAL CONTEXT

EXPERIENCE

UNOFFICIAL TRAINING

CLASSROOM TRAINING

UNOFFICIAL DOCUMENTATION

OFFICIAL DOCUMENTATION

SOFTWARE

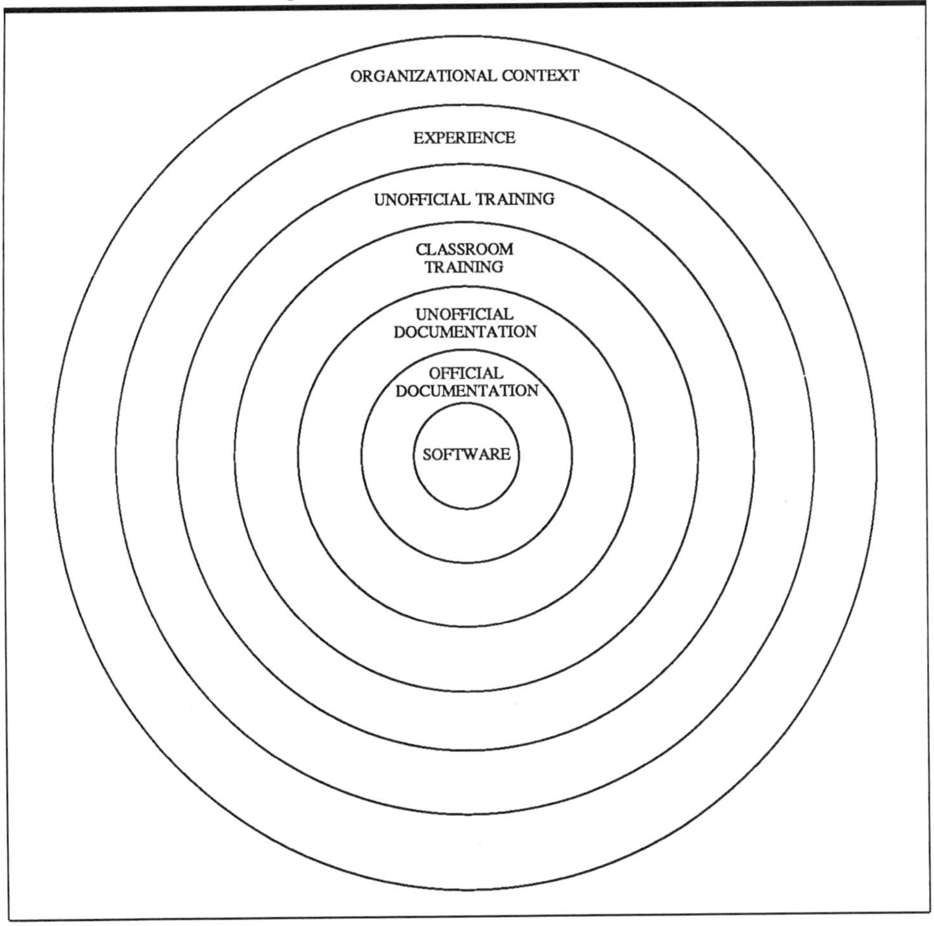

Added to this documentation is classroom training or participation in demonstrations and tutorials. Here, too, official training is accompanied by unofficial training: hints from other users, tips picked up by watching someone else use the system, and shortcuts discovered by experimenting with undocumented operations.

Next, your background works in combination with training, documentation, and the organization in which you work to give you a personalized view of the system, how it functions, and how it fits in with the way in which your job is performed.

The way in which a system is *intended* to be understood can differ drastically from the way in which *you* understand it if additional influential factors color your perception. Trainers must tailor training and documentation to the abilities and backgrounds of those being trained. For example, training for users with no computer experience will be very different from that for users with extensive computer experience. Likewise, documents written for operators with a college education should be more advanced than documents for operators with a high-school reading level. If the audience for training is ignored, training can be counterproductive.

An actual example can be helpful. On an office automation project, the trainers assumed that all users would be secretaries. The training classes and materials included many large passages that were to be typed and then worked with on the screen. However, many technical employees requested word processing training; they wanted to prepare their long reports online instead of writing them with pen and paper for a secretary to type. The technical employees were scheduled to take the same course as secretaries, and both types of employees were mixed within a class.

The training courses were a disaster. The technical employees could not type fast, and so they tended not to do the exercises. Thus, they learned little from the class. In addition, they were embarrassed about their inability to type; after class, they tended to avoid the secretaries with whom they had taken the class. Needless to say, very few of the technical employees used the automated system. At the same time, the secretaries were hesitant to make mistakes or ask silly questions in front of the technical employees. The secretaries tended to be quiet and not ask for help during class. Thus, the secretaries also did not learn as much in class as they could have. The solution was a complete redesign of the training classes. One class was created for typists and another for non-typists.

11.8
KEEPING DOCUMENTION UP-TO-DATE

Traditionally, a major emphasis in software development projects has been adherence to schedule; the developers may curtail the documentation effort in order to deliver the system on time. In this case, much of the documentation is written *after* the system is already in place at the customer site. If documentation is not explicitly required, it may even be abandoned.

However, previous chapters have pointed out many instances where documentation is the mortar binding one stage of the project to others. For example, the program design documents are the basis from which the coded modules are written. Similarly, the test team develops test plans and scripts from user manuals and system requirements documents. A mistake or omission can affect not only the quality of the final product but also the development schedule.

Thus, documentation must be written throughout development and should always be kept up-to-date. This is easier said than done. Programmers are notorious for coding first and documenting later, especially when being pressured to adhere to a schedule. On a large software development project with a great deal of communication among the members of the development team, it is impossible for documentation to wait.

11.9

CHAPTER SUMMARY

This chapter has explored the realities of system development. Although great pains are taken to estimate and plan a project, to track its progress, and control the course of development, there are always problems that arise unexpectedly. By knowing what some of these problems are, we may be able to anticipate and avoid them. At the very least, we will know that we are not the first developers beset by a particular problem.

No matter where customer needs originate, we as software engineers have not been very good at estimating how long it will take to build a system to meet those needs. One of the stumbling blocks has been the way in which we estimate. Unless we take estimation seriously and devote resources to it just as we do to the other facets of development, we will not improve our estimates. Models and metrics are needed to predict and track the progress of a project; then a measurement team should be designated to make estimates and perfect their estimating skills.

Phased development, while easing some problems (such as user comfort with the system), can add others. Increased configuration management is the most visible and critical aspect of phased development, and the controls needed to move from one phase to the next must be put in place at the very beginning of the life cycle.

Ideally, requirements are discussed and documented at the beginning of a project, and the goal of development is to build a system to meet those requirements. However, long or complex projects may involve requirements that change as development progresses. Prototyping can help to identify requirements early, but building the prototype may take a great deal of time. Communication problems among staff and with the customer can contribute to misunderstanding and may result in the need to revise requirements.

When building a system over a long period of time, the technology can change and make the system out of date. Thus, the customer may insist on using new technology to build the system. Or, a new product may not perform as described by the vendor. The discrepancy can result in redefining requirements, redesigning the system, or rewriting code.

No matter how automated or technologically impressive the system development process becomes, it is still based on the contributions of the people involved in the development. Personnel problems may seem irrelevant but do make a great difference in the timeliness and quality of the final product. To many, the peer review process is uncomfortable. Add to peer interaction the inflexibility of many people when dealing with those of different work styles, and problems are compounded. We must also realize that users, developers, and trainers bring to the system their own context for understanding and using it.

Finally, we noted that documentation is the glue that binds together the stages of development. Unless documentation is kept up-to-date and is written to address its intended audience, it can slow or stop communication and lead to errors in the resulting system.

11.10

EPILOG

Software engineering is exciting. Its technological component challenges us to use the most current tools and techniques to help our customers solve their problems. Its human component challenges us to understand the people behind the procedures and to build systems that increase user comfort as well as capability. The methods and guidelines presented in this text form software engineering's foundation. However, ongoing research yields new methods and techniques, making software engineering a growing, changing field.

As a software engineer, you can look forward to using your skills to help others solve problems. In addition, you will be evaluating projects—yours and others—to determine their success or failure. You will continue research into questions whose answers will make us better software engineers:

1. What characteristics of a system make it difficult to develop?
2. What characteristics can we measure to help us in estimating the cost and schedule of a project?
3. How can we automate requirements specification to lead to more successful system design?
4. How can we build more flexible systems?
5. How can we use artificial intelligence in designing and developing systems?
6. For systems that have already been built, how can they be modified or structured to make maintenance easier?

In general, you will examine new developments in computer science and try to apply them to the software engineering problems you encounter. Thus, as a software engineer, you must be an expert in understanding *technology*, *people*, and *change*.

11.11

EXERCISES

1. The director of a software development project is working with the system designers to design a module that will sort a very large list. The director asks designers Tom, Barbie, Ethel, and Don to choose an appropriate sorting algorithm. Tom is concerned about the project schedule and suggests the first algorithm that comes to mind. Barbie can't make up her mind because she is still researching to find out what all the possible sorting algorithms are. Ethel is afraid to choose one algorithm for fear that the choice will displease other members of the design team. Don suggests an algorithm that he has used before and likes. Explain how the designers' choices reflect their work styles. With such a variety of work styles on one team, explain how work style inflexibility may lead to a less-than-successful design.

2. Consider a term project that you have developed for one of your classes. It is likely that you were provided with a set of requirements by your professor at the beginning of the term or semester, and development of the project progressed as the course went on. Review the requirements and rate them in terms of their criticality to the project. Then, describe the probable impact on the project schedule and total effort if each requirement had been changed a week after you received the assignment; two weeks after; five weeks after. Could your design have been changed to help avoid the problems generated by changing requirements?

3. As a student, the place in which you do your program design and development is likely not to be a quiet, private office. List the distractions in the place where you work. Then estimate the time taken by each distraction (e.g., average time for phone call) and the time required to recover from the distraction and be fully productive again. Total all estimates and calculate how much of the time you spend working on programs is fully productive. What can you do in terms of distractions to improve your productivity?

4. Your professor has asked you to write a program to translate ASCII characters to EBCDIC. Estimate how long it will take you to write such a program. Explain how your estimate will change if:

   a. You must write it in a language you do not yet know

   b. You must write it on a computer with which you are not familiar

   c. You use no software tools

   d. You must use a software tool with which you are not familiar

   e. You do not know what ASCII and EBCDIC are.

REFERENCES

[ALF77] M. Alford, "A Requirements Engineering Methodology for Real-Time Processing Requirements," *IEEE Transactions on Software Engineering*, SE-3(1) (January 1977): 60–69.

[ALF85] M. Alford, "SREM at the Age of Eight; The Distributed Computing Design System," *IEEE Computer*, 18(4) (April 1985): 36–46.

[BAI64] E. Bairdain, "Research Studies of Programmers and Programming," unpublished study, (New York) 1964.

[BAC69] C. W. Bachman, "Data Structure Diagrams," *Data Base—The Quarterly Newsletter of SIGBDP*, 1(2) (Summer 1969).

[BAK72] F. T. Baker, "Chief Programmer Team Management of Production Programming," *IBM Systems Journal*, 11(1) 1972.

[BAL81] R. Balzer, *Gist Final Report*, Information Sciences Institute, University of Southern California, (February 1981).

[BAR84] D. W. Barron and J. M. Bishop, *Advanced Programming*, John Wiley and Sons, (New York) 1984.

[BEL71] L. A. Belady and M. M. Lehman, "Programming System Dynamics or the Metadynamics of Systems in Maintenance and Growth," *IBM Research Report*, RC 3546, (September 1971).

[BEL72] L. A. Belady and M. M. Lehman, "An Introduction to Growth Dynamics," in W. Freiberger (ed.), *Statistical Computer Performance Evaluation*, Academic Press, 1972.

[BEN86] J. Bentley, *Programming Pearls*, Addison-Wesley, (Reading, Massachusetts) 1986.

[BOE78] B. W. Boehm, *Characteristics of Software Quality*, Elsevier North-Holland, (New York) 1978.

[BOE81] B. W. Boehm, *Software Engineering Economics*, Prentice-Hall, (Englewood Cliffs, New Jersey) 1981.

[BOE84] B. W. Boehm, T. E. Gray and T. Seewaldt, "Prototyping Versus Specifying: A Multi-project Experiment," *IEEE Transactions on Software Engineering*, SE-10(3) (March 1984).

[BOH66] C. Bohm and G. Jacopini, "Flow Diagrams, Turing Machines and Languages with Only Two Formation Rules," *Communications of the ACM*, 9(5) (May 1966).

[BRA85] G. Bray and D. Pokress, *Understanding Ada*, John Wiley and Sons, (New York) 1985.

[BRO75] F. P. Brooks, Jr., *The Mythical Man-Month*, Addison-Wesley, (Reading, Massachusetts) 1975.

[CAI75] S. H. Caine and E. K. Gordon, "PDL—A Tool for Software Design," *Proceedings of the National Computer Conference*, 1975.

431

[CAS80] P. M. Cashman and A. W. Holt, "A Communication-Oriented Approach to Structuring the Software Maintenance Environment," *ACM SIGSOFT Software Engineering Notes*, 5(1) (January 1980).

[CHA74] N. Chapin, "A New Format for Flowcharts," *Software—Practice and Experience*, 4(4) 1974.

[CLA81] J. Clapp, "Designing Software for Maintainability," *Computer Design*, (September 1981).

[CON84] J. Connell and L. Brice, "Rapid Prototyping," *Datamation*, 30(15) (August 1984).

[CUR79] W. Curtis et al., "Measuring the Psychological Complexity of Software Maintenance Tasks with the Halstead and McCabe Metrics," *IEEE Transactions on Software Engineering*, SE-5(3) (March 1979).

[DEM78] Thomas DeMarco, *Structured Analysis and System Specification*, Yourdon Press, (New York) 1978.

[DEM82] Thomas DeMarco, *Controlling Software Projects*, Yourdon Press, (New York) 1982.

[DEM85] T. DeMarco and T. Lister, "Programmer Performance and the Effects of the Workplace," *Proceedings of the Eighth International Conference on Software Engineering*, IEEE, (London) 1985.

[DIJ68] E. Dijkstra, "Go To Statement Considered Harmful," *Communications of the ACM*, 11(3) (March 1968).

[DOD77] Department of Defense, *Automated Data Systems Documentation Standards*, 13 (September 1977).

[ELM73] W. R. Elmendorf, "Cause-Effect Graphs in Functional Testing," *IBM Report*, TR-00.2487, IBM Systems Development Division, (Poughkeepsie, New York) 1973.

[ELM74] W. R. Elmendorf, "Functional Analysis Using Cause-Effect Graphs," *Proceedings of SHARE XLIII*, (New York) 1974.

[EST80] R. Esterling, "Software Manpower Costs: A Model," *Datamation*, (March 1980): 164–170.

[FAG76] M. Fagan, "Design and Code Inspections to Reduce Errors in Program Development," *IBM Systems Journal*, 15(3) 1976.

[FAI85] R. Fairley, *Software Engineering Concepts*, McGraw-Hill, (New York) 1985.

[FJE79] R. K. Fjeldstad and W. T. Hamlen, "Application Program Maintenance Study: Report to Our Respondents," *Proceedings of GUIDE 48*, (Philadelphia, Pennsylvania) 1979.

[FLO67] R. W. Floyd, "Assigning Meanings to Programs," in J. T. Schwartz, ed., *Mathematical Aspects of Computer Science*, American Mathematical Society, (Providence, Rhode Island) 1967.

[FRE75] P. Freeman, "Toward Improved Review of Software Designs," *Proceedings of the National Computer Conference*, 1975.

[FRI81] F. L. Friedman and E. B. Koffman, *Problem Solving and Structured Programming in FORTRAN*, Addison-Wesley, (Reading, Massachusetts) 1981.

[GAN79] C. Gane and T. Sarson, *Structured Systems Analysis: Tools and Techniques*, Prentice-Hall, (Englewood Cliffs, New Jersey) 1979.

[GRE76] T. Green et al., "Program Structures, Complexity and Error Characteristics," in *Computer Software Engineering, Polytechnic Press*, (New York) 1976.

[HIL67] F. S. Hillier and G. J. Lieberman, *Introduction to Operations Research*, Holden-Day, (San Francisco) 1967.

[HOA71] C. A. R. Hoare, "Quicksort," *Computer Journal*, 5(1) 1971.

[HUG78] Charles Hughes, C. P. Pfleeger and L. Rose, *Advanced Programming Techniques*, John Wiley and Sons, (New York) 1978.

[IBM74] IBM Corporation, *HIPO—A Design Aid and Documentation Technique*, GC 20-1851, IBM Corporation, (White Plains, New York) 1974.

[IEE83] IEEE, *Standard Glossary of Software Engineering Terminology*, IEEE Standard 729, 1983.

[IVI77] E. L. Ivie, "The Programmer's Workbench—A Machine for Software Development," *Communications of the ACM*, 20(10) (October 1977).

[JAC83] M. Jackson, *System Development*, Prentice-Hall, (Englewood Cliffs, New Jersey) 1983.

[JAC85] J. Jacky, "The 'Star Wars' Defense Won't Compute," *Atlantic Monthly*, (June 1985): 18–30.

[JOH78] D. Johnson, C. Kolberg, J. Sinnamon, "Programmable System for Software Configuration Management," *Proceedings of CompSAC 1978*, IEEE Computer Society, (Chicago) (November 1978).

[JON77] T. Capers Jones, "Programmer Quality and Programmer Productivity," *IBM Technical Report* TR-02.764 (January 1977).

[JOY85] E. J. Joyce, "The Art of Space Software," *Datamation*, (November 15, 1985): 30–34.

[JUN59] C. Jung, *The Basic Writing of C. G. Jung*, Modern Library, (New York) 1959.

[KAN85] R. Kannan, G. E. Hinton, A. Hisgen, R. S. Wallstein, Letter to the Editor, *Atlantic Monthly*, (September 1985): 4–8.

[KER76] B. W. Kernighan and P. J. Plauger, *Software Tools*, Addison-Wesley, (Reading, Massachusetts) 1976.

[KER78] B. W. Kernighan and P. J. Plauger, *The Elements of Programming Style*, McGraw-Hill, (New York) 1978.

[KLI84] R. Kling and S. Iacono, "The Control of Information Systems Developments After Implementation," *Communications of the ACM*, 27(12) (December 1984).

[KNU73] D. Knuth, *The Art of Computer Programming*, Volume 3: Sorting and Searching, Addison-Wesley, (Reading, Massachusetts) 1973.

[KUL85] D. Kull, "Designs on Development," *Computer Decisions*, 17(7) (April 9, 1985).

[LEH80] M. M. Lehman, "Programs, Life Cycles and Laws of Software Evolution," *Proceedings of the IEEE*, 68(9) (September 1980).

[LIE78] B. P. Lientz, E. B. Swanson, G. E. Tompkins, "Characteristics of Applications Software Maintenance," *Communications of the ACM*, 21(6) (June 1978).

[LIE80] B. P. Lientz and E. B. Swanson, *Software Maintenance Management*, Addison-Wesley, (Reading, Massachusetts) 1980.

[LIE81] B. P. Lientz and E. B. Swanson, "Problems in Application Software Maintenance," *Communications of the ACM*, 24(11) (November 1981).

[MAN83] William Manchester, *The Last Lion*, Little-Brown, (Boston) 1983.

[MCC76] T. McCabe, "A Software Complexity Measure," *IEEE Transactions on Software Engineering*, SE-2(12) (December 1976).

[MCC78] G. McCue, "Architectural Design for Program Development," *IBM Systems Journal*, 17(1) 1978.

[MCM84] S. McMenamin and J. F. Palmer, *Essential Systems Analysis*, Yourdon Press, (New York) 1984.

[MIL72] H. D. Mills, "On the Statistical Validation of Computer Programs", FSC-72-6015, IBM Federal Systems Division, (Gaithersburg, Maryland) 1972.

[MOD79] Modular Computer Systems, Inc., *MAX POWER PAC Product Description*, 1650 W. McNab Road, (Fort Lauderdale, Florida) 1979.

[MOR79] M. S. Moriconi, "A Designer/Verifier's Assistant," *IEEE Transactions on Software Engineering*, SE-5(4) (July 1979).

[MYE75] G. J. Myers, *Reliable Software Through Composite Design*, Petrocelli/Charter, (New York) 1975.

[MYE76] G. J. Myers, *Software Reliability*, John Wiley and Sons, (New York) 1976.

[MYE79] G. J. Myers, *The Art of Software Testing*, John Wiley and Sons, (New York) 1979.

[NAN64] B. Nanus and L. Farr, "Some Cost Contributors to Large-Scale Programs," *AFIPS Proceeding of the SJCC*, 25 (Spring 1964): 239–248.

[NAS73] I. Nassi and B. Shneiderman, "Flowchart Techniques for Structured Programming," *SIGPLAN Notices*, ACM (August 1973).

[NAT83] National Science Foundation, *The Process of Technological Innovation*, (Washington, D.C.) 1983.

[NAU66] P. Naur, "Proof of Algorithms by General Snapshots," *BIT*, 6(4) 1966.

[NOR63] P. V. Norden, "Useful Tools for Project Management," *Operations Research in Research and Development*, John Wiley and Sons, (New York) 1963.

[OVE71] R. K. Overton et al., *A Study of Fundamental Factors Underlying Software Maintenance Problems: Final Report*, Hanscom Air Force Base Report NTIS Numbers AD739479 and AD739872, 1971.

[PAR83a] G. Parikh and N. Zvegintzov, *Tutorial on Software Maintenance*, IEEE Computer Society, (Silver Spring, Maryland) 1983.

[PAR71] D. Parnas, "Information Distribution Aspects of Design Methodology," *IFIP Congress Proceedings*, (Ljubljana, Yugoslavia) 1971.

[PAR72] D. Parnas, "On Criteria to Be Used in Decomposing Systems into Modules," *Communications of the ACM*, 15(12) (December 1972).

[PAR79] D. Parnas, "Designing Software for Ease of Extension and Contraction," *IEEE Transactions on Software Engineering*, SE-5(2) (March 1979).

[PAR85] D. Parnas, "Software Aspects of Strategic Defense Systems," *Datamation*, 28 (12) (December 1985).

[PAR80] F. N. Parr, "An Alternative to the Rayleigh Curve Model for Software Development Effort," *IEEE Transactions on Software Engineering*, SE-6(3) (May 1980).

[PET73] W. W. Peterson, T. Kasami and N. Tokura, "On the Capabilities of While, Repeat and Exit Statements," *Communications of the ACM*, 16(2) (August 1973).

[PFL85] S. L. Pfleeger and D. W. Straight, *Introduction to Discrete Structures*, John Wiley and Sons, (New York) 1985.

[PUT78] L. Putnam, "A General Empirical Solution to the Macro Software Sizing and Estimation Project," *IEEE Transactions on Software Engineering*, SE-4(4) 1978: 345–361.

[PUT80] L. Putnam, *Software Cost Estimating and Life Cycle Control: Getting the Software Numbers*, IEEE, (New York) 1980.

[REN85] B. Rensburger, "The Software Is Too Hard," *The Washington Post National Weekly Edition*, (November 11, 1985): 10–11.

[RIC74] F. R. Richards, *Computer Software: Testing, Reliability Models and Quality Assurance*, NPS-55RH74071A, Naval Postgraduate School, (Monterey, California) 1974.

[ROC75] M. J. Rochkind, "The Source Code Control System," *IEEE Transactions on Software Engineering*, SE-1(12) (December 1975).

[ROS77] D. T. Ross, "Structured Analysis (SA): A Language for Communicating Ideas," *IEEE Transactions on Software Engineering*, SE-3(1) (January 1977): 16–34.

[ROS85] D. T. Ross, "Applications and Extensions of SADT," *IEEE Computer*, 18(4) (April 1985): 25–34.

[SAC68] H. Sackman, W. J. Erikson, and E. E. Grant, "Exploratory Experimental Studies Comparing Online and Offline Programming Performance," *Communications of the ACM*, 11-1 (January 1968): 3–11.

[SAM69] J. E. Sammet, *Programming Languages: History and Fundamentals*, Prentice-Hall, (Englewood Cliffs, New Jersey) 1969.

[SAW85] K. Sawyer, "The Mess at the IRS," *The Washington Post National Weekly Edition*, (November 11, 1985): 6–7.

[SCH83] L. Scharer, "User Training: Less is More," *Datamation*, (July 1983): 175–182.

[SHO75] M. L. Shooman and M. Bolsky, "Types, Distribution and Test and Correction Times for Programming Errors," *Proceedings of the 1975 International Conference on Reliable Software*, IEEE, (New York) 1975.

[SHO83] M. L. Shooman, *Software Engineering*, McGraw-Hill Book Company, (New York) 1983.

[SID84] Charles H. Sides, *How to Write Papers and Reports About Computer Technology*, ISI Press, (Philadelphia, Pennsylvania) 1984.

[SOF83] SofTech Microsystems, Inc., *p-System Program Development*, Sage Computer Systems, (Reno, Nevada) 1983.

[STE74] W. Stevens, G. Myers, and L. Constantine, "Structured Design," *IBM Systems Journal*, 13(2) 1974.

[TEI77] D. Teichroew and E. A. Hershey III, "PSL/PSA: A Computer-Aided Technique for Structured Documentation and Analysis of Information Processing Systems," *IEEE Transactions on Software Engineering*, SE-3(1) (January 1977): 41–48.

[TIC79] W. F. Tichy, "Software Development Control Based on Module Interconnection," *Proceedings of the Fourth International Conference on Software Engineering*, IEEE Computer Society, (Long Beach, California) 1979.

[VAN80] E. C. Van Horn, "Software Must Evolve," in H. Freeman and P. M. Lewis II, *Software Engineering*, Academic Press, 1980.

[WAL77] C. Walston and C. Felix, "A Method of Programming Measurement and Estimation," *IBM Systems Journal*, 16(1) 1977: 54–73.

[WEI71] Gerald M. Weinberg, *The Psychology of Computer Programming*, Van Nostrand Reinhold, (New York) 1971.

[WEI74] G. M. Weinberg and E. L. Schulman, "Goals and Performance in Computer Programming," *Human Factors*, 16(1) (February 1974).

[WEI82] Gerald M. Weinberg, *Rethinking Systems Analysis and Design*, Little, Brown and Co., (Boston) 1982.

[WEI85] Edmond H. Weiss, *How to Write a Usable User Manual*, ISI Press, (Philadelphia, Pennsylvania) 1985.

[WHI84] D. Whieldon, "Prototyping: Shortcut to Applications," *Computer Decisions*, 16(6) (June 1984).

[WIR71] N. Wirth, "Program Development by Stepwise Refinement," *Communications of the ACM*, 14(4) (April 1971).

[YEH82] Raymond Yeh, "Requirements Analysis—A Management Perspective," *Proceedings of COMPSAC '82*, 410–416.

[YOU78] E. Yourdon and L. Constantine, *Structured Design*, Prentice-Hall, (Englewood Cliffs, New Jersey) 1978.

[YOU82] Edward Yourdon, *Managing the System Life Cycle*, Yourdon Press, (New York) 1982.

[ZEL78] M. V. Zelkowitz, "Perspectives on Software Engineering," *ACM Computing Surveys*, (June 1978).

[ZIM85] J. A. Zimmer, *Abstraction for Programmers*, McGraw-Hill, (New York) 1985.

INDEX